Introducing Speech and Language Processing

This major new textbook provides a clearly written, concise and accessible introduction to speech and language processing. Assuming knowledge of only the very basics of linguistics and written specifically for students with no technical background, it is the perfect starting point for anyone beginning to study the discipline. Students are introduced to topics such as digital signal processing, speech analysis and synthesis, finite-state machines, automatic speech recognition, parsing and probabilistic grammars, and are shown from a very elementary level how to work with two programming languages, C and Prolog. The accompanying CD-ROM contains all the software described in the book, along with a C compiler, Prolog interpreter and sound file editor, thus providing a self-contained, one-stop resource for the learner. Setting a firm grounding in speech and language processing and an invaluable foundation for further study, *Introducing Speech and Language Processing* is set to become the leading introduction to the field.

JOHN COLEMAN is Director of the Phonetics Laboratory and Reader in Phonetics at Oxford University, having previously worked on speech technology at the universities of Hull and York, and AT&T Bell Laboratories. His previous books are *Phonological Representations* (Cambridge University Press, 1998) and *Acoustics of American English Speech* (Springer-Verlag, 1993).

Cambridge Introductions to Language and Linguistics

This new textbook series provides students and their teachers with accessible introductions to the major subjects encountered within the study of language and linguistics. Assuming no prior knowledge of the subject, each book is written and designed for ease of use in the classroom or seminar, and is ideal for adoption on a modular course as the core recommended textbook. Each book offers the ideal introductory material for each subject, presenting students with an overview of the main topics encountered in their course, and features a glossary of useful terms, chapter previews and summaries, suggestions for further reading, and helpful exercises. Each book is accompanied by a supporting website.

Books published in the series
Introducing Phonology David Odden
Introducing Speech and Language Processing John Coleman

Forthcoming:
Introducing Phonetic Science Michael Ashby and John Maidment
Introducing Sociolinguistics Miriam Meyerhoff
Introducing Morphology Maggie Tallerman and S. J. Hannahs
Introducing Historical Linguistics Brian Joseph
Introducing Second Language Acquisition Muriel Saville-Troike
Introducing Language Bert Vaux

Introducing Speech and Language Processing

JOHN COLEMAN
University of Oxford
Phonetics Laboratory

CAMBRIDGE
UNIVERSITY PRESS

PUBLISHED BY THE PRESS SYNDICATE OF THE UNIVERSITY OF CAMBRIDGE
The Pitt Building, Trumpington Street, Cambridge, United Kingdom

CAMBRIDGE UNIVERSITY PRESS
The Edinburgh Building, Cambridge, CB2 2RU, UK
40 West 20th Street, New York, NY 100114211, USA
477 Williamstown Road, Port Melbourne, VIC 3207, Australia
Ruiz de Alarcón 13, 28014 Madrid, Spain
Dock House, The Waterfront, Cape Town 8001, South Africa

http://www.cambridge.org

First published 2005
Reprinted 2005

Printed in the United Kingdom at the University Press, Cambridge

Typeface Swift 9/12 pt   *System* Quark Express™   [TB]

A catalogue record for this book is available from the British Library

Library of Congress Cataloguing in Publication data

Coleman, John (John S.)
Introducing speech and language processing/ John Coleman.
     p.   cm. — (Cambridge introductions to language and linguistics)
Includes bibliographical references and index.
ISBN 0 521 82365 X – ISBN 0 521 53069 5 (pbk.)
1. Speech processing systems.   I. Title.   II. Series.
TK7882.S65C618   2004
006.4′54–dc22   2004048599

ISBN 0 521 82365 X hardback
ISBN 0 521 53069 5 paperback

Contents

Acknowledgements and copyright notices

The production of a textbook such as this is very much a team effort involving many people besides the author. I reserve my greatest thanks for the students who have followed my introductory courses on speech and language processing during the last ten years. Their interest in and enthusiasm for the subject sustained my efforts to put these lectures into publishable form, and their critical comments and questions led to many improvements. I would also like to thank my secretary, Celia Glyn, who patiently transcribed an early set of recordings of the classes, thus laying down the foundation of the text. Equally, my ability to develop these course materials, and even write the textbook, is due to the technical support of Andrew Slater and other computing support staff in my department. In particular, the DTW program in chapter 6 is abbreviated from code developed by Andrew, in relation to research we have conducted together (Slater and Coleman 1996).

From Cambridge University Press, I was encouraged first by Christine Bartels, then by Andrew Winnard and Juliet Davis-Berry to get on and finish it! The reviewers that Cambridge engaged to comment in detail on the manuscript deserve praise as well as thanks for their thorough critical commentaries. Their suggestions and complaints were most valuable. In addition, Robin Coleman provided valuable help in compiling the index.

Much of the material on the CD-ROM is copyright and is provided for use under licence only by the owner of the book. Some of the material was written by others, and is only included here with their permission under terms stated in the relevant files on the disk. For classroom use, multiple copies of the software may be made with permission from the Copyright Clearance Centre. Otherwise, copying and distribution of any of the material on the CD-ROM is prohibited.

For the non-copyright intellectual property of all the methods of speech and language processing that are explained in the following pages, I trust that the citations of prior work will be acceptable indicators of my indebtedness to earlier workers in the field, with respect to whom we are all students.

CD-ROM and companion website

The CD-ROM included with this book contains all the software used in the course, including:

- Two programming languages (C and Prolog)
- A sound file editor and a text file editor
- All of the program listings printed in the text, and a few extras
- Licence details

Neither Cambridge University Press nor John Coleman make any warranties, express or implied, that the programs contained in this book and on the CD-ROM and companion website are free of error, or are consistent with any particular standard of merchantability, or that they will meet your requirements for any particular application. They should not be relied on for solving a problem whose incorrect solution could result in injury to a person or loss of property. If you do use the programs in such a manner, it is at your own risk. The authors and publisher disclaim all liability for direct or consequential damages resulting from your use of the program.

I may improve the software in future, as may other developers of the software included on the disk. Consequently, revised versions of the software, or links to revised or alternative resources, may be made available through the companion website, www.islp.org.uk. Information about bugs in the software that may be found after publication will also be placed there, so if any of the programs appear to be defective, please check there for a possible upgrade before attempting to contact me. (You can send email to me by visiting the companion website.)

Because material on the internet changes so frequently, there are no URLs (i.e. addresses of web pages) in the text, except for www.islp .org.uk. Instead, I have provided some links to useful websites at www.islp.org.uk.

1 Introduction

CHAPTER PREVIEW

KEY TERMS

computational linguistics

speech technology

signal processing

practical exercises

hardware

free software

This chapter briefly describes what the book is about, who it is aimed at, and why the subject is a useful one to study. It also describes the computational resources you will need in order to follow the practical work: basically just an ordinary PC with a CD-ROM reader and a sound card.

1.1 About this book

This is a **first, basic, elementary and short textbook in speech and natural language processing for beginners with little or no previous experience of computer programming.** The subject is, of course, somewhat technical, and there are many other textbooks that are much more technical, aimed, for example, at computer science or electrical engineering students. This book, in contrast, is aimed at beginners, including: arts, humanities and social sciences students of language, such as linguistics and psychology students; speech science students, that is, those studying communication disorders, or training for careers in speech and language therapy; as well as beginning science and engineering students seeking a quick entry-point to the main methods of the field. I have taught the course to arts students (specifically, graduate students of linguistics) several times. Since they had little technological expertise, I expect that the course may be useful for other beginners. I have expended a great deal of care and attention on trying to make it suitable for beginners, while still covering enough ground to be useful and interesting. (One caveat to that is that it is *primarily* written for language, speech and linguistics students. Consequently, I shall assume some prior knowledge of basic linguistics. See section 1.4 for more details.) I have also designed this book so that someone working alone could use it, if no formal course were available.

1.2 Purpose of this book

Languages are large and slippery entities to get to grips with, and staying on top of the data requires us to use the best tools for the job. Today, the computer is one of the most important of those tools. Many language technologies are becoming widely available on the internet, or as standard components of computer operating systems, including spelling and grammar correction, speech recognition and synthesis, and machine translation. The engineers that develop these systems value the input of linguistics graduates, especially those with some understanding of the methods commonly in use. Similarly, computational techniques have been adopted with advantage in an increasingly wide range of areas of language. A practical knowledge of these techniques can suggest powerful new analysis methods with which to study various aspects of language.

Speech processing and natural language processing are two exciting new subjects of growing relevance. They are subjects that provide new insights and tools for the analysis and generation of physical properties of sounds and the implementation of grammars in testable, working models. Unfortunately, however, existing textbooks in these subjects are mostly unsuitable for the typical student of language and speech, who normally has little experience of computer programming and no prior knowledge of digital signal processing or computational linguistics. Those textbooks assume more mathematical or programming background than is reasonable to expect of some students, especially those who are new to the subject. Furthermore, although researchers in these two areas have begun to take note of each other's work, there continues to be a division between signal processing courses, which are normally taught in electronic engineering degrees, and computational linguistics, which is mainly directed to students of computer science or linguistics. Also, computational linguistics textbooks tend to concentrate on syntactic and semantic processing: while I shall not neglect those areas, this book also gives as much attention to phonological processing, in order to make a bridge between speech and natural language processing. This textbook provides students with a grounding in the subject that will enable them to progress to more technical books and papers if they wish. Suggestions for further reading and carefully selected background readings, and numerous exercises, are given throughout.

1.3 Some reasons to use this book

There are several reasons why students of language, in particular, may benefit from this text book:

- First, some understanding of acoustic theory is now expected of all phonetics students: the time when subjective phonetic transcriptions were deemed an adequate record of speech for many purposes has long since passed. For instance, the discovery of 'covert contrasts' (i.e. measurable but hardly noticeable differences between sounds) cannot be overlooked in the study of adult and child language (Dinnsen 1985; Nolan 1992; Peng 2000; Scobbie et al. 2000), studies of sound change and slips of the tongue (Mowrey and Mackay 1990).
- Second, in experimental phonetics, the standard tools provided in speech analysis packages are often either insufficient – how can we measure the degree of nasality or aspiration? – or impossible to use correctly without understanding the computations involved in standard techniques, such as spectral analysis or pitch tracking.
- Third, in phonology, an understanding of the phonetic grounding is essential. Without it, a student has no resources with which to critically consider the distinctive features, or the concepts of gradient contrast, phonetic distance and near merger. Much of the literature on acoustic features (e.g. Jakobson, Fant and Halle 1961) would be unintelligible, which partly explains the widespread avoidance of acoustics in phonological theory.
- Recent computational linguistic work on probabilistic grammars is having a profound impact on linguistic theory (Klavans and Resnik 1996; Bod et al. 2003), including theoretical phonology (Coleman 2000b), morphology (Sproat et al. 1996; Goldsmith 2001) and syntax (Schabes 1992; Bod 1998) – but only for those people who study it! Linguistic theory in the 1960s–1990s tended to focus on key examples, such as the ambiguity of 'the man saw the boy in the park with a telescope', the intuitive ungrammaticality of certain sentences, or

the mismatch between the phonological and morphological bracketing of 'ungrammaticality'. From the perspective of spoken language processing, though, we might ask whether there is any point expending a great deal of effort writing rules to describe such unproductive derivations as *hymn* ⇒ *hymnal*, or *electric* ⇒ *electricity* (Halle and Mohanan 1985), when the output forms are easily (and arguably more plausibly) simply stored/memorized. Faced with a word or a sentence that can be parsed in many ways (under any theory), how do we choose the right analysis, without hand waving or appealing to unexplained principles of 'pragmatics'? When writing rules in syntax or phonology, how do we deal with the fact that parsing is not deterministic?

- A great deal of the practice of linguistics concerns the grammar of a particular language, where a reasonable degree of *coverage* is required, as well as *consistency* and *correctness*. Languages are large, and the grammar-writer's goals of coverage, consistency and correctness are more easily reached by using computational tools. **Corpus-based linguistics** has moved on from being a minority interest of the 1960s and 1970s to become the common practice of computational linguistics today.

- Although the analytical techniques set out in this book were mostly developed in the first place by communications engineers and computer scientists, from whom we have much to learn, there is much that students of language can offer in return to the emerging field of spoken-language processing. Questions raised by linguists that are profoundly relevant to the subject include: What is the extent of a phonological contrast (Kelly and Local 1986; Hawkins and Slater 1994, West 1999)? Given the existence of phonological neutralization (Trubetzkoy 1969) and the non-uniqueness of phonemic analyses of a language (Chao 1934), is it reasonable – or reliable – to use phonemic transcriptions in speech technology? Does syllable structure help in speech recognition (Church 1983, 1988) or synthesis (Coleman 1992)? What about morphology? To what extent does our knowledge of word-structure and its effects depend on word grammar or analogy/similarity to other words (Bailey and Hahn 2001)? How do we assign stress to words we have not encountered before (Coleman 2000a)?

My personal motivation for writing this book rests on a refusal to let the old sociological divide between arts and sciences stand in the way of a new wave of spoken language researchers with a foot in both camps. I do not expect a reader to metamorphose into a signal processing or computational linguistics wizard – not straight away, anyway. But if, by following this course, you can understand what our speech and natural language processing colleagues in the Computer Science or Electronic Engineering departments are talking about, and if you can tinker with the programs in order to try them out, and/or adapt them to your own purposes, I will feel that the book has succeeded.

1.4 What's in the book (and what's not)

This book, the accompanying CD-ROM and the companion website contain text, lecture notes, and all the software for a short introductory course of eight two-hour classes, covering both speech and natural language processing in an integrated fashion. The CD-ROM contains all the program and data files used in the book, so you won't need to type them out by hand. Almost no prior experience of computation is assumed, beyond general computer literacy and some familiarity with a PC for word processing, use of the Windows user interface, and the practical operation of hardware, such as powering on and off, and use of disks. On the other hand, since my students also follow courses in phonetics (including acoustic phonetics), phonology, syntax, semantics and other areas of linguistics, I have assumed the reader has some training in some of these areas, and I shall not attempt to repeat material that may be found in other introductory textbooks on language.

A note for Mac and Unix users

The course software was originally developed for use in a Unix environment and has been transferred to PCs in order to reach a wider readership. In order to make this book suitable for beginners, and at the same time marketable, I have written it for PC/Windows users only. The software can be compiled and run on other machines, or under other operating systems, provided that the user has appropriate technical support on which to call.

Every effort has been taken to ensure that the course could be followed by someone who is a newcomer to spoken language processing, whether a student on a first course, a lecturer preparing such a course, or even a reader working alone without additional formal instruction. The emphasis from the outset is on practical exercises in the use and modification of computer programs written in C and Prolog, in order that students will rapidly gain confidence and acquire new skills.

Programming languages for speech and language processing

This course uses two programming languages, C and Prolog, because they have different advantages. C is particularly good for working with numbers, such as digital sound recordings, whereas Prolog is particularly good for work with the more abstract structures of language and logic. When I say 'use', I mean 'tinker about with': this is *not* a textbook in computer programming, though I do present and pick apart a number of useful, working programs, and there are a number of programming exercises. The main aim is to give students the confidence to *use, dissect* and *adapt* the programs on offer to their own purpose. By seeing how they work, the theory comes alive and you learn to alter them to suit your own interests. As a side-effect of tinkering, you will most likely also become increasingly proficient at programming. More importantly, you may gain the confidence to delve into programs in any *other* programming languages you may come across. A good deal of work on speech is done in Pascal, Fortran, C++ and (increasingly) Java; and work on language in Lisp and Perl, to name a few other languages you may encounter in the literature. Though many people find particular languages more suited to particular areas of work, in general, almost any program can be written in *all* of these languages. This means that it is important to be fairly flexible about what programming languages you may use. As with human languages, it is best to have an open and accepting attitude, and not think that you must attain perfect fluency in one language before you will even consider using another.

The text explains from first principles the operation of many useful programs, including:

Speech processing

1. How to record sound on your computer using digital audio.
2. How to generate sounds from numbers.
3. How to calculate various properties of recorded sounds, such as overall average volume.
4. How to manipulate digital recordings, for example, how to reduce a mains hum or a tape hiss in order to clean up a low-grade tape recording.
5. How to determine the frequency spectrum of part of a signal, to find some of the acoustic characteristics of speech sounds, using Fourier analysis.
6. How to calculate the pitch of a speech signal, using the cepstral method and the autocorrelation method.
7. How to determine which parts of a speech signal are voiced and which are voiceless.
8. How to encode speech signals using linear predictive coding (LPC), and some of the uses of such an encoding.
9. How to simulate the generation of speech using a formant synthesizer and an LPC synthesizer.
10. How to compare and evaluate the similarities between two stretches of speech, using dynamic time warping, one method of automatic speech recognition.
11. How speech recognizers work.

Natural language processing

1. How to use finite-state transducers to compute relationships between descriptions on two different levels, including: (a) speech signals and

phonetic labelling (a second method of automatic speech recognition); (b) phonetic and phonemic labelling; (c) phonemic and orthographic labelling.
2. How a kind of probabilistic finite-state transducer, Hidden Markov Models, can be used to *learn* the relationships between descriptions on two different levels.
3. How to work out syllable structure, metrical structure, word structure (morphology) and sentence structure (syntax) using phrase structure grammars and parsers.
4. When a parser provides several possible structural analyses, how to determine their relative likelihood, using probabilistic grammars.

What is *not* covered

Sufficient material is provided to enable the reader to branch off into the further study of either speech processing or natural language processing, using one of the more technical textbooks in those areas, such as Harrington and Cassidy 1999 or Jurafsky and Martin 2000. In order to keep the book to nine chapters, certain topics had to be omitted. I have therefore not included anything on connectionist methods (neural networks), machine learning, semantic processing, machine translation or discourse representation. (If you want to find out about these subjects, I recommend McLeod et al. 1998, Morgan and Scofield 1991 and Jurafsky and Martin 2000.) The chapters on syntactic parsing using phrase structure grammars do not follow any specific theory of grammar, but focus instead on the computation of hierarchical constituent structures of the kind encountered in almost all mainstream varieties of grammar, as well as morphology and phonology. I have tried to be fairly non-partisan throughout, but to provide the reader with a set of techniques and an armoury of useful computational tools with which to experiment.

Tinkering

An essential feature of this course is that I encourage you to try out the programs in the form in which I have given them, to see them in operation, and then tinker with them to adapt and alter them in various ways. In my view, tinkering is an invaluable part of the process of developing a deep understanding of how computational methods work. Theory is fine, of course, but there is no substitute for practice. And this is not a computer science textbook. (For that reason, I have no qualms about simply leaving out important topics that are, quite frankly, just too hard for an introductory course.)

On a related point, don't be afraid to tinker with programs you don't really understand. If, after reading the text and looking at a program listing, it is still a mystery, don't worry! That is no reason not to try the program out. After all, most of the time we use a computer we are running programs that we know nothing about. So, a partial understanding of a program is better than none at all. And by tinkering and using the program, you may come to understand its every line very well.

1.5 Computational set-up needed for this book

All the software can be run on a standard (preferably, reasonably new) PC with a CD-ROM reader and a sound card. No expensive special-purpose hardware or software is required or assumed. To be specific, you need to have the following:

1. A PC with a 486 or, preferably, Pentium processor running the Windows 95 or more recent Windows operating system. The software has not been checked for use on an older processor or other operating systems, although with a little technical expertise or support it could be got to work on other machines or under other operating systems.

2. For the speech processing chapters, a sound card, with the ability to record and play audio files with the suffix '.wav' is needed. An amplifier and loudspeaker or headphones will be needed for audio playback, and a microphone (or player for audio recordings) will be needed for input. The miniature microphones built in to some PCs are only just good enough for speech processing, and built-in miniature loudspeakers do not do justice to the high-fidelity audio signals we shall be considering. The small loudspeakers sold for use with multimedia PCs are sometimes adequate, as are the usual kind of stereo headphones provided with portable cassette or CD players (though hi-fi headphones would be preferable). Inexpensive microphones for home audio recording, karaoke, music performance and so on are widely available from home audio and music stores. Some microphones will also require amplification to the level required for 'line input': though audio cards often accept a microphone input, they are usually specifically intended for use with 'PC mikes', not ordinary dynamic microphones. You may also need an adapter, as most microphone cables end in a ¼-inch jack plug, but most PC sound cards have a socket for a *miniature* jack plug.

3. A CD-ROM drive, in order to copy the textbook software onto your computer.

4. A reasonable amount of memory (256 Mb should be OK).

5. For users of shared-access computers, such as those provided by university computing services or departments, the appropriate privileges for installation of the course software, and a quota of file space for temporary storage. Note that the software on the CD-ROM takes up 30 Mb. In chapter 2 I explain why the digital storage of medium quality audio signals requires very large files, generally much larger than the size of text files. For instance, a file of 1 megabyte will store only 32 seconds of speech at a sampling rate of 16000 samples per second and 16-bit resolution, the lowest specification that we usually consider adequate for speech processing work. For study purposes, therefore, at least a few megabytes of disk space will be required. For serious experimental work with speech, hundreds or thousands of megabytes of disk space is typically needed. Fortunately, new computers nowadays

have disk drives with a capacity measured in gigabytes (thousands of megabytes), plenty for working with speech.

6. Although they are not essential to the course, a connection to the Internet and software such as a web browser or ftp will be useful for accessing archives of publicly available software, including the additional course software on the companion website, www.islp.org.uk. I shall assume you have Internet access.

A number of free or inexpensive software products not provided on the CD-ROM are also mentioned in various chapters. In time, these will inevitably be revised or withdrawn, so additional information and links on the book website will provide updated information.

1.6 Computational skills that are necessary in order to use the book

You need to know a little about how to use a PC:

1. How to power it up (and, if necessary, how to start Windows).
2. How to use the mouse and keyboard.
3. How to attach a microphone or tape player (for input) and loudspeaker or headphones (for output).
4. How to use Windows to manage your files.
5. If the computer is your own (or if you otherwise have the privileges to do so), how to transfer files from the CD-ROM or floppy to your own disk.
6. How to open a Command Prompt window (i.e. exit to DOS or run a DOS program).
7. It is helpful also to know how to use a web browser to inspect a remote site and use it to download publicly available software.
8. How to type plain text to a file.
9. If something doesn't work as you think it should, you'll need somewhere to turn for help. (Refer to the Acknowledgements section for a notice concerning the terms under which the software is supplied.)

Computer programs are written as plain text, that is, without the kind of formatting that word processors can provide, such as bold face, italics, underlining, different fonts or sizes of fonts. Plain text uses just the letters of the alphabet, numbers, punctuation marks and a small number of special characters, such as the space, tab, carriage return and linefeed characters. Each of these can be represented by a computer as a number: the convention for numbering characters is given in the Appendix, the ASCII table ('ASCII' stands for American Standard Code for Information Interchange). To write a file of plain text, it is best to use a simple text editor, such as Notepad or WordPad. Some commercially available C and Prolog packages also include a text editor. There are also many publicly available shareware or free software products, such as PFE (see next section). If a text editor is not available, it is also possible to make plain text files using most word processors, by adhering to the following guidelines:

1. Type text in any font, using only ordinary keystrokes, not special combinations of keys. Use of the shift key is fine, but special characters generated using combinations of the Control (Ctl), Alt, Alt Gr or Windows key with other keys should not normally be used.
2. Different fonts, sizes or colours of fonts, bold, underline, italics, subscripts, superscripts etc. should not be used.
3. When the file is to be saved (either when typing is complete or when, after a few minutes' work it is desired to save a backup), a plain text version should be saved rather than a version in the word processor's proprietary format. For example, in Microsoft Word, do *not* save the file as a .doc file, or in Word Perfect, do *not* save the file as a .wpf file. To save a file as plain text in Microsoft Word, pull down the 'File' menu, select 'Save As', and then select 'Text Only' under the 'Save as type' menu. (Note that a file saved as 'file.c' in this way is actually named 'file.c.txt' by Windows! If you really want it to be called 'file.c', it is best to use a proper text editor, such as PFE, not a word processor.)

1.7 Free software suggestions

Although the book software is complete, it would certainly be useful to start to collect some other software tools, such as speech processing packages, text corpora and so on. At the time of writing, a number of useful software products are available either at no cost or as shareware, at a reasonable registration cost, and can be downloaded from many ftp archives. While I am happy to recommend these, I expect that the details on the companion website about their availability will inevitably change quite soon. Consequently, for more up-to-date information about how to get this software, consult the website, www.islp.org.uk.

1.8 Book structure

Roughly speaking, there are two 'strands' to the book, one on speech processing and the other on natural language processing. The speech processing program examples are written in C, and the natural language processing program examples are written in Prolog. Consequently, some chapters in each strand can be studied independently of the other strand. But in an effort to bring the two strands together into a more unified treatment of the subject, there are three places in particular at which the two strands are brought together. First, chapter 5, on finite-state machines, provides example applications in language processing (phonology, orthography and syntactic categorization) and at the speech–language (acoustics–phonology) interface. This chapter is a foundation for chapter 6 (on speech recognition techniques) and chapter 7 (on Hidden Markov Models), as well as the more language-oriented chapter 9. Chapter 9 itself brings together the speech and language strands, as it presumes an understanding of finite-state probabilistic models (from chapters 6 and 7) and non-probabilistic syntactic parsing (from chapter 8). Figure 1.1 provides a map of the course, showing the dependencies between the chapters.

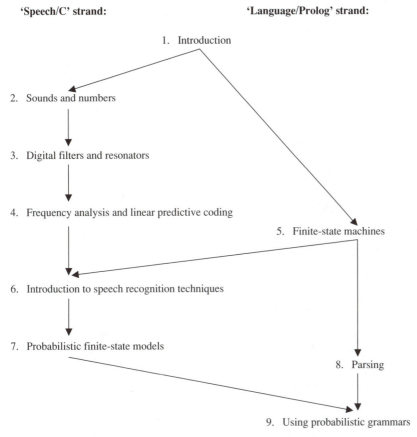

'Speech/C' strand: **'Language/Prolog' strand:**

1. Introduction

2. Sounds and numbers

3. Digital filters and resonators

4. Frequency analysis and linear predictive coding

5. Finite-state machines

6. Introduction to speech recognition techniques

7. Probabilistic finite-state models

8. Parsing

9. Using probabilistic grammars

FIGURE 1.1
Dependencies between the chapters

Reading in preparation for the next chapter

If you are a diligent student and have time to do some reading before turning to the next chapter, you might like to do some preparatory reading. Johnson 1997: 22–33 is a very readable account of digital signals at about the same level as this textbook.

2 Sounds and numbers

CHAPTER PREVIEW

In this chapter, we become familiar with the idea of a digital representation of a signal. We begin with a home-work assignment, to list (by hand) some values of a cosine wave, and then plot them on graph paper. We then look at a simple computer program for achieving the same pur-pose. The cosine wave that is generated can be converted to an audible bleep, or displayed on the screen using a waveform editor.

KEY TERMS

cosine wave
digital signal
sampling
quantization
binary numbers
data types
program
array

2.1 Preparatory assignments

If exercises 2.1 and 2.2 give you any problems, don't let them stop you from moving on to exercise 2.3, which only requires 'pencil and paper'.

Exercise 2.1 Checking the sound output on your computer

On the CD-ROM there is a file called `cosine.wav`. If you double-click on it, Windows ought to recognize that it is a sound file, and if the audio playback is set up properly on your computer, you ought to be able to hear a bleep, if you have headphones or loudspeakers plugged into the output jack on your sound card.

Exercise 2.2 Looking at the sound file using a waveform editor

If you have installed a sound editing program (such as Cool Edit) on your system, try running it, opening `cosine.wav`, and looking at the waveform of the file. (It may be informative to select a short portion, of say 0.05 s duration, and 'zoom in' on that, by setting the viewing range accordingly. In Cool Edit 2000 you do this in the View menu.) If that is successful, take a look at a speech file: `joe.wav`. Obviously, it looks and sounds different from the cosine wave.

Main questions of this chapter

The question we shall focus on for the remainder of this chapter is: *How does that work?* What kind of information is in those computer sound files? And how can they be turned into *actual, audible sounds?* To answer these questions, we shall set ourselves the task of *creating* a sound file like `cosine.wav`. In order to do that, it will be useful to review what we may (or may not!) have learned in school about cosines and waves. Here goes!

Exercise 2.3

Complete the second, third and fourth columns of table 2.1. Use a table of cosines (e.g. table 2.2), and/or a pocket calculator.

Exercise 2.4

Using 1 mm squared graph paper, plot $32000 \times \cos(i \times 17°)$ on the shorter dimension against i on the longer dimension. Hint: use a scale of 500 units to 1 small square on the shorter dimension, i.e. 10 small squares = 5000 units, and 10 small squares to 1 unit on the longer dimension. Put 0 in the middle, with values in the range -35000 to $+35000$ below and above. Another way of phrasing this exercise is: sketch a cosine wave, taking samples at 17° intervals.

Table 2.1. Worksheet for exercise 2.3			
i	$i \times 17°$	$\cos(i \times 17°)$	$32000 \times \cos(i \times 17°)$, rounded to the nearest whole number
0	0°	1	32000
1	17°	0.956304	30601
2	34°	0.829037	26529
3	51°	0.629320	20138
4	68°	0.374606	
5	85°	0.087155	
6	102°	−0.207911	
7	119°	−0.484809	
8	136°	−0.719339	
9	153°	−0.891006	
10	170°	−0.984807	
11			
12			
13			
14			
15			
16			
17			
18			
19			
20			
21	357°		
22	374° (= 360° + 14°; same as 14°)		
23	391° (= 31°)		
24	408° (= 48°)		
25	425° (= 65°)		
26	442° (= 82°)		
27	459° (= 99°)		
28	476° (= 116°)		

Table 2.2. A table of cosines

Degrees	Radians	Cosines	Degrees	Radians	Cosines
1	0.017453	0.999847	33	0.575958	0.838670
2	0.034906	0.999390	34	0.593411	0.829037
3	0.052359	0.998629	35	0.610865	0.819152
4	0.069813	0.997564	36	0.628318	0.809016
5	0.087266	0.996194	37	0.645771	0.798635
6	0.104719	0.994521	38	0.663225	0.788010
7	0.122173	0.992546	39	0.680678	0.777145
8	0.139626	0.990268	40	0.698131	0.766044
9	0.157079	0.987688	41	0.715584	0.754709
10	0.174532	0.984807	42	0.733038	0.743144
11	0.191986	0.981627	43	0.750491	0.731353
12	0.209439	0.978147	44	0.767944	0.719339
13	0.226892	0.974370	45	0.785398	0.707106
14	0.244346	0.970295	46	0.802851	0.694658
15	0.261799	0.965925	47	0.820304	0.681998
16	0.279252	0.961261	48	0.837758	0.669130
17	0.296705	0.956304	49	0.855211	0.656059
18	0.314159	0.951056	50	0.872664	0.642787
19	0.331612	0.945518	51	0.890117	0.629320
20	0.349065	0.939692	52	0.907571	0.615661
21	0.366519	0.933580	53	0.925024	0.601815
22	0.383972	0.927183	54	0.942477	0.587785
23	0.401425	0.920504	55	0.959931	0.573576
24	0.418879	0.913545	56	0.977384	0.559192
25	0.436332	0.906307	57	0.994837	0.544639
26	0.453785	0.898794	58	1.012290	0.529919
27	0.471238	0.891006	59	1.029744	0.515038
28	0.488692	0.882947	60	1.047197	0.5
29	0.506145	0.874619	61	1.064650	0.484809
30	0.523598	0.866025	62	1.082104	0.469471
31	0.541052	0.857167	63	1.099557	0.453990
32	0.558505	0.848048	64	1.117010	0.438371

Table 2.2. (*cont.*)					
Degrees	Radians	Cosines	Degrees	Radians	Cosines
65	1.134464	0.422618	97	1.692969	−0.121869
66	1.151917	0.406736	98	1.710422	−0.139173
67	1.169370	0.390731	99	1.727875	−0.156434
68	1.186823	0.374606	100	1.745329	−0.173648
69	1.204277	0.358367	101	1.762782	−0.190808
70	1.221730	0.342020	102	1.780235	−0.207911
71	1.239183	0.325568	103	1.797689	−0.224951
72	1.256637	0.309016	104	1.815142	−0.241921
73	1.274090	0.292371	105	1.832595	−0.258819
74	1.291543	0.275637	106	1.850049	−0.275637
75	1.308996	0.258819	107	1.867502	−0.292371
76	1.326450	0.241921	108	1.884955	−0.309016
77	1.343903	0.224951	109	1.902408	−0.325568
78	1.361356	0.207911	110	1.919862	−0.342020
79	1.378810	0.190808	111	1.937315	−0.358367
80	1.396263	0.173648	112	1.954768	−0.374606
81	1.413716	0.156434	113	1.972222	−0.390731
82	1.431169	0.139173	114	1.989675	−0.406736
83	1.448623	0.121869	115	2.007128	−0.422618
84	1.466076	0.104528	116	2.024581	−0.438371
85	1.483529	0.087155	117	2.042035	−0.453990
86	1.500983	0.069756	118	2.059488	−0.469471
87	1.518436	0.052335	119	2.076941	−0.484809
88	1.535889	0.034899	120	2.094395	−0.5
89	1.553343	0.017452	121	2.111848	−0.515038
90	1.570796	0	122	2.129301	−0.529919
91	1.588249	−0.017452	123	2.146754	−0.544639
92	1.605702	−0.034899	124	2.164208	−0.559192
93	1.623156	−0.052335	125	2.181661	−0.573576
94	1.640609	−0.069756	126	2.199114	−0.587785
95	1.658062	−0.087155	127	2.216568	−0.601815
96	1.675516	−0.104528	128	2.234021	−0.615661

Table 2.2. (*cont.*)

Degrees	Radians	Cosines	Degrees	Radians	Cosines
129	2.251474	−0.629320	161	2.809980	−0.945518
130	2.268928	−0.642787	162	2.827433	−0.951056
131	2.286381	−0.656059	163	2.844886	−0.956304
132	2.303834	−0.669130	164	2.862339	−0.961261
133	2.321287	−0.681998	165	2.879793	−0.965925
134	2.338741	−0.694658	166	2.897246	−0.970295
135	2.356194	−0.707106	167	2.914699	−0.974370
136	2.373647	−0.719339	168	2.932153	−0.978147
137	2.391101	−0.731353	169	2.949606	−0.981627
138	2.408554	−0.743144	170	2.967059	−0.984807
139	2.426007	−0.754709	171	2.984513	−0.987688
140	2.443460	−0.766044	172	3.001966	−0.990268
141	2.460914	−0.777145	173	3.019419	−0.992546
142	2.478367	−0.788010	174	3.036872	−0.994521
143	2.495820	−0.798635	175	3.054326	−0.996194
144	2.513274	−0.809016	176	3.071779	−0.997564
145	2.530727	−0.819152	177	3.089232	−0.998629
146	2.548180	−0.829037	178	3.106686	−0.999390
147	2.565634	−0.838670	179	3.124139	−0.999847
148	2.583087	−0.848048	180	3.141592	−1
149	2.600540	−0.857167	181	3.159045	−0.999847
150	2.617993	−0.866025	182	3.176499	−0.999390
151	2.635447	−0.874619	183	3.193952	−0.998629
152	2.652900	−0.882947	184	3.211405	−0.997564
153	2.670353	−0.891006	185	3.228859	−0.996194
154	2.687807	−0.898794	186	3.246312	−0.994521
155	2.705260	−0.906307	187	3.263765	−0.992546
156	2.722713	−0.913545	188	3.281218	−0.990268
157	2.740166	−0.920504	189	3.298672	−0.987688
158	2.757620	−0.927183	190	3.316125	−0.984807
159	2.775073	−0.933580	191	3.333578	−0.981627
160	2.792526	−0.939692	192	3.351032	−0.978147

Table 2.2. (*cont.*)					
Degrees	Radians	Cosines	Degrees	Radians	Cosines
193	3.368485	−0.974370	225	3.926990	−0.707106
194	3.385938	−0.970295	226	3.944444	−0.694658
195	3.403392	−0.965925	227	3.961897	−0.681998
196	3.420845	−0.961261	228	3.979350	−0.669130
197	3.438298	−0.956304	229	3.996803	−0.656059
198	3.455751	−0.951056	230	4.014257	−0.642787
199	3.473205	−0.945518	231	4.031710	−0.629320
200	3.490658	−0.939692	232	4.049163	−0.615661
201	3.508111	−0.933580	233	4.066617	−0.601815
202	3.525565	−0.927183	234	4.084070	−0.587785
203	3.543018	−0.920504	235	4.101523	−0.573576
204	3.560471	−0.913545	236	4.118977	−0.559192
205	3.577924	−0.906307	237	4.136430	−0.544639
206	3.595378	−0.898794	238	4.153883	−0.529919
207	3.612831	−0.891006	239	4.171336	−0.515038
208	3.630284	−0.882947	240	4.188790	−0.5
209	3.647738	−0.874619	241	4.206243	−0.484809
210	3.665191	−0.866025	242	4.223696	−0.469471
211	3.682644	−0.857167	243	4.241150	−0.453990
212	3.700098	−0.848048	244	4.258603	−0.438371
213	3.717551	−0.838670	245	4.276056	−0.422618
214	3.735004	−0.829037	246	4.293509	−0.406736
215	3.752457	−0.819152	247	4.310963	−0.390731
216	3.769911	−0.809016	248	4.328416	−0.374606
217	3.787364	−0.798635	249	4.345869	−0.358367
218	3.804817	−0.788010	250	4.363323	−0.342020
219	3.822271	−0.777145	251	4.380776	−0.325568
220	3.839724	−0.766044	252	4.398229	−0.309016
221	3.857177	−0.754709	253	4.415683	−0.292371
222	3.874630	−0.743144	254	4.433136	−0.275637
223	3.892084	−0.731353	255	4.450589	−0.258819
224	3.909537	−0.719339	256	4.468042	−0.241921

Table 2.2. (cont.)

Degrees	Radians	Cosines	Degrees	Radians	Cosines
257	4.485496	−0.224951	289	5.044001	0.325568
258	4.502949	−0.207911	290	5.061454	0.342020
259	4.520402	−0.190808	291	5.078908	0.358367
260	4.537856	−0.173648	292	5.096361	0.374606
261	4.555309	−0.156434	293	5.113814	0.390731
262	4.572762	−0.139173	294	5.131268	0.406736
263	4.590215	−0.121869	295	5.148721	0.422618
264	4.607669	−0.104528	296	5.166174	0.438371
265	4.625122	−0.087155	297	5.183627	0.453990
266	4.642575	−0.069756	298	5.201081	0.469471
267	4.660029	−0.052335	299	5.218534	0.484809
268	4.677482	−0.034899	300	5.235987	0.5
269	4.694935	−0.017452	301	5.253441	0.515038
270	4.712388	0	302	5.270894	0.529919
271	4.729842	0.017452	303	5.288347	0.544639
272	4.747295	0.034899	304	5.305800	0.559192
273	4.764748	0.052335	305	5.323254	0.573576
274	4.782202	0.069756	306	5.340707	0.587785
275	4.799655	0.087155	307	5.358160	0.601815
276	4.817108	0.104528	308	5.375614	0.615661
277	4.834562	0.121869	309	5.393067	0.629320
278	4.852015	0.139173	310	5.410520	0.642787
279	4.869468	0.156434	311	5.427973	0.656059
280	4.886921	0.173648	312	5.445427	0.669130
281	4.904375	0.190808	313	5.462880	0.681998
282	4.921828	0.207911	314	5.480333	0.694658
283	4.939281	0.224951	315	5.497787	0.707106
284	4.956735	0.241921	316	5.515240	0.719339
285	4.974188	0.258819	317	5.532693	0.731353
286	4.991641	0.275637	318	5.550147	0.743144
287	5.009094	0.292371	319	5.567600	0.754709
288	5.026548	0.309016	320	5.585053	0.766044

Table 2.2. (*cont.*)					
Degrees	Radians	Cosines	Degrees	Radians	Cosines
321	5.602506	0.777145	341	5.951572	0.945518
322	5.619960	0.788010	342	5.969026	0.951056
323	5.637413	0.798635	343	5.986479	0.956304
324	5.654866	0.809016	344	6.003932	0.961261
325	5.672320	0.819152	345	6.021385	0.965925
326	5.689773	0.829037	346	6.038839	0.970295
327	5.707226	0.838670	347	6.056292	0.974370
328	5.724679	0.848048	348	6.073745	0.978147
329	5.742133	0.857167	349	6.091199	0.981627
330	5.759586	0.866025	350	6.108652	0.984807
331	5.777039	0.874619	351	6.126105	0.987688
332	5.794493	0.882947	352	6.143558	0.990268
333	5.811946	0.891006	353	6.161012	0.992546
334	5.829399	0.898794	354	6.178465	0.994521
335	5.846852	0.906307	355	6.195918	0.996194
336	5.864306	0.913545	356	6.213372	0.997564
337	5.881759	0.920504	357	6.230825	0.998629
338	5.899212	0.927183	358	6.248278	0.999390
339	5.916666	0.933580	359	6.265732	0.999847
340	5.934119	0.939692	360	6.283185	1

2.2 Solutions

The solution to exercise 2.3 is given in table 2.3. Figure 2.1 shows the solution to exercise 2.4.

Figure 2.1 is not a cosine wave, but a digital representation of a cosine wave. It consists of samples of a cosine wave selected at angular increments of 17°.

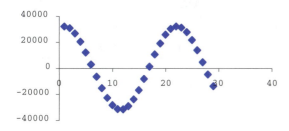

FIGURE 2.1
Solution to exercise 2.4

Table 2.3. Solution to exercise 2.3			
i	$i \times 17°$	$\cos(i \times 17°)$	$32000 \times \cos(i \times 17°)$, rounded to the nearest whole number
0	0°	1	32000
1	17°	0.956304	30601
2	34°	0.829037	26529
3	51°	0.629320	20138
4	68°	0.374606	*11987*
5	85°	0.087155	*2788*
6	102°	−0.207911	*−6654*
7	119°	−0.484809	*−15514*
8	136°	−0.719339	*−23019*
9	153°	−0.891006	*−28513*
10	170°	−0.984807	*−31514*
11	*187°*	*−0.992546*	*−31762*
12	*204°*	*−0.913545*	*−29234*
13	*221°*	*−0.754709*	*−24151*
14	*238°*	*−0.529919*	*−16958*
15	*255°*	*−0.258819*	*−8283*
16	*272°*	*0.034899*	*1116*
17	*289°*	*0.325568*	*10418*
18	*306°*	*0.587785*	*18809*
19	*323°*	*0.798635*	*25556*
20	*340°*	*0.939692*	*30070*
21	357°	*0.998629*	*31956*
22	374° (= 14°)	*0.970295*	*31049*
23	391° (= 31°)	*0.857167*	*27429*
24	408° (= 48°)	*0.669130*	*21412*
25	425° (= 65°)	*0.422618*	*13523*
26	442° (= 82°)	*0.139173*	*4453*
27	459° (= 99°)	*−0.156434*	*−5006*
28	476° (= 116°)	*−0.438371*	*−14028*

Measuring angles in radians

There is a slight difference between the second column of table 2.1 and table 2.2: the second column of table 2.2 is not in degrees; it is in radians. The radian, like the degree, is an angular measure. Consider a circle (figure 2.2). One complete trip round the circle is 360°. If the radius of the circle is 1 unit long, the circumference is 2π units in length (because the length of the circumference is $2\pi r$, and $r = 1$). A radian is the angle made by a portion of the circumference one radius in length. Mathematicians say that one radian is the angle subtended by one radius. There are 2π radians in a complete trip round the circle, so 2π radians is 360°. One radian is $360°/2\pi$ and 2π is just over 6 (roughly 6.28) so there are just over 6 radians in a circle. Each one is just under 60° (roughly 57.3°).

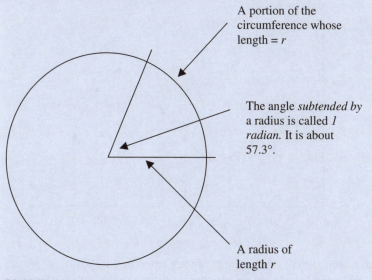

A portion of the circumference whose length = r

The angle *subtended by* a radius is called *1 radian*. It is about 57.3°.

A radius of length r

FIGURE 2.2
Angular measure in radians

Notice on table 2.3 that 360° falls between the 21st and 22nd rows (ignoring row 0). In column 3, around about the 21st or 22nd row, when we have gone once round the circle (one cycle), the cosine is close to 1. The difference between degrees and radians may seem minor, but it is important to know about because radian measure is more commonly used in signal processing than degrees. In fact radian measure is more commonly used in mathematics than degrees because it is a 'natural' division of the circle, whereas 360° is just an arbitrary number of small divisions of the circle, arising from the (mistaken) belief of ancient astronomers that there were 360 days in the year!

2.3 Sampling

So figure 2.1 is not a cosine wave but an approximation to a cosine wave. It is an approximation in two ways: first, we selected particular samples at particular angles. This is the first step in making a digital representation of a signal: to sample it. Although the *x*-axis (the horizontal axis) of figure 2.1 represents angles, we could just as well label it with units of time. Then, samples would be measurements made at time intervals, as in figure 2.3. Sampling usually means measuring some quantity at small intervals of time, but for certain kinds of speech processing programs we often represent time using angles! One cycle is 360°, so if you are generating or analysing a signal with a frequency of, say 100 cycles per second (100 hertz, abbreviated Hz), 360° corresponds to 1/100 s (0.01 s, or 10 ms), so 1° corresponds to 0.000027 s (0.027 ms), and 1 ms corresponds to 36°.

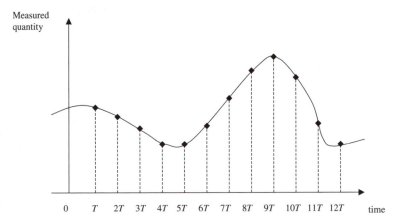

FIGURE 2.3
Sampling at intervals of time *T* (a standard diagram, adapted from Embree, Paul, *C Language Algorithms for Digital Signal Processing*, 1st edition, © 1991 480. Reprinted by permission of Pearson Education, Inc., Upper Saddle River, NJ.)

For speech signals, the quantity we are interested in is the *air pressure*, because sound waves are air pressure waves. But in fact we do *not* measure air pressure: we use a microphone to convert air pressure waves into a changing voltage, and then we measure that voltage. Or rather, a computer measures the voltages, using an analogue-to-digital conversion device (an A–D converter), such as a sound card.

2.4 Quantization

Now in theory you could sample a signal at *discrete* intervals of time (e.g. every 0.1ms), with each measurement taken from a *continuous* range of values. You could use real numbers at each point in time for this quantity, but that is not possible with computers: the number of decimal places in a number is limited in practice by the size of the working memory in the computer's central processing unit. Consequently, as well as sampling in time when we digitize the signal, we also have to quantize the signal, for example the voltage at the input to the A–D converter (figure 2.4).

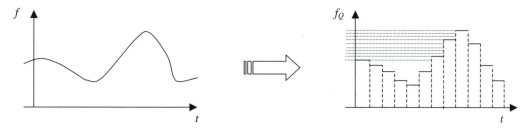

FIGURE 2.4
Sampling and quantization (digitization) maps a continuously varying signal into a finite number of discrete values at discrete intervals of time.

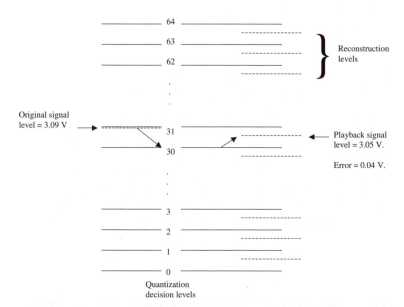

FIGURE 2.5
Quantization and reconstruction of a digital signal (adapted from Embree, Paul, *C Language Algorithms for Digital Signal Processing*, 1st edition, © 1991 480. Reprinted by permission of Pearson Education, Inc., Upper Saddle River, NJ.)

Figure 2.5 shows why the quantized signal is not an *exact* representation of the original continuous signal. Suppose you have 64 discrete quantization levels and suppose the input voltage can be between 0 and 6.4 Volt. So, level 1 is 0.1 V, level 2 is 0.2 V, and so on, up to level 64 = 6.4 V. Consider what happens at a moment when the input signal is just below 3.1 V, say 3.09 V. Quantization rounds intermediate values down to the nearest whole quantity, so in this case, 3.09 V will be rounded down to level 30. The inverse of the quantization operation is called **reconstruction**, the assignment of a particular output level to each quantization level. (Reconstruction is used to play back a digitized signal, to convert it from digital to analogue form, using a D–A converter.) In this case, the reconstruction level of each value is at the mid point of its range of input values. Thus, inputs from 3.0–3.1 V are assigned to level 30. The reconstruction of this level is therefore 3.05 V. The reconstructed output 3.05 V is not an entirely faithful reproduction of the original level, 3.09 V, but it is near enough. It is accurate to within 1 quantization level (in this case 0.1 V), and it can be out by no more than half a level (0.05 V). So, our ability to represent the original level accurately depends on how many discrete quantization levels we use. We can have arbitrarily many of them: 64, as here, is a very small number, just to keep the example simple. To represent 64 numbers (e.g. from 0 to 63) only requires 6 bits, whereas speech signals are typically quantized to a resolution of 12 or 16 bits. One of those 16 bits can be used to denote the sign: whether the signal is positive or negative. The remaining 15 bits provide 2^{15} discreet quantization levels. With the sign bit, that gives 2^{15} positive and 2^{15} negative levels. 2^{15} is about 32000, so that is why column 4 on table 2.1 in the homework was scaled to an interval of plus or minus 32000. 64000 discrete levels is enough for quite a high fidelity representation of speech.

Student: What is the definition of a *bit*?

A bit is a zero or a one, a binary digit.

Binary numbers

Although computers use binary numbers, we shall hardly bother with them most of the time. However, it is essential to understand what size of decimal number can be stored with a binary number of a certain number of bits. With one bit, we can represent two (2^1) numbers, 0 and 1. Two bits allow us to represent four (2^2) numbers: 00 (= decimal 0), 01 (decimal 1), 10 (= 2) and 11 (= 3). Four bits allow us to represent 16 (2^4) numbers (e.g. 0 to 15, or −8 to +7, if we want to use both negative and positive numbers), as listed in table 2.4.

Table 2.4. Four-bit binary numbers

Binary	Decimal	Binary	Decimal	or (for *signed* integers)
0000	0	1000	8	−8
0001	1	1001	9	−7
0010	2	1010	10	−6
0011	3	1011	11	−5
0100	4	1100	12	−4
0101	5	1101	13	−3
0110	6	1110	14	−2
0111	7	1111	15	−1

Note that if we use negative as well as positive numbers, the *sign* (i.e. + or −) takes 1 bit to represent: for example, we could use 0 to mean negative and 1 to mean positive. Thus, with 4 bits we can represent 16 positive numbers, or 8 negative and 8 positive numbers. Zero is considered as a positive number.

8 bits (1 byte) allows 256 (2^8) numbers to be represented (e.g. 0 to 255 or −128 to +127). 16 bits (2 bytes) can encode 2^{16} numbers (e.g. −32768 to 32767). Instead of 'hundreds, tens and units', the places of digits in a binary number represent powers of two: from right to left, ones, twos, fours, eights etc. We shall use 16-bit binary numbers so frequently in this course that it is as well to have a simple name for them: we shall call them short integers, for reasons that will become clear a little later.

So, we can make the quantization arbitrarily fine by having just as many bits as we need to model the number of discrete quantization levels that we want. If we want to model a signal between 0 and 10 V to an accuracy of 1 mV (1 millivolt, i.e. 0.001 V), fine: that is possible, as long as we employ 10000 discrete levels. A similar condition applies to the sampling rate. Obviously it is limited in part by how fast we can measure things using electronics (just as the quantization resolution is limited by how accurately we can measure the signal), but in principle you can make the sampling rate as frequent as you need for your purpose. If the quantity that you are measuring is changing fairly slowly, you only need to sample at a relatively slow rate. Speech signals change very rapidly, however. An idea of how rapidly we need to sample them can be given by considering the highest frequency event in a speech signal. In high frequency fricative sounds such as [s] we can hear frequencies of several kilohertz. (One kilohertz – 1 kHz – is one thousand cycles per second.) We are not talking about hundreds of kilohertz, though: it is not ultrasound.

Now, there is a theorem (an equation) that tells us what sampling rate we need to use in order to capture a particular frequency. Put the other way round, with a given sampling rate there is an upper limit to the frequency that you can measure. We shall look at this theorem in the next section.

2.5 The sampling theorem

Suppose we have a cosine wave like the one in figure 2.1, and suppose we were to take samples very frequently, as we did in exercise 2.3. 'Very frequently' means we take samples many times more frequently than the frequency of the signal that we are looking at, so if it is a 100 Hz signal we might take 1000 samples per second. Then we will have ten samples per cycle. That will give us a fair approximation, as in figure 2.6 (b); however, it is a pretty rough and ready representation of the signal, I hope you will

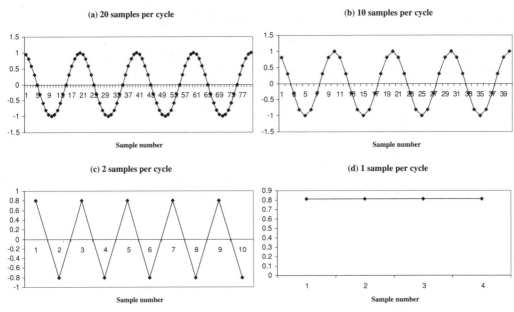

FIGURE 2.6
Accuracy of representation of a signal at different sample rates, relative to the frequency

agree. The question is: what is the lowest frequency that we can sample at? What is the lowest sampling rate that we can get away with? Now let us go to the other extreme: suppose we took only *one* sample per period. It doesn't matter where in the cycle it is, so let us say that it is just after the crest. This is shown in figure 2.6 (d): it is not a very good representation of the signal because it is just a constant value. If the sampling frequency were slightly more or slightly less than one sample per cycle, the reconstructed signal would not be flat, but it would still be a poor representation of the signal. So a sampling rate of about one sample per cycle is not very good. If we take at least two samples per cycle (let's say we take one just before the peak and one just after the trough, as in figure 2.6 (c)), the reconstruction will still not be a very high fidelity model of the original signal. The shape is a bit wrong – more triangular than sinusoidal – but it does at least go up and down at the same frequency as the signal that we are modelling. So, two samples per cycle is the lowest sampling rate that we can get away with. Thus, we need at least 200 samples per second to model a signal with a frequency of 100 Hz. If the sampling rate is greater we will get a better approximation to the signal. In other words, if f is the frequency of the signal, the sampling rate must be at least $2f$. The sampling rate, f_S, has to be greater than or equal to $2f$. Another way of looking at this is that the highest frequency that we can capture, f_{max}, is ½ f_S. This is known as the **Nyquist frequency**.

Let's look at a practical example of this. Most computers nowadays have analogue-to-digital conversion circuits in them (for instance, in the sound card) that can sample input signals at various sampling rates. For analysis of speech signals, we might record a signal and digitize it at a sampling rate of 16000 samples per second. Therefore, the highest frequency that you can reliably record at that sampling rate is 8 kHz (i.e. 8000 Hz). You can choose to digitize your signal at other, perhaps higher, rates. Audio CDs are recorded at a higher rate, 44100 samples per second, but the upper limit of frequency resolution is always half the sampling rate. The highest frequency that can be captured at that rate is 22.05 kHz. Note that hardly anyone can hear sounds above 20 kHz, anyway, which is why recordings on CDs sound so good: they capture the entire frequency range of human hearing.

2.6 Generating a signal

Now, in this chapter, we are not so much interested in *analysing* signals as *modelling* them, by which I mean building *working* models, which really means being able to generate signals, not just describe them. So we shall generate a wave, or rather, a file that contains a sequence of numbers – the fourth column of table 2.3 – representing the cosine wave in figure 2.1. We are going to generate a sequence of numbers such that when you play that sequence back, by sending those numbers to a digital-to-analogue converter at 8000 samples a second it will come out as a sound, a 200 Hz bleep lasting 1 second. The program that generates the sequence of numbers is called `simple_coswave.c` (listing 2.1, below). It is written in a programming language called C. When `simple_coswave.c` is compiled, it generates another program called `bleep.exe`, which only the computer can understand. When you run `bleep.exe`, it generates an output file called `cosine.dat` that consists of 8000 16-bit integers. When you play `cosine.dat` at 8000 samples per second, the frequency of the sound will be 200 Hz.

Compilation

Student: And what exactly do you mean by 'compile'?
In computing, 'compile' means 'translate'. A compiler is a program that translates your program, written in a programming language such as C, into a form the computer can understand, i.e. in the machine code for that particular computer. There are normally two steps to compilation. First, the original program is translated into object code, an intermediate level of representation. Then, the object code is translated into machine code. Often, a program is defined in several separate files, each a separate module of the program. In that case, each file is compiled into object code, and then the several separate object code files are linked together and processed further to make a single executable program, expressed in machine code.

Machine code

For instance, the command to clear the 'carry' bit (i.e. the binary 'carry' digit – 0 or 1 – resulting from an addition or subtraction) in the instruction set of an Intel Pentium processor is the 1-byte binary number '11111000'. The command to add a 1-byte number n to the number in the 'accumulator' register is '00000100', followed by binary number n. It would be very time-consuming and tedious to have to write our programs in the machine language of a particular processor. Furthermore, machine language programs written for one kind of processor will not run on another. Consequently, we write programs using high-level programming languages, which we then automatically translate into the machine language of the particular processor using a compiler program.

Our C program is the same whatever machine we might run it on, but in order to be understood by a particular computer it has to be translated into a form that that computer understands. So an SGI workstation will need one C compiler, on a PC it will be a different one, on a Mac it will be a different one yet again, because they are different machines with different processor chips with different machine languages. If you don't have a compiler that is the right compiler for your machine then you can't compile the code, so you can't run the program. The CD-ROM accompanying this book includes the GNU C compiler, `gcc`, in particular a version called DJGPP that runs on PCs, in order to generate executable programs (`.exe` files). Instructions about how to install the C compiler are on the CD-ROM, in the file `readme.html`.

When we specify frequency in this program we are not going to specify it in hertz, because the pitch of the bleep represented by `cosine.dat` will depend on how fast you play it back. Just like an LP record, if you play it at one speed it comes out at one pitch, and if you play it at a higher speed the pitch is higher. So consequently we won't specify the frequency in absolute terms, in Hz; we will specify it as *a fraction of the sampling rate*. The frequency we want is f, but in the program we are going to express that as `freq`. The size of this number is f/f_s which means 'frequency divided by the sampling frequency'. If the sampling frequency is 8000 Hz and `freq` is a half, the frequency of the generated signal will be half the sampling rate, that is 4000 Hz. If we set `freq` to a quarter, we mean 2000 Hz; if we set it to an eighth then we mean 1000 Hz; if we set it to 0.025 (i.e. one fortieth), we mean 200 Hz. Now if you played that file back at a different playback rate, if you played it back at 10000 samples per second, a `freq` of 0.025 would mean 250 Hz, so the frequency of the output sound would be different, a bit higher.

The program `coswave.c` is written in C, a high-level programming language. Actually, compared with some other high-level programming languages (such as Prolog, which we will use in chapters 5, 8 and 9), C is pretty low level, that is, close to the level of the machine language. One of the disadvantages of that is that it makes C programs a bit difficult to follow at times, but one of the benefits is that you can specify how you want numbers to be represented in the computer (there are lots of different ways of doing that), and many other important details. In some other programming languages you can't always do that. We do not *just* want to generate a sequence of numbers: we want to generate a sequence of binary numbers that the computer's digital-to-analogue converter will be able to reconstruct as the levels of the output voltage. The numbers are going to have to be 16-bit, signed, binary integers. In C, you can easily get the numbers in the right form. The downside of that is that the program has to specify what form we want the numbers to be in, and we have to keep track of the type of each number in our programs. Another nuisance in working with this language is that every variable and every data structure that we use has to have memory allocated to it by the program. (**Data structures** are *arrangements of information*, like tables, sequences, lists, trees, matrices and so on.) All the variables and data structures that the program uses have to go somewhere in the computer's memory, and the compiler has to ensure that the appropriate amount of memory is allocated for them. With some other programming languages you do not have to worry about things like that – the compiler will sort out the memory for you – but C is not so obliging. The program has to state what kind of numbers are going to be stored in each variable, and how big each data structure is, so that the compiler can employ the appropriate amount of memory. However, C gives us great power to do some of this stuff, and as it is also the *lingua franca* of computer programming as well, it is worth studying a little. (There are lots of books on C, but Kernighan and Ritchie 1988 is the definitive reference, which I recommend.)

2.7 Numeric data types

Now, there are numbers and numbers and numbers. For instance, you already know about the difference between integers (whole numbers) and decimals. Let's consider decimal numbers for a minute. A decimal number can have arbitrarily many digits after the decimal point. You can have however many decimal places you want, but there is a limit to the number of decimal places on a computer, dictated in part by how much memory you have got in which to store all of those digits after the decimal point. No computer can allow you to work with decimal numbers with an *unlimited* number of decimal places. They all have to set some limit on how many decimal places you can have, because the storage capacity of a computer's memory, however large, is always finite. Consequently, for decimal numbers (often called **floating point** numbers) there are two main types in C. The ordinary ones are called **floats**: they use 32 bits of storage, which allows you up to only 7 significant decimal digits (i.e. on most computers, numbers in the range $\pm 1.18 \times 10^{-38}$ to 3.4×10^{38}). Double precision decimals (**doubles**) have twice as many bits, 64 bits, which gives you 16 significant digits and an even bigger range of numbers. The relationship between how many bits you have and how many decimal places you have got is not something to worry about in this book. It varies from one

Table 2.5. Some types of numbers in C

		Word size of computer		Range
		16-bit (e.g. 486 PC)	32-bit (e.g. Pentium PC)	
Integer types				
char	1 byte	8 bits	8 bits	−128 to 127 (or 0 to 255, for unsigned char)
int	word-sized integer	16 bits	32 bits	(as for short and long, according to word size)
short (or short int)	fixed size, 2-byte integer	16 bits	16 bits	−32768 to 32767 (0 to 65535, for an unsigned short)
long (or long int)	fixed size, 4-byte integer	32 bits	32 bits	−2147483648 to 2147483647 ($\pm 2.2 \times 10^9$), or $\pm 4.3 \times 10^9$, for an unsigned long
Floating point types (decimals)				
float	single precision	32 bits	32 bits	$\pm 1.18 \times 10^{-38}$ to $\pm 3.4 \times 10^{38}$
double	double precision (more decimal places)	64 bits	64 bits	$\pm 2.23 \times 10^{-308}$ to $\pm 1.79 \times 10^{308}$

machine to another, in any case. In this program we will use doubles, so whenever you see the term double, that means a decimal number. In summary, there are two types of decimal numbers in C, called float and double (see table 2.5). So when you employ a variable for a decimal number in the program, you need to say at the beginning whether it is a float or a double.

When we use wave files made of integers, it makes sense to use the short data type, as a short integer occupies 16 bits, irrespective of the type of the computer. To add a further complication, though, when 2 bytes are used to store a short integer, some programs put the lower 8 bits (units, twos, fours etc.) before the higher 8 bits (the 'little endian' or 'Intel' convention), and some the other way round (the 'big endian' or 'Motorola' convention). For example, 700 is expressed as a 16 bit binary number as:

0000001010111100

Since this takes two bytes to store, it can be broken up into two parts, each of one byte:

00000010	10111100
big end	little end

In the computer's memory chips, either the little end can be stored first, or the big end. In 'little-endian' (Intel) convention, the bytes are stored in the order

10111100
00000010

Whereas Motorola prefers the big-endian order:

00000010
10111100

We shall use the 'Intel' convention, as a standard.

> *Student: Why do we need to know this?*
> You'll see in Exercise 2.5 that when you want to look at or play a
> sound file that is encoded in binary you need to know (and tell the
> software you're using) what byte-order convention has been used. If
> you get the bytes in the wrong order, the sound file will not sound
> at all right.

For decimal numbers like radians and cosines, which have decimal places,
we shall use floating-point variables. We shall also represent the frequency
of a signal as a proportion of the sampling rate, rather than a certain number of hertz: frequencies expressed in this way will typically have fractional
values such as 0.025, so they will be stored using doubles as well. But the
sample number and also the number of samples in the output are just integers. With whole numbers you do not need to worry about decimal places,
of course. The size of your whole numbers is also determined by how many
bits you use to store them, though. This may seem like a troublesome detail,
but you don't want to use up too much memory if your program actually
deals with small numbers. So in table 2.5 there are four types of variables
for storing integers, char, int, short and long. A char is always 8 bits
long. They can only be used for rather small numbers, such as the numbers
that are assigned to ASCII characters (see appendix) which is why that data
type is called char. The value of a char must be between 0 and 255,
because it is 8 bits long. From 0 to 255 is too small a range to store, for example, sample numbers, because we usually want to process several seconds of
speech, which will require tens or hundreds of thousands of samples. It is
usually advisable to avoid the int datatype, even though they are bigger
than a char: they have 16 bits on a 16 bit machine but 32 bits on a 32 bit
machine, so they vary depending on what kind of computer you have got.
We don't want that because we want to be able to run this software on
different machines without having to rewrite the program. So actually a
short is a better type of variable to use for storing integers because they are
of fixed size, 16 bits. Similarly, a long is fixed at 32 bits. That holds good
across different computers, so using short and long for integers helps to
ensure portability of the software from one computer to another. Although
it is a bit more of a fuss having to say whether an integer variable is short
or long, it is better to be explicit.

2.8 The program

Listing 2.1

```
#include <stdlib.h>
#include <stdio.h>
#include <math.h>

/* COSWAVE.C - Generates a cosine wave: 8000 samples, 1 s, 200 Hz */    5
/* (when played at 8000 samples/s), called cosine.dat            */

int main()
{
    int length, status, i;                                              10
    short int *x;           /* a pointer to the array of samples */
    float freq;
    double arg, twopi;
    FILE *file_id;
                                                                        15
    length = 8000;
    freq = 0.025;
    twopi = 8.0*atan(1.0);              /* calculate 2*PI        */
    arg = twopi * freq;
                                                                        20
/* allocate the sample array and set its cells to zero          */
    x = (short int *) calloc(length,sizeof(short int));
    if(!x) {
        printf("Unable to allocate space for samples\n");
        exit(1);                                                        25
    }

/* Loop over the length of the array of samples                 */
    for (i = 0 ; i < length ; i++)
        x[i] = (short int) 32000 * cos(i*arg);                          30

    file_id = fopen("cosine.dat","wb");
    if(file_id == NULL) {
        printf("Unable to open file\n");
        exit(1);                                                        35
    }
    status = fwrite(x,sizeof(short int),length,file_id);
    if(status < length) {
        printf("Unable to write all samples\n");
        exit(1);                                                        40
    }
    fclose(file_id);
    return 0;
}
```

Now here, in listing 2.1, is the program. It is one of the simplest C programs that does anything useful that I have ever seen. We will study it in several pieces.

> To assist in our dissection of the program, every fifth line of the program is numbered in the right-hand margin, in blue. Note that these line numbers are not part of the program: unlike some programming languages, such as BASIC or FORTRAN, line numbers are not used in C. Blank lines are numbered as well as those that actually contain text.

There is a line-by-line annotated description of the code in the file `coswave_notes.txt`, included on the CD-ROM, but a line-by-line description doesn't help you break the program down logically and really understand it. Note that any text starting with a `/*` and ending with a `*/` is a comment, just a description of what that bit of the program does. Comments are completely ignored by the compiler: they just make the program a little more readable by humans. They remind the author of the program and help to inform a user what certain lines of the program do.

2.9 Structure of a loop

It is quite useful to begin by focussing on lines 29–30; this is where the main work actually all gets done. The part that actually generates a sequence of numbers is called a 'for' loop:

```
for (i = 0 ; i < length ; i++)
    x[i] = (short int) 32000 * cos(i*arg);
```

(It is called a *loop* because it does the same action over and over again. The flowchart in figure 2.7 illustrates the loop, which is followed until the counter variable `i` is no longer less than the limit variable, `length`.)

Line 29 begins with the word 'for' followed by something in brackets. The 'for' command specifies an iterative procedure: an instruction to do something over and over again. (It is just one of several iterative commands in C.) The part in brackets, 'i = 0 ; i < length; i++', is some information that (indirectly) tells the computer how many times to loop. It specifies what to do at the start of the loop, how to decide when to finish, and what to do to the loop counter on each step of the loop. Line 30 is the computation that is to be performed over and over again. So the part in brackets is the control specification for the loop, and the following line is the computation that must be repeated again and again by the loop. The three parts of the control specification, separated by semicolons, are these:

1. First, there is a variable `i`, which we shall use as a counter for the *i*th sample of the cosine wave, just as we did in exercise 2.3.

   'i = 0'

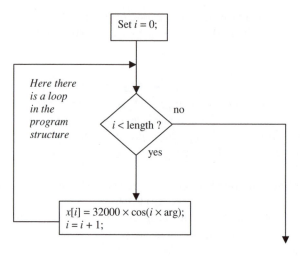

FIGURE 2.7
Flowchart for lines 29–30

means that *i* starts off with the value 0. That is a somewhat arbitrary starting point: it could just as well have been 1.

2. The second part, the **continuation condition** says that while *i* is less than the length of the signal that we wish to generate, continue to repeat the loop.

3. On each pass through the loop, the counter is modified according to the third expression: 'i++' means increment *i* by 1. '++' is an operation that has been provided in C because you so often have loops that add 1 each time you go through. So instead of saying 'let $i = i + 1$' (which is not a meaningful C expression), 'i++' is a useful shorthand for that. (Note that in C, as in many other programming languages, '$x = y$' does *not* mean that *x* and *y* are equal. It means 'ignore whatever value *x* may already have, and set *x* to the value of *y*'. Thus, '$i = i + 1$' would be a perfectly acceptable alternative to 'i++', even though in ordinary arithmetic there are no values of *i* for which $i = i + 1$.)

So in this example the control specification of the loop has the counter i to which it will add 1 every time it performs the computation in the loop, until i is no longer less than the length of the signal. We set the variable length to 8000 on line 16. If we were to increase that value, the 'for' loop would be repeated more times. (Notice that line 10 says 'int length, status i'. That is where we specify that length, status, and i are integers.)

Let us now have a look at what is computed on each cycle of the loop, on line 30:

```
x[i] = (short int) 32000 * cos(i*arg);
```

The expression x[i], sometimes pronounced '*x* of *i*', means the *i*th sample of the signal. Line 30 says that the *i*th sample is $32000 \times \cos(i \times arg)$. Note

the use of '*' instead of '×', to mean 'multiply'. arg is the angular increment: it was 17° in exercise 2.3, whereas in this case it is $2\pi \times$ freq (see line
19). So line 30 calculates $i \times$ the angular increment, takes the cosine of that
and multiplies it by 32000. The values of the cosine function are decimal
numbers (in this case, doubles, because arg is declared to be a double on
line 13), so the values of cos(i*arg) will also be decimal numbers. For
example, when $i = 1$, cos($i \times arg$) is just over 0.157, times 32000 is a little
more than 5026.5482. That is not an integer, but we want to make a signal
that is a sequence of 16-bit integers, so we must round it down to make it
short. That is what the expression '(short int)' after the '=' sign on line
30 does: it turns the result of the calculation 32000 * cos(i*arg) into
a short integer by just dropping all of the decimal part and storing the
whole number part as a short integer, that is, 2 bytes. So, x[i] is also a
short integer.

2.10 Structure of an array

Let me explain more about x[i], and what the square brackets mean. x
is a variable: it refers to a chunk of memory that we allocated for storage
of a sequence of numbers. It is a type of **array**. Being a sequence, it is a one-
dimensional array. Arrays are not necessarily one-dimensional. They can
be two-dimensional arrays (e.g. for tables) or *n*-dimensional arrays for
more complex kinds of data. Arrays are basically *n*-dimensional arrangements of a particular type of objects, in this case, integers, short ints.
(This is defined in line 11.) So x is just a one-dimensional sequence of
shorts.

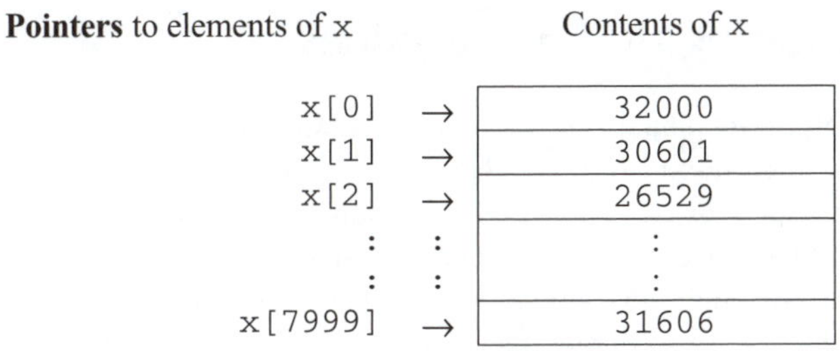

Pointers to elements of x   Contents of x

x[0]	→	32000
x[1]	→	30601
x[2]	→	26529
:	:	:
:	:	:
x[7999]	→	31606

FIGURE 2.8
Structure of a typical one-
dimensional array, x

The first element in it is referred to as x[0], and the *i*th element is called
x[i]. The final element of an array *a* of *n* elements is a[n-1], note,
because the first element is numbered a[0].

Now an array, such as x, has to be stored somewhere in the computer's
memory, so in the program we have to tell the compiler how much memory we need in which to store this array. That is done in line 22, after the
comment 'allocate the sample array ...'.

```
/* allocate the sample array and set its cells to zero    */
    x = (short int *) calloc(length,sizeof(short int));
```

`calloc` is an instruction for allocating memory. The first argument of `calloc` specifies how many cells there will be, and the second specifies how many bytes of memory each cell requires. In this case, the number of cells is specified by `length`, which is set to 8000 on line 20, so `x` has 8000 cells in it. Each cell is the size of a `short int`. The `calloc` command allocates a chunk of memory for `x`. `calloc` sets aside enough memory so that as we generate each sample it will have a place in the computer's memory to go. You can picture `x` as a sort of grid or table, as in figure 2.8, where each sample goes into a cell. Each cell in the table is given an **address**, that is, a number indicating its specific location in the computer's memory.

The cells are consecutive, and the address of the first cell is very special, as it is also the address of the whole array. The address of the first cell can be referred to by this notation with an ampersand at the beginning, `&x`. We can use that address to refer to an array as a whole. If we want to submit the array to a function or procedure, we can refer to the array by its first element, and that is sufficient to pass the array to another part of the program. The program can pass the *whole grid* around, from one function to another. The numbers are not taken out of the grid and moved somewhere else: they are kept wherever they are in the computer's memory. But by passing the address round, you can tell other parts of the program where the array is, that is, where it begins. Other than that, we are not normally interested in the address – the actual location in memory – of an array or its cells. To recap, the following may be a useful reference.

`*x`   A pointer to the first cell of `x`.
`x[0]`   Contents of the first cell of `x`.
`x[i]`   Contents of cell *i*+1.

2.11 Calculating the cosine values

Immediately before the loop, there is a little calculation in line 19 to work out the angular increment, `arg`. We also have to calculate 2π because C doesn't even provide π or 2π as a pre-defined quantity. To compute 2π, we use the fact that the tangent of a 45° angle is 1, in combination with the fact that there are eight 45° angles in a complete circle (figure 2.9). Therefore, 45° is $2\pi/8$ (i.e. ¼π) radians. So, tan $2\pi/8$ = 1, $2\pi/8$ = arctan 1, so 2π = 8 × arctan 1. Line 18 expresses this in C as:

```
twopi = 8.0*atan(1.0);          /* calculate 2*PI   */
```

Alternatively, it is just as easy to replace line 18 by:

```
twopi = 6.2831853071795864769252886676655901;
```

or even define the value of `twopi` when it is declared, in line 13.

We also need to work out the relationship between the angular increment from one sample to the next, given the frequency of the signal that we want to generate. 2π radians is one cycle, so the angular increment from one sample to the next is 2π times the frequency ratio, `freq`. The frequency of the signal is expressed as a proportion of the sampling frequency.

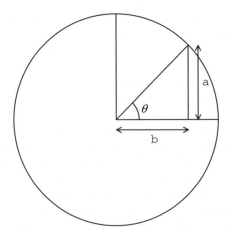

FIGURE 2.9
Working out the value of
2π using trigonometry
tables

In a right-angled triangle, tan θ = a/b. If a = b, θ=45° = $^1/_4\pi$ radians, and tan θ = 1, 2π = 8θ, and θ = arctan 1. Therefore, 2π = 8 × arctan 1.

So, multiplying 2π by `freq` gives us the angular increment appropriate to the frequency of cosine wave we want to generate.

Student: You said that frequency is expressed as a ratio?
Yes, this program doesn't use hertz at all; it refers to frequencies using proportions of the sampling rate. So, suppose the sampling rate is 8000 samples per second. For a bleep with a frequency of 200 Hz, `freq` = 200/8000 = 0.025. For a frequency of 100 Hz, `freq` = 0.0125.

2.12 Structure of the program

Now, lines 29–42, especially the `for` loop, are the most interesting part of the program. Let's go back to the beginning and get the big picture, though.

There is some stuff at the beginning (lines 1–3), the '#include' statements, which refer to the names of other files, library files containing various functions and general-purpose C programs that are frequently required by all sorts of different programs. `stdlib` refers to the standard library; `stdio` is the library of standard input and output functions; `math` is the library of mathematical functions. The trigonometric functions cos and atan are defined in the `math` library, for instance, and the commands to open, write and close a file are defined in the `stdio` library. These libraries are part of the ANSI standard for C, and are always available in respectable C compilers. The '#include' statements are examples of C macros. When we compile this program, the first thing the compiler does is to run a program called the C pre-processor. Statements beginning with '#' are instructions to the C pre-processor. The C pre-processor *replaces* lines that begin with '#include' by the entire contents of the files that are named after #include. So in this case the C pre-processor inserts pre-prepared programs for the functions defined by reference to stdlib.h, `stdio.h`, and `math.h` into your program, to save you from having to type in your own definitions of how to compute cosines, or how to do standard input and output functions like writing data to the disk.

> *Student: So the header lines tell the compiler where it can find all the right tools to be able to make the program work.*

So when you compile a program, you typically do not compile just one program, you usually compile a list of several programs. As we have seen, the program contains a number of '`#include`' statements that refer to other files. This compiler thus pulls together a collection of fragments of C code to form the complete program. They get compiled and linked together to form the executable file, the translation of your program into machine language. It is fairly normal that when you compile a program you have to link several pieces of program together. (We shall see some examples of this in later chapters, as we build up more complicated procedures out of simpler functions defined in earlier chapters.) If they are not all there or if they are not all correct the whole compilation process can go wrong even if your program is correct. If a library file, or some other `#include`d file is missing, it can't compile it.

After the macros and title, the program has a function called `main`, which is defined in lines 8–45. The definition begins at the left parenthesis in line 9 and ends with the corresponding right parenthesis in line 45. A C program is made up of one or more functions, one of which must be called `main`. Roughly speaking, a function is a chunk of code that computes a procedure: `main` is the function with which a program starts. In lines 10–14 the names of the variables used in this function and their types are *declared*. Two of the variables, `length` and `freq`, are assigned constant values (see lines 16–17); two others, `twopi` and `arg`, are also assigned constant values, by slightly more complicated calculations that were discussed above. Note that it is possible to declare the values of a variable when its type is declared. Thus, we could shorten lines 10–14 as follows:

```
int length = 8000, status, i;
short int *x;
float freq = 0.025;
double arg, twopi;
FILE *file_id;
```

2.13 Writing the signal to a file

When lines 29–30 are executed, the cells of the array `x` all get their values filled in. After generating the sequence of cosine values, they must be written to a disk file. This is done in lines 32–42:

```
file_id = fopen("cosine.dat","wb");
if(file_id == NULL) {
    printf("Unable to open file\n");
    exit(1);
}
```

```
status = fwrite(x,sizeof(short int),length,file_id);
if(status < length) {
     printf("Unable to write all samples\n");
     exit(1);
}
fclose(file_id);
```

fopen is one of the standard functions defined in the stdio library. It is used to open the file cosine.dat, in order to write to it (indicated by 'w'). The 'b' in 'wb' informs the operating system that the file to be written is a binary file, not a text file.

Before you run the program, there is no such file as cosine.dat. (Or if there is already a file of that name, fopen deletes it and opens a new file called cosine.dat.) It gives it the file name, or at least, it tries to. If it succeeds, it makes a file number (which we don't need to worry about) and assigns it to the variable file_id (on line 32). file_id is a file identification number, and is purely internal to the workings of the program. It is not something we need to bother about very much, except that we want to know whether it exists or not because if the file is created and opened successfully, if the fopen function succeeds, file_id will end up with a numerical value. The fact that that value exists tells us that the disk file was opened properly. However, if there wasn't enough space left on the disk, or if an invalid address was given for the file, or some other such problem arose, what would happen is that file_id would have the value NULL (i.e., 0), meaning that the fopen function has failed.

> *Student: What would that actually look like? Would it just display a warning message like 'Error opening file cosine.dat'?*
>
> The error message is defined on line 34: 'Unable to open file' is all that it will tell you.

On line 33 we check to see whether or not file_id is NULL, and if it is, we write an error message and call the function exit with the value 1, indicating a particular kind of error. 'exit(1)' tells the operating system to display a particular kind of error message, a disk error in this case. (In the expression 'printf("Unable to open file\n")', the symbol '\n' is C shorthand for the 'new line' character.)

'A == B' means 'A equals B'. '==' is a logical operator, meaning that the value of the expression 'A == B' has the value true (or 1) if and only if A equals B. (Recall that 'A = B' means 'set the value of A to that of B', which is quite different.)

Another common way of writing 'file_id == NULL', often encountered in C programs, is '!file_id'. '!' means 'not'. So, if file_id is NULL (i.e. 0), '!file_id' evaluates to 'true' (or 1). Thus, the statement 'if(!file_id) {...};' will have the same effect as lines 33–34. This kind of expression is used in line 23.

However if `file_id` does exist then no problem, the program just carries on. It doesn't exit, because the disk space is fine. The file has been opened correctly, and the program can then write the signal to the file. That is what the function `fwrite` on line 41 does. It writes the array `signal` as a sequence of `short ints`, of length `length`. `fwrite` knows what file to write it to because the file identifier `file_id`, the internal number that `fopen` returned, is given as the fourth argument of `fwrite`. Every time the program writes a file, `file_id` could be a different number, but we don't need to worry about that because it is internal to the program. It is generated in line 32 and then we use that number to refer to the file in lines 33, 37 and 42.

If an error occurs while writing the file, `status`, the variable in which is stored the return value of `fwrite`, will be less than the third argument of `fwrite`. So line 38 checks whether `status` is less than `length`, and if so, ends the program with an error message. Otherwise, all being well, the command in line 42 closes the file. And that is the end of the program.

`signal_out`: a useful utility function

The code in lines 32–42 to write an audio file to disk will be useful in many other programs to be presented in later chapters. Consequently, we can package it up as a function `signal_out` that takes a file-name `outfile`, an array of samples `x_out` and a specification of the size of the array `size` (so that the function knows how many samples to write to disk), as follows:

```
void signal_out(int size, short int *x_out, char
*outfile) {
    FILE *fid;
    int status;
    fid = fopen(outfile,"wb");
    if(fid == NULL) {
        printf("Can't open %s\n",outfile);
        printf("It may be in use by another
        application.\n");
        exit(1);
    }
    status = fwrite(x_out,sizeof(short
    int),size,fid);
    if(status < size) {
        printf("Error writing %s\n",outfile);
        exit(1);
    }
    else printf("%s written OK\n",outfile);
    fclose(fid);
}
```

Student: I am not entirely clear what you mean by the address of an array like x. Are addresses all numerical?

Yes: they are numbers referring to actual memory locations in the computer's hardware.

Student: So calloc *sets up a load of places numerically for where this stuff is going to go, is that what it is doing?*

Yes. That is perhaps not something that I have explained very well. A computer memory can be pictured as a sequence of cells, each cell holding one object. Each cell has an *address*, the computer's numbering of that memory location. We need to know the address in memory of each object that we need to store, so we need to keep track of two things: the addresses and what we are storing at each address.

Student: So we refer to the address of an array by using variable names, but the computer will do it with a number.

Yes, that is right, the address of the beginning of the array.

Student: OK, I see.

Chapter summary

We began by plotting selected values of the cosine function, to see how a wave could be represented as a sequence of numbers. In order to get a practical understanding of how sounds can be stored, manipulated or generated on a computer, we then examined a short program to generate a cosine wave sound file. In order to generate the sequence of cosine values, we used a loop structure in the C programming language.

Further exercises

Exercise 2.5. **Compilation**

Now I have explained the program, you are advised to compile and run it. The precise formulation of the expression to compile it will depend on your operating system, where you have put the file, and which C compiler you are using.

On a PC running Windows, using the C compiler provided on the CD-ROM that accompanies this book, however, proceed as follows. It is recommended, if you have not already done so, to make a folder on your C: drive, called SLP, and copy coswave.c to that folder. First, open a Command Prompt window. (In older versions of Windows, this is called an MS-DOS window. From the ⟪start⟫ menu, look under the 'Programs ▶' menu.) When the Command Prompt window opens, you will need to change to the right directory by typing, e.g., cd slp ⟪ENTER⟫. (⟪ENTER⟫ means 'press the Enter key', of course. On your computer, this might be labelled Enter, or Return, or with a bent arrow like ↵. You know the key I mean.)

Next, compile the program to object code (refer back to Section 2.6 if you're unsure what this means) by typing gcc -c coswave.c ⟪ENTER⟫

All being well, the compiler will not respond with any warnings or error messages. All that should happen is that the computer will print a blank line and then come back with a prompt again. The output of this step is a file called `coswave.o`, which you cannot understand. (To see if it is there, type `dir coswave*` (ENTER).) Next, compile this object file to an executable program. You can give it whatever name you want: I suggest:

```
gcc -o bleep.exe coswave.o (ENTER)
```

Once again, nothing much should happen on screen. However, behind the scenes, gcc should have made a file called `bleep.exe`. Once again, you can type `dir bleep*` (ENTER), to check that it's there, if you like.

Now, you can run `bleep.exe`, in two different ways. First, still working in the MS-DOS Prompt window, you can just type `bleep` (ENTER). Again, nothing much appears to happen, though if you type `dir cos*`, you should see that as well as `coswave.c` and `coswave.o`, there is now a file called `cosine.dat`, the size of which should be 16000 bytes (i.e. 8000 short integers, remember?). Alternatively, since `bleep.exe` is an executable program, you can run it under Windows. For instance, from the desktop, by clicking on the 'My Computer' icon, then on the C: drive icon and then on the icon for the SLP folder, you should be able to find an icon for the application 'bleep'. Clicking on that icon (or double-clicking, depending on your desktop preferences) will run the program. Doing so will cause a new MS-DOS window to appear, then almost immediately afterwards it will disappear again. The file `cosine.dat` should now have been created.

Either way, `cosine.dat` is still not quite usable, because it is a 'raw' binary data file: it is not in any recognized audio file format. Fortunately, utilities are available in many operating systems for converting raw audio files to a variety of standard audio file formats.

Using 'Cool Edit', for instance, you can follow the following steps to play the cosine.dat audio file:

1. Start Cool Edit. (For example, from the [start] menu, select 'Programs ►', then 'Cool Edit 2000 ►', then 'Cool Edit 2000'. However, your computer's configuration could be different, so you may need to start it in a different way. Alternatively, if there is a shortcut on the desktop, click on it.)
2. Pull down 'File/Open . . .' and, if necessary, navigate to the right folder.
3. At the bottom of the 'Open a Waveform' window, in the 'Files of type:' field, pull down 'All files (*.*)'
4. Double click on the file `cosine.dat`.
5. Since `cosine.dat` is not in a recognized audio file format, a window pops up with the title 'Interpret Sample Format As'. Select the sample rate 8000, channels: mono, and resolution: 16-bit.
6. In the 'Raw Data (no header)' window that pops up, next select 'Data formatted as 16 bit, Intel PCM (LSB,MSB)'.
7. All being well, the cosine wave should now be displayed. Clicking on the 'play' button (► or Alt+p) causes it to be played over the sound card as a short audible bleep.

Exercise 2.6. Recording and displaying speech waveforms

As well as looking at and listening to `cosine.dat`, examine the speech wave `joe.dat`, a recording of a sentence containing many of the phonemes of English. The speech in this file is the same as in `joe.wav`, mentioned in exercise 2.2. What sampling rate was used in that recording? (The resolution is 16 bits and the bytes are in the 'Intel' byte ordering convention.) Is it the same sample rate as `cosine.dat`?

Exercise 2.7.

In section 2.4 I stated that '2^{15} is about 32000'. What is the *exact* value? (Reminder: 2^{15} is short for $2 \times 2 \times 2 \times 2 \times 2 \times 2 \times 2 \times 2 \times 2 \times 2 \times 2 \times 2 \times 2 \times 2 \times 2$.)

Exercise 2.8.

Alter line 30 of `coswave.c` as follows:

```
{x[i] = (short int) 32000 * cos(i*arg);
printf("%d %d\n",i,x[i]);}
```

What is the effect of this change when `coswave.c` is compiled again and `bleep` is run? Note that if more than one expression is to be computed on each pass through the loop, as in this case, they must be grouped together using curly brackets.

`printf` is a formatted print command. Its first argument, '%d %d\n', is a string specifying the format of the output. The remaining arguments, `i` and `x[i]`, are variables whose values are to be used in the output of the print command. The first 'd indicates that the first variable, `i`, should be printed as an integer. The second %d indicates that the second variable, `x[i]`, is also to be printed as an integer. In the expression '%d %d\n', note that there is a single-character space between the two instances of %d, indicating that the two values of the two variables should be separated by a single space. The expression \n stands for 'new line' (meaning 'carriage return, line feed'). Remember, though, that if you want to go back to generating actual audible signal files, you'll need to go back to the original version of the program.

Exercise 2.9.

See what happens if the space and new line symbol are *not* included in the format specification of the previous exercise.

Exercise 2.10.

Modify the program's sampling rate, tone frequency and duration of the signal generated.

Exercise 2.11.

Exercise 2.8 writes out the sample number and sample value. By redirecting that output to a file, those numbers can be stored and inspected. This can easily be done in the MS-DOS Prompt window by typing, e.g.

```
bleep >cosine.txt
```

(You can call the text file anything you like.) Now you can examine the text file with an editor like PFE, or WordPad, or even import it into Excel. Figure 2.10 shows a plot of the first 1000 samples, made using the Excel graph tools.

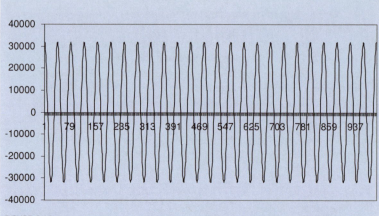

FIGURE 2.10
Excel plot of part of `cosine.txt`

What are the differences between the output and the signal file? *Hint:* the character string '12' is not the same as the binary number 1100, even though they mean the same thing.

Further reading

From the vast array of books on the C programming language, I recommend Kernighan and Ritchie 1988 in particular. This is very close to being the standard manual on C, partly because Dennis Ritchie designed the first version of C in the 1970s.

Reading in preparation for the next topic

For some preparation concerning digital filtering, see Johnson 1997: 16–37.

Klatt 1980 is not exactly an easy read, but since we shall examine a C version of the Klatt synthesizer at the end of the next chapter, some 'reading ahead' may be useful. An electronic version of that paper is provided on the CD-ROM, in the file Software/SLP/Klatt1980.pdf.

3 Digital filters and resonators

CHAPTER PREVIEW

KEY TERMS

integral

average

RMS amplitude

filter

resonator

formant

synthesis

In the previous chapter we saw how a sound wave can be represented digitally, as a sequence of numbers. Now, we shall consider certain numerical operations on digital representations of sound waves. Through digital filtering, we can suppress or enhance components of a sound in particular frequency ranges. In this way, we can also synthesize speech sounds. We shall look at an example of such a speech synthesis method, the Klatt formant synthesizer.

3.1 Operations on sequences of numbers

In the previous chapter we generated a sequence of numbers, representing a cosine wave. In this chapter we shall consider some operations on such digital signals. Once you have a signal represented as a sequence of numbers, you can perform numerical operations on it. Let's call the sample number i and the value of the ith sample $x[i]$, rather as in `coswave.c`. Some of the numerical operations we can perform on such a sequence of numbers are useful and interesting. Some of them are already familiar to you: for instance, if you have a list of numbers you can add them up and get the sum of $x[i]$, written $\Sigma x[i]$, which is also called the integral. It is a measure of the overall energy in the signal (i.e. overall loudness). Obviously, the sum will be bigger the longer the signal is, so it is often more sensible to divide that quantity by the number of samples in the signal, n, which in other words is computing the average value of all of the samples, a measure of the average amplitude:

$$\frac{\Sigma x[i]}{n}$$

This is a better measure of the signal amplitude because it does not increase according to the overall length of the signal, but it is still problematic because the signal has both positive and negative values, so the negative values will tend to counteract the positive. We could use the absolute (i.e. unsigned) values of the samples, $|x[i]|$ in the sum, but a more widely used measure of average amplitude is the root mean square (RMS) amplitude: for each sample (positive and negative alike) $x[i]$, first calculate the square, $x[i]^2$: this makes a sample value of, say, -9 more comparable with a positive value, for example 8, as $(-9)^2$ is 81 and 8^2 is 64, so -9 is in a sense a bigger amplitude than 8. Now, take the average of the sequence of squared values, for a certain number of samples n:

$$\frac{\Sigma x[i]^2}{n}$$

This will be a number that is not to the same scale as the numbers in $x[i]$, because of the squaring operation. So finally, take the square root:

$$\sqrt{\frac{\Sigma x[i]^2}{n}}$$

This is the root of the mean of the square of n signal values, root mean square: RMS.

3.2 A program for calculating RMS amplitude

Listing 3.1 gives a C program for calculating the RMS amplitude of a signal file named by the user when the command is invoked with the usage: `rms filename`. It will work with a file of shorts in 'Intel' format. The sampling frequency does not matter.

Listing 3.1

```c
#include <stdio.h>
#include <math.h>
#include "slputils.c"

/* RMS.C */                                                            5

/* Reads a signal (a sequence of shorts in "Intel" format) from
a disk file into an array, x. The length of the signal is returned in
*length. Calculates and prints out the root mean square amplitude of
the signal. */                                                        10

int main(int argc, char *argv[]) {
    short int *x, *signal_in();
    char *infile;
    int i, *length, n;                                                15
    float rms = 0.0, sum = 0.0;

    if (argc ! = 2) {
        printf("usage: rms input_file\n");
        exit(1);                                                      20
    }
    infile = argv[1];
    x = signal_in(infile,length);
    n = *length;
                                                                      25
    for (i=0;i<n;i++)
        /* Square x[i] and add it to the sum-so-far */
        sum += (float) x[i] * (float) x[i];
    rms = sqrt(sum/ (float) n);
    printf("The RMS amplitude of %s is %.2f\n",infile,rms);           30
    return 0;
}
```

You can compile this program with the Gnu C compiler (e.g. DJGPP) as follows:

```
gcc -c rms.c
gcc -o rms.exe rms.o
```

Then you can use it with signal files (user input is in italics). For example:

```
C:\SLP>rms cosine.dat
The RMS amplitude of cosine.dat is 22627.02

C:\SLP>rms joe.dat
The RMS amplitude of joe.dat is 1862.10
```

A few words of explanation about this program are in order. The #include library file stdio.h is needed in order to print out the result at the end. The square root function `sqrt` is defined in the `math` library. The line `#include "slputils.c"` tells the C pre-processor to include a program that I have written: it contains various utility functions, such as the `signal_out` function that was defined at the end of section 2.13. Here, the function `signal_in` is used, as discussed below.

The main function is called with two arguments: (1) an integer, `argc`, which counts the number of 'words' in the command to run the program, and (2) a pointer to an array of characters (a string, in fact), `argv`, each element of which is a word of the command. For instance, if your command is `rms  joe.dat`, `argv[0]` will point to the string 'rms' and `argv[1]` will point to 'joe.dat'. Thus, we can use `argv[1]` to deal with the right file.

The expression 'if (argc ! = 2)...' checks that the command has the right number of arguments (i.e. that a filename is provided), and if not, informs the user of the right usage.

The expression 'x = signal_in(infile);', defined in `slputils.c`, opens the file, works out how long the signal is (by reading shorts until the end of the file is reached), initializes the array x so that it has the right number of elements, and then reads the signal in again, one short at a time, putting each one in x. (x is returned to this program as the *result* of the function `signal_in`: it was declared at the start of `main` to be a pointer to an array of shorts.)

A 'for' loop is used to step through x , squaring each x[i], converting the square to a `float` (to allow for big numbers, and later decimal division), and adding the result to sum. The syntax 'a += b;' is C shorthand for 'a = a+b;'. After the loop, sum will be the sum of squares of all the samples. Then, RMS is calculated as 'sqrt(sum/(float) n);', that is, the square root of sum/n. The number of samples, n, is converted to a `float`, so that 'normal' decimal division is possible.

3.3 Filtering

Sums and averages are fine, of course, but they provide only one number for your entire signal. We are often interested in obtaining not a single measurement of an entire signal, but a quantity that changes in time as the signal progresses. So, if we are interested in the volume of a signal, we may be more interested in how it goes up and down as the signal goes on, changing through time. In this case, we want to transform the input sequence into a sequence of numbers as the output. As before, let's call the input to these operations $x[i]$, where i is the sample number n. We can refer to particular samples of x, for example, the first sample $x[0]$, the tenth sample $x[9]$, or even expressions such as $x[i-1]$, which means the sample before $x[i]$, or $x[i+m]$, meaning the sample that is m samples later than $x[i]$.

In what follows, we shall look at operations that transform an input sequence $x[n]$ into an output $y[n]$. (The choice of letters is arbitrary.) As a first example, consider a *local* averaging operation, where we go through the signal from $x[0]$ to $x[k]$, calculating the average of every (say) four successive samples:

(3.1)
$$y[n] = \tfrac{1}{4} x[n] + \tfrac{1}{4} x[n-1] + \tfrac{1}{4} x[n-2] + \tfrac{1}{4} x[n-3]$$

This operation is called **running means of 4**. (Since this equation works on a sample $x[n]$ and the three previous samples, the minimum value of n is 3.) Equation 3.1 is a **moving average**, not an average for the whole signal. The idea of a moving average is this: you take consecutive samples and work out what the average is for that short extract of the signal. So you add them up and divide by 4. (In equation 3.1 the division is done by multiplying each term by $\tfrac{1}{4}$, which comes to the same thing.) For it to be a *moving* average we do that for the first four samples, samples 1–4, and then for 2–5, and then from 3–6, and so on through the signal. We move through the signal, so there is one value in the output for every group of four in the input. In fact there will not be quite as many samples in the output as in the input. If there are m samples in the input, there will be $m-3$ samples in the output, because the first value of $y[n]$ that can be calculated is $y[3]$. Easy, isn't it?

For this example, I picked *four* to be the number of samples used in the average out of the air, but it could be ten or a hundred or two or whatever.

Now let's consider what that kind of operation does to a signal like a speech signal, where one sample may be quite different from the next, because there are some quite high frequency events in the signal. So on figure 3.1 there are ten arbitrarily chosen different sample levels for ten successive samples of $x[n]$. The moving average, $y[n]$ is shown as a dashed line.

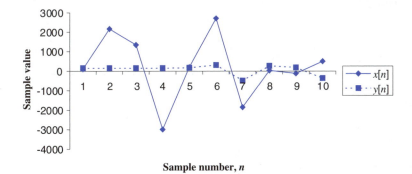

FIGURE 3.1
A portion of a signal and its running mean of 4

The first sample, $x[1]$, is a little above the average, and $x[2]$ is far above the average. $x[3]$ is somewhere between the two and $x[4]$ is in the other direction, a big negative value, well below average. The average, $y[n]$, of course lies somewhere in the middle of those levels, so it doesn't show quite the same rapid sample-to-sample variations that you get in the input, $x[n]$, though over longer intervals (longer than four samples) the average value may be higher or lower, depending on the amplitude of the signal. Consequently, $y[n]$ reflects the grosser, slower-changing aspects of $x[n]$, but not the finer, faster-changing details of $x[n]$.

So those grosser, more slowly changing aspects of the input won't be affected by the averaging; whereas very fast local changes in the input signal (inside the four-sample moving window) are affected by the averaging operation. Think about what that means in terms of frequency: the faster changing events are the higher frequency components of the signal and the slower changing events are the lower frequency aspects of the signal. High frequency events involve faster changes from one sample to the next, so it is the more rapidly changing, higher frequency components of $x[n]$ that are affected by this averaging operation. Those higher frequency changes from one sample to the next are *smoothed* out as it were by the averaging. We say they are filtered out, meaning that they are diminished, possibly eliminated from the signal. Because the higher frequency components are filtered out but the lower frequency components are unaffected, what we have, therefore, is called a low pass filter. So equation 3.1 is a digital version of the older analogue electronic circuits that performed this same function, filtering out the high frequencies and leaving the low frequencies unaffected. The acoustic effect of low pass filtering is like turning the treble control down, so that you get a less hissy/squeaky, more muffled sound. The output sounds like the input except that it is more muffled: muffled in terms of having less treble rather than muffled in volume – it has about the same overall loudness.

3.4 A program for calculating running means of 4

A program implementing running means of 4 is given in `meansof4.c` (listing 3.2):

Listing 3.2

```
#include <stdlib.h>
#include <stdio.h>
#include <math.h>
#include "slputils.c"
                                                                    5
/* MEANSOF4.C - Filters infile to produce outfile using running
means of 4 with coefficients b1-b4. */

int main(int argc, char *argv[]) {
    char *infile, *outfile;                                        10
    int i, *length;
    short int *x, *y, *signal_in();
    void signal_out();

    /* Coefficients for running means of 4 */                      15
    float b[4] = {0.25, 0.25, 0.25, 0.25};
```

```
    if (argc != 3) {
        printf("usage: meansof4 input_file output_file\n");
        exit(1);                                                    20
    }
    infile = argv[1];
    outfile = argv[2];

    x = signal_in(infile,length);                                   25
    y = (short *) calloc(*length,sizeof(short int));

    for (i = 4; i < *length; i++)
        y[i] = (int) (b[0]*x[i]+b[1]*x[i-1]+b[2]*x[i-2]+b[3]*x[i-3]);
    signal_out(length,y,outfile);                                   30
    return 0;
}
```

This program is very similar to rms.c in many respects. It uses two file-names, taken from the command line and referred to by the array elements argv[1] and argv[2]. It uses a small array of four floats to store the four multipliers:

```
float b[4] = {0.25, 0.25, 0.25, 0.25};
```

It is not necessary to put the multipliers in an array in this way: doing so merely makes it a bit easier to change or tinker with them, to try other values.

Having read in the input file using the function signal_in(infile) and determined its length, memory is allocated for the output signal y, using the expression:

```
y = (short *) calloc(length,sizeof(short int));
```

The calculation of the values of each y[i] is performed by a loop over an equation just like 3.1:

```
y[i] = b[0]*x[i]+b[1]*x[i-1]+b[2]*x[i-2]+b[3]*x[i-3];
```

The program can be compiled, as before, by using the commands:

```
gcc -c meansof4.c
gcc -o meansof4.exe meansof4.o
```

Its effects on a signal can then be examined. For instance, meansof4 joe.dat joe_means.dat generates an output file that can be heard to be a little quieter in the higher frequencies. Figure 3.2 shows the spectrum of [ʃ] from 'shoe' at frame 20100 of joe.dat compared with the spectrum at the corresponding point in joe_means.dat. It is obvious that above about 3000 Hz there is less energy in joe_means.dat, especially around 4000 Hz. The [ʃ] even sounds quieter in joe_means.dat. (If you don't understand what a spectrum is, you should examine, e.g., Johnson 1997. This topic will come up again in chapter 4.)

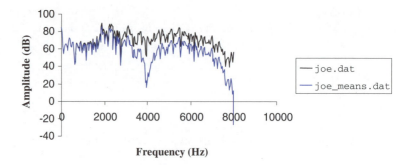

FIGURE 3.2
Spectrum of [ʃ] before
and after means-of-4
filtering

3.5 Smoothing over a longer time-window

Now, four samples is a very short time-window. In a signal sampled at 16000 samples per second, four samples is just one four-thousandth of a second (0.25 ms). So events of less than a quarter of a millisecond are smoothed out, that is, frequency components over 4 kHz. This can be seen quite easily in figure 3.2: the amplitude of [ʃ] in `joe_means.dat` is about the same as that in `joe.dat` up to 4 kHz, but it is lower above 4 kHz. Now if you want to smooth out frequency components at lower frequencies than the 4 point moving average reaches, to smooth over a larger slice of the signal, we have to expand the time window that we look at in the moving average. There are two ways of doing this: one is the obvious way, which is simply to increase the number of samples in the formula, using 10 points or 100 points (see table 3.1).

3.6 Avoiding the need for long windows

For low-pass filtering at low frequencies, there is a clever technique for avoiding having very long averaging windows, which is to make y[n], the output at frame n, depend in part on *its own previous values*, not just previous values of the input. So the definition of the filter is actually **recursive**, since it refers to its own previous value, not just previous values of the input.

The acoustic effects of such a filter are very tricky to understand at the simple level that we have been working at so far. I'm not going to go into that because it is beyond the scope of this book. However, I hope that you can see that the value of the output at point n depends in part on its own previous value, which is in turn dependent on its previous value, and so on down the chain of previous samples. Consequently, you can have filtering effects that go in a chain through the signal. They can be quite long-domain in that even though the definition of the filter equation only makes reference to a few previous values of the input, the filter has an effect over a relatively longer portion of the signal.

Filters of this second kind are actually used very commonly because they require fewer terms in their definition *and* they are very simple to

Table 3.1. Low pass filter cut-off frequencies

No. of samples m in the moving average	Low pass filter cut-off frequency (Hz) (for an input signal with 16000 samples/s $= 16000/m$)
2	8000
3	5333
4	4000
5	3200
6	2666
7	2286
8	2000
10	
12	
16	
20	
24	
30	
40	
50	
80	
120	
160	

implement. Their general form, which we have already pretty much constructed, is:

(3.2)
$$y[n] = b_0 x[n] + b_1 x[n-1] + b_2 x[n-2] + \cdots + b_k x[n-k]$$
$$- a_1 y[n-1] - a_2 y[n-2] - \cdots - a_j y[n-j]$$

Let's go through this equation step by step. First of all, $y[n]$ is dependent upon previous values of x, so it is dependent on $b_0 x[n]$ (i.e. some constant b_0 times $x[n]$), $b_1 x[n-1]$, $b_2 x[n-2]$, up to $b_k x[n-k]$. So there are up to k previous values of x, each one of which is weighted by a multiplier b_m. In equation 3.1, the a multipliers were all 0 and the b multipliers were all 0.25 for b_0 to b_3: for an average you always have the same multiplier for each previous term. But we don't necessarily have to do that: we can actually have different multipliers, making different previous samples contribute to the output to a greater or lesser extent. For instance, we might want to say the further you go back in time the less of an influence, so the fourth previous sample should have less of an effect on the

Table 3.2. Filter coefficients for a 5th order low pass Butterworth filter

f_{8000}	f_{16000}	f/f_s	b_0	b_1	b_2	b_3	b_4	b_5	a_1	a_2	a_3	a_4	a_5
50	100	0.0125	2.74E−9	1.37E−8	2.74E−8	2.74E−8	1.37E−8	2.74E−9	−4.8729	9.4997	−9.2613	4.5152	−0.8807
60	120	0.015	6.74E−9	3.37E−8	6.74E−8	6.74E−8	3.37E−8	6.74E−9	−4.8475	9.4016	−9.1192	4.4237	−0.8585
70	140	0.0175	1.44E−8	7.19E−8	1.44E−7	1.44E−7	7.19E−8	1.44E−8	−4.8221	9.3041	−8.9789	4.3339	−0.837
80	160	0.02	2.77E−8	1.38E−7	2.77E−7	2.77E−7	1.38E−7	2.77E−8	−4.7967	9.2072	−8.8404	4.2458	−0.816
90	180	0.0225	4.93E−8	2.46E−7	4.93E−7	4.93E−7	2.46E−7	4.93E−8	−4.7713	9.111	−8.7036	4.1594	−0.7955
100	200	0.025	8.25E−8	4.12E−7	8.25E−7	8.25E−7	4.12E−7	8.25E−8	−4.7459	9.0154	−8.5687	4.0746	−0.7755
120	240	0.03	2.00E−7	1.00E−6	2.00E−6	2.00E−6	1.00E−6	2.00E−7	−4.695	8.8261	−8.304	3.9099	−0.737
140	280	0.035	4.22E−7	2.11E−6	4.23E−6	4.23E−6	2.11E−6	4.22E−7	−4.6442	8.6394	−8.0461	3.7514	−0.7004
160	320	0.04	8.04E−7	4.02E−6	8.04E−6	8.04E−6	4.02E−6	8.04E−7	−4.5934	8.4551	−7.7949	3.5989	−0.6657
180	360	0.045	1.42E−6	7.08E−6	1.42E−5	1.42E−5	7.08E−6	1.42E−6	−4.5426	8.2733	−7.5503	3.4522	−0.6326
200	400	0.05	2.34E−6	1.17E−5	2.34E−5	2.34E−5	1.17E−5	2.34E−6	−4.4918	8.0941	−7.3121	3.311	−0.6011
250	500	0.0625	6.74E−6	3.37E−5	6.74E−5	6.74E−5	3.37E−5	6.74E−6	−4.3649	7.6566	−6.7437	2.9813	−0.5291
300	600	0.075	1.58E−5	7.92E−5	1.59E−4	1.59E−4	7.92E−5	1.58E−5	−4.238	7.2344	−6.2125	2.6821	−0.4655
350	700	0.0875	3.24E−5	1.62E−4	3.24E−4	3.24E−4	1.62E−4	3.24E−5	−4.1112	6.8272	−5.7164	2.4109	−0.4094
400	800	0.1	5.98E−5	2.99E−4	5.98E−4	5.98E−4	2.99E−4	5.98E−5	−3.9845	6.4349	−5.2536	2.1651	−0.3599
450	900	0.1125	0.0001	0.0005	0.001	0.001	0.0005	0.0001	−3.858	6.0572	−4.8222	1.9426	−0.3163
500	1000	0.125	0.0002	0.0008	0.0016	0.0016	0.0008	0.0002	−3.7315	5.6939	−4.4205	1.7411	−0.2778
600	1200	0.15	0.0004	0.0018	0.0037	0.0037	0.0018	0.0004	−3.4789	5.0098	−3.6995	1.3942	−0.2138

700	1400	0.175	0.0007	0.0036	0.0072	0.0072	0.0036	0.0007	−3.2269	4.3811	−3.0782	1.1112	−0.1641
800	1600	0.2	0.0013	0.0064	0.0128	0.0128	0.0064	0.0013	−2.9754	3.806	−2.5453	0.8811	−0.1254
900	1800	0.225	0.0021	0.0106	0.0211	0.0211	0.0106	0.0021	−2.7246	3.2832	−2.0902	0.6948	−0.0955
1000	2000	0.25	0.0033	0.0164	0.0328	0.0328	0.0164	0.0033	−2.4744	2.811	−1.7038	0.5444	−0.0723
1200	**2400**	**0.3**	**0.0069**	**0.0347**	**0.0693**	**0.0693**	**0.0347**	**0.0069**	**−1.9759**	**2.0135**	**−1.1026**	**0.3276**	**−0.0407**
1400	2800	0.35	0.0129	0.0645	0.129	0.129	0.0645	0.0129	−1.4797	1.4037	−0.6809	0.1919	−0.0221
1600	3200	0.4	0.0219	0.1097	0.2194	0.2194	0.1097	0.0219	−0.9853	0.9738	−0.3864	0.1112	−0.0113
1800	3600	0.45	0.0349	0.1745	0.349	0.349	0.1745	0.0349	−0.4923	0.7183	−0.1733	0.0688	−0.0047
2000	4000	0.5	0.0528	0.2639	0.5279	0.5279	0.2639	0.0528	0	0.6334	0	0.0557	0
2250	4500	0.5625	0.0839	0.4196	0.8392	0.8392	0.4196	0.0839	0.6155	0.766	0.2213	0.0764	0.0061
2500	5000	0.625	0.1275	0.6377	1.2755	1.2755	0.6377	0.1275	1.2323	1.1667	0.5207	0.1459	0.016
2750	5500	0.6875	0.1875	0.9375	1.8751	1.8751	0.9375	0.1875	1.8516	1.8438	0.9825	0.2873	0.0351
3000	6000	0.75	0.2689	1.3447	2.6894	2.6894	1.3447	0.2689	2.4744	2.811	1.7038	0.5444	0.0723
3250	6500	0.8125	0.3788	1.8942	3.7885	3.7885	1.8942	0.3788	3.1011	4.0869	2.8014	0.9902	0.1435
3500	7000	0.875	0.527	2.6351	5.2702	5.2702	2.6351	0.527	3.7315	5.6939	4.4205	1.7411	0.2778
3750	7500	0.9375	0.7274	3.6368	7.2736	7.2736	3.6368	0.7274	4.3649	7.6566	6.7437	2.9813	0.5291

Table 3.3. Filter coefficients for a 5th order high pass Butterworth filter

f_{8000}	f_{16000}	f/f_s	b_0	b_1	b_2	b_3	b_4	b_5	a_1	a_2	a_3	a_4	a_5
45	90	0.005625	0.9444	−4.7221	9.4441	−9.4441	4.7221	−0.9444	−4.8856	9.549	−9.3331	4.5616	−0.8919
55	110	0.006875	0.9325	−4.6624	9.3249	−9.3249	4.6624	−0.9325	−4.8602	9.4506	−9.19	4.4692	−0.8695
65	130	0.008125	0.9207	−4.6035	9.2071	−9.2071	4.6035	−0.9207	−4.8348	9.3528	−9.0488	4.3785	−0.8477
75	150	0.009375	0.9091	−4.5454	9.0908	−9.0908	4.5454	−0.9091	−4.8094	9.2556	−8.9094	4.2896	−0.8264
85	170	0.010625	0.8976	−4.4879	8.9759	−8.9759	4.4879	−0.8976	−4.784	9.1591	−8.7718	4.2024	−0.8057
95	190	0.011875	0.8862	−4.4312	8.8625	−8.8625	4.4312	−0.8862	−4.7586	9.0631	−8.6359	4.1168	−0.7854
110	220	0.01375	0.8695	−4.3475	8.695	−8.695	4.3475	−0.8695	−4.7204	8.9205	−8.4355	3.9915	−0.756
130	260	0.01625	0.8476	−4.2382	8.4765	−8.4765	4.2382	−0.8476	−4.6696	8.7324	−8.1742	3.8299	−0.7185
150	300	0.01875	0.8263	−4.1317	8.2633	−8.2633	4.1317	−0.8263	−4.6188	8.5469	−7.9197	3.6744	−0.6828
170	340	0.02125	0.8055	−4.0277	8.0555	−8.0555	4.0277	−0.8055	−4.568	8.3639	−7.6718	3.5248	−0.6489
190	380	0.02375	0.7853	−3.9263	7.8527	−7.8527	3.9263	−0.7853	−4.5172	8.1834	−7.4304	3.3809	−0.6166
225	450	0.028125	0.751	−3.7548	7.5097	−7.5097	3.7548	−0.751	−4.4284	7.8734	−7.0231	3.1422	−0.564
275	550	0.034375	0.7045	−3.5223	7.0447	−7.0447	3.5223	−0.7045	−4.3015	7.4436	−6.4736	2.828	−0.4963
325	650	0.040625	0.6607	−3.3037	6.6073	−6.6073	3.3037	−0.6607	−4.1746	7.0289	−5.9602	2.5432	−0.4366
375	750	0.046875	0.6196	−3.098	6.1959	−6.1959	3.098	−0.6196	−4.0479	6.6292	−5.481	2.285	−0.3839
425	850	0.053125	0.5809	−2.9044	5.8088	−5.8088	2.9044	−0.5809	−3.9212	6.2442	−5.0341	2.0511	−0.3374
475	950	0.059375	0.5444	−2.7222	5.4443	−5.4443	2.7222	−0.5444	−3.7947	5.8737	−4.6178	1.8393	−0.2964

550	1100	0.06875	0.4937	−2.4687	4.9373	−4.9373	2.4687	−0.4937	−3.6051	5.3448	−4.0468	1.5589	−0.2438
650	1300	0.08125	0.4329	−2.1643	4.3286	−4.3286	2.1643	−0.4329	−3.3528	4.6886	−3.3772	1.2455	−0.1874
750	1500	0.09375	0.3788	−1.8942	3.7885	−3.7885	1.8942	−0.3788	−3.1011	4.0869	−2.8014	0.9902	−0.1435
850	1700	0.10625	0.3309	−1.6546	3.3091	−3.3091	1.6546	−0.3309	−2.8499	3.5382	−2.3086	0.783	−0.1095
950	1900	0.11875	0.2884	−1.4419	2.8837	−2.8837	1.4419	−0.2884	−2.5994	3.0408	−1.889	0.6155	−0.0832
1100	2200	0.1375	0.2334	−1.167	2.3339	−2.3339	1.167	−0.2334	−2.2249	2.3882	−1.3772	0.4238	−0.0544
1300	2600	0.1625	0.174	−0.8699	1.7399	−1.7399	0.8699	−0.174	−1.7275	1.6856	−0.8727	0.2515	−0.0302
1500	3000	0.1875	0.1275	−0.6377	1.2755	−1.2755	0.6377	−0.1275	−1.2323	1.1667	−0.5207	0.1459	−0.016
1700	3400	0.2125	0.0915	−0.4577	0.9153	−0.9153	0.4577	−0.0915	−0.7387	0.8245	−0.2723	0.0859	−0.0076
1900	3800	0.2375	0.0639	−0.3197	0.6394	−0.6394	0.3197	−0.0639	−0.2461	0.6546	−0.0842	0.059	−0.0022
2200	4400	0.275	0.0349	−0.1745	0.349	−0.349	0.1745	−0.0349	0.4923	0.7183	0.1733	0.0688	0.0047
2400	4800	0.3	0.0219	−0.1097	0.2194	−0.2194	0.1097	−0.0219	0.9853	0.9738	0.3864	0.1112	0.0113
2600	5200	0.325	0.0129	−0.0645	0.129	−0.129	0.0645	−0.0129	1.4797	1.4037	0.6809	0.1919	0.0221
2800	5600	0.35	0.0069	−0.0347	0.0693	−0.0693	0.0347	−0.0069	1.9759	2.0135	1.1026	0.3276	0.0407
3000	6000	0.375	0.0033	−0.0164	0.0328	−0.0328	0.0164	−0.0033	2.4744	2.811	1.7038	0.5444	0.0723
3300	6600	0.4125	0.0007	−0.0036	0.0072	−0.0072	0.0036	−0.0007	3.2269	4.3811	3.0782	1.1112	0.1641
3600	7200	0.45	5.98E-05	−2.99E-04	5.98E-04	−5.98E-04	2.99E-04	−5.98E-05	3.9845	6.4349	5.2536	2.1651	0.3599

current value of the output than say the second previous value. We might want to make the multiplier for values further back in the signal smaller than those nearer, with intermediate values in between. Well, there are various possibilities we could explore and they have different effects on the nature of the filtering, the acoustic effects of the filter. So I use the b variables, b_0, b_1, b_2 and so on to denote the multipliers of the previous values of the input. b_0 has a fixed value, but it may be the same as or different from b_1, which may be the same as or different from any of the other bs. In equation 3.1 the b values are all the same, 0.25. And in equation 3.2 we also have previous values of the output, $y[n-1]$ to $y[n-j]$, also being taken into account. Just as the previous values of the input are multiplied by bs, previous values of the output can be taken into the equation, multiplied by as. In our moving average example, equation 3.1, we did not refer to any previous values of the output, so all of the as were zero, and we had 3 previous terms. There were 4 bs in all, but they were all equal to 0.25.

The kind of filter in equation 3.2 is called an Infinite Impulse Response (IIR) filter. Sometimes they are called recursive filters. If all the as are zero, as in equation 3.1, it is called FIR: Finite Impulse Response. There are two kinds of digital filters, but the only difference between IIR and FIR is whether you refer to previous values of the output. The FIR is thus a special case of the IIR; you can get an FIR filter by using an IIR filter with all the as set to zero.

Now this is interesting and useful, because although we are not going to get deeply into the mathematics of these filters (because it is rather difficult), by choosing appropriate values of the bs and as and how many previous values of x and y you use, you can design a digital filter that has the desired frequency selectivity. We can set the range of frequencies that the filter excludes at a particular value. We can also design high pass filters, that allow high frequencies through but reduce or exclude low frequencies, below a certain frequency called the cut-off frequency. By combining a high pass filter with a low pass filter, we can also design band pass filters that allow frequencies within a certain range, but filter out higher and lower frequencies outside that range, the pass band.

Table 3.2 gives values of as and bs for a 5th order low pass Butterworth filter at a selection of frequencies relevant to speech applications. Refer to the first column, labelled f_{8000}, if the sampling rate of the signal is 8000 samples/s, and find the desired low-pass cut-off frequency (in hertz). Reading along the row will give the relevant bs and as. If the sampling rate is 16000 samples/s, use the second column. For other sampling rates f_s, divide the desired cut-off frequency f by the sampling rate f_s, and use the third column to find the right row. For example, to filter out frequencies above 3.3 kHz if the sampling rate is 11025 Hz, $f/f_s = 0.299$. This is very close to 0.3, for which the coefficients are 0.0069, 0.0347, 0.0693, 0.0693 . . . (the highlighted row).

Coefficients for high pass filters are given in table 3.3. For band pass filters, you can either use a combination of a high pass filter and a low pass filter, or a second-order resonator as described in section 3.8 below.

3.7 IIR filters in C

The program filter.c given in listing 3.3 is very little different from meansof4.c, given earlier. (I have italicised the differences to highlight them.) Note that in the line 'float a[6] = {0, -1.2323, 1.1667...};', the first value is always 0. Table 3.2 only gives values for a_1–a_5, represented in this C program as the array elements a[1] to a[5].

Listing 3.3

```
#include <stdlib.h>
#include <stdio.h>
#include <math.h>
#include "slputils.c"

/* FILTER.C
Filters infile to produce outfile using a fifth-order IIR filter with
coefficients a1-a6 and b1-b6. (For an FIR filter, set a[0..5] to 0.)
*/

int main(int argc, char *argv[]) {
   char *infile, *outfile;
   int *length, i;
   short int *x, *y, *signal_in();
   float *yf;
   void signal_out();

   /* Coefficients for a high-pass filter */
   /* (>3 kHz at 16000 samples/s) */
   float a[6] = {0, -1.2323, 1.1667, -0.5207, 0.1459, -0.0160};
   float b[6] = {0.1275, -0.6377, 1.2755, -1.2755, 0.6377, -0.1275};

   if (argc != 3) {
      printf("usage: filter input_file output_file\n");
      exit(1);
   }
   infile = argv[1];
   outfile = argv[2];

   x = signal_in(infile,length);
   y = (short *) calloc(*length,sizeof(short int));
   yf = (float *) calloc(*length,sizeof(float));

   for (i = 5 ; i < *length ; i++) {
      yf[i] = (int) (b[0]*x[i] + b[1]*x[i-1] + b[2]*x[i-2]
         + b[3]*x[i-3] + b[4]*x[i-4] + b[5]*x[i-5] - a[1]*yf[i-1]
         - a[2]*yf[i-2] - a[3]*yf[i-3] - a[4]*yf[i-4] - a[5]*yf[i-5]);
      y[i] = (short int) yf[i];
   }
   signal_out(length,y,outfile);
   return 0;
}
```

This program can easily be altered to the desired cut-off frequency by putting different values into the arrays a and b. Numbers in scientific notation (such as 5.98E−4, meaning 5.98×10^{-4}, i.e. 0.000598) can be entered as is: thus a declaration like 'float b[6] = {5.98E-5, 2.99E-4, 5.98E-4, 5.98E-4, 2.99E-4, 5.98E-5};' is fine in C.

3.8 Structure of the Klatt formant synthesizer

To conclude this chapter, we'll look at the structure of a speech synthesizer that uses a large number of bandpass filters in order to create complex sound waves that can sound similar to speech (provided that you set the filters to the right frequencies). A block diagram of the synthesizer in question, the Klatt formant synthesizer (Klatt 1980), is given in figure 3.3.

It generates synthetic speech signals on the basis of tables of control parameters. An example of such a parameter table is the file riy.par, which is designed for synthesis of the consonant–vowel sequence [ɹiː]. Part of that file is shown in table 3.4. (The parameter names listed along the top row are not included in the file. There are more parameters in table 3.4 than are mentioned in Klatt 1980, because the implementation is based on further revisions to the Klatt synthesizer introduced by Klatt and Klatt 1990. I shall not discuss those additions here: I shall only describe part of the basic 1980 version.) Each row of the table gives the control parameters for one frame (usually, as in this case, a 5 ms interval).

Each parameter controls some part of the synthesizer, as in figure 3.3.

For most of the components shown as rectangular boxes on this diagram, the synthesizer uses a large number of IIR filters of a very simple kind: second order bandpass filters of the form:

(3.3)
$$y[t] = Ax[t] + By[t - 1] + Cy[t - 2].$$

This is a specific version of equation 3.2, with $b_0 = A$, $b_1 \ldots b_k = 0$, $a_1 = B$, $a_2 = C$ and $a_3 \ldots a_j = 0$. Klatt uses the letters A, B and C instead of b_0, a_1 and a_2 so I will stick with his notation. Also, instead of $[t]$ he writes nT, meaning some multiple n of the sample-to-sample time interval T, but that is just an insignificant difference in notation. The values of A, B and C are determined by the frequency f, and bandwidth w of each filter according to the equations:

(3.4)
$$C = -e^{2\pi wT}$$
$$B = 2e^{\pi wT} \cos(2\pi/T)$$
$$A = 1 - B - C$$

The synthesizer uses filters of this kind for two main purposes. The first purpose is for modelling the glottal wave, and the second purpose is for

Table 3.4. The first 19 frames of `riy.par`

Parameter	1	2	3	4	5	6	7	8	9	10	11	12	13	14	15	16	17	18	19
GAIN (dB)	70	70	70	70	70	70	70	70	70	70	70	70	70	70	70	70	70	70	70
AVP (dB)	0	0	0	0	0	0	0	0	0	0	0	0	0	0	0	0	0	0	0
AB (dB)	0	0	0	0	0	0	0	0	0	0	0	0	0	0	0	0	0	0	0
ANP (dB)	0	0	0	0	0	0	0	0	0	0	0	0	0	0	0	0	0	0	0
B6P (Hz)	1000	1000	1000	1000	1000	1000	1000	1000	1000	1000	1000	1000	1000	1000	1000	1000	1000	1000	1000
A6 (dB)	0	0	0	0	0	0	0	0	0	0	0	0	0	0	0	0	0	0	0
B5P (Hz)	200	200	200	200	200	200	200	200	200	200	200	200	200	200	200	200	200	200	200
A5 (dB)	0	0	0	0	0	0	0	0	0	0	0	0	0	0	0	0	0	0	0
B4P (Hz)	250	250	250	250	250	250	250	250	250	250	250	250	250	250	250	250	250	250	250
A4 (dB)	0	0	0	0	0	0	0	0	0	0	0	0	0	0	0	0	0	0	0
B3P (Hz)	170	170	170	170	170	170	170	170	170	170	170	170	170	170	170	170	170	170	170
A3 (dB)	0	0	0	0	0	0	0	0	0	0	0	0	0	0	0	0	0	0	0
B2P (Hz)	110	110	110	110	110	110	110	110	110	110	110	110	110	110	110	110	110	110	110
A2 (dB)	0	0	0	0	0	0	0	0	0	0	0	0	0	0	0	0	0	0	0
B1P (Hz)	90	90	90	90	90	90	90	90	90	90	90	90	90	90	90	90	90	90	90
A1 (dB)	0	0	0	0	0	0	0	0	0	0	0	0	0	0	0	0	0	0	0
SKEW	0	0	0	0	0	0	0	0	0	0	0	0	0	0	0	0	0	0	0
AF (dB)	0	0	0	0	0	0	0	0	0	0	0	0	0	0	0	0	0	0	0
TILT (dB)	0	0	0	0	0	0	0	0	0	0	0	0	0	0	0	0	0	0	0
ATURB (dB)	40	40	40	40	40	40	40	40	40	40	40	40	40	40	40	40	40	40	40
KOPEN	30	30	30	30	30	30	30	30	30	30	30	30	30	30	30	30	30	30	30
ASP (dB)	0	0	0	0	0	0	0	0	0	0	0	0	0	0	0	0	0	0	0
BNP (Hz)	100	100	100	100	100	100	100	100	100	100	100	100	100	100	100	100	100	100	100
FNP (Hz)	250	250	250	250	250	250	250	250	250	250	250	250	250	250	250	250	250	250	250
BNZ (Hz)	100	100	100	100	100	100	100	100	100	100	100	100	100	100	100	100	100	100	100
FNZ (Hz)	250	250	250	250	250	250	250	250	250	250	250	250	250	250	250	250	250	250	250
B6 (Hz)	1000	1000	1000	1000	1000	1000	1000	1000	1000	1000	1000	1000	1000	1000	1000	1000	1000	1000	1000
F6 (Hz)	4900	4900	4900	4900	4900	4900	4900	4900	4900	4900	4900	4900	4900	4900	4900	4900	4900	4900	4900
B5 (Hz)	200	200	200	200	200	200	200	200	200	200	200	200	200	200	200	200	200	200	200
F5 (Hz)	3850	3850	3850	3850	3850	3850	3850	3850	3850	3850	3850	3850	3850	3850	3850	3850	3850	3850	3850
B4 (Hz)	250	250	250	250	250	250	250	250	250	250	250	250	250	250	250	250	250	250	250
F4 (Hz))	3300	3300	3300	3300	3300	3300	3300	3300	3300	3300	3300	3300	3300	3300	3300	3300	3300	3300	3300
B3 (Hz)	170	170	170	170	170	170	170	170	170	170	170	170	170	170	170	170	170	170	170
F3 (Hz)	2650	2650	2650	2650	2650	2650	2650	2650	2650	2650	2650	2650	2650	2650	2650	2650	2650	2650	2650
B2 (Hz)	110	110	110	110	110	110	110	110	110	110	110	110	110	110	110	110	110	110	110
F2 (Hz)	1890	1890	1890	1890	1890	1890	1890	1890	1890	1890	1890	1890	1890	1890	1890	1890	1890	1890	1890
B1 (Hz)	90	90	90	90	90	90	90	90	90	90	90	90	90	90	90	90	90	90	90
F1 (Hz)	680	680	680	680	680	680	680	680	680	680	680	680	680	680	680	680	680	680	680
AV (dB)	0	0	0	0	0	0	0	0	0	0	0	0	0	0	0	0	0	0	0
F0 (0.1 Hz)	0	0	0	0	0	0	0	0	0	0	0	0	0	0	0	0	0	0	0

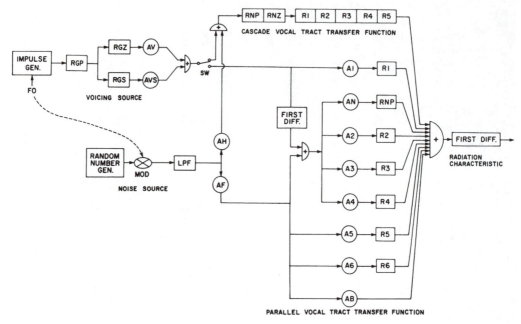

FIGURE 3.3
Block diagram of Klatt's formant synthesizer, reprinted with permission from D. H. Klatt (1980) Software for a cascade/parallel formant synthesizer. *Journal of the Acoustical Society of America* **67(3),** 971–95. Copyright 1980, Acoustical Society of America. Digital resonators (band pass filters) are indicated by the prefix *R* and amplitude controls by the prefix *A*. Each resonator R_n has an associated resonant frequency control parameter F_n and a resonance bandwidth control parameter B_n.

filtering specific frequency components from that glottal wave in order to model the resonant frequencies of the vocal tract. We will look first at how the synthesizer models the glottal wave. (The full program listing is too long to go through every line here, but I shall focus on the main steps in the synthesis process. Nevertheless, it is worth referring to the file `simple_parwave.c` while reading the description that follows.) The function `impulsive_source` (defined in `simple_parwave.c`) generates an impulse sequence, which is a sequence of spikes (in this implementation one sample with value 13000000, followed by one of -13000000) separated by 0's, as in figure 3.4. The spacing between the impulses is every four samples for voiceless speech (figure 3.4); for voiced speech the interval between impulses is the period of the fundamental frequency of the desired glottal wave (figure 3.5), as specified by the control parameter F0.

So if we use a sampling rate of 10000 samples per second (which is quite usual in Klatt synthesis), in order to generate a glottal wave with a fundamental frequency of 100 Hz, the period from one spike to the next is 100 samples. By changing the number of 0's that intervene between the spikes you can model the slowly changing rate of vibration of the vocal cords. Figure 3.6 shows the value of the variable `voice`, at line 183 of the function `parwave`, illustrating the actual impulse sequence generated on the basis

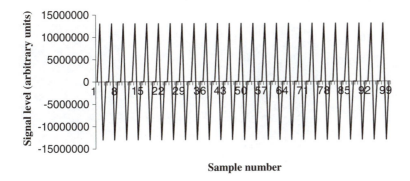

FIGURE 3.4
Impulsive source during voiceless frames

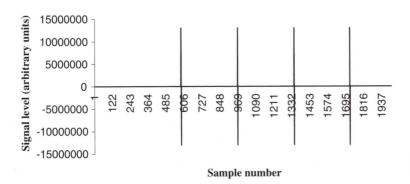

FIGURE 3.5
Impulsive source during voiced frames

of the parameter file `riy.par`. The impulses come very rapidly at the start and at the end, because the initial and final silences (before and after the actual utterance of [ɹiː]) are voiceless. In this portion, therefore, the impulse train is of the type shown in figure 3.4. In the middle portion, corresponding to the [ɹiː] portion, the impulse train is of the type appropriate for voicing, as in figure 3.5.

Note that the impulses are further apart at the start of the voiced portion (i.e. during the [ɹ]), compared with the middle (the beginning of the [iː]), because the frequency of the voicing is lower. At the end of the [iː], the impulses become further and further apart again, indicating a drop in the frequency of voicing. The spacing between impulses is calculated according to the F0 control parameter, which for `riy.par` is plotted in figure 3.7.

Klatt's design alters the amplitude of the impulse train by multiplying it by the amplitude of voicing (AV) parameter. The effect of this and subsequent filtering is to remove the very rapid impulses associated with voicelessness (because they are multiplied by AV, which is 0 for voicelessness), and to smooth out the spikes so that they are more like real glottal waveform pulses, as in figure 3.8.

The resulting glottal waveform for `riy.par` is shown in figure 3.9. The spectrum of this synthetic glottal waveform around the middle of the vowel (sample 3260, using a sampling rate of 8000 samples/s) is shown in figure 3.10.

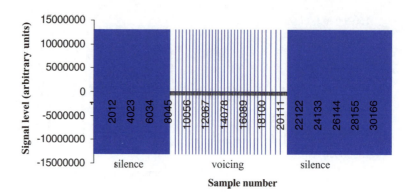

FIGURE 3.6
Impulse source generated
from riy.par

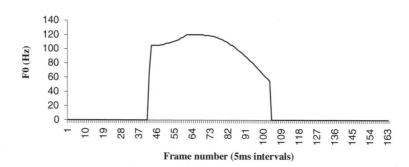

FIGURE 3.7
F0 parameter specified in
riy.par

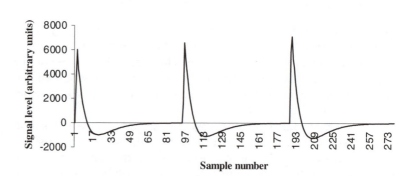

FIGURE 3.8
Synthetic glottal pulses

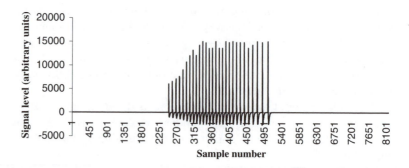

FIGURE 3.9
Synthetic glottal wave-
form generated from
riy.par

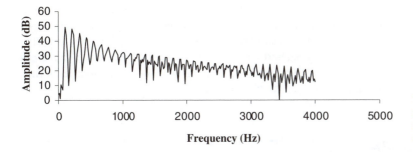

FIGURE 3.10
Spectrum of synthetic
glottal waveform
(512-point FFT, Hanning
window)

This glottal waveform is then put through the cascade of resonators (i.e. bandpass filters) R_1 to R_n. (n, usually 5, can be specified by the user at the command line.) Each resonator is a bandpass filter, which allows through the signal around a particular formant frequency, as specified by the parameters F1 to Fn, but attenuates (i.e., reduces the loudness of) other frequencies. The spectrum of the [iː] waveform at the output of the first four resonators is shown in figure 3.11. Note that there is an extra peak in the spectrum of each successive output.

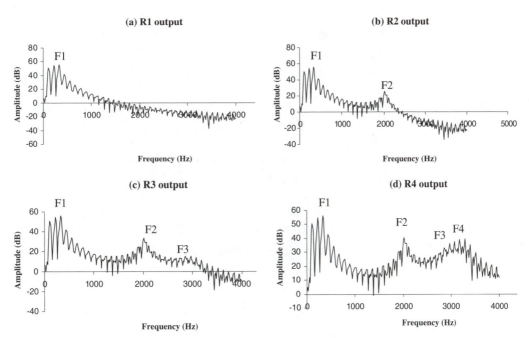

FIGURE 3.11
Effect of filtering the glottal wave at successive formant frequencies

When supplied with appropriate parameters, the Klatt synthesizer is capable of generating quite realistic-sounding synthetic speech, especially for short utterances. But analysing natural speech in order to determine formant frequencies, amplitudes and bandwidths, and other parameters, such as the amplitude of friction, is a very demanding task. (Some techniques are described in Coleman and Slater 2001.) In the next chapter we shall examine some of the necessary analysis techniques, as well as an alternative approach to speech analysis and synthesis that is capable of generating very realistic synthetic speech, without the difficulties of finding parameters for the Klatt synthesizer.

Chapter summary

In this chapter, we started to look at some ways in which digital signals can be manipulated on a computer. After some simple examples, such as calculating average and RMS amplitudes, we looked in detail at filtering: the selection of certain ranges of frequencies, and the reduction or elimination of other frequencies. Then, we saw how a formant synthesizer uses a combination of band pass filters at different frequencies to model the resonant frequencies of the vocal tract. In this way, speech-like sounds can be artificially generated.

Exercises

Exercise 3.1
Complete table 3.1.

Exercise 3.2
If we are interested in the perception of intonation, we might low pass filter a speech signal at, say, 200 Hz, in order to create a somewhat muffled version of a recording, which preserves the pitch of the original. How many samples would a moving average filter need to include in order to attain this cut-off frequency?

Exercise 3.3
Try it. Adapt the program `meansof4.c` into a new program `meansof80.c`. Hints: Instead of the equation:

```
y[i] = b[0]*x[i]+b[1]*x[i-1]+b[2]*x[i-2]+b[3]*x[i-3];
```

don't bother with the array b, and use a loop to add up the `x[i-n]`'s:

```
for (n=0;n<80;n++) y[i] += x[i-n]/80;
```

Don't forget to initialize `y[i]` to 0 before the loop. (If you get completely stuck, sneak a peek at `meansof40.c`.)

Exercise 3.4
Suppose we have digitized a cassette tape recording at 16000 samples/s. Unfortunately, there is an annoying high-pitched 'tape hiss' in the recording, as in the file `hissy.dat`. However, we decide that we can live with a recording that only goes up to 5500 Hz, because the most important features of speech are below that frequency. What size of moving-average window is needed?

Exercise 3.5

Try it. Adapt `meansof4.c` to make a filter for reducing tape hiss. Compare the results of cleaning up `hissy.dat` using a moving-average filter with the results of using a low-pass IIR filter with a cut-off frequency of 5000 Hz.

Exercise 3.6

Compile the simple version of the Klatt synthesizer given on the CD-ROM, `simple_klatt.c`, as follows:

```
gcc -c simple_parwave.c

gcc -c simple_klatt.c

gcc -o sklatt.exe simple_klatt.o simple_parwave.o
```

Test it out by synthesizing `riy.par` using the command `sklatt -i riy.par -o riy.dat -r 2`. You can then play and listen to `riy.dat`. (You will need to know that the sampling rate is 11025 Hz.)

Exercise 3.7

The data for figure 3.9 was generated using the command `sklatt -i riy.par -o figure3.9.txt -n 0 -q`. The figure was plotted by importing `figure3.9.txt` into Microsoft Excel. You can generate a glottal signal file using the command `sklatt -i riy.par -o riy_voice.dat -n 0 -r 2`, which you can then play and listen to! It sounds just like a buzz, with the right duration and pitch for [ɹiː], but no articulation.

Further reading

Most of the literature on digital filtering is *much* more technical than this chapter, so I shall not make any specific recommendations here. For more on the Klatt speech synthesizer, see Klatt 1980 and Klatt and Klatt 1990. Some techniques for estimating the control parameters for the Klatt synthesizer are described in Coleman and Slater 2001.

Reading in preparation for the next chapter

Johnson 1997: 33–47 and 85–9; Wakita 1996, especially pp. 470–8.

4 Frequency analysis and linear predictive coding

CHAPTER PREVIEW

In this chapter we look at programs for analysing various acoustic parameters from speech signals, including spectral analysis, linear predictive coding, two methods of f_0 analysis and two methods of formant frequency estimation.

KEY TERMS

spectrum

Fourier transform

window

cepstrum

pitch tracking

voicing detection

autocorrelation

linear prediction

4.1 Spectral analysis

The subject of this chapter is the extraction of various acoustic parameters from speech signals. In the last chapter we saw how, by using filters as resonators, we could model the resonances of the vocal tract. In combination with a specification of the fundamental frequency of vocal cord vibration (the pitch of the voice as it rises and falls), we could construct a signal that was a good synthetic imitation of a natural speech signal. The question arises as to how we are to derive the necessary frequency, bandwidth and pitch parameters from analysis of natural speech. For the first half of this chapter that is what we are going to be looking at.

First of all, let's consider the analysis of the resonances, the frequency components of natural speech. A simple method for getting information about the resonances of the vocal tract is spectrography, a technique familiar from experimental phonetics. The original spectrographs were hardware devices in which a single tuneable filter was used to analyse an input signal by scanning through the range of possible frequencies in speech (Koenig, Dunn and Lacy 1946), by looking at the strength of the signal at each particular frequency, just as you might take a transistor radio and scan through the different radio frequencies to pick out the strong radio stations and the weak radio stations. The technique of extracting different frequency components from a complex wave, such as a speech wave, has been mathematically well understood for a long time: this is the technique of Fourier analysis. The French mathematician Jean Baptiste Joseph Fourier (1768–1830) developed methods by which any signal, however complex, can be analysed as the sum of a (possibly large) number of much simpler signals, for instance the sum of a set of simple cosine waves, each of which with a particular frequency, bandwidth, amplitude and phase with respect to the other frequency components. However, although Fourier analysis was being applied to speech analysis by the end of the nineteenth century, implementing computations to extract the individual frequency components of a wave by a Fourier analysis was very challenging until the arrival of the Fast Fourier Transform (FFT) algorithm, a numerical analysis method developed by Cooley and Tukey in the mid-1960s. (Their method had also been independently discovered many times by earlier workers.) The (re)discovery of the Fast Fourier Transform algorithm opened the way to its pervasive use as a method of frequency analysis in speech processing, where hitherto we had had to rely mainly on the hardware method of spectrography.

4.2 Spectral analysis in C

Listing 4.1 gives a program for computing the spectrum of a portion of a signal at a stated sample number. Like the other program listings in this book, it is included on the CD-ROM. For the calculation of the FFT, it uses the function four1, which is from Press et al. 1992: 507–8. Compile it in the usual way, to produce an executable file called spectrum.exe, as follows:

```
gcc -c spectrum.c
gcc -o spectrum.exe spectrum.o
```

Since the other program files it needs (`slputils.c` and `four1.c`) are `#included` at the start, there is no need to compile them separately. This done, you can get the spectrum around a certain sample of a signal file using an expression of the form:

```
spectrum filename.dat sample_number
```

For example, to get the spectrum at around sample 15000 of `joe.dat` (the middle of the vowel [ɑ] of 'father'), type:

```
spectrum joe.dat 15000
```

Listing 4.1

```
#include <stdio.h>
#include <math.h>
#include <stdlib.h>
#include "slputils.c"
#include "four1.c"                                                    5

/* SPECTRUM.C                                                      */
/* Spectral analysis using a 512-point FFT                        */

int main(int argc, char *argv[])                                    10
{
    short int *x_in, *signal_in();
    char *infile, *sampleno, *endcp;
    int sample, i, *length;
    float wvalue, twopi, arg, logpsd[512];                          15
    float data[1024];               /* 512 complex data points    */
    void four1();

    if (argc != 3) {
        printf("usage: spectrum input_file sample_number [ > output_file ]\n");
        exit(1);
    }
    infile = argv[1];
    sampleno = argv[2];
                                                                    25

    x_in = signal_in(infile,length);
    sample = (int) strtoul(sampleno,&endcp,10);

/* Windowing using 512-point Hanning window and coercion to floats  */
                                                                    30
    twopi = 8.0*atan(1.0);                         /* calculate 2*PI */
    arg = twopi/511.0;
    for (i=0;i<=511;i++) {
```

```
        wvalue = 0.5 - 0.5*cos(arg*i);
        data[2*i] = (float) (x_in[sample+i-256] * wvalue);          35
        data[2*i+1] = 0.0;
    }
    four1(data-1,512,1);
                                                                    40
/* In the log power spectral density, magnitudes are in dB       */
/* in steps of SampleRate/512 Hz (31.25Hz at 16000 samples/s).   */

    printf("f (Hz)\tAmplitude (dB)\n");
                                                                    45
    for (i=0;i<=256;i++) {
        logpsd[i] = data[2*i];
        logpsd[i] *= logpsd[i];
        logpsd[i] += SQR(data[2*i+1]);
        logpsd[i] = 10*log10(logpsd[i]);                           50
        printf("%d\t%.2f\n",(int) (i*31.25),logpsd[i]);
    }
    return 0;
}
```

The program uses the function `signal_in` to read a signal from the input file into a variable, `x_in`, and a sample number `sample`. A 512-sample portion of the signal from `sample-256` to `sample+255` is windowed using a Hanning window, the FFT is calculated, then the log power spectral density, which is written as lines of text to the standard output. (If any of this terminology is unclear to you, don't worry: I shall now describe each step in turn.)

As with many of our programs, a good portion of the code is taken up with declaring variables (lines 12–17) and reading in the data specified by the arguments to the `spectrum` command. For example, lines 19–23 check that no arguments are missing, and assigns them to variables; lines 27–8 reads in the signal, and line 28, '`sample = (int) strtoul(sampleno,&endcp,10);`', converts `sampleno` (a string of ASCII numerals) to `sample` (an integer). The `strtoul` function, which converts <u>str</u>ings <u>to</u> <u>u</u>nsigned <u>l</u>ong integers, is defined in the C standard library `stdlib`.

Windowing

The real signal processing is done in the second half of the program, lines 31–54. First, a portion of the signal from 256 samples before `sample` until 255 samples after `sample` is multiplied by a Hanning window: a function based on one cycle of a cosine, that goes smoothly from 0 at the beginning to 1 in the middle and back to 0 at the end (figure 4.1).

When a portion of the signal is multiplied by this function, its ends smoothly diminish in amplitude. Figure 4.2a shows a 512-sample portion of `joe.dat` around sample 15000, and figure 4.2b the result of multiplying that portion by the Hanning window. Note, in particular, that there

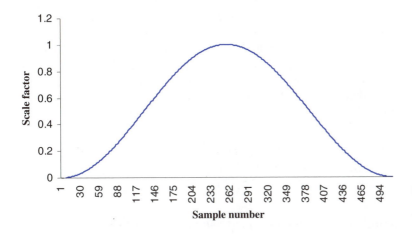

FIGURE 4.1
512-point Hanning
window data

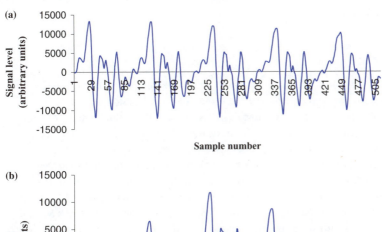

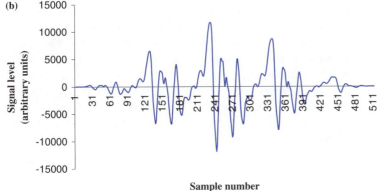

FIGURE 4.2
(a) 512-sample extract
from `joe.dat`, centred
on sample 15000.
(b) 512-point Hanning
windowed portion of
`joe.dat`, centred on
sample 15000.

are five large pulses in figure 4.2a, of which the first is the largest. In figure 4.2b, however, the effect of the Hanning window is to dramatically
reduce the size of the first and last pulses, with the result that the signal
extract is at its greatest amplitude around the middle. Various kinds of
windowing function have been proposed in the signal processing literature: for examples see Press et al. 1992 or Embree and Kimble 1991.

The windowed portion of the signal is converted from integers to floats and put into the even-numbered cells of data, an array of 1024 cells. This is the array of data that is submitted to the four1 function. So x_in[frame-256] goes into data[0], x_in[frame-255] goes into data[2], and so on until x_in[frame+255] goes into data[1022]. The odd-numbered cells of data are set to zero. This is all done using the following code, from lines 33–37:

```
for (i=0;i<=511;i++) {
    wvalue = 0.5 - 0.5*cos(arg*i);
    data[2*i] = (float) (x_in[sample+i-256] * wvalue);
    data[2*i+1] = 0.0;
}
```

In this extract, a loop is set up to count i from 0 up to 511. wvalue is the value of the Hanning window at sample i. The final two lines put samples of x_in into even-numbered cells of data and zeroes the odd-numbered cells.

Complex numbers

If you don't already know about complex numbers, you can skip this paragraph without losing the thread of the discussion.
The reason why data has twice as many cells as the number of samples in the portion we are analysing is because the FFT is defined to work with complex numbers. We represent complex numbers as a pair of two floats, one for the real part and one for the imaginary part. In the input speech signal, all of the samples are real, so they go into the even-numbered cells, the real part of each of the 512 complex data-points used by the four1 function. See Press et al. 1992: 508 for details, but note that our scheme of numbering of array cells in the standard C manner as data[0] to data[1023] differs from the convention used by Press et al. of unit-offset numbering from data[1] to data[1024]. Which is why on line 39 we pass the data array to the four1 function using the reference data-1! Either convention is as good as the other, however.

With the data array loaded up in the right way, it is passed in line 41 to the four1 function. The result of calculating the Fourier transform of the input is returned by the four1 function in the data array too: that is, it replaces the input samples. Each number in the Fourier transform shows the strength of the signal at a particular frequency, but the relationship between data points and frequencies is rather strange (purely as a side-effect of the way the FFT is calculated). data[0] and data[1] relate to frequency zero, and can be ignored. data[2] to data[513] map on to increasingly higher frequencies. The remaining cells, from data[514] to data[1023] contain a mirror-image, in reverse order, of the lower half of the array, and can be ignored. The frequency interval (in Hertz) between one cell and the next is the sampling rate divided by 512; thus, it is 31.25 Hz for a signal sampled at 16000 samples/s. The frequency (in Hertz) of cell `i-1` is `i` times the frequency interval.

In lines 46–52 we use the values of the Fourier transform to calculate the power at each frequency, in decibels. Using a `for` loop that counts from 0 to 256, we print the frequency and amplitude at each multiple of the frequency interval. Since it is text output, we can redirect it to a file, using the MS-DOS (or Unix) ">" operator. For instance: `spectrum joe.dat 15000 >joe_spec.txt` sends the output to the file `joe_spec.txt`, the beginning of which looks like this:

```
f (Hz)     Amplitude (dB)
0          85.41
31         80.14
62         68.83
93         83.72
125        108.82
156        113.09
187        105.27
218        75.24
250        84.23
281        104.84
312        107.46
343        98.14
```

Text data such as this can be processed by other software. For example, by importing `joe_spec.txt` into Microsoft Excel, it was easy to plot figure 4.3.

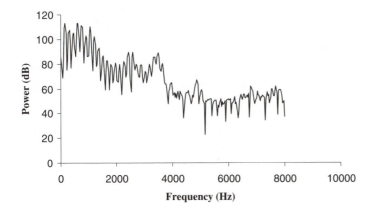

FIGURE 4.3
Spectrum of portion of `joe.dat`, centred on sample 15000

Such a plot is known more technically as the **power spectral density**, though it is usually referred to as the **spectrum**, for short.

Exercise 4.1
If you have any other software capable of spectral analysis, compare the outputs. For instance, the output of spectral analysis at the same point using Cool Edit is

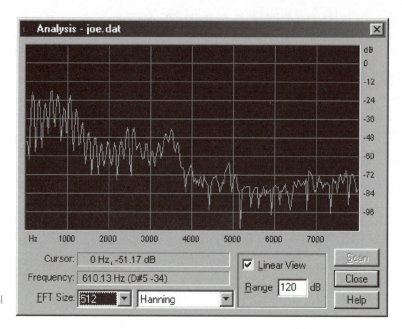

FIGURE 4.4
A spectral analysis in Cool
Edit

shown in figure 4.4. Naturally, it is not different from figure 4.3 in any important respects. (One small difference is that the power scale in figure 4.3 goes from 0 to 120 dB, whereas the Cool Edit scale goes from −120 to 0 dB, i.e. the 0 dB reference point is taken to be the maximum amplitude signal.)

You will appreciate that if we had some method of picking out the peaks from such a spectrum, i.e. the resonant frequencies of the vocal tract, we would have a way of estimating the formant frequencies. There is a problem in accurately estimating formant frequencies, however, which is evident in figure 4.5a (from Noll 1967: the same figure is also reproduced in Wakita 1996).

The spectra in figures 4.3, 4.4 and 4.5a contain two kinds of peaks. First there are many little narrow peaks, each of which is an integral multiple of the fundamental frequency. We call these peaks harmonics. And then there are larger, or rather perhaps we should say wider peaks (shown by a dashed line in figure 4.5a), which represent the resonances of the vocal tract. Our ability to plot, or to compute the location in the frequency domain of the resonances of the vocal tract is somewhat impaired by the presence of the smaller peaks, the harmonics. Where a harmonic happens to coincide with a resonant frequency, that is, where the resonant frequency of the vocal tract happens to be an integral multiple of the fundamental frequency, we get a fairly well defined formant peak. But where the resonant frequency happens to be a little off a harmonic frequency, finding the resonant peak may be somewhat difficult. So it would be useful to have a method for separating out the location of the harmonic peaks from the location of the underlying resonances, the

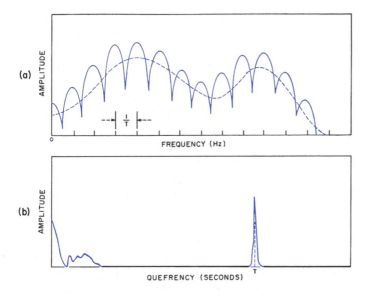

FIGURE 4.5
(a) Spectrum of a
voiced speech segment;
(b) the cepstrum of (a).
Reprinted with permis-
sion from A. M. Noll
(1967) Cepstrum pitch
determination. *Journal of
the Acoustical Society of
America* **88**, 1299–1312.
© 1967, Acoustical
Society of America.

resonant peaks. The second technique that we are going to look at in this chapter, cepstral analysis, enables us to do this, to separate the harmonic peaks from the resonances. By separating out the harmonic peaks it enables us to get a good estimate of the pitch, since the harmonics occur at integral multiples of the fundamental. It does not really help us to get a better estimate of the resonant frequencies of the vocal tract (the formants), however. We shall return to that subject at the end of the chapter.

4.3 Cepstral analysis

The technique of cepstral analysis is fairly well described in Wakita (1996). One way of approaching the idea of the cepstrum is to consider first the spectral representation that we have in figure 4.5a, a standard power spectral density function displayed on a logarithmic scale. Suppose that we were to ignore for a moment the fact that the horizontal axis is a frequency scale; after all, that is just a label that we give to the graph. Suppose that the graph we are looking at here were a short segment of a signal in the time domain, a short time-varying signal. We want to find the distance between the smaller peaks, as well as the distance between the larger peaks. In the time domain, that would amount to determining the frequency of the smaller vibrations and the frequency of the larger vibrations. If this were a time domain signal we could do a Fourier analysis of it, and that would tell us the frequency of the higher frequency events (the little peaks) as well as the lower frequency events (the big peaks). The higher frequency peaks represent the harmonics and the lower frequency peaks represent the underlying resonances. So if we were to take a Fourier analysis of this graph, that would give us a technique for separating out the narrow harmonic peaks from the broad resonance peaks. So, having applied the Fast Fourier Transform once, to get the power spectrum, if we apply it again, a second time, we will be able to measure the time interval between the little peaks and the time interval between the big peaks. However since we are mapping not from the time domain to the frequency domain on this second application, but from the frequency domain back into the time domain, the operation that we use is not an FFT as such, but an *inverse* Fast Fourier Transform. This will have the same separation effect but will take us from the frequency domain back into the time domain. What is this time domain that arises as the result of performing an inverse Fast Fourier Transform to a log power spectral density? Well, it is called quefrency, a term coined by Bogert et al. 1963 that is intended to denote the inverse of frequency in some respect, the inverse of frequency being a time domain unit. On the horizontal axis of figure 4.5b it is given in seconds, though as we shall see the units of quefrency will turn out to be *samples* of the original signal. The quefrency of the spike that we see representing the fundamental frequency will turn out to be the *period* (in samples) of the fundamental frequency of the original signal. You can see in figure 4.5b the result of applying an inverse Fast Fourier Transform to a log power spectrum. There is one sharply demarcated spike at around T seconds on the scale, which is the spike representing the fundamental frequency. If $T = 8.4$ ms, for instance, the frequency will be 119 Hz, since $f = 1/T$. At the left-hand end of the horizontal axis, that is quefrencies of events with a very much smaller period, we have peaks that represent the resonances of the vocal tract. Note that there is a very clear separation between the fundamental frequency and the resonances. That is because the fundamental frequency, the period of the glottal wave may be of the order of say 10 milliseconds, whereas the period – if that is the right word to use – the time taken for each oscillation of the resonators is very much shorter. At a sampling rate of 8000 samples a second, a resonance at 4000 Hz, for instance, would have a period of just 2 samples, a quarter of a millisecond. So that is the idea of cepstral analysis.

4.4 Computation of the cepstrum in C

So much for the theory: now let's look at some actual examples of the computation, in C. Since we have already found out how to compute the power spectral density, we are already in a position to compute the next step, to take the inverse Fast Fourier Transform of the logarithm of the power spectral density, that is the cepstrum. Listing 4.2 gives a C program, `cepstrum.c`, for doing this. Just like `spectrum.c` (listing 4.1), it expects a file name and a sample number as its two arguments, and it gives the cepstrum in text form, as a list of paired quefrency and amplitude values. Also, since quefrencies are easily converted to frequencies, it prints out the corresponding frequencies too, for convenience.

Listing 4.2

```
#include <stdio.h>
#include <math.h>
#include <stdlib.h>
#include "slputils.c"
#include "four1.c"                                              5

/* CEPSTRUM.C                                               */
/* Cepstral analysis                                        */
/* An extension of spectrum.c                               */
                                                              10
/* Reads a signal from a disk file into a variable, x_in, and a  */
/* frame number n. Windows the signal using a Hanning window,    */
/* calculates the FFT, the log power spectral density, and then  */
/* the inverse Fourier transform. The lower half is written as a */
/* text stream to the standard output.                      */  15

int main(int argc, char *argv[])
{
      short int *x_in, *signal_in();
      char *infile, *frameno, *endcp;                         20
      int frame, i, *length;
      float wvalue, twopi, arg, logpsd[1024];
      float data[1024];             /* 512 complex data points    */
      void four1();
                                                              25
      if (argc != 3) {
            printf("usage: cepstrum input_file frame_number [>
            output_file ]\n");
            exit(1);
      }                                                        30
      infile = argv[1];
      frameno = argv[2];

      x_in = signal_in(infile,length);
      frame = (int) strtoul(frameno,&endcp,10);                35

      /* 512-point Hanning windowing and coercion to floats     */
      twopi = 8.0*atan(1.0);                    /* calculate 2*PI */
      arg = twopi/511.0;

      for (i=0;i<=511;i++) {                                   40
            wvalue = 0.5 - 0.5*cos(arg*i);
            data[2*i] = (float) (x_in[frame+i-256] * wvalue);
            data[2*i+1] = 0.0;
      }
                                                              45
      four1(data-1,512,1);

/* So far, this is all the same as spectrum.c                */

      for (i=0;i<=511;i++) {                                   50
```

```
        logpsd[2*i] = data[2*i];
        logpsd[2*i] *= logpsd[2*i];
        logpsd[2*i] += SQR(data[2*i+1]);
        logpsd[2*i] = 10*log10(logpsd[2*i]);
        logpsd[2*i+1] = 0.0;                                    55
    }

/* This is additional to spectrum.c                            */

    four1(logpsd-1,512,-1);                    /* Inverse FFT */  60

    printf("Quefrency (ms)\tf (Hz)\tAmplitude\n");
    for (i=2;i<256;i++)
        printf("%f\t%.1f\t%f\n",i*0.0625,16000.0/i,logpsd[2*i]);
    return 0;                                                  65
}
```

The first noteworthy difference between cepstrum.c and spectrum.c is that the array in which the spectrum is stored, logpsd, has 1024 cells, not 512, because it is submitted to the four1 function. The values of the spectrum go into the even-numbered cells, logpsd[2*i], and the odd-numbered cells, logpsd[2*i+1], are set to 0.0.

The four1 function is used twice, first to calculate the spectrum, and then towards the end, to calculate the inverse Fourier transform. The third argument, -1, in the expression 'four1(logpsd-1,512,-1);' indicates that the inverse transform is required. As before, four1 puts its result back in the array supplied to it, in this case logpsd. In the printout of quefrency, the lower half of the inverse Fourier transform has 256 values, representing a quefrency range from 1 sample to 256 samples. The duration of 1 sample (at 16000 samples/s) is 0.0625 ms, so the quefrency of the i the value is i times 0.0625, corresponding to a frequency of $16000/i$.

Compile cepstrum.c as for spectrum.c, above:

```
gcc -c cepstrum.c
gcc -o cepstrum.exe cepstrum.o
```

As with spectrum.c, the textual output of cepstrum can be redirected to a text file. Figure 4.6 was made by importing the cepstrum of joe.dat around sample 15000 into Microsoft Excel.

A large peak is apparent in the upper panel of figure 4.6 at a quefrency of about 7 ms. The plot of the same cepstrum on the frequency scale (the lower plot in figure 4.6) is less revealing. The spike is clearly very close to 0 Hz, but because the scale goes up to 8 kHz we cannot see much more than that. Other peaks in the range 0–2 kHz correspond to vocal tract resonances, but we cannot tell their frequencies with precision. On the other hand, inspection of the quefrency data around the 7 ms point reveals that the actual quefrency of the biggest spike is at 6.5625 ms, corresponding to a frequency of 152.4 Hz. That is the fundamental frequency – the frequency of voicing – for that portion of the vowel.

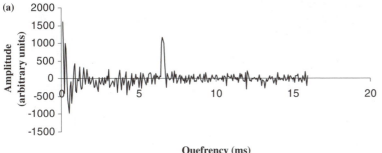

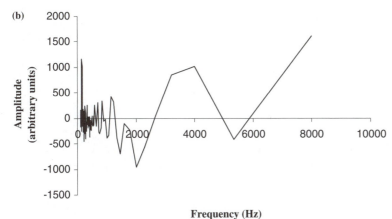

FIGURE 4.6
Real cepstrum of portion of `joe.dat`. Above: quefrency scale; below: frequency scale.

4.5 Pitch tracking using cepstral analysis

To conclude this discussion of cepstral analysis, let us consider a modification of `cepstrum.c`, such that it works right the way through a file, calculating the cepstrum every 80 samples (every 5 ms at 16000 samples/s) and writing out the f_0 each time.

Listing 4.3

```
#include <stdio.h>
#include <math.h>
#include <stdlib.h>
#include "slputils.c"
#include "four1.c"                                              5

/* CEPSTRAL_F0.C                                          */
/* Pitch (f0) tracking using cepstral analysis            */
/* An extension of cepstrum.c                             */
                                                              10
/* Reads a signal from a disk file into a variable, x_in. */
/* f0 is written as a *text* stream to the standard output. */
```

```
int main(int argc, char *argv[]) {
    short int *x_in, *signal_in();                                      15
    char *infile, *frameno, *endcp;
    int i, *length;
    void four1(), cepstral_f0();
    float max_f0;
                                                                        20
    if (argc != 2) {
        printf("usage: cepstral_f0 input_file [ > output_file ]\n");
        exit(1);
    }
    infile = argv[1];                                                   25
    x_in = signal_in(infile,length);

    printf("Sample\tf_0 (Hz)\n");
    for (i=79;i<319;i+=80) printf("%d\t0\n",i);
    for (i=319;i<*length-256;i+=80)                                     30
        cepstral_f0(i,x_in,max_f0);
    return 0;
}

void cepstral_f0(int frame, short int *x_in, float max_f0) {           35
/* Given a pointer to a signal *x_in and a frame number, returns the
pitch. */

    float data[1024];                      /* 512 complex data points  */
    float wvalue, twopi, arg, max, logpsd[1024];                       40
    int i;

/* Windowing using 512-point Hanning window and coercion to floats */

    twopi = 8.0*atan(1.0);                 /* calculate 2*PI          */ 45
    arg = twopi/511.0;
    for (i=0;i<=511;i++) {
        wvalue = 0.5 - 0.5*cos(arg*i);
        data[2*i] = x_in[frame+i-256] * wvalue;
        data[2*i+1] = 0.0;                                             50
    }

    four1(data-1,512,1);

    for (i=0;i<=511;i++) {                                             55
        logpsd[2*i] = data[2*i];
        logpsd[2*i] *= logpsd[2*i];
        logpsd[2*i] += SQR(data[2*i+1]);
        logpsd[2*i] = 10*log10(logpsd[2*i]);
        logpsd[2*i+1] = 0.0;                                          60
    }

    four1(logpsd-1,512,-1);                        /* Inverse FFT        */

    max = 0.0;                                                         65
```

```
    max_f0 = 0.0;
    for (i=88;i<256;i++){
/* Work down from an upper limit of 180Hz (88 = 16000/180)          */
        if (logpsd[2*i] > max) {
            max = logpsd[2*i];                                       70
            max_f0 = 16000.0/i;
        }
    }
    printf("%d\t%.1f\n",frame,max_f0);
}                                                                    75
```

Although this is longer than any of the other programs we've seen so far, there is hardly anything new in it. It can be divided into three sections. First, lines 1 to 26 ('x_in = signal_in(infile,length);') are virtually the same as the beginning of spectrum.c and cepstrum.c. These lines read the input file into the array x_in.

Second, lines 35–75 package up the remainder of cepstrum.c into a function, cepstral_f0, that calculates the cepstrum at a particular frame (as in cepstrum.c), and then finds the biggest peak in the cepstrum below 400Hz. So, instead of printing out the whole cepstrum, it just gives the cepstral peak, which is the f_0 of that frame. Lines 65–74 find the peak in the cepstrum. The variable max provides working memory for the maximum value of the cepstrum so far, and max_f0 is the f_0 corresponding to that peak. The loop set up in line 67 counts i through each quefrency, from 88 samples (182 Hz) to 256 samples (62.5 Hz). To alter the range in which f_0 is sought, therefore, these limits can be changed. Lines 69–72 can be paraphrased as 'if the cepstral amplitude at the ith quefrency is greater than the maximum found so far, make it the new maximum, and recalculate the peak f_0 from the current quefrency'.

Third, lines 28–31, at the end of the main function, are the main addition to cepstrum.c. The loop 'for (i=319;i<*length-256;i+=80)' counts through the input signal from sample 319 as far as the sample that is 256 samples from the end, in jumps of 80 samples (5 ms). (Sample 319 is the 320th sample, or the very end of the fourth 80-sample interval.) Each time, it calls the function cepstral_f0, thus computing and printing the peak f_0 for that frame. Because the cepstrum computation uses a window of 512 samples centred on the current sample, the first cepstrum cannot be computed until at least 256 samples into the signal, and no later than 256 samples from the end of the signal. Since the frames are at 80-sample intervals, the first frame is at the first multiple of 80 after 256, which is sample number 319 (taking account of the fact that the first sample is numbered 0). Figure 4.7 shows the result of applying cepstral_f0 to joe.dat. (Once again, the text stream printed out by cepstral_f0 was redirected to a text file and imported into Excel to plot this graph.)

It is evident that this method of f_0 tracking suffers from the limitation that it will find f_0 values even during voiceless portions, causing the f_0 track

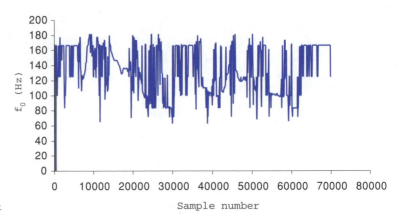

FIGURE 4.7
f_0 estimate from `joe.dat`

to fluctuate wildly, within the prescribed limits. These measurements are quite useless, but if we had a way of working out which parts of the signal were voiced and which voiceless, we could set the f_0 track to zero during the voiceless portions. The rising pitch of the vowel of 'joe' (around samples 7000–10000) and the falling pitch of '(f)ather' (around samples 14000–19000) are evident. Closer inspection shows that the f_0 tracking works well in shorter voiced portions, too.

So, it would be useful to have a program that automatically worked out which samples were in voiced speech and which were in voiceless speech, generating a signal with only two possible values: 0 (for voiceless samples) and 1 for voiced samples. Then, if we multiply the f_0 signal (such as that in figure 4.7) by the voicing signal, f_0 would be set to 0 in voiceless samples. We would thus 'mask out' the voiceless portions, and get the frequency of vibration of the vocal cords only during speech that is really voiced. In the next section I shall present a method for achieving this.

4.6 Voicing detection

The idea behind the method of voicing detection in the program `voicing.c` is that in voiced speech there is more energy in lower frequencies (e.g. frequencies below, say, 400 Hz), whereas in voiceless speech there is not much energy in this frequency range. It suffers from the obvious limitation that if the recording is not clean and contains any low-frequency environmental noise (such as a motor running in the background, or even electrical interference from an AC power supply, such as a 50 or 60 Hz 'mains hum'), it will not work properly: it will classify the whole signal as voiced. (Such noise can sometimes be eliminated by high-pass filtering at the right frequency.) Also, for recordings made with a poor-quality microphone, such as those taken from a telephone, in which low frequencies are not picked up well, it will not work. However, experience shows that this method works fairly well with clean, good quality recordings. The program is given in listing 4.4.

Listing 4.4

```
#include <stdlib.h>
#include <stdio.h>
#include <math.h>
#include "slputils.c"
                                                                    5
/* VOICING.C                                                   */
/* Low-pass filters infile using a 400Hz low-pass filter.     */
/* Calculates running rms amplitude over a 100-sample window. */
/* Outputs voiced/unvoiced decision per sample, to outfile.   */
                                                                    10
int main(int argc, char *argv[]) {
    char *infile, *outfile;
    int *length, i;
    short int *x, *y, *signal_in();
    float *yf, *yfsqr, *sumsq;                                      15
    void signal_out();

 /* Coefficients for a low-pass filter                        */
 /* (<400 Hz at 16000 samples/s)                              */
float a[6] = {0, -4.4918, 8.0941, -7.3121, 3.311, -0.6011};         20
float b[6] = {2.34E-6, 1.17E-5, 2.34E-5, 2.34E-5, 1.17E-5, 2.34E-6};

    if (argc != 3) {
        printf("usage: voicing input_file output_file\n");
        exit(1);                                                    25
    }
    infile = argv[1];
    outfile = argv[2];

    x = signal_in(infile,length);                                   30
    y = (short *) calloc(*length,sizeof(short int));
    yf = (float *) calloc(*length,sizeof(float));
    yfsqr = (float *) calloc(*length,sizeof(float));
    sumsq = (float *) calloc(*length,sizeof(float));
                                                                    35
    for (i = 6 ; i <= *length ; i++) {
        yf[i] = (b[0]*x[i] + b[1]*x[i-1] + b[2]*x[i-2]
            + b[3]*x[i-3] + b[4]*x[i-4] + b[5]*x[i-5] - a[1]*yf[i-1]
            - a[2]*yf[i-2] - a[3]*yf[i-3] - a[4]*yf[i-4] - a[5]*yf[i-5]);
        yfsqr[i] = yf[i]*yf[i];                                     40
    }

/* sumsq is used to store sums of squares                      */
    for (i = 1; i<=158; i++) sumsq[i] = sumsq[i-1]+yfsqr[i];
    for (i = 159 ; i <= *length ; i++)                              45
        sumsq[i] = (sumsq[i-1] - yfsqr[i-160]) + yfsqr[i];
    for (i = 0; i <= *length; i++)
        y[i] = (sqrt(sumsq[i]/160) > 600);   /* threshold          */

    signal_out(length,y,outfile);                                   50
    return 0;
}
```

This program is an extension of `filter.c`, which we saw in chapter 2. The a and b coefficients define a 400 Hz low pass Butterworth filter, and are taken from table 3.2. After each output sample `yf[i]` is calculated, the square of that value is calculated and stored in the vector `yfsqr`, by the line 'yfsqr[i] = yf[i]*yf[i];'. Then, the squares are summed for each interval of 160 samples (i.e. 10 ms at 16000 samples/s). For the first 159 samples, though, from sample 0 to 158, the sum of squares so far (i.e. since sample 0) is calculated instead. This is done by adding the square of the current sample, `yfsqr[i]`, to the sum of squares calculated up to the previous sample, `sumsq[i-1]`:

```
for (i = 1; i<=158; i++)
sumsq[i] = sumsq[i-1]+yfsqr[i];
```

Now, the sum of n numbers from `x[i-n]` to `x[i]` is easily calculated by a loop: for example, 'for (j = i-n; j <= i ; i++) sum = sum+x[j];'. However, if this summation is repeated for successive values of `i`, that is, moving through `x`, a lot of processor time will be wasted, as $n-1$ numbers summed on the previous iteration will be summed again, as the following example shows. Suppose we want to calculate a running sum of 8 numbers from the sequence 14, 15, 16, 17, 18, 19, 20, 21, 22, 23, 24. On the first iteration, the sum will be $14+15+16+17+18+19+20+21$. On the second iteration, the sum will be $15+16+17+18+19+20+21+22$. Note that all but the last number in this sequence, i.e. $15+16+17+18+19+20+21$, has already been calculated on the previous iteration, which was 14 plus $(15+16+17+18+19+20+21)$! That is, seven additions are repeated for every sample. The same kind of needless replication of calculations will occur on every iteration:

Sequence	14	15	16	17	18	19	20	21	22	23	24
Items 1 to 8	14	15	16	17	18	19	20	21			
Items 2 to 9		15	16	17	18	19	20	21	22		
Items 3 to 10			16	17	18	19	20	21	22	23	

A rather cunning bit of programming is used to make sure that this wasteful recalculation is avoided. The idea is that instead of summing from term `i-n` to `i` on each iteration, we take the sum calculated on the previous iteration, `sum[i-1]`, subtract the first term of *that* sum, `x[i-1-n]`, and add the current term `x[i]`. In the context of the voicing program, the running sum of squares of `yf[i]` is calculated by the line:

```
for (i = 159 ; i <= *length ; i++)
     sumsq[i] = (sumsq[i-1] - yfsqr[i-160]) + yfsqr[i]);
```

The processing saving is immense: for a window of 160 items, 159 additions would be repeated on each sample. Since the length of the signal can easily be tens of thousands of samples long, millions of unnecessary recalculations can be avoided.

When all the sums of squares have been calculated, the output signal `y[i]` is calculated by dividing the sum of squares at sample `i` by 160, to obtain the mean sum of squares, and the square root is taken. This gives the RMS amplitude of the sample, which is compared to a threshold value of 600. The expression 'sqrt(sumsq[i]/160) > 600' has the value 1 (true) if sqrt(sumsq[i]/160) is greater than 600 and 0 (false) if sqrt(sumsq[i]/160) is not greater than 600. Thus, according to the following lines, y[i] will be 1 if the RMS amplitude is over 600 units (i.e. voiced) and 0 if it is not (i.e. voiceless).

```
for (i = 0; i <= *length; i++)
    y[i] = (sqrt(sumsq[i]/160) > 600);   /* threshold */
    signal_out(length,y,outfile);
```

The value of 600 was determined by experimentation to be a good level at which to set the threshold. It assumes that the signal being analysed is normalized to the range ±32000, that is, almost the full range of short integers. A recording does not necessarily satisfy this assumption, but you can normalize a signal in *filename*.dat to this range using the program normalize.c. For example, once you have compiled normalize.c to produce normalize.exe, in MS-DOS you can type 'normalize *filename*.dat *normfile*.dat' to produce a normalized file. Even so, it may be necessary to alter the threshold value 600, for recordings in which voicing is weak, for instance, but this is easy to do.

The voicing signal joe_voice.dat produced by using voicing.c to analyse a normalized version of joe.dat is shown in figure 4.8. joe_voice.dat was used to mask joe_norm.dat, by multiplying each sample of joe_norm.dat by the corresponding sample of joe_voice.dat (using the program multiply.c, supplied on the CD-ROM). The cepstral f_0 signal in figure 4.9 was then obtained from joe_norm_voiceonly.dat.

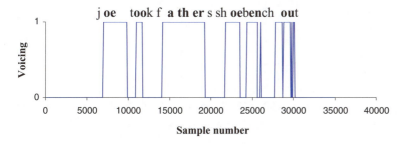

FIGURE 4.8
Voicing of part of joe.dat

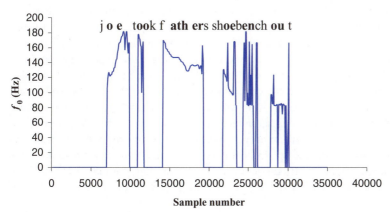

FIGURE 4.9
Cepstral f_0 of part of joe_norm.dat, masked by the voicing estimate

4.7 f_0 estimation by the autocorrelation method

Figure 4.10 shows the f_0 of the first part of joe.dat, as estimated using a different pitch-tracking method, the **autocorrelation** method. Comparison with figure 4.9 shows that this method is somewhat more stable. As with cepstral_f0, in order to use this method we must specify upper and lower limits of the f_0 range: in this case the maximum f_0 was set at 180 Hz and the minimum at 80 Hz. These limits are not appropriate for all speakers, however, and may need to be altered. A drawback of the program autocorr_f0.c presented in listing 4.5 below is that it estimates an f_0 value every sample, not just every 80 samples (as in cepstral_f0.c). This makes it very slow to run – it takes 10 seconds to analyse 1 second of speech on my computer – though it would not be difficult to alter it so that it only estimates f_0 value every 80 samples (see exercise 4.2 below). However, as it is an accurate method, it can be quite useful to have an f_0 estimate every sample. If desired, the resulting f_0 signal can always be re-sampled at 80 sample intervals, using the utility program to_frames.c. This takes a signal file as its argument and generates a text stream, on the standard output. Every 80th sample of the input is output on a separate line.

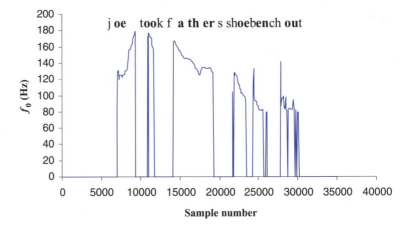

FIGURE 4.10
f_0 of part of joe.dat, estimated by the autocorrelation method, then masked by the voicing estimate

The idea behind the autocorrelation method is illustrated in figure 4.11. The top panel, (a), shows a 1024-sample portion of the first vowel ([əʊ]) of joe.dat. Consider the sample at the time marked by the vertical line, which is close to the peak of a voicing pulse in (a). Panel (b) shows the same portion, shifted to the right (i.e. later in time) by 50 samples. The sample lying on the vertical line in (a) – call it $x[t]$ – is 50 samples later than the sample on the line in (b), $x[t-50]$. Those two samples have rather different magnitudes, as indeed are $x[t]$ and $x[t-50]$ for *all* values of t. If we were to calculate an overall measure of the difference between $x[t]$ and $x[t-50]$ for all t, it would be a big discrepancy. Panel (c) shows the same portion again, shifted backwards by 90 samples, compared to (a). $x[t]$ in (a) is aligned with $x[t-90]$ in (c). Note that they are also very different

(a) Portion of a vowel

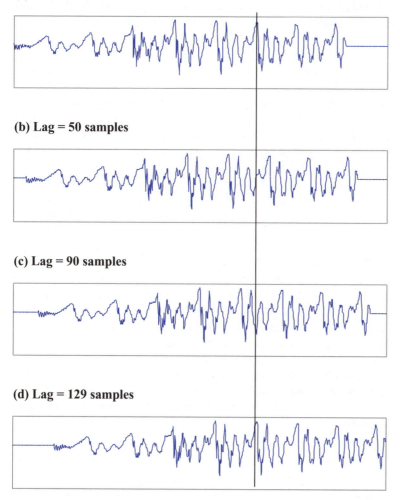

(b) Lag = 50 samples

(c) Lag = 90 samples

(d) Lag = 129 samples

FIGURE 4.11
Illustration of the degrees of similarity between a portion of a signal (a) and time-shifted copies of that portion (b–d).

values: the sample on the line in (c) is close to a dip in the signal, and has a large negative value. The difference between all samples in (a) and all samples in (c) is once again high.

Now compare (a) with (d), which is shifted by 129 samples. At that size of shift, the peaks of (d) are pretty well aligned with the peaks of (a), and likewise for the troughs. There is still *some* degree of difference between the two signal portions, but at this time-lag, the difference is low. If we were to carry on shifting, and consider a shift of, say 170 samples, we would find that the degree of difference between (a) and a time-delayed copy is again greater than that of (d). The time-lag of 129 samples between (a) and (d) is the size of shift that is necessary in order to make a copy of (a) most like itself. We say that the correlation between the copy, (d), and (a) – the *auto-correlation*, since (d) is a copy of (a) – is greatest at the lag at which the difference between the signal and its copy is smallest.

The reason why a lag of 129 samples gives rise to the smallest difference between (a) and its copy is because the voicing pulses in the signal recur at a 129-sample interval. At a sampling rate of 16000 samples/s, 129 samples is $16000 \div 129 = 124.031$ Hz.

This gives us the basis of a method for accurately calculating the frequency of voicing pulses. For each sample in a signal, consider a time-window of (say) 256 samples either side of that sample. Now, calculate the overall difference between that 512-sample portion and copies of itself shifted by every time lag from −512 samples through to +512 samples. That's an awful lot of computing: 1024 separate comparisons (excluding time lag 0!), for just one sample. Still, if we can do it fast enough it will be worth it if it yields an accurate estimate of f_0, which it does.

The program uses the function 'correl(data,data,512,ans);' near the end of listing 4.5 to calculate the correlation between each 512-sample portion of the signal (referred to by the pointer variable data) and itself at every lag from −512 samples to +512 samples. This function is defined in correl.c, taken from Press et al. 1992: 546. It uses an FFT and an inverse FFT to calculate the autocorrelation function efficiently, but further explanation is beyond the scope of this book. The magnitude of the autocorrelation at each lag is returned in the array ans, so that ans[j] gives the 'strength' of the autocorrelation at lag j. ans has 1025 cells: ans[0] is the correlation at lag 0, ans[1] to ans[512] give the autocorrelation at lags 1 to 512, respectively, and ans[513] to ans[1024] the autocorrelations at lags −512 samples up to −1 sample. Because we are interested in f_0, we inspect ans to determine the maximum autocorrelation in the range of lags specified by the variables top and bot, corresponding to the range of f_0's expected in speech.

Listing 4.5

```
#include <stdio.h>
#include <math.h>
#include <stdlib.h>
#include "slputils.c"
#define SR 16000          /* Sampling Rate                    */  5
#define MINF0 80
#define MAXF0 180


/* AUTOCORR_F0.C                                              */
/* Pitch prediction by short-time autocorrelation. f0_out (the */  10
/* sample-by-sample f0 track) is written to outfile.          */

int main(int argc, char *argv[])
{
    short int *x_in, *signal_in(), *f0;                          15
    char *infile, *outfile;
    int i, j, *length, maxlag, bot=SR/MINF0, top=SR/MAXF0;
    void four1(), correl(), signal_out();
```

```
      float *data, ans[1025], *x_in_f, max;

      if (argc != 3) {
         printf("usage: autocorr_f0 input_file output_file\n");
         exit(1);
      }
      infile = argv[1];
      outfile = argv[2];

      x_in = signal_in(infile,length);
/* Make a floating-point versions of x_in, called x_in_f, and     */
/* allocate space    for f0                                       */
      x_in_f = (float *) calloc(*length,sizeof(float));
      for (i=0;i<*length;i++) x_in_f[i] = (float) x_in[i];
      f0 = (short int *) calloc(*length,sizeof(short int));

      for (i=0;i<=1024;i++) ans[i] = 0;

      printf("Working ...\n");
      for (i=0;i<512;i++) f0[i] = 0;
      for (i=0;i<(*length)-512;i++) {
         data = x_in_f+i-1;
         correl(data,data,512,ans);

         maxlag = SR/MAXF0;
         max = 0;
         for (j=top;j<=bot;j++) {
            if (ans[j] > max) {
               maxlag = j;
               max = ans[j];
            }
         }
         f0[i+512] = SR/maxlag;
/* i+512 to offset lag introduced by windowing                    */
         if (f0[i+512] >= MAXF0) f0[i+512]=0;
      }
      signal_out(length,f0,outfile);
      return 0;
}
```

The program works as follows. First the input file is read into the vector
x_in. Then, memory is allocated for a floating-point version of x_in,
x_in_f, and for an f0 array of the same length as x_in. After the array
ans and the first 512 samples of f0 are zeroed, the heart of the program
is the following loop:

```
      for (i=0;i<(*length)-512;i++) {
         data = x_in_f+i-1;
         correl(data,data,512,ans);

         maxlag = SR/MAXF0;
         max = 0;
```

```
    for (j=top;j<=bot;j++) {
        if (ans[j] > max) {
            maxlag = j;
            max = ans[j];
        }
    }
    f0[i+512] = SR/maxlag;
/* i+512 to offset lag introduced by windowing */
    if (f0[i+512] >= MAXF0) f0[i+512]=0;
}
```

The counter variable `i` counts through the samples of the input from 0, the beginning, to `*length-512`, that is, 512 samples from the end (so that the autocorrelation calculations near the end of the signal never try to access samples beyond the end of the signal).

Exercise 4.2.

If you change the first line of this loop to '`for (i=0;i<(*length)-512;i+=80)`', the autocorrelation will only be calculated every 80 samples, making the program run much faster. If you do this, use a smaller array for `f0`, and instead of writing `f0` to a signal file, write out the values of `f0` as text output. (See line 74 of `cepstral_f0.c` for an example of how to do this.)

Instead of *copying* samples from `x_in` to `data` for the `correl` function to work on, we exploit the fact that arrays are passed to functions using a *pointer* to the array. So, we only have to tell `correl` where it can find its data, and we can do that by giving it the address of samples in `x_in`, without copying them to another array. We use the pointer variable `data` to refer to the beginning of each 512-sample portion of `x_in` that we want `correl` to work on. The expression '`data = x_in_f+i-1;`' can be read as 'the data is to be found at the `i`th sample of `x_in_f`. (The −1 is because `correl` expects the first sample to be at `data[1]`, not `data[0]`, whereas `x_in_f` begins at sample 0.)

Next we call the function `correl`, and then we inspect `ans` to find the lag at which the autocorrelation is greatest (within the f_0 range of interest). Bearing in mind that small lags correspond to high frequencies and large lags correspond to low frequencies, we inspect the array cells `ans[j]` from j = top to j = bot. `top`, the smallest lag of interest, is earlier defined to be `SR/MAXF0`, and `bot`, the largest lag of interest, is `SR/MINF0`. `SR`, the sampling rate, `MAXF0` and `MINF0` are `#defined` in the header, so that when the program is compiled these symbols are actually replaced by the numbers 16000, 180 and 80 respectively. With these values, `top` is 88 samples and `bot` is 200 samples. Thus, rather than looking through all of `ans` to find the maximum autocorrelation, we restrict the search to the range from `ans[88]` to `ans[200]`.

To find the autocorrelation peak within that range, we use the variable `max` to store 'the highest magnitude of the autocorrelation found so far'. We set it to 0 initially, and then use a loop that counts j from `top` to `bot`. On each iteration, if `ans[j]` is greater than the previously found `max`, we set maxlag to j and max to ans[j], updating the highest magnitude found so far:

```
max = 0;
for (j=top;j<=bot;j++) {
    if (ans[j] > max) {
        maxlag = j;
        max = ans[j];
    }
}
```

When the end of this loop is reached, maxlag will be set to the lag at which the autocorrelation is greatest. SR/maxlag gives the corresponding f_0, which we write to f0[i+512]. (The offset of 512 is to keep samples of f0 in step with samples of x_in.) Any f_0 values found to be at the upper limit of the range are assumed to be out of range, that is, probably unvoiced, and are set to zero.

When compiling the program, it is necessary to compile and link correl.c and nrutil.c too. For example:

```
gcc -c autocorr_f0.c
gcc -c nrutil.c
gcc -c correl.c
gcc -o autocorr_f0.exe nrutil.o correl.o autocorr_f0.o
```

4.8 Linear predictive coding

The next topic that I want to look at is another extremely important innovation in the computational analysis of speech signals, **linear predictive coding**. To understand the relevance and utility of linear predictive coding it is worthwhile looking back to the state of the art in the 1960s when the technique was developed. Even using Fast Fourier Transforms to extract resonances from a speech signal, keeping track of the resonances as they change in time – tracking the formant peaks – was a difficult and challenging computational problem. So decomposing a speech signal into a set of resonances and a changing pitch signal of some kind according to the source–filter model, while being a theoretically elegant and attractive decomposition of a speech wave, is in practice difficult to compute. Linear predictive coding offers us a much simpler approach to the decomposition of speech signals into a number of *analysis parameters*. We will look at the nature of those analysis parameters and their relationship to some more familiar parameters of speech shortly. Let's consider first the nature of linear prediction.

Schroeder (1985) gives a little about the history of linear prediction. The originators of the technique, Bishnu Atal and colleagues, were originally working not on speech signals, but on television pictures, two-dimensional images changing in time. One way of representing such an image is as a two-dimensional matrix of numbers, each representing the brightness of one spot on the screen, each pixel. The representation of a single image would require a very large matrix of numbers, and to represent a changing sequence of images, many images per second, would require huge quantities of data to represent television images in digital form. However that approach to the representation of images in digital form overlooks a fact about images: the brightness of any particular point is *not* independent of the brightness of neighbouring points in the image, because on a television image there are *regions* of light and dark and different shades in between. The brightness of a pixel is usually not very different from the brightness of its neighbours. In other words there is a strong correlation between the brightness of any given pixel and the brightness of its neighbours.

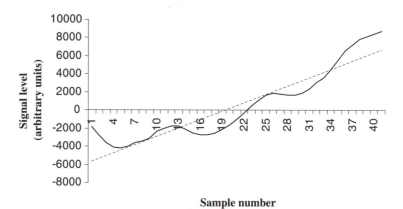

FIGURE 4.12

Portion of a signal (solid line) modelled by linear regression (dashes)

The same holds true for speech signals, as we can see in figure 4.12. There is a strong correlation between the magnitude of a signal at any given sample and the magnitude of the immediately preceding samples. The magnitude of the signal at each sample is often predictable by considering the magnitude of the signal for the preceding few samples, as we can see if we examine a section of the signal (figure 4.12). That is a very local kind of correlation. Of course if we predict the value of the magnitude of the signal at one point in time on the basis of linear regression from the preceding samples, the actual magnitude of the signal in that sample might be something different from our prediction. The prediction could be in error one way or the other, too high or too low. In figure 4.12, for example, the equation of the linear regression line (dashed) is $x[t] = 308.35\ t - 5928.8$, so for the next point, $t = 41$, we predict that $x[t]$ will be 6714. In fact, the actual value is 8738. However if we take the *difference* between the predicted value and the actual value, the size of the difference between the prediction and the actual value is in general very much less than the magnitude of the signal itself at that point. In this case, the difference is -2024, an underestimate. As we go through the signal making predictions as to what the next value of the signal is going to be based upon the previous handful of samples, our prediction will be more or less in error. But if we *store* the errors as a separate signal the combination of the predicted signal (according to the predictor coefficients) and the stored error accurately encodes the original signal. The amount of information that we need to store can be

(a) First 32000 samples of `joe.dat`

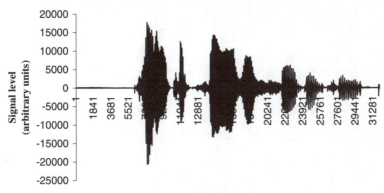

Sample number

(b) First 32000 samples of `joe_err.dat`

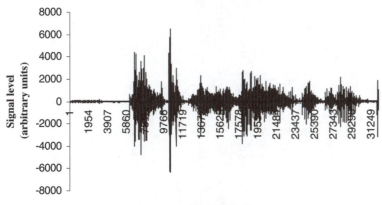

Sample number

(c) First 32000 samples of `joe_1pc.dat`

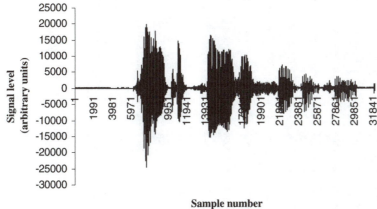

Sample number

FIGURE 4.13
Linear prediction of a signal

Table 4.1. LPC coefficients for the first 18 frames (90 ms) of joe.dat

a_1	a_2	a_3	a_4	a_5	a_6	a_7	a_8	a_9	a_{10}	a_{11}	a_{12}	a_{13}	a_{14}
0.529507	0.214570	0.157968	−0.015645	−0.098790	0.102021	0.073432	0.053835	0.046884	−0.095953	−0.125095	−0.003316	−0.068915	0.211290
0.663435	0.235670	0.057659	−0.173204	−0.022757	0.085107	0.071049	−0.046500	0.051426	0.073784	0.001921	−0.075364	0.023511	0.013053
0.660165	0.181547	−0.026792	−0.130653	−0.037969	0.159775	0.005743	−0.047008	−0.010137	0.149722	0.202995	−0.162092	−0.074751	0.116651
0.421265	0.137616	0.126946	0.166275	−0.006271	0.053303	0.124907	−0.041883	0.016269	0.008911	0.073567	0.045266	−0.049689	−0.102131
0.651959	0.037576	0.199862	−0.045865	−0.009035	0.037421	0.109637	0.063807	−0.125036	0.052322	−0.049273	0.136695	−0.050734	−0.029301
0.699839	0.110381	0.205427	−0.090266	−0.217306	0.027334	0.145426	0.147045	0.008613	−0.248360	−0.053345	0.073251	0.034594	0.132024
0.659970	−0.067966	0.051772	0.092589	0.054614	0.085508	−0.116219	0.165014	0.007561	0.156107	0.035027	−0.043373	0.116442	−0.217553
0.465469	0.081698	0.053311	−0.003915	−0.002184	0.030224	0.105007	0.015475	0.017796	0.119037	0.070655	0.095783	−0.002592	−0.066286
1.023540	−0.409890	−0.007197	0.103930	−0.095082	−0.025607	0.123147	0.115771	0.055260	−0.304300	0.331231	0.028615	−0.205308	0.253941
0.630019	−0.043888	0.041295	0.093989	−0.001065	0.035442	0.092332	0.192455	−0.083449	0.123295	0.066693	−0.092346	0.008203	−0.087634
1.490039	−1.112880	0.614489	−0.219688	0.066938	0.043352	−0.075506	0.469913	−0.385509	0.220238	−0.167493	0.193481	−0.201832	0.046835
0.815097	−0.052690	0.117007	0.070670	−0.027797	0.042454	0.061282	−0.224938	0.173743	−0.066700	−0.035761	0.235775	−0.058357	−0.100508
0.997877	−0.196260	0.065919	0.020758	0.132399	−0.093126	−0.058893	−0.035998	0.035271	0.022649	0.015407	0.133469	−0.098020	0.023992
0.731185	−0.017871	−0.006013	−0.027752	−0.014516	0.073702	0.195654	0.131934	−0.119576	−0.061715	0.119068	0.037813	−0.017445	−0.058698
0.846576	−0.071224	−0.041400	−0.159512	−0.027687	0.253058	0.067785	−0.067398	−0.013547	0.070412	0.155887	0.035387	−0.095780	0.035486
0.902853	0.029868	−0.093316	−0.235631	−0.011643	0.214349	−0.013349	0.001981	0.057237	0.044977	0.007268	−0.101246	0.188820	−0.016132
0.843041	0.008629	0.085922	−0.060910	−0.097063	−0.007466	0.038094	0.127368	0.038659	0.028170	−0.046284	−0.007526	0.064399	−0.039740
0.977338	−0.399232	0.166142	0.014792	−0.089576	0.340422	−0.068083	−0.017606	0.104285	0.078625	−0.091262	−0.017864	−0.068480	0.026332

significantly less than simply storing the value of each successive sample. We will look at why that is shortly.

So we are going to estimate or approximate the magnitude of the current sample as a linear combination of the previous p samples, as in figure 4.12. Equation 4.1 expresses this idea.

(4.1)
$$x[t] = -a_1 x[t-1] - a_2 x[t-2] - a_3 x[t-3] \cdots - a_p x[t-p] + e[t]$$

p is called the **order** of the predictor: it is typically 12 to 18 samples or thereabouts. We predict that the current sample is the sum of the previous p samples, each multiplied by some weighting factor a_1, a_2 and so on to a_p, the a coefficients, also called **predictor coefficients**. However I said before that the prediction is only an approximation to the actual value of the current sample, and the difference between the predicted value and the current sample is an error quantity, $e[t]$. The sequence of error values when equation 4.1 is used to model a signal is called the **prediction residual**, that is, that part of the current sample that is not well represented by the weighted sample of p previous samples. Now we compute p coefficients for each sample, say 12 coefficients, and in addition we calculate the prediction residual, for every sample. On the face of it this may seem to be hardly an improvement in the economy of our representation of the signal. But it is not as problematic as it sounds for two reasons. First, the magnitude of the prediction residual as I said before is very much smaller than the magnitude of the original signal, so the error signal can be stored with fewer bits of information than the original signal. Second, we don't need to compute 12 coefficients for *every sample* in our representation of the speech, because the coefficients *change very slowly*, that is, more slowly than the original signal changes. The coefficients collectively encode the slowly changing resonances of the vocal tract: slowly changing, that is, compared to the very fast rate at which the speech signal changes. So instead of saving 12–18 coefficients per sample, we only need to save that many coefficients at about 10 millisecond intervals (every 80th sample for signals at 8000 samples/s). However, the LPC coefficients and the residual do not necessarily take up less memory, especially if the sample rate of the signal is high (e.g. 16000 samples/s) or if a relatively high prediction order is used, in order to get a good quality of the encoding. (A 14th-order LPC encoding of `joe.dat` takes up 165468 bytes, 24682 bytes more than `joe.dat`. Using signals sampled at a lower sampling rate does not help much, either: a 14th-order LPC encoding of `joe10k.dat` – `joe.dat` down-sampled to 10000 samples/s – takes up 112195 bytes, or 24201 bytes more than `joe10k.dat`.)

Let's consider a real example. A comparison between `joe.dat` and `joe_err.dat` is given in figure 4.13. Figure 4.13 (a) is the waveform of `joe.dat` and (b) is the prediction residual. (c) is the waveform that would be generated by the linear prediction coefficients alone, that is, without adding back the linear prediction residual. The values of the predictor coefficients themselves are not shown on this figure. To give an idea of what they are like, table 4.1 gives the values of the first 18 frames.

Note that the prediction residual, in figure 4.13 (b), is a lower-amplitude signal than the original: you can see that its vertical axis is on a smaller scale than figure 4.13 (a). The residual has sharp spikes at regular intervals, corresponding to the glottal pulses of the speech wave. Thinking back to the definition of the predictor model (equation 4.1), we can see that the spikes occur in the prediction residual at those points in the speech wave at which the signal is changing direction in a very extreme fashion. At those points, the linear prediction idea does not work very well. That is why we get a big error, which shows up as a spike in the prediction residual. As the spacing of those spikes occurs at the fundamental frequency of the original speech, the occurrence of a spike in the prediction residual is again highly correlated with the location of spikes on previous cycles. So by estimating the pitch, we could remove (or at least reduce) the spikes from the prediction residual. Practically all that is left in the prediction residual after pitch prediction is just residual noise.

4.9 C programs for LPC analysis and resynthesis

In the previous section I did not discuss how the LPC coefficients are actually calculated. The *idea* is very simple: for each frame (of 5–10 ms duration) we need to find p parameters, a_1 to a_p such that the error term $e[t]$ is as small as possible. However, to put this into practice requires a knowledge of mathematics beyond the level of this book (see Schroeder 1985: 55–6 for the details). And in general, we do not need to understand the method in order to use it in practice. My program lpcana.c, for instance, provided on the CD-ROM and listed in listing 4.6, uses the function memcof, taken from Press et al. 1992: 568–9. This takes a vector of data (a frame of, e.g., 80 consecutive samples), the size of each frame n, and the number of desired coefficients m (i.e. the prediction order), and returns an array d containing the m coefficients. (It also returns the mean square error, though we do not use this, as we have to calculate the sample-by-sample error anyway, in order to obtain the residual.) Since it is quite a large program, I shall break it up into pieces and describe each piece in turn.

Listing 4.6

```
#include <stdio.h>
#include "slputils.c"
#define k 14              /* Number of coefficients */
```

The statement '#define k 14' tells the C preprocessor to substitute the number 14 in place of the symbol k, wherever it appears in the code below. To compile a version of this program for a larger or smaller prediction order, therefore, this statement can be altered accordingly. Note that k is therefore not a variable, but a symbol that gets replaced by a constant during compilation.

Listing 4.6 (*continued*)

```
/* LPCANA.C                                                          */
/* Reads a signal from a disk file into a variable, x_in.            */
/* Steps through x_in, 80 frames at a time, computes k LPC coefficients */
/* in array c, writes the LPC residual to errfile, and the coefficients */
/* (as floats) to coeffs.                                            */

int main(int argc, char *argv[])
{
    short int *x_in, *signal_in(), *e;
    char *infile, *errfile, *coeffs;
    int frame, n_frames, i, j, n, prev, next, *length = 0;
    float data[81], *xms, d[k+1], *c, *x_in_f, *lp;
    void signal_out();
    void memcof();
    FILE *fid;
```

There are a lot of variables to take stock of here. infile and errfile are pointers to the character arrays in which the file *names* of the input signal and the error signal, respectively, are stored. Those signals are stored as arrays of short integers, indexed by the pointer variables x_in and e. signal_in() and signal_out() are functions for reading and writing the input and output files, and memcof() is the function that computes the predictor coefficients, given a frame of data. The 80 samples of a single frame are put in cells 1–80 of the array data, which must therefore be assigned 81 cells (though in fact data[0] is unused). The k predictor coefficients are returned in the array d, from cells d[1] to d[k]. Thus, d must be allocated k+1 cells, even though d[0] is unused. memcof also returns xms, a pointer to the mean square error: though we are not interested in it, I kept it as I did not want to alter the definition of memcof, so as not to spoil its generality. length is a pointer to a variable containing the number of samples in the input signal, and is returned by the function signal_in(). n_frames is to store the number of 80-sample frames (calculated below).

It would be sufficient to store the LPC coefficients in an array of k × n_frames cells. However, in order to improve the quality of the prediction model (i.e. to reduce the size of the error), this program calculates an array c containing k coefficients for *every sample* of the input. We can picture c as a table of k columns and *length rows. For k = 14, for example, the numbering of cells in c can be illustrated as in table 4.2.

Thus, coefficient a_j of sample *i* will be stored in cell c[(i-1)*k+j-1]. The program uses memcof to estimate the coefficients for every 80 samples, and places them in the last row of the frame (row 80, row 160, etc., starting at c[1106], c[2226] ...). All of the other values are calculated by linear interpolation, between the value at the end of the previous frame (prev) and the value at the end of the next frame (next). The code for this calculation will be given further on, though not discussed at length, as it is fairly uninteresting.

Table 4.2. Numbering of cells in the matrix of coefficients, c

	c[0]	c[1]	c[2]	c[3]	c[4]	c[5]	c[6]	c[7]	c[8]	c[9]	c[10]	...	c[13]
Frame 0													
	c[14]	c[15]	c[16]	c[17]	c[18]	c[19]	c[20]	c[21]	c[22]	c[23]	c[24]	...	
	...												
sample 1	c[(i-1)*k]	...											
	...												
sample 79	c[1106]												
Frame 1	c[1120]												
	...												
sample 159	c[2226]												
Frame 2	c[2240]												
	...												

Listing 4.6 *(continued)*

```
if (argc != 4) {
    printf("usage: lpcana input_file lp_error_file lp_coeffs_file\n");
    exit(1);
}
infile = argv[1];
errfile = argv[2];
coeffs = argv[3];

x_in = signal_in(infile,length);
n_frames = (*length)/80;
```

The previous block of code is sufficiently similar to pieces of earlier programs as to need no further comment. In the next few lines, a copy of the array x_in is made, x_in_f, in which each sample in x_in is converted from a short int to a float. This is because memcof requires floats to work on. Because the size of x_in is not known until the program is run (and it will differ from one input signal to another), the sizes of the arrays x_in and x_in_f, c, lp and e are also not known. But when the signal is read in, the value indexed by length can be used to work out how much storage is needed for each of these variables. Then, the library function calloc can be used to set aside space for these arrays:

Listing 4.6 *(continued)*

```
/* Make a floating-point version of x_in, called x_in_f     */
    x_in_f = (float *) calloc((*length),sizeof(float));
    for (i=0;i<(*length);i++)
        x_in_f[i] = (float) x_in[i];
    c = (float *) calloc((*length)*k,sizeof(float));

fid = fopen(coeffs,"wb");
```

Now we are ready to step through the input signal, taking each successive frame of 80 samples, passing them to memcof, getting back k coefficients, and putting them into the right row of c. So:

```
for (frame=0;frame<n_frames;frame++) {
```

'for each frame, from 0 to n_frames ...'

```
    for (j=0;j<=79;j++) data[j+1] = x_in_f[80*frame+j];
```

'take each sample j, from 0 to 79, and copy it into the data array (from cell 1 to cell 80).'

```
    memcof(data,80,k,&xms,d);
```

'Submit the 80 samples in data to memcof to get the k coefficients for that frame in the vector d.'

```
for (j=0;j<=k-1;j++) {
    c[(frame+1)*80*k-k+j] = d[j+1];
    fwrite(&d[j+1],sizeof(float),1,fid);
}
}
fclose(fid);
```

'Finally, copy each coefficient from d into c, and write it to the coeffs file.' The coefficients go into the row of c that is immediately before the next frame. Now, each frame takes up 80*k cells, so the next frame begins at cell (frame+1)*80*k. So, the row before the next frame starts at (frame+1)*80*k-k. Each coefficient, in d[j+1], goes into cell (frame+1)*80*k-k+j.

At this point, instead of storing the coefficients in c, we could just write them to the coeffs file as each one is calculated for each frame, and finish. Instead, as I mentioned above, this program goes on to interpolate intermediate values of each coefficient:

Listing 4.6 (*continued*)

```
/* For the first frame, use the first analysis vector for every sample */
    for (i=0;i<=78;i++) {
        for (j=0;j<=k-1;j++) c[i*k+j] = c[79*k+j];
    }
/* For frames 1..n_frames, interpolate the intermediate LPC vectors */
    for (frame=1;frame<n_frames;frame++) {
        prev = frame*k*80-k;
        next = prev+k*80;
        for (i=0;i<79;i++) {
            for (j=0;j<=k-1;j++) {
            c[prev+k+k*i+j] = c[prev+j]+((float) i/80.0)*(c[prev+j]-
c[next+j]);
            }
        }
    }
```

Having calculated k coefficients for every sample in x_in_f, we are now in a position to model x_in_f using the linear prediction equation. First, we allocate storage for the predicted signal lp and the error signal e, both of which are made of floats:

```
/* Model x_in_f and calculate the error                              */
    lp = (float *) calloc((*length),sizeof(float)); /* predicted signal */
    e = (short int *) calloc((*length),sizeof(short int));
```

Here's how we generate the linear prediction signal and the corresponding error signal. First, a loop is set up to zero the first k values of e. Then,
a loop counts i through all the samples from k to the end. We set j to
(i-1)*k, the array index of the start of the ith row of c.

```
for (i=0;i<k;i++)  e[i] = 0;
for (i=k;i<(*length);i++) {
    j = (i-1)*k;
    lp[i] = 0;
```

We cannot include a sum like equation 4.1 in the program, because we
don't know in general how many terms it will have, as k can be altered.
So, we set up an inner loop, counting n from 0 to k−1. For each n, we calculate just one term of equation 4.1 and add it to a running total, lp[i]:

```
for (n=0;n<=k-1;n++)  lp[i] = lp[i]-c[j+n]*lp[i-n-1];
lp[i] = -lp[i];
```

The error at sample i, e[i] is just the difference between the actual value
of the signal, x_in_f[i], and the predicted value, lp[i]. The value of
e[i], which is a float, is converted to a short int and put into the ith
cell of e as it is calculated. e[i] is added to lp[i] so that the overall error
of lp does not accumulate. When the loop is complete, the error array is
written to errfile, using signal_out.

Listing 4.6 (*continued*)

```
        e[i] = (short int) x_in_f[i]-lp[i];
        lp[i] += e[i];
    }
    signal_out(length,e,errfile);
    return 0;
}
```

We might also write out lp, though we do not do so here, because we can
reconstruct the original signal from the error file and the file of coefficients using the program lpcsyn.c. This is almost identical to
lpcana.c, except that: (1) instead of calculating the residual signal and
the coefficients, they are read in from files; (2) the end of the loop in the
preceding program fragment is replaced by the following lines:

Listing 4.7

```
    x_out[i] = (short int) lp[i]+e_in[i];
    lp[i] += e_in[i];
    }
signal_out(length,x_out,outfile);
```

That is, instead of calculating the error by subtracting `lp` from `x_in_f`, `x_out` is calculated by adding the error, `e_in`, to `lp`. The output is `x_out`, the modelled signal. (`x_out` will need to be declared at the beginning of the program, and memory allocated for it, in the same way as for `x_in` and `e`.) Since the error is the discrepancy between the original signal and `lp`, adding the error to `lp` reconstructs the original signal exactly. The result is a *perfect* (synthetic) copy of the original.

4.10 Trying it out

The function `memcof`, which this program uses, is defined in the file `memcof.c`. This, in turn, refers to a utility file `nrutil.c`. Thus, to compile `lpcana.c`, it is also necessary to compile `nrutil.c` and `memcof.c`, and then link all three object files together, as follows:

```
gcc -c nrutil.c
gcc -c memcof.c
gcc -c lpcana.c
gcc -o lpcana.exe nrutil.o memcof.o lpcana.o
```

The program `lpcana.exe` can be used to generate a file of coefficients and the corresponding error signal. For instance, `lpcana joe.dat joe_err.dat joe_coeffs.dat` generates the error signal shown in figure 4.13 (b) and the coefficients shown in part in table 4.1. Then, `lpcsyn joe_err.dat joe_coeffs.dat joe_syn.dat` will generate the synthetic reconstruction of `joe.dat`.

It is instructive to listen to these signals. The residual, `joe_err.dat`, is almost intelligible, though it is a very rough, whispery version of the original input. The synthetic reconstruction, `joe_syn.dat`, is identical to `joe.dat`.

4.11 Applications of LPC

Speech can be synthesized (or perhaps we should say *resynthesized*) by providing either the prediction residual or a synthetic version of the residual, together with the predictor coefficients. In the simplest method of synthesis, we first work out which portions of the original signal are voiced and which are unvoiced. For the voiced parts of the signal, the error can be modelled by an impulse source that approximates the sequence of spikes seen in the prediction residual. To do this, we mainly need to make sure that the spacing between the spikes is right for the desired frequency of voicing (as described in section 3.8, for the Klatt synthesizer – the idea is the same). In this way we can alter the pitch contour to a fair degree, if we wish. The voiceless parts of the signal can be modelled with white noise of roughly the right amplitude.

Generating voiced speech with an impulse source in LPC tends to produce synthetic speech that is rather 'buzzy'. Other forms of excitation have also been investigated. Atal also demonstrated that an improvement could be made to the quality of LPC-synthesized speech by using multi-pulse excitation, that is, modelling each pitch period with several impulses per period. For the voiceless parts, higher fidelity synthesis can be attained by spectral analysis of segments of the prediction residual. If we use a library of stored spectra, each of which is given a reference number, we could describe the spectrum of each portion of the residual signal by the number of the most similar stored spectrum. A synthetic version of the residual can then be made from a sequence of spectral reference numbers, pulling each spectrum out of storage by its code number. That method is the code-book excitation method of linear prediction, usually referred to by the acronym CELP (code-book excited linear prediction). It yields a fairly naturalistic encoding and resynthesis of speech, for which reason it is used in a variety of communications contexts, such as military communications. See, for example, Tremain 1982, concerning LPC-10, 'the US government standard linear predictive coding algorithm', or Campbell et al. 1991, concerning the US Federal Standard 1016 CELP coder. Further useful information, including software, is available from the comp.speech FAQ web site, a link to which is included on the web site for this course.

Coding of this kind is suitable for use in the transmission of speech through telephone wires or other kinds of telecommunication links, such as mobile telephony (e.g. the GSM coding standard) and 'Internet phones'. In these applications, the listener isn't usually aware that the speech that they are hearing is a synthesized *reconstruction* of an *encoded* version of the speaker's speech!

One of the benefits of linear prediction, perhaps the main benefit, is that it is easy to compute: getting the coefficients from natural speech is not difficult. Contrast this with formant synthesis, or articulatory synthesis: for both of these, obtaining the synthesizer parameters from natural speech is extremely challenging, making these synthesis methods impractical for many purposes. Finding linear predictor coefficients is simply a question of minimizing the size of the prediction residual. A number of algorithms have been developed to do this, as Schroeder (1985) and Wakita (1996) discuss.

The mathematical relationship between linear prediction coefficients and more familiar acoustic parameters such as formant frequencies and bandwidths has also been studied at some length. The mathematics of the relationship between prediction coefficients and formant frequencies and bandwidths is too complex to cover in this course. But the method is very simple. Consider a single frame of linear prediction coefficients, for instance, 10 coefficients relating to the 80-sample frame around sample 8000 of `joe8k.dat`. (That frame falls in the middle of the [ɑ] of 'father'.) Those coefficients are plotted in figure 4.14. We scale these numbers up (by multiplying them by 15000) and add zeroes at the start and end, to make a signal portion 512 samples long, as in figure 4.15.

The Fourier transform of this brief, blip-like signal has a very smooth spectrum, as figure 4.16 illustrates. It has amplitude peaks at 343–390 Hz (i.e. centred on 356 Hz), 2656 Hz, and 3656 Hz. Those figures are the first,

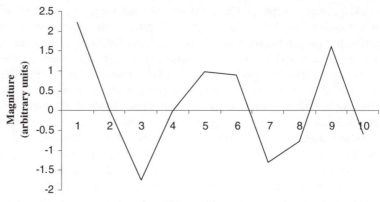

FIGURE 4.14
Ten LPC coefficients from
[ɑ] in `joe8k.dat`

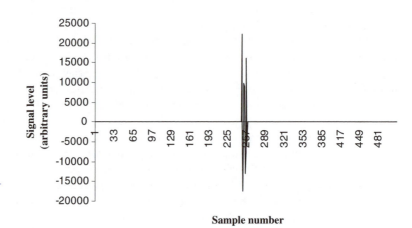

FIGURE 4.15
The same ten LPC coeffi-
cients scaled up and
zero-padded to 512
samples

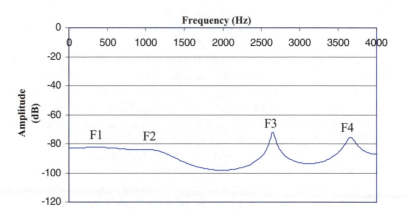

FIGURE 4.16
LPC spectrum of [ɑ]

third and fourth formants of the vowel: the analysis does not resolve the difference between F1 and F2 adequately, though. Because it is so easy to measure formants in this way, linear prediction has become a standard method for automatic formant tracking.

A program that implements this method is provided in `lpc_spectrum.c`. I shall not give a listing or discuss its operation in detail here, as it merely puts together techniques we have seen already: the explanation above must suffice. When compiling it, it must be linked with `nrutil.o` and `memcof.o`, as we saw with `lpcana.c` above. When compiled, `lpc_spectrum` takes two arguments, a signal file name and the sample number of interest, and outputs the spectrum as text to standard output, as with `spectrum.c` in section 4.2. Figure 4.16 was plotted from the output of `lpc_spectrum`.

In the field of speech recognition, too, linear predictive coding has proved to be a very useful way of storing the reference templates for stored words in a speech recognition system. Early speech recognition systems worked by comparing an input speech signal to a vocabulary of stored speech signals one word at a time, and you cannot do that comparison simply by comparing the raw signals with some kind of stored signals, one for each word in the vocabulary. But by comparing the linear prediction coded version of the input speech with the linear prediction coding of the stored words, a number of successful speech recognition methods were developed. To this day linear predictive coding and the derivatives of the technique continue to be used in the storage of the vocabulary in speech recognition systems.

Chapter summary

In this chapter we examined some more powerful speech processing methods. First, we saw how to do spectral analysis using the Fast Fourier Transform. We then examined two methods of pitch tracking: cepstral analysis and autocorrelation analysis. In order to set the pitch tracks to zero during unvoiced speech, we examined a simple but reasonably effective method of voicing detection. Then we looked at a very powerful and important method for numerically modelling speech signals: linear prediction. Encoding and decoding of speech signals using linear prediction can be used for speech synthesis, and is also used in telephony (especially in mobile phones). Finally, we saw how linear prediction can be used for spectral analysis.

Further exercises

Exercise 4.3

Record a sentence and analyse its pitch using `cepstral_f0` and `autocorr_f0`. Which method seems to be the more stable? Analyse the voicing of the same sentence using `voicing`. What are the upper and lower limits of your pitch range, during the voiced portions?

Exercise 4.4

Copy `lpcana.c` to `lpcana2.c`. Amend `lpcana2.c` so that it writes out `lp` rather than `coeffs`. Compare the `lp` files with some original audio recordings.

Exercise 4.5

Examine `joe.dat` (or another recorded signal) to determine the approximate location of each vowel. Write down the sample numbers of points approximately ¼ and ¾ of the way through each vowel. Use `lpc_spectrum` to estimate the first three formants of each vowel. Compare them to published tables of vowel formants, such as those in Olive et al. 1993.

Further reading

Most of the topics covered in this chapter are described (without implementation in software) in Wakita 1996. For more about Fourier analysis in C and the Fast Fourier Transform, see Press et al. 1992: 496–510 and 537–53. For more on windowing, see Press et al. 1992: 553–8. Cepstral analysis is well described by Wakita 1996, autocorrelation pitch tracking by Johnson 1997: 33–6 and Linear Predictive Coding by Johnson 1997: 40–4 and Schroeder 1985. The C implementation given in this chapter is closely based on Press et al. 1992: 564–72.

Reading in preparation for the next chapter

Chomsky 1957: 18–20.

CHAPTER PREVIEW

The previous chapters concentrated on signal-oriented methods for speech processing. In this chapter, our attention turns to language processing, starting with finite-state machines. These are rather simple computational devices applicable to various kinds of language-processing tasks. We examine a variety of examples of their use.

KEY TERMS

language processing

automata

finite state

Prolog

transducers

phonology

syntax

5.1 Some simple examples

A finite-state machine is an abstract computing device. (You will some-times see the terms 'finite-state automaton' or 'finite-state transition network' instead, which mean the same thing as finite-state machine.) We will look at some concrete implementations of finite-state machines and the uses to which they are put in due course. In fact, it is reasonable to say that finite-state machines are nowadays the most important computational technique in spoken language processing. They are used in relating signals to word transcriptions, in morphological and syntactic processing, and even in machine translation. The uses of these abstract computing devices are many and varied, and the particular purposes that we will put them to here are representative examples, mainly applications involving speech and the structure of words. So I am going to begin by looking at some examples that are concerned with *phonotactics*, that is, the well-formedness of sequences of phonological symbols. So rather than working on signals, we are going to start off by looking at the use of these machines for processing sequences of symbols. This is at a slightly higher level of abstraction than in the previous chapters, but as we go on I shall try to make the link between symbolic representations and representations of signals. I shall show how the two levels can be integrated using a particular kind of finite-state machine. That will lay the groundwork for some other work that comes up in chapter 7, on probabilistic finite-state machines and their use in modelling speech signals.

Gazdar and Mellish (1989) give a little example of a finite-state machine: a laughing machine, that is, a machine that generates or recognizes sequences of the letter 'h' followed by 'a', repeated any number of times and terminated by an exclamation mark (figure 5.1). This machine will generate or recognize sequences such as 'ha!', 'haha!', 'hahaha!' and so on. It is not capable of recognizing any other strings, and so if we provide any other strings as the input to this machine they will not be accepted: the machine is incapable of dealing with them.

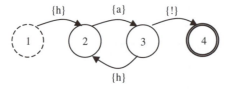

FIGURE 5.1

A laughing machine

A finite-state machine works rather like a board game in which you move a piece from one position to the next in order to get from one side of the board (the start) to the other (the end). There is a start state (state 1, marked by a dashed circle), and one or more end states (marked by a double-ringed circle): in figure 5.1 there is only one end state, state 4. The machine is allowed to move from one state to another according to the arrows, which are marked with labels (sets of symbols). The machine is used to **generate** strings by writing out one of the symbols on the arrow as you pass from one state to the next. Alternatively, the machine can be used to **accept** (i.e. recognise) strings input to the machine by checking off a symbol from the beginning of the string if it is among the set of symbols with which the arrow is labelled. The set of strings you can generate or accept by moving from the start to the end is the language defined by the machine.

Jurafsky and Martin (2000: 34) give a similar simple example. They present a finite-state machine that defines a 'sheep language'. The words of their 'sheep language' start with a *b* and then have two or more *a*s and an exclamation mark. Thus, 'baa!', 'baaa!' and 'baaaaaaaaaaa!' are sheepish words, but 'ba!', 'baba!' and 'micro-organism' are not. The sheeptalk machine is reproduced in figure 5.2.

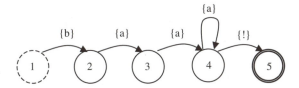

FIGURE 5.2
A sheeptalk machine
(After Jurafsky, Daniel;
Martin, James H., *Speech
and Language Processing:
An Introduction to Natural
Language Processing,
Computational Linguistics
and Speech Recognition*,
1st edition, © 2000.
Reprinted by permission of
Pearson Education, Inc.,
Upper Saddle River, NJ.)

So, a finite-state machine is an abstract computing device – an imaginary computing device, if you like, though we will see some concrete implementations shortly – consisting of (1) a set of states, (2) one of which is distinguished as the start state, (3) some of which are distinguished as end states, and (4) a set of labelled **transitions** between states.

5.2 A more serious example

The previous examples are instructive and easy to understand, but real spoken languages are much more complex, of course. Figure 5.3 gives an example of a machine that models (i.e. generates or recognizes) a set of monosyllabic words in a language rather like English. It is not completely right for English, but it is similar to the sequences of consonants and vowels that can occur in English monosyllables; it's an approximation to English. The labels on the transitions are sets of phoneme symbols, so this machine generates or recognizes phonemic transcriptions of monosyllabic words. (A key to the transcription system is given in table 5.1, below.)

I shall call this machine NFSA1, which stands for 'non-deterministic finite-state automaton 1'. The set of states abstractly represents the set of separate conditions the machine can be in. There are 16 states in NFSA1. When we implement this abstraction as a real, working program, the computer will actually pass through a succession of states of the program during its execution. So state 1 represents the state that the machine is in

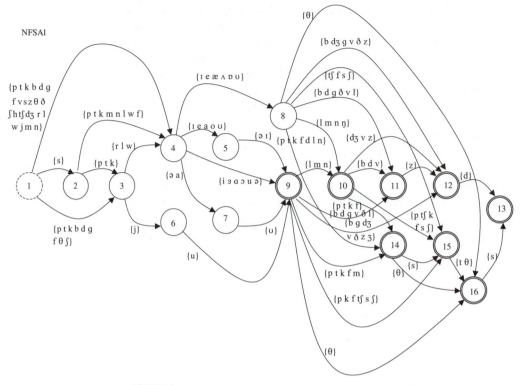

FIGURE 5.3
NFSA1: a finite-state model of English-like monosyllables

when you start the program, the end states represent the actual states that the program can be in at its end, and the intermediate states represent the intermediate steps in the execution of the program. They don't necessarily correspond to lines or chunks of the program: they show the actual states that the machine is in as it is executing the program. The way in which the start state is shown with a dashed circle and the end states are shown with a double circle is just a bit of notation: you could use whatever notation you want, and different authors do use different notations. The arcs (arrows) drawn between one state node and the next represent the transitions of the machine from one state to the next that are allowed by that machine. The arcs are labelled with sets of letters of the International Phonetic Alphabet in this case, although symbols from any set of symbols could be used. Later on I shall look at examples with labels in normal spelling, pairs of symbols from different alphabets, and even vectors of LPC coefficients!

As I said, the way in which the machine works is a bit like a game in which you can move from one state to the next if the first symbol of the string that you are looking at is one of the labels of the transition arrow. So, for instance, starting at state 1 we can go to state 2 if the string we are looking at begins with the phoneme s, or we can go to state 3 if the string we are looking at begins with p, t, k, b, d, g, f, θ or ʃ. The rule about how we move from one state to another is: you can go from one state to another if the beginning of the string that you are processing starts with one of the symbols in the set of symbols with which the arrow is labelled. When you get to the end of the arrow, you move on past that symbol in the string. So for the next state you look at the first symbol of the *rest* of the string, after the one that we looked at in the previous transition. Let's consider the actions that this machine might go through in processing the string s, t, r, ɪ, ŋ. We start in state 1, looking at the first symbol, s. There are two routes we can take: we can either go to state 2 because s is on the arrow from 1 to 2, or we can go to state 4 because s is included in the label on the arrow from 1 to 4. We must decide which way to go – that is why the machine is called **non-deterministic**. (If there were only one possible path to take at every node, it would be **deterministic**.) For now, it doesn't matter how we decide which way to path. We could follow them in numerical order, or we could choose randomly. Let's go to state 2. The next letter of the input string is t. Well, that is OK: we can move to state 3. Then we see an r; that's OK because there is a legal transition to state 4. Then we see an ɪ and there are two ways in which we can move: we can go to state 5 or to state 8. I'm going to take the path to state 8 because it is the one that will end up working out (though a computer would not be able to see that!). In state 8 we see an ŋ next: that takes us to state 10. State 10 is an end state, and the rule about end states is that you can finish if there is nothing left of the string by the time that you reach the end state. There are no more letters left in the input string, so we can stop there. We say that the machine **accepts** or **recognizes** the string s, t, r, ɪ, ŋ. This particular machine accepts almost all the monosyllabic words in Mitton 1992, a machine-readable English dictionary, apart from a few very unusual words, mostly foreign words such as *Gdansk, Khmer, Pjerm* and *schmaltz*. It also accepts a very large number of words that are not actual, meaningful English words, but that are similar to existing words. Examples are **sprɛŋkst** ('*sprenkst*'), **splɔnd** ('*splawned*'), **strɒlkt** ('*strolked*'), **trʌltθ** ('*trultth*') and **blem**. It also accepts and generates a large number of words that are quite un-English, such as **tlʊɪmv**. Whether or not a high degree of overgeneration is acceptable depends on the application. It is often preferable to design a system that accepts a wide range of unforeseen inputs than to constrain the input so much that even inputs that ought to be acceptable are rejected.

Let's consider an input string that the machine will not accept: s, g, r, ɪ, n, t. We can get to state 2 with s, but the next symbol, g, is not one of the symbols listed in any of the transitions out of that symbol. Now what do we do? Well there are several things we could do. The first idea we shall consider is that at that point the machine just stops. It doesn't reach the end; it stops and says that you have failed. The machine doesn't recognize a string if at some point the conditions for the next symbol to be accepted aren't met. The string s, g, r, ɪ, n, t – or any other string beginning with s, g – isn't acceptable by this machine.

If you wanted NFSA1 to accept **sgrɪnt** or **ʃnæps** (*schnapps*) or **gdænsk** (*Gdansk*) you would have to alter the machine in some way. There is another possibility, though, concerning what to do if the next symbol in the input isn't listed on any of the transition labels. Rather than just giving up and stopping, the machine can backtrack (go back) along the arrow that it just followed and see if there are any other routes out of the previous state that would also be acceptable. For example, when analysing s, t, r, ɪ, ŋ, if we had first decided to move from state 1 to state 4, we would not be able to go on from state 4 because the next symbol, t, is not on any of the transitions out of state 4. But that does not mean that s, t, r, ɪ, ŋ, is an unacceptable string: it's just that we were pursuing the wrong route through the machine. If we backtrack to state 1 and try a different route through the network, we can eventually accept the string. If, when you have explored every possible route, you find that you *still* can't reach an end state with no symbols left, the string isn't acceptable by *any* route through the network. At that point we say, 'no, the string we are analysing is ungrammatical (or unacceptable)'.

Student: But if you are at state 3 can you backtrack all the way to state 1? Yes, you can; if the input was pɪt and you went from state 1 to state 3, you could backtrack from 3 to 1 in one go. You can backtrack as much as is necessary, but you must backtrack one step at a time, and you must retrace the transition you took. You can't backtrack arbitrarily far in one go; you have to backtrack to the previous state, and then you try other routes forward. If they don't work out, you can backtrack further back, and you *could* end up getting back to state 1, and be unable to proceed through the network any further. For example, if the input is sprɪmθ ('sprimth'), we can go from state 1 to 2, 3, 4, 8, and 10, but then we cannot go any further, as θ is not on any of the labels of the transitions out of state 10. Backtracking to 8 is no help, though if we go back to 4 we can try 5 instead. But that's no good: m is not listed on the transition out of 5. So back to 4, and no other ways forwards. Back to 3, 2, still no good. Right back to 1: we could try going from 1 to 4 instead, but it is a fool's errand: we cannot get any further. sprɪmθ is just no good.

5.3 Deterministic and non-deterministic automata

We will make use of this backtracking method in the implementation of the machine below. Note that this method is only relevant to nondeterministic FSAs: in deterministic FSAs, by definition, there is only ever one move you can make for each symbol in the input. In a deterministic finite-state machine, in each state there is only ever (at most) one transition that you can make for a given input symbol, there are never any cases like state 1 of NFSA1 where if the next symbol is s, p, t, k, b, d, g, f, θ or ʃ there are two ways you can go. Or at state 8 if the next symbol is l, there are three ways you can go. This is a non-deterministic finite-state machine, because you sometimes can't determine the right way to go forwards. You would have to toss a coin or something, and choose one. In a *deterministic* finite-state machine there is no need for backtracking: at each step there is only one way you can go forward, for a given input string, so there is no need for backtracking.

Figure 5.4 shows a deterministic variant of NFSA1 that accepts (or generates) almost exactly the same set of strings. To make DFSA1, a few changes to NFSA1 had to be made. Some extra states had to be introduced (these are shaded) and some extra transition arcs (those with broken lines). Also, the transition labels had to be altered. Additionally, we have allowed for the possibility of **empty transitions:** that is, moves forwards without reading a symbol from the input string (or, equivalently, reading the empty symbol, "). For example, to read the string sʌn (*sun*), the first symbol is s, so the machine must go from state 1 to state 2. Then, the next symbol is ʌ. This is not in the transition label from state 2 to 3, nor in the transition label from 2 to 4. But the empty symbol " is in the transition label from 2 to 4, so we can go to state 4. Now ʌ is still the first symbol of the remainder of the input string: from state 4 we can go to state 8b. Then,

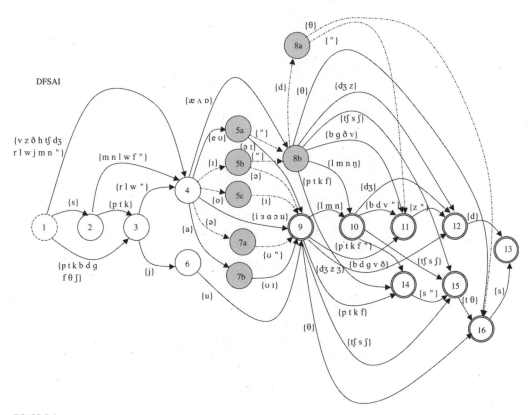

FIGURE 5.4
DFSA1: a deterministic version of NFSA1

reading n, we can go to state 10. As 10 is an end state and there are no letters left, we can stop: sʌn is acceptable.

Non-deterministic FSAs are no more or less powerful than deterministic ones, in the sense that for any language that can be accepted by a non-deterministic machine, a deterministic machine can be constructed that accepts it, and vice versa. Furthermore, a non-deterministic machine can be automatically turned into an equivalent deterministic machine: Hopcroft et al. 2000 gives details.

We only use backtracking in non-deterministic finite-state machines, where at some points there might be two or more options to take. So if we take one route and it turns out not to have been right, we can backtrack and explore other possibilities. So backtracking enables us to implement a kind of parallel processing. We can't actually *do* the processing in parallel, following different routes at the same time, but we can explore various possibilities one after the other until we have exhausted all the possible paths through the network, if necessary. If we reach an end state before exploring the whole graph, then fine, the string is acceptable, and we can stop there.

5.4 Implementation in Prolog

An implementation of this example is given in listing 5.1. This particular implementation is in Prolog, a programming language that is quite easy to understand, but one that is very different from C. Some of the most salient differences are listed in the following text box, though you don't need to study this now in order to go on. A good Prolog interpreter, SWI-Prolog, is provided on the CD-ROM, and there is a helpful website that goes with it (see the companion website to this book for a link).

Some differences between Prolog and C

1. Prolog programs are not normally compiled: they are interpreted. That means that you start the Prolog interpreter, and then you can type in one definition or question at a time. Or you can put your definitions and questions in a file and run it, in which case the Prolog interpreter will go through them one at a time just as if you were typing them in.
2. There is no 'main' procedure: if your program defines various predicates (which are somewhat like C functions), you can tell the interpreter to call (i.e. run) *any* of them. This means that there are many ways of running a program. It depends on what you ask the interpreter to do.
3. There is no 'pre-processor' (a feature peculiar to C). To incorporate one program file within another (as with the C #define *filename* pre-processor command), in Prolog we talk of 'consulting' that file, expressed either as 'consult(*filename*).' or '[*filename*].',

depending on the implementation of Prolog you are using. (Note that Prolog clauses end with a full stop, whereas in C they are terminated with a semicolon. The punctuation is different in other respects too. Instead of C's {. . .}, for instance, you can use (. . .) in Prolog, though it is usually not necessary.)

4. The data type of a variable does not need to be declared in advance (hooray!). In fact, a variable can be used to hold objects of various kinds. However, there are fewer numeric types than in C, and they do not relate to the actual storage of different kinds of numbers in the computer's memory. If you write anything to a file, it will be written as an ASCII description of the object: this is true even of integers and floating point numbers! The difference between variables and constants is shown typographically: variable names begin with a capital letter or the underscore symbol __. Anything else is a constant. (To make a constant that begins with a capital letter, you can put it in single quotes. Anything in single quotes is a constant.) Thus, John is a variable, john is a constant, 'John' is a constant and __constant is a variable (because it begins with an underscore). A, B, C, X, X1, String, What, Result and Anything are typical variables. ASCII letters and numbers are constants, as are operator symbols like +, <, and the reserved words of the language such as consult, is and name.

5. The content of a variable is only fixed within a clause (i.e. it is local to each function). Thus, if I use the variable A in two clauses, there is not necessarily any connection between them.

6. Prolog is a logic programming language. One clause calls another by a process of logical inference called theorem proving. This means that you do not need to tell the interpreter the order in which the clauses in a program should be executed. Also, contradictory, inconsistent, illogical programs fail, whereas in C it is unfortunately easy to write illogical programs.

There are several good textbooks on Prolog; some titles are recommended in the 'further reading' section at the end of this chapter.

There are several main ways to represent strings in Prolog that we could use. For this implementation, we shall write a string as a list of letters, separated by commas and enclosed in square brackets. For example, we will encode pet as [p,e,t]. Non-roman IPA letters will need to be expressed using some kind of translation into ASCII symbols. I shall use the encoding in table 5.1, which is based on that used in Mitton 1992, with one modification: 'C' and 'J' are used instead of Mitton's 'tS' and 'dZ'. This avoids an unnecessary complication with the machine: it is not very important or necessary, though. Capital letters, like the capital T, or the capital C, and so on, should be enclosed in single quotes in

Table 5.1. An encoding of some IPA symbols into Prolog atoms and ASCII

IPA	Prolog encoding	ASCII encoding	English examples	IPA	Prolog encoding	ASCII encoding	English examples
p	p	112	**p**ot, s**p**ot	ɪ	'I'	73	**p**it
t	t	116	**t**ot, s**t**ock	e	e	101	**p**et, h**ea**d
k	k	107	**c**ot, so**ck**, **qu**ay, **k**ey	æ	'&'	38	**p**at
b	b	98	**b**et	ʌ	'V'	86	p**u**tt, c**u**t, bl**oo**d
d	d	100	**d**ebt	ɒ	0	48	**p**ot
g	g	103	**g**et, **gu**ard	ʊ	'U'	85	p**u**t, f**oo**t, w**o**lf
tʃ	'C'	67	**ch**urch, e**tch**	ə	'@'	64	**the**, **an**
dʒ	'J'	74	**j**u**dge**	i	i	105	f**ee**t, h**ea**t
f	f	102	**f**it, o**ff**, s**ph**ere	eɪ	e, 'I'	101, 73	f**a**te, r**ai**d, m**ay**
θ	'T'	84	**th**ick	aɪ	a, 'I'	97, 73	p**ie**, m**y**
s	s	115	**s**it, ki**ss**, **ps**ych	ɔɪ	o, 'I'	111, 73	**t**oy, qu**oit**
ʃ	'S'	83	**sh**ip, qui**che**	u	u	117	f**oo**d, bl**ue**
h	h	104	**h**ot	ju	j, u	106, 117	n**ew**, c**ue**, **you**
v	v	118	**v**et, gi**ve**	əʊ	'@', 'U'	64, 85	g**o**, t**oe**, t**oa**d
ð	'D'	68	**th**is	aʊ	a, 'U'	97, 85	c**ow**, l**ou**d
z	z	122	**z**oo, si**z**e	ɪə	'I', '@'	73, 64	**p**ier, **p**eer, **f**ear
ʒ	'Z'	90	rou**ge**	eə	e, '@'	101, 64	**p**air, **p**ear, **c**are
m	m	109	**m**et	ɜ	3	51	v**er**se, f**ur**, f**ir**
n	n	110	**n**et, **kn**ot	ʊə	'U', '@'	85, 64	**t**our
ŋ	'N'	78	si**ng**, thi**nk**	ɔ	'O'	79	**or**, l**aw**, t**au**t
l	l	108	**l**et, te**ll**	ɑ	'A'	65	**t**ar
r	r	114	**r**ot, w**r**ite				
w	w	119	**w**et				
j	j	106	**y**et				

Prolog if they are to be used as constants, because capitals in Prolog represent variables. When we want to use capital letters as constants we have to put them in single quotes. Thus, ʃəʊ is encoded as the list ['S','@','U']. Note that 0 (zero), used to encode IPA ɒ, and 3 (three), representing IPA ɜ, do not need to be put in quotes, because numerals are constants anyway.

Listing 5.1. A Prolog implementation of NFSA1

```
/* NFSA1.PL    A nondeterministic finite-state automaton to      */
/*             recognize English-like monosyllabic phoneme strings */

accept(String):- move(s1,String).
                                                                     5
move(State,Symbol):-
     transition(State,Symbol,end).
move(StateA,[Symbol|Rest]):-
     transition(State1,Symbol,StateB),
     move(StateB,Rest).                                              10

/* Enumerate all acceptable strings */

loop:- accept(A), write(A), nl, fail.
                                                                     15
transition(s1,s,s2).
transition(s1,p,s3).
transition(s1,t,s3).
transition(s1,k,s3).
transition(s1,b,s3).                                                 20
transition(s1,d,s3).
transition(s1,g,s3).
transition(s1,f,s3).
transition(s1,'T',s3).
transition(s1,'S',s3).                                               25
transition(s1,p,s4).
transition(s1,t,s4).
transition(s1,k,s4).
transition(s1,b,s4).
transition(s1,d,s4).                                                 30
transition(s1,g,s4).
transition(s1,f,s4).
transition(s1,v,s4).
transition(s1,s,s4).
transition(s1,'T',s4).                                               35
transition(s1,'D',s4).
transition(s1,'S',s4).
transition(s1,h,s4).
transition(s1,'C',s4).
transition(s1,'J',s4).                                               40
transition(s1,r,s4).
transition(s1,l,s4).
transition(s1,w,s4).
transition(s1,j,s4).
transition(s1,m,s4).                                                 45
transition(s1,n,s4).
transition(s2,p,s3).
transition(s2,t,s3).
transition(s2,k,s3).
transition(s2,p,s4).                                                 50
```

```
transition(s2,t,s4).
transition(s2,k,s4).
transition(s2,m,s4).
transition(s2,n,s4).
transition(s2,l,s4).                                    55
transition(s2,w,s4).
transition(s2,f,s4).
transition(s3,r,s4).
transition(s3,l,s4).
transition(s3,w,s4).                                    60
transition(s3,j,s6).
transition(s4,'I',s5).
transition(s4,e,s5).
transition(s4,'&',s5).
transition(s4,o,s5).                                    65
transition(s4,'U',s5).
transition(s4,'@',s7).
transition(s4,a,s7).
transition(s4,'I',s8).
transition(s4,e,s8).                                    70
transition(s4,'&',s8).
transition(s4,'V',s8).
transition(s4,0,s8).
transition(s4,'U',s8).
transition(s4,3,s9).                                    75
transition(s4,'A',s9).
transition(s4,'O',s9).
transition(s4,u,s9).
transition(s4,i,s9).
transition(s4,'@',s9).                                  80
transition(s5,'@',s9).
transition(s5,'I',s9).
transition(s6,u,s9).
transition(s7,'U',s9).
transition(s8,l,s10).                                   85
transition(s8,m,s10).
transition(s8,n,s10).
transition(s8,'N',s10).
transition(s8,b,s11).
transition(s8,d,s11).                                   90
transition(s8,g,s11).
transition(s8,'D',s11).
transition(s8,v,s11).
transition(s8,l,s11).
transition(s8,b,s12).                                   95
transition(s8,'J',s12).
transition(s8,g,s12).
transition(s8,v,s12).
transition(s8,'D',s12).
transition(s8,z,s12).                                  100
transition(s8,p,s14).
transition(s8,t,s14).
```

```
transition(s8,k,s14).
transition(s8,f,s14).
transition(s8,d,s14).                                              105
transition(s8,l,s14).
transition(s8,n,s14).
transition(s8,'C',s15).
transition(s8,f,s15).
transition(s8,s,s15).                                              110
transition(s8,'S',s15).
transition(s8,'T',s16).
/* State 9 is an end state if there are no more letters left */
transition(s9,[],end).
transition(s9,l,s10).                                              115
transition(s9,m,s10).
transition(s9,n,s10).
transition(s9,b,s11).
transition(s9,d,s11).
transition(s9,g,s11).                                              120
transition(s9,v,s11).
transition(s9,'D',s11).
transition(s9,l,s11).
transition(s9,b,s12).
transition(s9,'J',s12).                                            125
transition(s9,g,s12).
transition(s9,v,s12).
transition(s9,'D',s12).
transition(s9,z,s12).
transition(s9,'Z',s12).                                            130
transition(s9,p,s14).
transition(s9,t,s14).
transition(s9,k,s14).
transition(s9,f,s14).
transition(s9,m,s14).                                              135
transition(s9,p,s15).
transition(s9,k,s15).
transition(s9,f,s15).
transition(s9,'C',s15).
transition(s9,s,s15).                                              140
transition(s9,'S',s15).
transition(s9,'T',s16).
/* State 10 is an end state if there are no more letters left */
transition(s10,[],end).
transition(s10,b,s11).                                             145
transition(s10,d,s11).
transition(s10,v,s11).
transition(s10,'J',s12).
transition(s10,v,s12).
transition(s10,z,s12).                                             150
transition(s10,p,s14).
transition(s10,t,s14).
transition(s10,k,s14).
transition(s10,f,s14).
```

```
transition(s10,p,s15).                                              155
transition(s10,k,s15).
transition(s10,'C',s15).
transition(s10,f,s15).
transition(s10,s,s15).
transition(s10,'S',s15).                                            160
/* State 11 is an end state if there are no more letters left */
transition(s11,[],end).
transition(s11,z,s12).
/* State 12 is an end state if there are no more letters left */
transition(s12,[],end).                                             165
transition(s12,d,s13).
/* State 13 is an end state if there are no more letters left */
transition(s13,[],end).
/* State 14 is an end state if there are no more letters left */
transition(s14,[],end).                                             170
transition(s14,s,s15).
transition(s14,'T',s16).
/* State 15 is an end state if there are no more letters left */
transition(s15,[],end).
transition(s15,t,s16).                                              175
transition(s15,'T',s16).
/* State 16 is an end state if there are no more letters left */
transition(s16,[],end).
transition(s16,s,s13).
```

The program is very simple, even though it is quite long. It has two parts: first, there are four statements or clauses, each of which has a left hand part and a right hand part separated by ':-', which means *if*. 'A :- B.' can be read as 'A if B', or 'A is true if B is true', or 'in order to prove A, prove B'. Note that each clause ends with a full stop. So the first statement, 'accept(String):- move(s1,String).', means 'accept a string (held in the variable String) if there is a move from state 1 (s1) that takes you through the String'. So that is a definition of acceptance or acceptability.

Then, there are two clauses in lines 6 to 10 that define a move through the automaton. The first defines the special case of a final move; the second defines non-final moves. The definition of a final move is:

```
move(State,Symbol):- transition(State,Symbol,end).
```

(Line breaks, such as those after the ': – ' in line 6 or 8 of listing 5.1, are ignored by the Prolog interpreter.) This clause can be read as 'there is a move from a State past a Symbol if there is a transition from State to the end via that Symbol'. The largest part of the program is a long list of statements about what kinds of transitions are permitted in this automaton: these statements define the entire content of the automaton NFSA1. States are represented s1 ... s16, though *any* sixteen distinct symbols would do.

Consider the transitions from state 9 to state 11. On figure 5.3 I drew a single transition arrow from node 9 to node 11 with a set of six letters {b d g v ð l} on the one arrow. But in listing 5.1 there are six different transitions from state 9 to state 11, each mentioning a single symbol:

```
transition(s9,b,s11).
transition(s9,d,s11).
transition(s9,g,s11).
transition(s9,v,s11).
transition(s9,'D',s11).
transition(s9,l,s11).
```

So that is why there are six conditions, six statements in the group of rules for transitions from state 9 to 11, any one of which is a legal transition. It is as if we interpret figure 5.5 (a) as (b), and similarly for all the other transitions with multiple labels. With only one symbol per transition arrow, we can dispense with set braces.

(a) Single arrow, multiple labels   **(b) Multiple arrows, single labels**

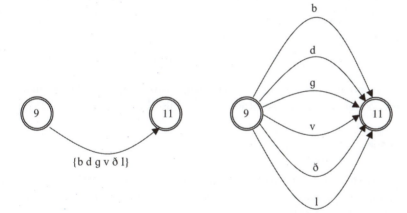

FIGURE 5.5
Interpretation of multiple labels

Digression

Alternatively, we could use the predicate `member`, which is built in to many versions of Prolog, to check whether the symbol is in the set of symbols on a transition arrow. For example, instead of the following six lines:

```
transition(s9,p,s15).
transition(s9,k,s15).
transition(s9,f,s15).
transition(s9,'C',s15).
transition(s9,s,s15).
transition(s9,'S',s15).
```

we could write just:

```
transition(s9,X,s15):- member(X,[p,k,f,'C',s,'S']).
```

If it is not built in to your version of Prolog, the following definition of member is standard:

```
member(H,[H|_]).
member(X,[_|T]):- member(X,T).
```

However, this approach makes the code run a little more slowly, and does not generalize as easily to other varieties of finite-state automata, such as those we will consider below.

Referring to figure 5.3, the following are examples of possibly final transitions: (1) from s6 to s9 via u, (2) from s10 to s11 via b, and (3) from s8 to s15 via tʃ. In the program, however, these are treated like non-final transitions, because whether a state is final or not depends not only on its own status, but also on the fact that there are no more symbols left in the string. The following clauses sanction the three transitions mentioned above:

```
transition(s6,u,s9).
transition(s10,b,s11).
transition(s8,'C',s15).
```

The fact that states 9, 11 and 15 (to name but three) are final states if there are no more letters left is encoded by the following clauses:

```
transition(s9,[],end).
transition(s11,[],end).
transition(s15,[],end).
```

Effectively, it is as if we had defined an additional state, called end, as in figure 5.6. Transitions from s9, s11, s15 and others to state end are permitted if all that remains of the string is nothing.

The second statement in the definition of move defines non-final moves:

```
move(StateA,[Symbol|Rest]):-
    transition(StateA,Symbol,StateB),
    move(StateB,Rest).
```

It is a recursive definition, because it includes move again. It can be read as follows: 'there is a move from any state, StateA through a string that starts with a Symbol and continues with the Rest of the string *if*: (1) there is a transition from StateA to some StateB via that Symbol, and (2) there is a move from StateB through the Rest of the string'. Briefly, that means you can go from state A to the end, if you can go from state A to state B and then from state B to the end. Note that the second argument of the first mention of move is a list, [Symbol|Rest]. There are two notations for lists (of e.g. characters) in Prolog. We have already

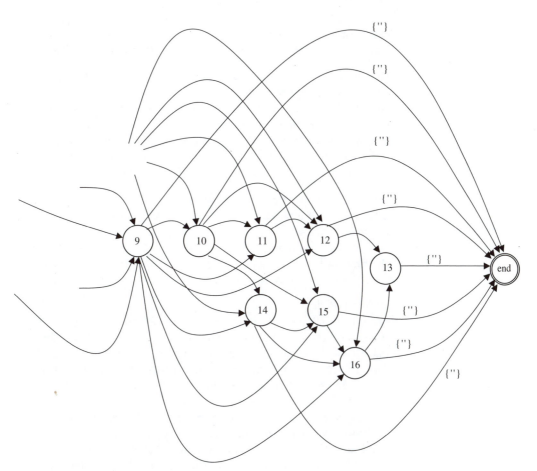

FIGURE 5.6
Treatment of final states in the Prolog implementation of NFSA1

seen the notation in which you explicitly state the items in the list, separated by commas, for example [p,e,t]. We can also describe a list by its first element(s) (the **head**) and the rest (the **tail**). The tail of a list is a list containing all the items in the list apart from the head. Thus, the head of [p,e,t] is p (not [p], note) and its tail is [e,t]. Another way of writing a list uses the symbol '|' to separate the head from the tail. For example, instead of [p,e,t] we could write [p|[e,t]]. (We could also write it as [p,e|[t]] or even [p,e,t|[]].)

The fourth clause is a loop to generate all the strings that the automaton accepts. I will discuss it further below.

Student: Can I just ask about the brackets? I am not quite sure what is the significance of ordinary parentheses and square brackets.
Parentheses are only used in this program to show the arguments of a predicate (i.e. function). Square brackets indicate a *list* of objects: in this

case we are using lists of letters to represent strings. The vertical bar is a notation that separates the beginning of a list from the rest of a list.

Student: So in the second clause of move, *the first symbol of the list is salient, and the rest is sort of unspecified?*

Yes, the `Rest` is dealt with in later steps. In each state we are only concerned with the first symbol of the part of the string we are working on. The rest of it is still to be processed. We can't look ahead and process letters in the string that are further on: we need to set them aside for processing by the later parts of the network.

Student: I mean, at state 1, at the beginning, if the letter is for instance m *(let's say the work is* mɪlk*), at this state if* m *is accepted, the rest is going to be processed in state 4?*

And the `Rest` will be `['I',l,k]`, in state 4. Then when we look at the first symbol, `'I'`, we can go to state 5 or 8. Now the `Rest` is just `[l,k]`. Suppose we go to state 5 . . .

Student: It is illegal.

Yes, it is illegal, because in state 5 there are no transitions that read the letter l. The rest of the string must begin with `'@'` or `'I'`. The machine will have to backtrack. But if the input string had been `[m,'I','@']` ('mere'), the rest of the string from state 5 would be `['@']`, and so in that case we could go to state 9, which is a possible end state.

So as we go through the string we can read letters off the beginning of the list, one by one, and as we do so we move from one state to the next. There are several end states, and if in those states the string that is passed to this state has no more letters left, it is the empty list, that is, an acceptable final move. And because that is an acceptable final move that isn't conditional upon any other moves, the program will finish at that point: it will terminate successfully.

Student: What does it actually do if you give it an illegal string. Suppose you get to state 9 and the first symbol in Rest is an 'I'?

Since Prolog works non-deterministically and this is a non-deterministic automaton, it will backtrack and attempt to find other routes through the network. If it reaches a point at which every route has been tried that it can legally get to, but it can get no further than that, the program will fail at that point. Each time Prolog processes a clause, it actually returns the answer either 'yes' or 'no', meaning 'yes, that is provable', or 'no, I can't prove that with these rules'. If it gets to an end state with no letters left, it has proved that the input string is acceptable, so the result will be 'yes'. But if after thrashing around and backtracking here, there and everywhere, and exploring the network without finding any way through it, it will say 'no'. Those are the two possible results of the predicate `accept`.

5.5 Prolog's processing strategy and the treatment of variables

I've been talking about this machine as an acceptor of strings: you put a string in, it follows some transitions through the machine and ends up with a decision about whether the string is acceptable or not. Interpreting the program as an acceptor, a recognizer, is actually only one view of the program's behaviour. Given a string, the machine will behave as an acceptor. But suppose we provide not a string but no information, just a variable, as the input to the machine. What it will then do is work its way through the transition network, and since a variable will match *any* of the symbols on the transition network, it will be able to trace any path through the network that it chooses. In doing so it will have followed a particular choice of letters on the arrows.

To understand this, let's think of an example in a different domain. In algebra you have symbols that stand in place of a whole set of other symbols that could have occurred in those places: we use *x* and *y* instead of actual numbers, for instance. In an expression like *x* + *y* = 10, *x* can be 1 and *y* 9, or *x* can be 2 and *y* 8. Or *x* could be 1024 and *y*, −1014. *x* can be any number: it stands for a range of possibilities. We can do that for strings as well: you can have variables like *x* and *y* representing not numbers but possible letters, without specifying which particular letters. You can have variables for any kind of object, representing a lack of any more specific information about that kind of object. In listing 5.1, the definition of a move does not refer to any particular symbol, but describes the string in question using the variables `Symbol`, to refer to the first letter of the string, and `Rest`. Within a clause, the value of a variable is the same on each mention, as illustrated by the lines in Figure 5.7. In this figure, solid lines are used to indicate that two instances of a variable have the same value, and dashed lines are used to indicate that two variables with different names but in the same position (e.g. the first and second arguments of the predicate `move`) have the same values, too.

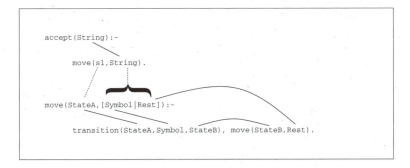

FIGURE 5.7
Sharing of values of variables within a clause is determined by name (solid lines) and between clauses is determined by argument position (dashed lines)

Now, if we ask the Prolog interpreter to prove 'accept([s,p,u,n]).', it will give the variable `String` the value [s,p,u,n]: this value is passed on to the `move` predicate, and the interpreter next attempts to prove:

```
move(s1,[s,p,u,n]).
```

Recall that there are two clauses in the definition of move: the interpreter tries each one in turn. It tries the first clause first:

```
move(State,Symbol):- transition(State,Symbol,end).
```

It can do this by assigning the constant s1 to the variable State and the list [s,p,u,n] to Symbol, leading it next to attempt to prove:

```
        transition(State,Symbol,end).
i.e.    transition(s1,[s,p,u,n],end).
```

The attempt will be fruitless, however, as nowhere in all the many definitions of the legal transitions of this machine is there one from s1 to end. Nor are there any transitions listed with more than one letter as the second argument. Thus, this clause cannot be proved, and the interpreter must backtrack.

But there is a second clause to the definition of a move, and this is now tried out. To prove 'move(StateA,[Symbol|Rest])' according to the second clause, the interpreter must first prove 'transition(StateA, Symbol,StateB)', and then prove 'move (State B, Rest).' To do this, s1 must be assigned to StateA, and [s,p,u,n] to [Symbol|Rest]. Bearing in mind what I said earlier about the structure of lists, that means that Symbol is instantiated to s and Rest is instantiated to [p,u,n]. So, the interpreter must prove 'transition(s1, s,StateB)'. Note that StateB is a variable, so it can in principle be set to anything (because Prolog variables are not limited to a specific data type, as C variables are). Among the many definitions of the transitions, there are two with s1 as the first argument and s as the second argument:

```
transition(s1,s,s2).
transition(s1,s,s4).
```

Once again, these are considered in turn. The first means that StateB must be set to s2. OK so far. That means that the interpreter must then attempt to prove 'move(StateB,Rest)', that is, 'move(s2,[p,u,n])'.

If we repeat this logic over again, we will soon come round to attempting to prove that 'transition(s2,p,StateB)', and thence 'move(s3, [u,n])'. However, the latter will not pan out, as there are no transitions out of s3 with u as the first symbol. So we backtrack to the second possibility for proving 'transition(s2,p,StateB)', which is 'transition(s2, p,s4)', which leads on to 'move(s4,[u,n])'. This is more profitable, as the program contains the statement 'transition (s4,u,s9)'. So, on we go with 'move(s9,[n])' as our new goal. Because of the definition 'transition(s9,n,s10)', we next attempt the goal 'move(s10,[])'. We have now used up all the letters in the input string as we moved from one state to the next. Fortunately, state 10 is an end state: the program contains the clause 'transition(s10,[],end)'. This matches the first clause of move, and does not ask for anything else to be proved. The search for a proof is now complete, as the following text box spells out.

Prolog's (eventual) proof of `accept([s,p,u,n])`.

1. `transition(s10,[],end).`
2. Therefore, `move(s10,[])`.
3. `transition(s9,n,s10).`
4. Therefore, `move(s9,[n])`.
5. `transition(s4,u,s9).`
6. Therefore, `move(s4,[u,n])`.
7. `transition(s2,p,s4).`
8. Therefore, `move(s2,[p,u,n])`.
9. `transition(s1,s,s2).`
10. Therefore, `move(s1,[s,p,u,n])`.
11. Therefore, `accept([s,p,u,n])`. Q. E. D.

Exercise 5.1. Trying it out

If you have SWI-Prolog installed on your computer, you should be able to start the Prolog interpreter in Windows and consult (i.e. load) `nfsa1.pl` just by double-clicking on its icon, in whatever folder you have put it. (Otherwise, double-clicking on the `nfsa1.pl` file icon may cause Windows to present the 'Open With' dialogue box, which says: 'Click the program you want to use to open the file "Nfsa1.pl". …'. You'll have to respond by selecting your Prolog interpreter.)

Alternatively, you can launch your Prolog interpreter (for example, by double-clicking on its icon, or clicking on the [start] menu, selecting '<u>P</u>rograms ▶', and then your Prolog interpreter's icon. If you don't see one, you probably haven't got one, and you will need to install one before going any further.

If you launch Prolog in this way, you'll need to consult `nfsa1.pl` manually, by clicking on the Prolog window and typing:

```
[nfsa1].
```

after the Prolog prompt, '?– '. If that doesn't work, you may have to give the full file name, e.g.

```
['nfsa1.pl'].
```

or the full directory name. (In SWI-Prolog, the Microsoft convention of using '\' in pathnames is not observed: instead, you must use '/'.) Thus, to load C:\SLP\nfsa1.pl, you type:

```
['C:/SLP/nfsa1.pl'].
```

Or you may have to use the built-in predicate `consult`:

```
consult('nfsa1.pl').
```

Some versions of Prolog for Windows (including SWI-Prolog) give you pull down menus for dealing with files. Whatever brand of Prolog interpreter you have, and however you consult the program file, you should then be able to try it out. Try the query:

```
accept([s,t,r,'I','N']).
```

Prolog should reply just:

```
Yes
?-
```

and is now ready for you to type in the next query.

Exercise 5.2

See if it will accept the pseudo-English words mentioned in section 5.2: **spreŋkst, splɔnd, strɒlkt, trʌltθ** and **blem**. What about the un-English word **tlʊimv**? What about **sgrɪnt** and **sprɪmθ**?

Hint: Remember to encode **ŋ, ɔ, ʌ, θ, u,** and **ɪ** using capital letters in single quotes, i.e. 'N', 'O', 'V', 'T','U' and 'I' respectively (see table 5.1).

Tip: In SWI-Prolog, you can recall earlier queries by using the 'up arrow' key. You can then modify an earlier query using the 'left arrow' and 'right arrow' keys, delete and backspace, and the other keys on the keyboard. Prolog will not process your query until you hit the Enter/Return key.

Exercise 5.3

If you forget to put the quotes round a capital letter, and type e.g.

```
accept([s,p,l,O,n,d]).
```

instead of:

```
accept([s,p,l,'O',n,d]).
```

Prolog will take the O to be a variable name. What happens? After it gives its response, press the semicolon key. What happens? Press it 11 more times, or until Prolog responds No. What's going on?

5.6 Generating strings

If we don't provide a string to the automaton, but just provide a variable, a variable will match *any* list of letters. So if we give a variable as the argument of accept, the machine can take any path it likes through the network from beginning to end. Since all we have given it to work on is a variable, it will always be able to get from any of the start states to any of the end states.

Instead of invoking this program by entering

```
accept([s,t,r,'I','N']).
```

where we give a particular string and ask 'is this sequence of letters acceptable?', we can enter

```
accept(X).
```

which means 'What X is acceptable?' Because X is unspecified, the machine will be able to follow any path from the start state to the end state as an instance of X. In following such a path, it will follow a particular set of transitions, each labelled with a particular symbol. So when the machine gets to the end state it will have picked some list of letters, and that list will be assigned to X. The first string it will accept in this way is [s, p, r, 'I', @], in fact. That is just the first path that it happens to follow through the network, because the first transition in the program out of s1 is to s2 via s, the first transition out of s2 is to s3 via p, the first transition out of s3 is to r via s4, and so on. In this way, the automaton can *generate* a string.

Exercise 5.4
Try it.

However, getting *one* result in this way perhaps isn't very satisfactory. For instance, we might want to generate *all* the strings acceptable to the automaton. So after the Prolog interpreter gives an answer, you can type ';', and that tells it to backtrack and consider another possible outcome. When it is forced to backtrack it goes back and generates another answer. First, the last transition will be reconsidered, which was the transition from state 9 to the end:

```
transition(s9,[],end).
```

The next transition out of state 9 in the program listing is:

```
transition(s9,[l],s10).
```

so the next solution it generates is:

```
X = [s, p, r, 'I', @, l]
```

Then if you enter ';' again it will go off and find another solution, and another. If you want to determine the full set of strings that an automaton generates you could be typing semi-colons all night, as in fact it generates 564498 strings. (Yes, I *have* generated them all.) So I have also provided a little predicate called `loop` (see listing 5.1 for the definition). If you enter

```
loop.
```

that calls:

```
accept(A), write(A), nl, fail.
```

meaning, 'accept a variable, type the contents of that variable out, start a new line and then fail'. The enforced failure at the end makes Prolog backtrack, and it will carry on looking for alternative solutions. There are no alternative solutions to `write(A)` or `nl`, but there are many, many alternative solutions to `accept(A)`. So Prolog will backtrack through the whole search space and it will generate all acceptable strings. (You may have to use Ctl-C to interrupt the program, or even close the Prolog window!)

Consequently, the program `nsfa1.pl`, like the abstract finite-state machine in figure 5.3, is completely non-committal about whether it is an accepting device or a generating device. It depends on what queries you give the interpreter to work on.

You can concoct slightly more exotic queries (as in exercise 5.3) where you give an incompletely specified string, such as `[s,t,r,X,'N']` and the solutions to that will provide various values of X. You can get it to generate either a single value of X that is phonotactically acceptable, or if you were to keep typing semicolons or write a bit of code like the `loop` predicate, you could get it to generate all possible values of X, insofar as the string is well formed according to the machine.

5.7 Three possibly useful applications of that idea

1. Alliteration. Suppose we want to find words that begin with the same consonant cluster as 'scrunch'. The following query will do the trick:

```
X = [s,k,r|_], accept(X).
```

The underscore symbol means 'the anonymous variable', that is, a variable whose contents we are uninterested in examining. (What happens if we just ask 'accept([s,k,r|_]).'?)

2. Riming. This is a bit difficult. Suppose we want a rime for 'munch'. The following will give some results, but not all:

```
X = [_,'V',n,'C'], accept(X).
```

Repeatedly replying to each solution by typing semicolons will generate every solution with one letter before '–unch'. But it will not yield, say, 'scrunch'. The best ways to get rimes with more than one letter before '–unch' is simply to make two further queries:

```
X = [_,_,'V',n,'C'], accept(X).
```

and

```
X = [_,_,_,'V',n,'C'], accept(X).
```

(There is an alternative that will generate all the rimes from one query, but it is very inefficient and slow.)

3. Palindromes. In the previous examples, a *template* list was constructed and submitted to accept. Other templates are possible. For instance, we can exploit the fact that every mention of a variable shares a value within a clause to make templates that are symmetrical. Words with this structure are palindromes. (In this case, they are phonemic palindromes, because NFSA1 cannot spell.) The only patterns of palindromes found in monosyllabic words are:

```
[C,V,C],     [C1,C2,V,C2,C1],        [C1,C2,C3,V,C3,C2,C1],
[C,V,V,C],   [C1,C2,V,V,C2,C1], and  [C1,C2,C3,V,V,C3,C2,C1].
```

The first solution to

```
X = [C1,C2,C3,V,C3,C2,C1], accept(X).
```

is

```
X = [s, p, l, 'I', l, p, s]
```

All the solutions with two V's in the middle are uninteresting, as the only identical sequence of V's acceptable to NFSA1 is 'I','I', which is not really English.

5.8 Another approach to describing finite-state machines

We have been talking about these machines on several different levels. I started off with pictures of networks with state nodes, arrows and labels. We should not confuse a **picture** of a network with the **abstract machine** that it depicts. The machine itself is not a network, but an abstract computing device. I shall not get into a discussion about it, but there is a huge literature on the algebraic structure and properties of abstract automata. (If you are really keen, see, e.g., Hopcroft et al. 2000.) For example, you may come across definitions like this:

A finite-state automaton A is a quintuple $(Q, \Sigma, q_0, F, \delta)$ where Q is a finite set of states $q_0, q_1, \ldots, q_N$, Σ is a finite alphabet of input symbols, q_0 is the start state, F is the set of final states, $F \subseteq Q$, and $\delta \subseteq Q \times \Sigma \times Q$, the transition function.

That definition should be taken outside and shot.

So pictures and algebraic structures are two levels of representation. A third level of representation is that of particular computer programs written in particular programming languages, the **implementations** of a finite-state machine. There are many ways to implement a specific, abstract finite-state machine, and many programming languages in which you could do it.

Table 5.2 gives a fourth representation of finite-state machine, a **symbol–state table**, or **state transition table**, as they are sometimes known. A state transition table is a two-dimensional table with the list of the symbols that may occur in the alphabet that the machine is capable of accepting listed along the top row, and the numbers of the states listed down the left-hand column. The entries in the table say what state to go to if the symbol at the head of a column occurs in the input. We start at the start state, state 1, which is the first line. If the first symbol in the string we are processing is a 'b', we look in the column of state numbers underneath 'b'. In row 1, in the 'b' column is the number 3, which means we then go to state 3. If the first letter of the input was 'v', we would go to state 4, and so on. Suppose it is 'v' and we go to state 4. We now look at the entries in line 4. If the next symbol is 'i' we must go to state 9. If the next symbol is 'h', we look at row 9, column 'h'. That cell contains 0, meaning that that is an illegal transition: 'vih' is an illegal string! So the entries in the table encode the transitions from one state to another state when viewing a particular symbol in the input. So the 'from' state number is the line number of the table, the

Table 5.2. Symbol–state table of DFSA1 (see figure 5.4). Final states are in bold italics.

	p	t	k	b	d	g	tʃ	dʒ	f	θ	s	ʃ	h	v	ð	z	ʒ	m	n	ŋ	l	r	w	j	i	ɪ	e	æ	a	ə	ɜ	u	ʊ	o	ɔ	ʌ	ɑ
1	3	3	3	3	3	3	4	4	3	3	2	3	4	4	4	4	4	4	4	4	4	4	4	4	9	5b	5a	8b	7b	7a	9	9	5a	5c	8b	8b	9
2	3	3	3	0	0	0	0	0	4	0	0	0	0	0	0	0	0	4	4	0	4	0	4	0	9	5b	5a	8b	7b	7a	9	9	5a	5c	8b	8b	9
3	0	0	0	0	0	0	0	0	0	0	0	0	0	0	0	0	0	4	0	0	0	4	4	6	9	5b	5a	8b	7b	7a	9	9	5a	5c	8b	8b	9
4	0	0	0	0	0	0	0	0	0	0	0	0	0	0	0	0	0	0	0	0	0	0	0	0	9	5b	5a	8b	7b	7a	9	9	5a	5c	8b	8b	9
5a																																					
5b																																					
5c	0	0	0	0	0	0	0	0	0	0	0	0	0	0	0	0	0	0	0	0	0	0	0	0	9	9	0	0	0	0	0	0	0	0	0	0	0
6	0	0	0	0	0	0	0	0	0	0	0	0	0	0	0	0	0	0	0	0	0	0	0	0	9	0	0	0	9	0	0	0	0	0	0	0	0
7a																																					
7b																																					
8a																																					
8b																																					
9	14	14	14	11	11	11	15	12	14	16	15	15	0	11	11	12	12	10	10	10	10	0	0	0	0	0	0	0	0	0	0	0	0	0	0	0	0
10	14	14	14	11	11	0	15	12	14	16	15	15	0	11	0	0	0	0	0	0	0	0	0	0	0	0	0	0	0	0	0	0	0	0	0	0	0
11																																					
12																																					
14																																					
15											13																										
16	0	0	0	0	0	0	0	0	0	0	0	0	0	0	0	0	0	0	0	0	0	0	0	0	0	0	0	0	0	0	0	0	0	0	0	0	0

'next' state numbers are entries in the table, and each column corresponds to the symbol that must be read in order to make a transition from one state to the next. Also, note that I have indicated which states are final, by writing those state numbers in bold italics. As you will see, I haven't filled in all the numbers for the entire network. I leave that as an exercise for anyone who wants to implement DFSA1 in this way for themselves. Although some lines are complete, note that line 6 actually only has one legal state transition in it, which means 'if you see a "u", and you are in state 6, you can go to state 9'. So another approach to the implementation of finite-state machines is to have such a table in a computer file, and then all you need is a little program that moves from one state to the next according to the entries in the table and the next symbol in the string. The program obviously would not care about what that table represents: it will work with any such table, so that is a nice general-purpose implementation of finite-state machines. The machine follows the moves given to it by the table, and the table could be changed in order to model different languages, or to use different symbols. (To represent non-deterministic machines in this way, it must be possible to have more than one number in each cell. Then, a way of picking one of them must be added, as well as a way of keeping track of which one was selected, so that on backtracking the other choices may be pursued.)

Well, we could stop at this point because those are the main things to learn about finite-state machines. But for the rest of the chapter I shall cover some other possibilities and some particular ideas for extensions, applications and so on.

5.9 Self-loops

In the automata we have looked at so far there aren't any self-loops. A self-loop is a transition from a state to itself. In figure 5.2 there is a loop from state 4 to itself. If the machine is in state 4 and sees the letter *a*, instead of going to state 5 it stays in state 4. The letter *a* is acceptable at that state but it doesn't advance the state of the machine. You might ask 'what is the use of that?' In the context of the previous discussion it may not appear to be very useful, but there is a general purpose device called a searcher, a finite-state machine with just two states (figure 5.8). A searcher is a machine that looks for a particular symbol, or perhaps a particular short sequence of symbols. Suppose, for instance, we have a string and it is however long it is, and want to look to see if it contains a '£' sign. We might even have a file of such strings: we might be searching through the files on your disk, looking for all of the files that have something to do with money. (A file is just a long string of characters.) What we need is a searcher. State 1 is labelled '$\Sigma - \{£\}$': Σ is the alphabet of the machine (the entire ASCII character set, for instance), and '$-$' means set difference, so '$\Sigma - \{£\}$' means 'all symbols apart from £'. In state 1, therefore, if the first symbol of the input *isn't* a £ sign, the machine stays in that state. It then examines the next symbol in the input. It can go to the second state if the first symbol is what it is that you are looking for, the pound sign. After it has found a £ sign we don't care what else it sees, so that could be anything: it might contain the £ sign, or it might not contain the £ sign, it could be any symbol in the alphabet, so state 2 is labelled 'Σ'. (Since 'Σ' is being used as the name of a set, rather than as a symbol that might occur in the machine's input, it is not enclosed in set braces, {...}.) State 2 is an end state.

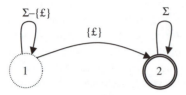

FIGURE 5.8
A machine that searches
for money

The machine will only get to state 2 if the input contains the £ sign. Therefore, the machine will only accept strings containing £.

Exercise 5.5

Think of an easy way to extend the machine in figure 5.8 in order to make it search for money in many currencies, e.g. dollars, yen or euros. What problem might arise in searching for prices in pence?

grep

Readers who are familiar with the Unix operating system are probably aware of *grep*, a program that searches through one or more files for a specific string or search pattern, using a finite-state method. It's like a more general version of the method presented here for searching for a currency symbol. MS-DOS has a similar but more restricted command, called 'find'. In the MS-DOS prompt window (i.e. command prompt window, in more recent versions of Windows), typing FIND 'string' *filename* causes the stated file(s) to be searched for all instances of the stated string.

Searchers can also be used in finite-state machines that model the application of phonological rules. When you apply a phonological rule of the form *cad* → *cbd* (i.e. *a* → *b* / *c—d*) to a string *x* you have to see whether the expression on the left-hand side of the rule, *cad*, matches the string *x* that you are applying the rule to. You can use a searcher for that (figure 5.9). Note that in state 2, if the next symbol is not *a*, you go back to the beginning of the search again. That is, a *c* that is not followed by an *a* does not get you very far. Nor does *ca* if *d* does not immediately follow (state 3).

So a searcher implements a pattern-matching operation. The larger machines that we looked at earlier on are also pattern-matching machines in that the set of strings that they will accept matches the patterns of well-formed syllable phonotactics of this English-like language. Weird and

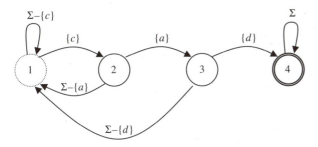

FIGURE 5.9
A schema for machines that search for phonological rule environments of the form *cad*. (For each rule, specific symbols must be substituted in place *c*, *a* and *d*.)

wonderful strings that violate what is acceptable by NFSA1 or DFSA1 are not recognized or accepted: they fail to match the machine's patterns.

5.10 Finite-state transducers (FSTs)

There is an interesting and useful generalization of finite-state machines in which the transition labels consist not just of single symbols, but of pairs of symbols. A finite-state machine of this kind is called a finite-state transducer, and works with two strings at a time. A transition is acceptable if one element of the label is the first symbol of one string and the other element of the label is the first symbol of the other string. In this way, correspondences between the symbols of one string and symbols of the other string can be related to another in sequence. The two strings that are processed by a finite-state transducer could have various interpretations or uses. For instance we might regard one of the strings as an input string, and the other as an output. Alternatively, we could regard two strings as the input, and the machine would then compute an alignment or set of correspondences between the two strings.

Let's look at some specific examples of this to show the use. First, we will consider a machine that relates orthographic representations (i.e. words written in normal spelling) to their phonemic transcriptions. It uses paired transition labels, joined by a colon, such as ph:f, th:θ, th:ð, sh:ʃ, c:k, ck:k, oo:ʊ, oo:u and x:ks. A symbol written by itself, for example s, abbreviates the same symbol on both sides of the relation, for example s:s. On either side of the semi-colon there may be single symbols or short sequences of symbols, to allow for the fact that two orthographic units can map onto one phoneme (e.g. sh:ʃ), or one orthographic unit may map onto two phonemes (notably x:ks). Figure 5.10 illustrates such a transducer, NFST1. It is based on NFSA1, and works with English-like monosyllables.

A Prolog implementation of NFST1 is given in the file `nfst1.pl`. The beginning of that program is given in listing 5.2. There are a few differences between `nfst1.pl` and `nfsa1.pl`. First, the definitions of `accept`, `move` and `loop` are altered so that they work with two strings simultaneously: an orthographic string and a phonemic string. Second, the representation of strings is different from that in listing 5.1. Instead of strings of constants, such as [s,t,r,'I','N'], this program represents a string as a list of ASCII character codes. For example, "S@U"

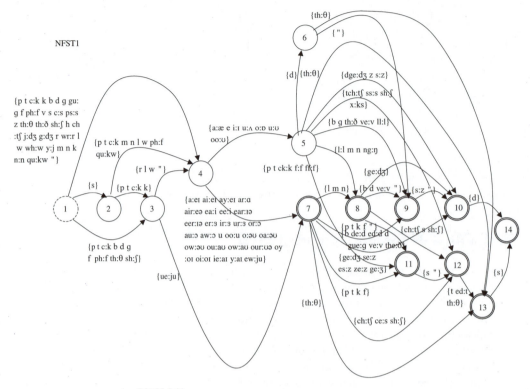

FIGURE 5.10

NFST1: a non-deterministic finite-state transducer for computing grapheme–phoneme relations in English monosyllables

(i.e. ʃəʊ) is encoded as the list [83, 64, 85], not ['S','@','U']. (This has several implementational advantages that I shall not discuss here.) Fortunately, this encoding is not as opaque as it may at first appear, because Prolog provides two mechanisms that help us use it easily. First, there is a special notation for lists of ASCII characters: a string of letters enclosed in double quotes is automatically represented as a list of ASCII codes by Prolog. Thus, if we write "S@U", it will be automatically translated by Prolog into [83, 64, 85]. The empty string, " ", is translated to the empty list [ ]. Second, the built-in predicate name converts (either way) between Prolog constants and lists of ASCII codes. Thus, the query:

```
?- name(X, [83, 64, 85]).
```

yields the answer:

```
X = 'S@U'
```

and

```
?- name('sgrint',X).
```

gives:

```
X = [115, 103, 114, 105, 110, 116]
```

This predicate is used to make the ASCII strings that may be generated by the machine more readable, so they can be printed out to the screen or to a file. (Note that name is now called `atom-codes` in the international standard definition of Prolog.)

Listing 5.2. Part of a Prolog implementation of NFST1

```
/* NFST1.PL    A nondeterministic finite-state transducer       */
/*             to relate English-like phoneme strings to spellings */

accept(OrthString,PhonString):-
      move(s1,OrthString,PhonString,[],[]),                          5
      name(Orth,OrthString), name(Phon,PhonString),
      write(Orth), write(' '), write(Phon), nl.

move(State1,Orth,Phon,[],[]):-
      transition(State1,Orth:Phon,end).                             10
move(State1,Orth,Phon,OrthRem,PhonRem):-
      transition(State1,OrthSym:PhonSym,State2),
      append(OrthSym,OrthRest,Orth),
      append(PhonSym,PhonRest,Phon),
      move(State2,OrthRest,PhonRest,OrthRem,PhonRem).               15

/* Enumerate all acceptable strings */

loop:- accept(A,B), fail.
                                                                    20
transition(s1,"s":"s",s2).
transition(s1,"p":"p",s3).
transition(s1,"t":"t",s3).
transition(s1,"c":"k",s3).
transition(s1,"b":"b",s3).                                          25
transition(s1,"d":"d",s3).
transition(s1,"g":"g",s3).
transition(s1,"f":"f",s3).
transition(s1,"ph":"f",s3).
transition(s1,"th":"T",s3).                                         30
transition(s1,"sh":"S",s3).
```

The treatment of empty transitions is a little different, as there are two circumstances to consider. First there is the case in which the state is an end state, and there are no more letters left. For example:

```
transition(s8,"":"",end).
```

Second, there is the case of an empty transition to the next state, though there are more letters remaining (a mechanism that helps to keep the machine a bit simpler). For example:

```
transition(s8,"":"",s9).
```

Now suppose that you provide only one of the input strings to `accept`, the one that corresponds to the symbols before the colon, a graphemic input string. For example:

```
?- accept("squeak",_).
```

The graphemic input string variable `OrthString` is instantiated with a particular sequence of symbols (in this case `"squeak"`, i.e. `[115, 107, 119, 105, 107]`), and `PhonString` is just an uninstantiated variable. Provided that `OrthString` is graphemically well formed (according to the definition of the machine), as the machine progresses through the network from one state to the next, it will successfully read off the graphemic side of the transition labels. As it does so it also can generate a record of the correspondences between the graphemes and the phonemes as it goes along. The sequence on the phonemic side is generated by the machine at the end as the result (just as was the case when we non-deterministically generated strings in section 5.6). The machine provides a method for mapping from orthography to phonemic transcriptions. Thus, Prolog's reply to the preceding query is to print out:

```
squeak skwik
```

that is, the paired orthographic and phonemic strings. (If you use a named variable, e.g. X, instead of the anonymous variable _, it will give the ASCII codes of each string too.)

It works the other way round too: by providing just a phonemic string, by keeping track of the transitions that the machine goes through and writing down the *first* symbol of each pair in the transition label, you can get a possible graphemic string corresponding to a given phonemic input. By responding to Prolog's output by entering a semicolon, additional solutions can be generated. For example:

```
?- accept(X,"f0ks").
focks f0ks

X = [102, 111, 99, 107, 115] ;
fox f0ks

X = [102, 111, 120] ;
phocks f0ks

X = [112, 104, 111, 99, 107, 115] ;
phox f0ks
```

Well, it doesn't necessarily give the right answer first time! But in that way we can find homophones.

Once again the machine is completely noncommittal as to whether it is mapping from graphemes to phonemes, or phonemes to graphemes. A third possibility, of course, is that you provide both a graphemic string and a phonemic string. In that case you can only get through the network if the grapheme to phoneme correspondences encoded in the transition work are accepted. So that is a way of asking the machine to determine whether the particular phonemic transcription is a valid phonemic transcription of the graphemic transcription, and vice versa, whether the graphemic string is a valid spelling of the phonemic transcription. The fourth possibility is when you specify neither of the two strings. You input a variable for both the graphemic string and the phonemic string. That will non-deterministically generate a correspondence between the spelling and pronunciation of a syllable. By backtracking, you can generate all spelling–sound correspondences for all the syllables of the language.

There is a caveat, though: the power of the machine is limited by how much of the string it can look at at each transition. The examples that we have had so far are correspondences between single symbols in one string and single symbols in the other, where a 'single symbol' might actually be ornate: it might be a digraph or a trigraph, but it is effectively interpreted by the machine as a single symbol. There is no look-ahead mechanism in a finite-state machine, so you can't peek ahead to see whether or not there is some letter coming up later in the string. However, there is a way to encode a kind of look-ahead, which is to actually make the symbols on the transitions longer sequences of letters. For instance, in dealing with spelling to phoneme relations we must consider the behaviour of 'magic e' (the letter *e* after a vowel and a consonant that makes the vowel long) in the English orthography. For example: s<u>i</u>t vs. s<u>i</u>te, c<u>a</u>n vs. c<u>a</u>ne, p<u>a</u>st vs. p<u>a</u>ste, r<u>o</u>t vs. r<u>o</u>te. The pronunciation of a vowel letter depends on whether or not there is an 'e' after the next consonant, further along the string. NFST1 does not deal with most cases of 'magic e' (apart from –ce, –de, –se and –ze in state 7), though it does accept an 'e' after certain consonants (i.e. –dge, –ve, –ge, –gue and –the) that has nothing to do with vowel length. The only way in which you can build those kinds of correspondences into a deterministic finite-state machine without adding a new processing mechanism is to use transition labels that are three or four letters long at a time, and relate three- or four-letter sequences to three or four phoneme symbols at a time, for example ast:/ast/, but aste:/eɪst/. So you overcome the fact that you can't compute non-local dependencies in a string by making them local, by using longer chunks. The bigger the chunks get, however, the greater the number of transitions you need to have, since there is a very large number of mappings between sequences of three or four letters and sequences of three or four phoneme symbols.

Student: You can get into trouble with that kind of thing though can't you? The letters 'a, m, e' correspond phonemically to /eɪm/, but suppose you give the machine the string 'c, a, m, e, r, a'? How is it going to process that? Is it going to first map the c into a /k/? Then it might hit an 'a' and think it is /æ/. But if it processes 'a, m, e' as a single unit, corresponding to /eɪm/, it will go wrong.

The trouble with orthography is that sometimes these doublets and triplets correspond to phonological units and sometimes they do not.

You are right. It doesn't present any *general* computational problems, but it does present problems for the implementation of that particular task. By making the chunks of strings that are processed on each step larger, we introduce non-determinacy into the network, because the number of possible transitions to the next states becomes larger the more letters that you have on each transaction. There are various solutions about what to do with the sequence of letters a, m, e. We could just accept the non-determinism, and then there will be no need to use such long substrings as transition labels. Alternatively, you can attempt to prioritize the choice of which transition to follow next. The usual scheme for doing that is to try to match the longest substrings first, on the theory that they are more specific, special cases. You make the shorter substring matches of a lower priority. But that is actually adding an ordering scheme to the basic finite-state mechanism. We would stay within the bounds of finite-state languages, but that would be a new, non-standard variant of the finite-state architecture. I raised this example to show one of the limitations of finite-state machines. It is a limitation that can be overcome, but it is an intrinsic limitation, in as much as things become more complicated the more of the string you try to scan in any one chunk.

5.11 Using finite-state transducers to relate speech to phonemes

The examples in the previous section are about relations between one kind of alphabetic string and another kind of alphabetic string, grapheme strings and phoneme strings. Or instead of grapheme to phoneme mappings, we could map graphemes to allophones directly if you wanted to, or from morphophonemes to allophones, or from virtually any alphabetic representation to any other alphabetic representation that corresponds to the first in a certain way. (The kinds of correspondences that can be computed using finite-state transducers are known as regular relations.) But the symbols in the transition labels do not have to be letters of the alphabet (*any* alphabet: Roman, phonetic, Arabic, Thai, etc.). *Any* finite set of symbols will do. One instance of special interest in speech processing is that we can treat a set of acoustic parameters, such as a vector of LPC predictor coefficients, taken together as *one symbol*. For example, frame 200 of `joe_coeffs.dat` is a vector of 14 LPC coefficients for (part of) the vowel /ɑ/ of 'father'. We could treat them as a single symbol, a set of features, if you like, as in phonology, and write:

$[\alpha] =$

$$\begin{bmatrix}
a_1: & 2.693137 \\
a_2: & -3.15723 \\
a_3: & 2.153815 \\
a_4: & -0.46244 \\
a_5: & -0.62918 \\
a_6: & 0.194162 \\
a_7: & 0.696667 \\
a_8: & -1.27494 \\
a_9: & 1.502201 \\
a_{10}: & -1.37626 \\
a_{11}: & 1.135756 \\
a_{12}: & -0.52237 \\
a_{13}: & -0.11574 \\
a_{14}: & 0.135437
\end{bmatrix}$$

The number of possible values and combinations of all the different coefficients is very large, so the alphabet of these complex symbols is certainly enormous, but it *is* finite. So, consider a transducer in which the symbols on one side of the transition labels are LPC vectors and on the other side phoneme symbols. Each pairing of a phoneme symbol with an analysis vector represents a phonemic *labelling* of that analysis vector. For example:

```
"A":[2.693137   -3.15723    2.153815   -0.46244    -0.62918
     0.194162   0.696667   -1.27494    1.502201   -1.37626
     1.135756   -0.52237   -0.11574    0.135437]
```

So how can we find out what the correspondences are? Well, the first step is to record a speech database and encode speech into the desired parameters. Then, you segment the speech into phonemes, and provide phonemic labels for each segment, as in the upper part of figure 5.11. (This is usually a painstaking, long, manual task, possibly requiring many person-months of work.)

Then for every 5 or 10 ms frame in every segment you associate that phoneme label with that frame. (This needs to be automated to be practical.) This means that a stretch of speech in the database that is a complete vowel, say, will consist of a certain number of frames, say 30 frames, and each of those frames will have the same vowel label, as in the lower part of figure 5.11. That part of the figure shows a segment of speech from the 204th 5 ms frame of joe.dat (towards the end of the /ɑ/ of 'father') to the 212th frame, shortly after the start of the /ð/. Below each frame number is a phoneme label for that 5 ms interval, and 14 LPC coefficients, a_1 to a_{14}. Time is in the horizontal dimension, and analysis features are in the vertical dimension.

From such a database, we can construct a set of transitions in which the alphabet on the speech side is an alphabet analysis of vectors, and the alphabet on the linguistic side is an alphabet of phoneme labels of the

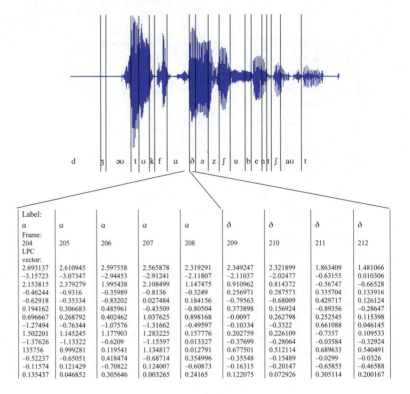

FIGURE 5.11

A phonemic labelling of a speech file

Label:								
ɑ	ɑ	ɑ	ɑ	ɑ	ð	ð	ð	ð
Frame:								
204	205	206	207	208	209	210	211	212
LPC vector:								
2.693137	2.610945	2.597558	2.565878	2.319291	2.349247	2.321899	1.863409	1.481066
−3.15723	−3.07347	−2.94453	−2.91241	−2.11807	−2.11037	−2.02477	−0.63155	0.010306
2.153815	2.379279	1.995438	2.108499	1.147475	0.910962	0.814372	−0.56747	−0.66528
−0.46244	−0.9316	−0.35989	−0.8136	−0.3249	0.256971	0.287573	0.335704	0.133916
−0.62918	−0.35334	−0.83202	0.027484	0.184156	−0.79563	−0.68009	0.429717	0.126124
0.194162	0.306683	0.485961	−0.43509	−0.80504	0.373898	0.156924	−0.89356	−0.28647
0.696667	0.268792	0.402462	1.037625	0.898168	−0.0097	0.262798	0.252545	0.115398
−1.27494	−0.76344	−1.07576	−1.31662	−0.49597	−0.10334	−0.3322	0.661088	0.046145
1.502201	1.145245	1.177903	1.283225	0.157776	0.202759	0.226109	−0.7357	0.109533
−1.37626	−1.13322	−0.6209	−1.15597	0.013327	−0.37699	−0.28064	−0.03584	−0.32924
135756	0.999281	0.119541	1.134817	0.012791	0.677501	0.512114	0.689633	0.540491
−0.52237	−0.65051	0.418474	−0.68714	0.354996	−0.35548	−0.15489	−0.0299	−0.0326
−0.11574	0.121429	−0.70822	0.124007	−0.60873	−0.16315	−0.20147	−0.65855	−0.46588
0.135437	0.046852	0.305646	0.003265	0.24165	0.122075	0.072926	0.305114	0.200167

ɑ:	ɑ:	ð:	ð:	ð:
2.565878	2.319291	2.349247	2.321899	1.863409
−2.91241	−2.11807	−2.11037	−2.02477	−0.63155
2.108499	1.147475	0.910962	0.814372	−0.56747
−0.8136	−0.3249	0.256971	0.287573	0.335704
0.027484	0.184156	−0.79563	−0.68009	0.429717
−0.43509	−0.80504	0.373898	0.156924	−0.89356
1.037625	0.898168	−0.0097	0.262798	0.252545
−1.31662	−0.49597	−0.10334	−0.3322	0.661088
1.283225	0.157776	0.202759	0.226109	−0.7357
−1.15597	0.013327	−0.37699	−0.28064	−0.03584
1.134817	0.012791	0.677501	0.512114	0.689633
−0.68714	0.354996	−0.35548	−0.15489	−0.0299
0.124007	−0.60873	−0.16315	−0.20147	−0.65855
0.003265	0.24165	0.122075	0.072926	0.305114

FIGURE 5.12

Part of a finite-state transducer that relates phoneme labels to LPC vectors

n $n+1$

usual kind. The transition labels are pairings of phoneme label with vectors of analysis features. We can disregard the frame numbers. For transitions from one vector to the next within a phoneme, we use self-loops, but for transitions from one phoneme to the next, we employ two separate states, as in figure 5.12. So the sequences of state transitions that the machine will accept are sequences of phoneme–frame correspondences.

Now, suppose we want to use such a machine to produce transcriptions on the basis of the speech analysis vectors. The basic idea is the same as when we were discussing grapheme-to-phoneme conversion earlier on. Then, if we didn't specify the graphemes but just provided the phonemes, NFST1 could compute the graphemes for us as it goes through the transition network. The same applies here: if we don't specify the phoneme labels but the set of correspondences between phoneme labels and frames is known and encoded in the machine, by presenting the machine with a sequence of analysis vectors we can recover the corresponding sequence of phoneme labels. Now consider a machine for transcribing vowel-consonant sequences that only recognizes one particular vowel-consonant sequence, /að/. The machine might only have two states, as in figure 5.12, with a very large number of self-loops from the state 1 to itself, each of which represents a possible vowel frame. In state 2, the consonant frames will be likewise represented by self-loops consisting of consonant symbols paired with acoustic parameter vectors. There will also be some particular vectors that have been observed at the transition from a vowel to a consonant. Provided we have multiple different tokens of /að/, there will be more than one transition from state 1 to state 2, all representing the change from /a/ to /ð/. For consistency let's give it the consonant label. There will be a great many self-loops in state 1, even if the machine only recognizes one vowel phoneme. And even if it only recognizes one consonant in state 2, there will be an awful lot of self-loops there, one for each distinct observed frame. If we enlarge the set of vowels and consonants that this machine recognizes, there will be an even greater number of self-loops, so the number of transitions in the machine will be very large. But the structure of the machine itself is extraordinarily simple: while the machine is seeing '/a/-type' frames it stays in state 1, and associates each vowel frame with the label /a/. Only if/when a '/ð/-type' frame is input can it make a transition from state 1 to state 2. Then if the frames after that continue to be of type /ð/, it will continue to generate a sequence of /ð/ labels. If the device works in the way that it is intended to, when given a sequence of frames as the input it will generate the corresponding sequence of phoneme symbols. A long sequence of *identical* symbols have to be contracted into a single label, so that the sequence of frame labels /aaaaaaaaaðððððððð/ will be abbreviated as /að/. So given the acoustic parameters of a speech signal, we could produce a hypothesis about what phonemes were input to the machine. It would be a rudimentary kind of speech recognition device; well, a kind of phonemic labelling device, at least.

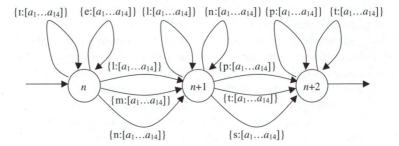

Student: Would a two-state machine like this handle VCC sequences?
No, but it would not take much to extend it to longer sequences.
You'd have a state for vowels, a state for the consonants that can
follow the vowel, and then a state for the second consonant in the
sequence, as in figure 5.13.
*Student: So the number of states in the machine is not tied to the number of
distinct phonemic symbols that it could output.*
That's right. I guess you could pursue that logic even further and say you
only need one state. But the reason for having separate states is to ensure
that only certain patterns of vowels and consonants are acceptable.

Now the question is, does it work? Well, yes it does, and no it doesn't. It
works after a fashion, but it doesn't work as well as we might like it to. For
the machine in figure 5.12 I picked a particular vowel and a particular consonant. But we are unlikely to want a machine that is so limited. We are
more likely to want a machine that can recognize different vowels and consonants. So in state n, as well as the /ɑ/-to-frame correspondences, we are
going to have some /e/-to-frame correspondences, and correspondences for
other vowels. Likewise, in state $n+1$ as well as /ð/-to-frame correspondences
we are going to have /p/-to-frame correspondences, and other consonants,
like in figure 5.13. Now the problem is going to come that it may so happen
that for some frame of the input that is spoken to the machine, that frame
may actually be more like an /ʌ/ than an /ɑ/. That could be the case, for
instance, at a vowel-to-consonant boundary where the spectrum of the
vowel is changing. Or even if it is not, even if it is just coincidence, a particular frame at a particular point in the input may happen to physically be
more like what had been stored away as an /ʌ/ frame, than an /ɑ/ frame.
What are we going to do about that? It might only cause a glitch at one
point, in which case the output might contain a sequence like /ɑɑɑɑɑʌɑɑɑ/.
That could be a remediable problem, because most of the symbols in the
output are /ɑ/s and only one of them is an /ʌ/, but the question is, how do
you cope with that? What we need is some kind of **confidence measure** that
tells us 'well, it is mostly /ɑ/'. We could count the number of times a letter
is continuously repeated in the output, and if there are more /ɑ/'s than /ʌ/'s
we might decide that it is an /ɑ/. But what if a changing sound really *was*

spoken? Maybe what the person said was 'eye', pronounced [ɑʌəi]. The whole business becomes a lot more tricky when we start talking about confidence measures, and asking what was the most likely input given a sequence of observations. Was it an /a/, a /t/, an /e/ or what? We have pushed this kind of machine to the limits of what it can achieve. In order to make this approach work, we need to add a probabilistic dimension to the machine, so that we can make judgements such as 'well, it is probably an /a/, and this sequence of frames is probably such and such a phoneme.' That is a topic for chapter 7, but I thought that I would raise it here as an indication that yes, the technique does work. It will slavishly compute sequences of symbols given sequences of frames in the input, but whether the sequences of symbols that it returns are quite what we are expecting or hoping to get is a different matter.

> *Student: Can you say 'if the frame is less than 5 or 10 milliseconds, it is really too short, so it doesn't count'?*
>
> Well, there are a variety of novel and imaginative ways in which we could try to resolve these problems, to try to get the device to perform how we want it to. These problems have taxed the minds of people working in speech recognition for years and years and a large number of bright ideas have been tried. Some improve the situation and some don't. But those considerations really take us beyond the scope of this chapter.
>
> *Student: As it stands, could it cope with double articulation? For example, when someone says 'apt', there is a short interval when the lips are closed for the /p/ and the tongue tip is raised for the /t/. Those two articulations actually overlap.*
>
> Yes, provided that the correspondences between symbols and analysis frames that are encoded in the transitions of the machines were included in the speech database, there is absolutely no reason why not. The machine does not care about the *linguistic plausibility* of the sequence of frames that it accepts. All that finite-state transducers do is to compute correspondences between descriptions on two different levels.

5.12 Finite-state phonology

Because of that fact, a number of people have proposed that finite-state transducers can be used in phonological modelling, which brings us back to the topic I started this chapter with. We can use finite-state transducers to compute the transitions between lexical (morphophonemic) representations and phonetic representations, as in standard generative phonology for instance. One of the attractive computational properties of finite-state machines is that you can cascade them: you can take the output of one machine and put it into the input of another machine. That is exactly the kind of thing that linguists want to do in standard generative phonology, where you compute the output of one rule, and take it as the input to another rule. So for each phonological rule you can build a little transducer, and then to represent the cascade of rewriting rules you can combine the transducers together. To cascade two transducers you can't just take the end states of one machine and join them to the start states of the next machine: that is not applying the rules in order, that is simply processing the first part of a string with one machine, and the rest of the string with a second machine. In order to cascade transducers you have to merge them in a way that I am not going to go into. It involves combining the sets of states and adding or removing transitions to collapse the two machines into one. There are some well-defined techniques for cascading two transducers because of which you can take a set of generative phonological rules and the order in which they are applied, build a transducer for each rule, and then cascade the whole set of transducers into a single large transducer, in which the effects of all of the rules have been worked out and combined together.

Let's consider an example, based on the standard phonological analysis of the alternation between *revise* ([ɹɪvɑɪz]) and *revision* ([ɹɪvɪʒən]). According to a commonly repeated generative phonological analysis (Chomsky and Halle 1968; Halle and Mohanan 1985), the short [ɪ] in the second syllable of *revision* is a shortened version of an underlying long /ii/, shortened because two more vowels follow ('trisyllabic shortening'). The diphthong in the second syllable of *revise* is the default realization of underlying long /ii/. Conventional (but simplified) rewrite rules for these two relationships are given in (5.1).

(5.1)   a. Trisyllabic shortening $V \rightarrow \emptyset \ / \ V - (C) \ V \ (C) \ V$
        b. Vowel shift $i \rightarrow a \ / - i$

(5.1) uses a combination of the environment symbols '/' and '—' to abbreviate the full forms in (5.2).

(5.2)   a. Trisyllabic shortening $V \ V \ (C) \ V \ (C) \ V \rightarrow V \ (C) \ V \ (C) \ V$
        b. Vowel shift $i \ i \rightarrow a \ i$

According to this analysis, (5.2a) has to be applied to the underlying form before (5.2b), because trisyllabic shortening bleeds vowel shift. Applied the other way round, the output would be wrong:

(5.3)   a. Correct rule ordering:

Underlying form	/riviiz/	/riviiz+iən/
Trisyllabic shortening	Not applicable	rivizion
Vowel shift	rivaiz	Not applicable
(Other rules)	. . .	. . .
Surface form	[ɹɪvɑɪz]	[ɹɪvɪʒən]

   b. Incorrect rule ordering:

Underlying form	/riviiz/	/riviiz+iən/
Vowel shift	rivaiz	rivaiz+iən
Trisyllabic shortening	Not applicable	rivazion
(Other rules)	. . .	. . .
Surface form	[ɹɪvɑɪz]	*[ɹɪvaʒən]

Let's reconstruct this analysis using finite-state transducers, and get rid of the need for rule ordering. Recall how we encoded in figure 5.9 a searcher for the left-hand side *cad* of rules of the form $a \rightarrow b \mid c$–d. Figure 5.14 extends this by encoding the rewrite part of the rule, $a \rightarrow b$, as the

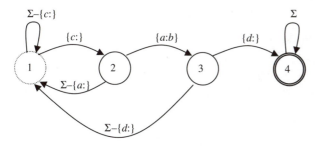

FIGURE 5.14

A schema for finite-state transducers that search for and map phonological rule environments of the form *cad* onto *cbd*, thus implementing rewrite rules of the general form $a \rightarrow b / c - d$

correspondence *a:b*. Note that the absence of a symbol on either side of the colon, for example *c:*, matches any symbol: we are not interested in what *c* or *d* map onto. Figures 5.15 and 5.16 give specific instances of how

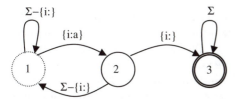

FIGURE 5.15

A transducer that encodes the vowel shift rule $i \rightarrow a / - i$

this transducer may be tailored to encode trisyllabic shortening and vowel shift. Note that, as in the conventional rule formalism, we use V to denote any vowel and C to denote any consonant. That is, {V:"} abbreviates {i:", e:", a:", o:", u:", ə:", ʌ:", ɒ:" …}.

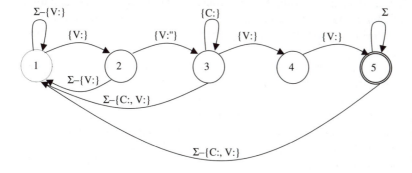

FIGURE 5.16

A transducer that encodes the trisyllabic shortening rule $V \rightarrow \emptyset/$ $V - (C) V (C) V$

The crucial difference between the two rule orders is that in the correct order, the two rules cannot *both* occur, whereas in the incorrect order, both rules incorrectly apply, to derive *[ɹɪvaʒən]. Thus the rules are in an *exclusive or* relationship: one or the other rule can apply, but not both. We

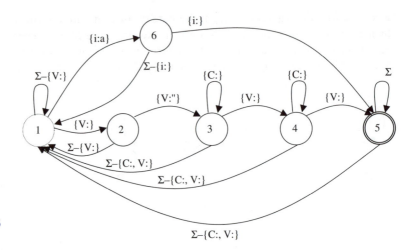

FIGURE 5.17
Result of combining the
transducers in figure 5.15
and figure 5.16

therefore combine the two transducers into a single machine (figure 5.17)
by establishing two separate paths from state 1 to state 5, such that either
the state sequence of one machine or that of the other, but not both, may
be followed.

The idea that standard phonological rules can be expressed as finite-
state transducers has been very influential in computational phonology. The theoretical potential of this approach was first noted by
Johnson (1972) and pursued in detail by Kaplan and Kay (1994) (a paper
known since 1981 from a conference presentation), Koskenniemi (1983)
and Karttunen (1983). The latter describes Kimmo, a system for automatically compiling two-level rules into finite-state transducers. More
recent implementations of 'finite-state toolboxes' include PC-KIMMO
(Antworth 1990) and the more general-purpose FIRE Lite toolkit (Watson
1999).

This work demonstrates (given appropriate caveats about the manner of
rule application) that we can dispense with intermediate levels of representation and rule ordering. As a consequence, this approach to computational phonology is called Two-Level Phonology: as the name suggests, it
employs only two levels of phonological representation, the lexical and surface levels.

I introduced transducers as a generalization of the finite-state machines
that work with pairs of symbols rather than single symbols. Once you take
that step, the floodgates are open: as well as working with pairs of symbols, you could compute correspondences between *any* number of symbols. Down that path lies a method for the computational implementation of autosegmental phonology, where you have to keep track of several
parallel tiers. This possibility was first informally proposed by Kay (1987),
and was further explored by Kornai (1991) and Wiebe (1992).

Kaplan and Kay (1994) acknowledge that cyclic rule application is a
problem for finite-state approaches to phonology, because one of the conditions that have to be placed on SPE rules in order to implement them
as finite-state devices is that a rule cannot reapply to its own input

(Johnson 1972). If that condition is not observed, SPE rules may have the power of context-sensitive grammars or even unrestricted rewriting systems. But if you impose the condition that a rule can't reapply to its own outcome at some later step in the derivation, the grammar is finite state. Kaplan and Kay argue that cyclicity is a contentious issue. There are certainly some unresolved issues as to whether or not cyclicity is dispensable. If it is always avoidable, then they are right, and most of phonology can be reduced to finite-state relations, but if they are wrong, that places a limitation on the circumstances in which finite-state methods are appropriate.

5.13 Finite-state syntactic processing

The literature on finite-state approaches to computational phonology is now quite large, so I have been rather selective about the references I have given. Before finishing, though, I want to mention one other example. I have been talking about phonetics, phonology and orthography, but the first use of these machines was in syntax. Figure 5.18 is an example of a finite-state machine for a subset of English expressions that might be used

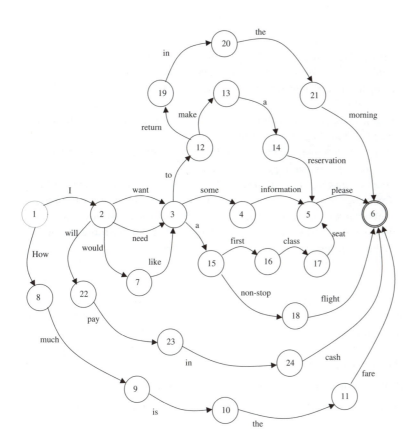

FIGURE 5.18

An example of a finite-state automaton for a small language (after Rabiner and Levinson 1981)

when booking an airline ticket. It is a simple kind of grammar that accepts certain sequences of words and not others. For certain kinds of applications that only use very simple languages, finite-state grammars are quite appropriate. In many circumstances where the range of messages that you want to recognize or generate is rather restricted, a finite-state machine might be more appropriate than a complex type of computational linguistic device, such as a full-blown linguistic parser of some sort. That is the case in many speech technology applications, where we are usually not so concerned with including all of the wonderful and elaborate sorts of linguistic constructions that one finds in generative grammar. You do not often find parasitic gaps in most people's requests for information, so a query like 'which files did you discard without reading?' may cause problems for such systems.

In chapter 2 of *Syntactic Structures*, Chomsky (1957) discusses three models of linguistic description. The first that he considers is a finite-state approach to syntax. He criticizes it, and shows a range of linguistic constructions that it can't handle. So it is ironic that in working linguistic systems in real life one finds finite-state methods being used more and more commonly, and often more successfully than more sophisticated kinds of linguistic parsers, which often just fall over, even though they are more theoretically respectable.

> *Student: But in all fairness what Chomsky was trying to say was that finite-state machines were not a general solution to syntactic problems. If you want to argue that they represent specific solutions to limited problems he might not argue with that.*
>
> That is true, you are dead right. But I think it is interesting historically that the wheel has turned full circle.
>
> *Student: Also the other argument he offered is that finite-state machines will produce a lot of junk that is not grammatical.*
>
> That is true too, but that is true of almost any linguistic theory. And if you over-constrain a grammar just a little too much, you can prevent a parser from accepting perfectly grammatical sentences. That is just as reprehensible as overgenerating, and can be far more annoying to a user, in practice!

But there is another issue, too, which is that the kinds of sentences with unbounded centre embedding that are widely cited as evidence that natural languages cannot be analysed with finite-state machines is easily addressed: they do not occur! To illustrate the importance of this, consider the following sentences:

(5.4)   The malt lay in the house that Jack built.

(5.5)   The malt that the rat ate lay in the house that Jack built.

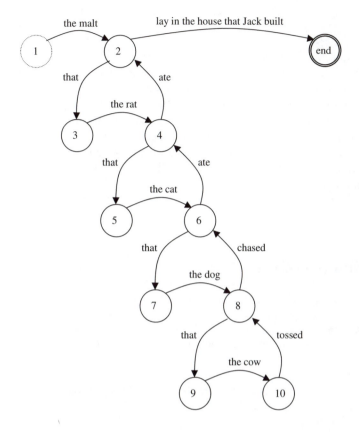

FIGURE 5.19
Centre embedding in a
state transition network

(5.6) The malt that the rat that the cat ate ate lay in the house that Jack
built.

(5.7) The malt that the rat that the cat that the dog chased ate ate lay in
the house that Jack built.

(5.8) The malt that the rat that the cat that the dog that the cow tossed
chased ate ate lay in the house that Jack built.

The syntactic structure of (5.4) to (5.8) can be expressed using a state
transition network of a kind similar to that used in finite-state automata, as in figure 5.19. But if there is no limit to the depth of the centre
embedding, this network is not a finite-state machine, as we cannot set
a finite limit to how many additional nodes lie below state 10. But is
that actually a problem? The degree of centre embedding exhibited in
examples (5.6) to (5.8) is rare to non-existent. So a network with no further embedding below node 10 would actually be capable of accepting
or generating (5.4) to (5.8) with a finite number of states. With this limitation, it would be a finite-state automaton. We shall return to this
issue at the end of chapter 7.

Chapter summary

In this chapter we examined a simple but very versatile computational device: finite-state machines. We saw how they could be used to generate or accept strings of symbols (sequences of letters or words). The twin labels used in finite-state transducers allow a variety of mappings between levels of analysis to be modelled too, making them suitable for grapheme–phoneme conversion, or for associating labels with speech signals. The theoretical presentations were illustrated with working computational implementations written in the Prolog programming language.

Further exercises

Exercise 5.6.

Extend `nfst1.pl` to deal with 'magic e' in the following words: ape, ate, cake, babe, made, age, ace, haze, came, cane, pale, haste, eke, theme, pipe, site, pike, jibe, glide, ice, size, rime, fine, tile, hope, rote, coke, robe, code, doge, hose, home, tone, sole, dupe, jute, puke, cube, rude, luge, fume, tune, rule.

Exercise 5.7.

Adapt figure 5.19 into a finite-state transducer by labelling the transitions with part-of-speech categories. Implement the result as a Prolog program in the style of `nfst1.pl`.

Further reading

There are several good textbooks on Prolog: for example, Clocksin and Mellish 2003, Pereira and Shieber 1987 or Sterling and Shapiro 1994 are all highly recommended. Many textbooks on formal language theory and the foundations of computer science have some discussion of finite-state machines. Few attain the gold standard set by Hopcroft et al. 2000; for clarity of presentation, however, Jurafsky and Martin 2000: 35–52 deserves special commendation. For more on finite-state *phonology*, see the references in section 5.12. For applications of finite-state methods to morphological analysis and syntactic parsing, see the papers in Kornai 1999.

6 Introduction to speech recognition techniques

CHAPTER PREVIEW

In this chapter we examine a selection of techniques that have been used in speech recognition systems. We examine one important pattern-matching technique, dynamic time warping, in some depth.

KEY TERMS

pattern-matching

decision tree

dynamic time warping

vector quantization

variability

6.1 Architectures for speech recognition

Automatic speech recognition is now a reliable and widespread technology. Simple speech recognizers that can recognize spoken digits or a few names are found in many mobile phones, for hands-free dialling. In many of them you can store the names of people that you call regularly, to make dialling speedier. Some automated services provided by businesses over the telephone network can recognize a number of words. These services can accept input from many speakers, a vast range of different voices. These systems, which recognize few words but can cope with many speakers, are rather different from dictation programs now available on PCs. These can transcribe fairly continuous speech, not just single words, as spoken by one or a small number of speakers.

In this chapter, we shall not look at full-blown, large vocabulary, continuous speech recognition systems. In the title, the word 'techniques' is crucial, because I want to concentrate more on the methods than on particular applications. A number of speech and language processing techniques have been discovered along the way towards arriving at the current state of automatic speech recognition technology, and most of these techniques are not widely discussed or mentioned in acoustic phonetics textbooks. We can learn some techniques from speech recognition and use them in other areas. I'll look at some applications later on, in section 6.4.

I'm going to cover three areas. First I want to take a look at the most widely used architectures for speech recognition, to give an overview of the field. Second, we shall look at dynamic time warping, a technique for manipulating the timing of speech signals. It is also a particular kind of pattern-matching technique. Third, we shall look at some applications and problems.

There are two principal architectures for speech recognition: one is the **knowledge-based** approach, in which you attempt to encode in a program the knowledge that an expert phonetician would use to decode a signal, by using their knowledge about speech acoustics and linguistic units to work out what was said. For example, what does the signal in figure 6.1 mean? What are its features, phonemes and words?

That architecture can be contrasted with the **pattern-recognition** or **pattern-matching** approach, in which the system is not given any explicit rules about language or speech. This kind of system is much less theory-laden (in terms of linguistic theory, that is) than a knowledge-based system. Instead, a pattern-matching system acquires most of its knowledge about speech and language by being **trained** on a large database of examples.

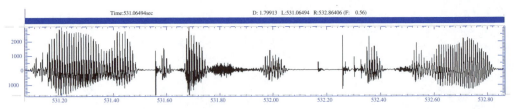

FIGURE 6.1
What are the features, phonemes and words of this signal?

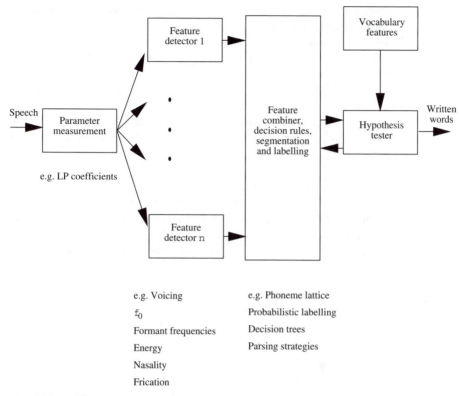

FIGURE 6.2
Structure of a typical knowledge-based speech recognition system (after Rabiner and Juang 1993: 45)

Figure 6.2 shows the structure typical of a knowledge-based system. First, there is a speech analysis component, which encodes the speech signal into some form of parametric representation, such as formant frequencies or linear prediction coefficients. Subsequent processing stages do not work on the raw signal, but on acoustic parameters derived from the signal. The second step is to try to determine some kind of acoustic properties of the speech. There is a list at the bottom of figure 6.2 of the sorts of properties we might look for in an acoustic-phonetic approach to speech recognition. If, without any prior experience, you were to think about how you would build a speech recognition device, maybe you would attempt to emulate what an acoustic phonetics expert might do. For instance, you might try to identify properties of the signal that correspond to phonetic features of one sort or another. You might look at how the pitch rises and falls, and how particular formants are changing, and what the overall energy is. If a part of the signal has lots of energy, it is probably a vowel; if it has rather little energy, it is probably a consonant. So we can employ a set of **feature detectors**, each of which is a little part of the program that 'knows' about one particular property of speech and identifies it. In this way, the program works out 'ah yes, this is a loud stretch, this is a quiet stretch, this is a high-pitched stretch, this is a low-pitched stretch, this is a nasal, this is not; here there is friction', and so on. So we have a number of independent 'expert' components, each of which 'knows' about some aspect of acoustic phonetics. Third, we need a way of pulling all those pieces of information together, to integrate the results of the feature detection and to classify each portion of the signal as being one sound or another. At this stage, we are moving towards the linguistic level of description. As soon as we start labelling parts of the signal with phonological features or phoneme labels, we are moving away from the signal level towards the linguistic level of representation. A variety of such techniques is listed in figure 6.2, some of which we shall look at in more detail as we go on.

Decision Trees

Let's look at the idea of feature detection and segmental labelling in a little more detail, and see what sort of things it might involve. Suppose we have a program that implements the decision procedure shown in figure 6.3, using what is called a decision tree. The program proceeds step by

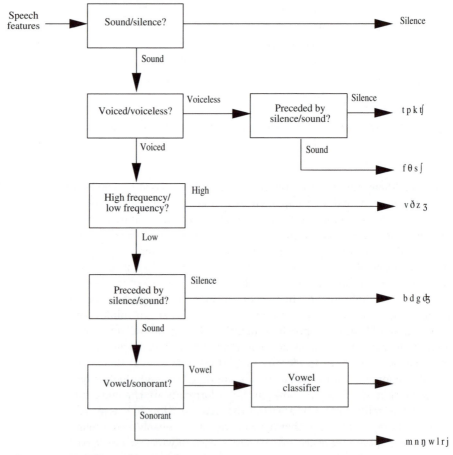

FIGURE 6.3
A decision tree for phoneme identification (after Rabiner and Juang 1993: 48)

step through the diagram, from top to bottom. At each node in the tree we make a decision, based upon the signal that we are looking at. Depending on the results of the simple decisions, at each step, we end up at the bottom of the tree with a **classification** of the sounds in terms of the properties we used to make the decisions.

Suppose a signal is input to the program. The program must examine the signal at successive intervals and label each interval. First, it needs to decide whether there is sound or whether there is not sound. There might actually be silence in the portion of the signal under consideration. So that is the first decision to make. If the signal is not silent, we might ask whether it is voiced or voiceless, by trying to work out whether or not the signal is periodic, perhaps (see section 4.6, previously). If it is voiceless, there is a further decision to make. We can look at whether or not the voiceless stretch is preceded by an interval of silence. If it is preceded by a period of silence, the silence is probably a stop closure, so we are probably dealing with a stop or an affricate: in English, one of /t/, /p/, /k/, /tʃ/. If a voiceless portion is preceded by sound, not silence, it could be a voiceless fricative. If an interval is voiced, we need to be able to distinguish between voiced fricatives and other voiced consonants – stops, sonorants and nasals – but again the classification is by making a decision at each step as to which class each portion of the signal falls into. Each decision is made by reference to one (or sometimes several) of the feature detectors.

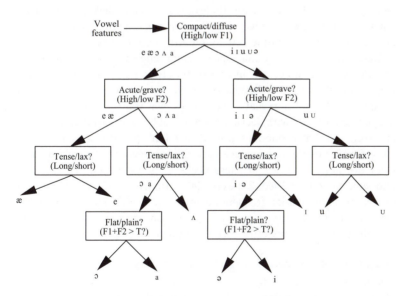

FIGURE 6.4
A decision tree for vowels (after Rabiner and Juang 1993: 47)

Figure 6.4 shows a decision tree for vowels. At the top level we might ask: 'Is F1 (the first formant) relatively high or relatively low?' If it is relatively high, we have a more open vowel. If it is relatively low, we have a closer vowel. Let's suppose that F1 is relatively high and we have a more open vowel. Then the program could look at F2 and consider 'is F2 high or is it low?' If it is relatively high we have a front vowel; if it is relatively low we have probably got a back vowel. Let's suppose F2 is relatively high, so we have a front vowel. In that case we can ask: 'Is the vowel that we are looking at long or short?' This begs the question of how you determine whether it is long or short. Once you have identified a certain portion of the signal, which you think is the vowel, you can measure it and ask: 'Is it long or is it short?' Well, if it is longer than a certain duration we'll say it is /æ/ and if it is relatively short we'll say it is /e/. Notice that there is a certain arbitrariness to what questions we ask at what points in the classification, and that the criteria that we use to distinguish one class from another represent only *distinctive* differences. There are of course other differences between /æ/ and /e/ than simply whether it is long or short. There are spectral differences as well, of course, but what we need to find is a set of classificatory questions, questions that can be implemented and that will work in the desired way most of the time. So there are two examples of decision trees, one for vowels and one for consonants.

The classification or decision tree is one of the main tools of knowledge-based speech recognition technology. A lot was learned from the research that went into building devices of this kind about various useful techniques for determining the phonetic properties of a signal. However, the performance of these systems was not as high as their developers hoped for, and the pattern-matching approach turned out to be better. One reason for this is that the decisions involved in a knowledge-based system are often unreliable. It is also difficult to integrate the results of several independent feature detectors. Nevertheless, research and development of systems using the knowledge-based approach is still ongoing, though it tends not to be used in commercial automatic speech recognition systems. However, for models of human speech comprehension and lexical access, knowledge-based systems continue to be attractive to academic speech researchers (Reetz 1999; Stevens 2002), whereas in commercial software companies, the solution that performs best *now* is always favoured. There is a general problem with decision trees: it can be very hard to recover from an error, and that is one reason why they don't perform so well. Correct identification of a phoneme depends on the correctness of maybe a dozen prior decisions. Only *one* of these needs to be wrong for the incorrect phoneme to be identified. For example, in figure 6.3, if we misjudge the difference between 'high frequency energy' and 'low frequency energy', we could easily misidentify an /m/ as a /v/, and confuse, say, 'man' with 'van'. It is difficult to institute error correction procedures for a system like this.

Other ways of combining the decisions

Student: Why aren't the decisions done all at once?
The classification questions could be evaluated all at once, but the problem we are talking about is how to integrate the *results* of the independent feature detectors. There are various ways in which we might do that. If you look at the results of each of the feature detectors sequentially, there are various permutations and choices as to which you consider first. It makes sense to try the most *reliable* classifications first, and save the less reliable classifiers until later on in the classification process. We hope that we can come to the

right conclusion earlier in the search using the most reliable classifiers. So, 'sound vs. silence' may be easier to determine than 'vowel vs. sonorant', for example. (Recall from section 4.6 how tricky it was to determine voicing!)

Classification and regression trees

Suppose we have a set of measurements of a number of parameters and a number of classification questions we want to settle, such as 'Is it a vowel or a consonant?' or 'Is it a nasal or non-nasal?' In order to make our speech recognition system work as well as possible, it would be useful to know what order to ask the questions in, and what shape the decision tree should have. As I have said, it is sensible to make the most reliable and accurate classifications first.

CART (classification and regression trees) is a general and automatic statistical method for generating decision trees, given a set of measurements and associated classifications (the training set). The CART algorithm works out how well each classification question divides up the training set. The question that best separates the data into two subsets – the best question – is taken as the topmost question of the tree. The algorithm then applies recursively to the two subsets, to determine which of the remaining classification questions best partitions the subsets, and so on until all the questions have been used to divide the data into a number of maximally distinct subsets. As a result, the algorithm finds the best decision tree for the training data. That decision tree can then be used to classify new, previously unseen data, such as the input to the recognition system.

For a technical explanation of the CART approach, see Huang et al. 2001: section 4.5.

Using a finite-state automaton to include phonotactic information

The strategy of using the most reliable classifiers first works quite well because we don't find *all* phoneme distinctions at every position in a word. For example, after a word-initial /t/, /p/ or /k/, we don't need to bother about the distinction between sonorants and obstruents, because only sonorants can occur in that context (in English). If the next sound has some of the characteristics of a voiceless obstruent, it must in fact be a voiceless pronunciation of a sonorant (a devoiced /r/, perhaps). Similarly, after a word-initial /st/, we don't need to pay any attention to the /r/-/l/ distinction, because /l/ cannot occur there. In that position, it is sufficient to identify the following sound as a sonorant consonant to work out that it must be /r/. Since there are a number of sound sequences that are *possible* words of English but that don't actually occur in the lexicon, you don't necessarily have to accurately identify every single phonological distinction at every place in a word. You only need *sufficient* information to be able to identify the word, so a sequential, ranked or weighted combination of the results is one way that has been tried. Of course, in order to take account of the combinatorial possibilities for different phonemes in a language, we need to augment the decision rules with some sort of phonotactic model, such as the finite-state transducer for vowel-consonant sequences we considered in the previous chapter, section 5.11 (figure 5.12). That system had two states, one representing the state of 'now dealing with a vowel', the other representing the state 'now dealing with a consonant'. There were many self-loops in each of those states, representing hypotheses about what the vowel or consonant is, given the particular frame of the signal being analysed. Between the two states was a transition denoting 'now moving from the analysis of a vowel into the analysis of a consonant'. (In the next chapter, we will expand upon that very simple architecture and generalize it.)

A model with two states such as figure 5.12 imposes a sequential organization on the patterns that it can accept, because first of all it is dealing with one part of the signal, and then it is dealing with the second part, so it is only able to deal with two-part signals, one part that begins with some vocalic material, and the second part which is consonantal. Those are the only kinds of signals that this machine can accept. However, the bipartite nature of the signals doesn't arise from the fact that it has two states, it arises from the fact that there is only one way of getting from state n to state $n+1$: there is only one arrow linking state n with state $n+1$. Because there is only one way of getting from one state to the next, the network divides into two halves. We could have a machine with many states in it, but which can be broken down into a smaller number of sub-networks, each of which might contain several states. For example, the syllable network in figure 5.3 can be divided into three functionally independent parts, one for initial consonants, one for medial vowels and one for final consonants. So, the sequences that a machine of that kind recognizes have to have a beginning, a middle and an end of a particular kind.

'Blackboard' architecture

Another technique for integrating the outputs of the feature detectors is to try to pool the results, using a blackboard architecture, where you share the output of all of the feature detectors (figure 6.5). Each classifier has access to the results of all of the feature detectors at the same time and can trade off one against the other, or make combinations: 'if there are properties A, B and C, but not D then the sound is X'. Such systems can be got to work, but there is a problem in formulating the rules for what combination of which acoustic properties corresponds to what phonological categories on the output side. What do we do when two classifiers disagree, for example? 'Looks like an /m/ to me', says one; 'looks like a /v/ to me' decides another: how do we tell which one is right? In addressing such problems during the last fifty years of speech recognition research, a lot of useful things have been learned, including negative results. Even techniques that have been tried and rejected are still useful to know about, I think – not necessarily for automatic speech recognition, but for doing certain kinds of speech analysis. When you know what the speech *is* that you

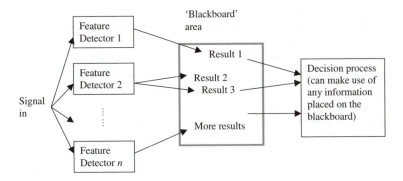

FIGURE 6.5
Schematic diagram of a
'blackboard' architecture

are looking at, you are not concerned about *identifying* the word, you know what the word is, but you might want to measure a certain property.

For instance, a problem I've worked on at various times is how to derive parameters for the Klatt synthesizer from natural speech (see Coleman and Slater 2001). In this case, I know what the words are that I want to synthesize: I just want to imitate them, not recognize them. In that case using some of these techniques for identifying individual acoustic parameters has proved fairly useful. To estimate the amplitude of friction, for example, it is useful to filter the speech into two bands, a high-frequency band (say, above 2 kHz) and a low-frequency band (say, below 2 kHz). The *ratio* of the RMS amplitudes of these two versions of the input is high when the input has a lot of energy at high frequencies, as is the case for fricatives. In fact, this ratio signal, when suitably scaled, can be used to model the frication component of speech rather well.

Role of the lexicon

So we have now looked at various details of the knowledge-based approach. For obvious reasons, Rabiner and Juang (1993) also call it the acoustic-phonetic approach, though one can envisage other kinds of measurements (such as video input) being used in a knowledge-based system as well. In figure 6.2 there was some kind of analysis phase, and once the program has decided what sounds the input speech consists of, it has a hypothesis about the sequence of phonemes in the word that is spoken into the system. Next, we can compare that hypothesis against the lexicon, and this may help us narrow down the search for the right word still further. For instance, some speech recognition applications have quite small vocabularies. Consider a system that is capable of recognizing the digits, zero to nine, a vocabulary of just ten words. In that case, one of the decisions that you might use is, 'are there two syllables or one?' There aren't very many two-syllable words in this lexicon, only 'seven' and 'zero', so you might then examine whether the word ends in a nasal or not. If it does, the word is 'seven', and if it doesn't, it is 'zero'. We do not have to identify *all* of the properties of the input word; you only need to look for a minimal subset of properties that is sufficient to uniquely distinguish the word from the other words in the vocabulary.

Crucially, you need to know what the set of words in the vocabulary is and how they differ in order to make the decision on the basis of such minimal information.

After segmentation and labelling, the system turns out sequences of phonemes, but then we cannot be sure that the sequence of phonemes that the system puts out are actual words of the language. If I say something and the system thinks that I said 'quog' (/kwɒg/), but 'quog' isn't in the lexicon, the hypothesis checker could find the word in the vocabulary that is most similar to the output of this hypothesis. It might be 'dog', or 'quick', or 'quark' – but which one to choose? In this situation, some other linguistic information could be useful. What are the previous and following words, for example? Is the application connected with particle physics or animals? Access to a lexicon (and grammar) can patch up some of the problems arising from the fact that the early stages of the speech analysis technique are not 100 percent reliable.

Student: When you say 'quog', does it decide that it is 'dog' because there is a phonotactic constraint, or. . . . ?

No: simply because 'quog' isn't in the dictionary, we can infer that if the output of the phoneme classifier isn't in the dictionary, that can't be the right word. So rather than going back and starting again from the beginning, the hypothesis checker considers, 'well, it must have been *something* like "quog", so what word in the dictionary is nearest to that?' Now, there are various ways to measure 'nearness': lowest number of phonemes different, lowest number of features different, or some measure of that kind. These are all measures of **minimum edit distance**. (The standard measure – the **Levenshtein distance** – is defined as the total number of insertions, deletions and substitutions minimally necessary to transform one sequence of symbols into another.) An algorithm for computing such minimum edit distances was proposed by Wagner and Fisher (1974). It employs **dynamic programming**, a technique that will be described for a different application in section 6.3 below.

6.2 The pattern-recognition approach

The type of system we have been considering employs many separate pieces of knowledge about speech, at the level of signals, at the level of patterns in the phonology, about the nature of distinctive features, and about what words there are in the vocabulary. An alternative approach, which as I said has been much more commercially successful than this method, is the **pattern-recognition approach** (figure 6.6). In the pattern-recognition approach we are not really interested in the phonetic or phonological structure of the input. We have a certain vocabulary that we want to be able to recognize, which in a modest system might only be ten words; in a grander system, a few hundred or many thousand words. For each word, we store one or more reference patterns. In a small-vocabulary system we might store several tokens of the actual pronunciations of each of the words in the vocabulary, spoken by a number of different speakers.

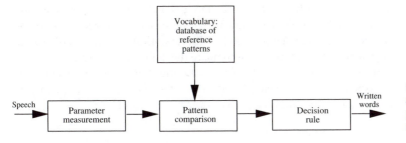

FIGURE 6.6
Architecture of the
pattern-recognition
approach

We could just store them digitally, like a digital recording of the whole word, or we could analyse them into acoustic parameters, using linear prediction coding, for instance. Rather than attempting to find out what the phonetic features are in those recordings, we simply use some kind of pattern-comparison method to compare the parameters of the speech input to the system with the parameters of speech stored in the vocabulary, a library of reference patterns. These are often whole word patterns, so the system isn't really concerned with the internal structure of words at all, let alone the internal structure of phonemes. I think it is precisely because the techniques of the pattern-recognition approach don't rely on linguistic and phonetic knowledge that they have so far had little impact on linguistics. Yet there is much of value to be learned from this approach to speech analysis, as we will see.

Pattern matching

The first problem to be addressed in the pattern-recognition approach is how to compare a **test** parameter from the input signal, for instance the **RMS** amplitude contour, with the corresponding trace in the stored **reference** pattern. It may be that the test pattern *x* for word *w* is actually quite close to reference pattern *y* for that word, or at least closer to it than to the reference pattern of any of the *other* words in the vocabulary. But one problem is that the stored pattern and the input signal are not necessarily precisely aligned in time. The speaker may pronounce the word – suppose it is the word 'seven' – and may say the initial [s] somewhat longer or shorter than the stored [s], and likewise for any of the other parts of the pronunciation of the word. If we just compare each analysis frame in the input with each frame in the reference pattern, frame for frame, due to natural variations in the rate of speaking and the duration of sounds, we could end up aligning the wrong frames from the input with the wrong frames of the reference pattern, because of the temporal 'elasticity' of pronunciations (figure 6.7). Therefore, we would like to have a way of matching the input word against the reference word in such a way that the key features of the parameter in question line up, so where we have a peak in the test parameter we want to line it up with a peak in the reference parameter, without paying too much attention to which frame it is in, as long as it is in more-or-less the right part of the word. If a peak is in the tenth frame of the input we don't necessarily want to compare that point to the tenth frame in the reference pattern if there is not also a corresponding peak in the tenth frame of the stored signal. We want the peaks and troughs in the test signal to line up with the peaks and troughs in the reference signal. We need to be a little bit flexible about the specific timing of peaks and troughs when we compare the input signal with the reference pattern. We want to allow parts of the input signal to be stretched or squashed when comparing it with the reference. One of the main techniques for doing that is called dynamic time warping.

6.3 Dynamic time warping

I'll describe the nature of the DTW (dynamic time warping) algorithm and how it works in some detail. There are many variants of the basic algorithm, in fact, each designed to improve it in some way (see, e.g., Sakoe and Chiba 1978). Here I shall present the simplest version, as implemented in the program dtw.c, which is included on the CD-ROM but, for reasons of space, is not printed out or discussed in detail here. In the DTW algorithm we compare two signals, that is, two sequences of numbers, the reference and the test. For example:

(a) (Input) test signal, $x[t]$:   1   1   2   3   2   0
(b) (Stored) reference signal, $y[t]$:   0   1   1   2   3   2   1
Sample-by-sample difference $x[t] -$ 1   0   1   1   −1   −2   undefined
$y[t]$:

In this example, both signals are similar in that they are single-peaked. However, the stored reference signal is longer than the test signal, and the peak is later. In other words, the two signals are not synchronized in time (figure 6.7).

Test pattern, x[t]

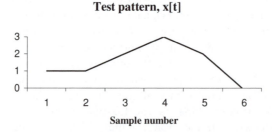

Sample number

Reference pattern, y[t]

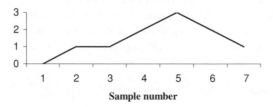

Sample number

FIGURE 6.7
A comparison of two
signals

Table 6.1.

y[t]								
	1	0	0	1	2	1	−1	
	2	−1	−1	0	1	0	−2	
	3	−2	−2	−1	0	−1	−3	
	2	−1	−1	0	1	0	−2	
	1	0	0	1	2	1	−1	
	1	0	0	1	2	1	−1	
	0	1	1	2	3	2	0	
		1	1	2	3	2	0	x[t]

We want to find out which points in the test signal correspond most closely to which points in the reference signal. To do that, we consider that each frame in the test signal might possibly correspond to *any* frame in the reference signal. Therefore, in the first step of the algorithm, we calculate some measure of the 'distance' between all pairs of frames from the two signals. By the 'distance' I mean how much one signal differs from the other, for a pair of frames. For instance, the distance between two peaks or two troughs is low, but if we compare a peak with a trough, the two signals are very dissimilar at that point, so we want the distance measure in such a case to be relatively high.

Step 1: Tabulate the distances

So the first step in the algorithm is to construct a matrix, d, in which we tabulate the distances between each frame in the test signal, $x[t]$, and every frame in the reference signal, $y[t]$. Table 6.1 is a simple example with just six frames in the test signal and seven frames in the reference signal. In this and subsequent tables, the test signal, $x[t]$, is written from left to right along the horizontal axis. The reference signal, $y[t]$, is written from bottom to top on the vertical axis, in accordance with the usual convention for plotting graphs.[1]

For each combination of frames in the two signals, we calculate a measure of the distance between the frames of the test and the reference. In this example, the distance measure used is the simple difference, $x[n] - y[m]$. These values are written in the cells of the matrix, as in table 6.1.

The numbers in the matrix d represent how different one signal is from the other for all pairs of frames. If we were to compare one signal with an exact copy of itself, so that every frame in the test signal was exactly the same as every frame in the reference signal, all along the diagonal there

---

[1] This is slightly different from the convention for numbering *matrices*, however. In matrices, rows are numbered from the top downwards, not from the bottom upwards. Of course, the order of rows does not greatly matter, as long as we are clear what we are doing. I shall use the 'graph plotting' convention so that the order of frames rows in the distance matrix has the same orientation as the way in which they are plotted on the y axis in figures such as table 6.2 and figure 6.10. In the program dtw.c, in fact, cell (x,y) of matrix d is coded in C as d[y][x].

Table 6.2.

$y[t]$									
	1	−1	0	0	1	2	1	0	
	2	−2	−1	−1	0	1	0	−1	
	3	−3	−2	−2	−1	0	−1	−2	
	2	−2	−1	−1	0	1	0	−1	
	1	−1	0	0	1	2	1	0	
	1	−1	0	0	1	2	1	0	
	0	0	1	1	2	3	2	1	
		0	1	1	2	3	2	1	$x[t]$

Table 6.3.

$y[t]$								
	1	0	0	1	2	1	0	
	2	1	1	0	1	0	2	
	3	2	2	1	0	1	3	
	2	1	1	0	1	0	2	
	1	0	0	1	2	1	1	
	1	0	0	1	2	1	1	
	0	1	1	2	3	2	0	
		1	1	2	3	2	0	$x[t]$

would be zeros, because the two paired frames would not be different at all. For other pairs of frames from different points in the signals, the differences are nonzero. This is shown in table 6.2, in which the zero distances between identical, matching frames are highlighted in colour. We see something similar in the distance matrix d in table 6.1. There are low numbers close to the diagonal, indicating which samples of $x[t]$ are closest in value to those of $y[t]$. These are also marked in colour. Further away from the diagonal towards the edges of the matrix there are higher numbers, 2s and 3s.

Instead of a simple subtraction, it is customary to use a symmetrical distance measure, such as $|x[t] - y[t]|$, the *unsigned* difference between $x[t]$ and $y[t]$, as in table 6.3. Turning negative values into positive ones has the advantage that the distance between, say, 3 and 1, is the same as the distance between 1 and 3.

So this matrix records the distance between each frame of the test signal and every frame of the reference signal. That still doesn't tell us how the two signals line up with one another, but it provides the basis for computing how they line up, which is the next step.

Step 2: Costing all alignments

We try to find a correspondence between frames in the test signal and frames in the reference signal that is as close to the diagonal as possible. The correspondence between one signal and another is encoded as a path – a sequence of cells – through the matrix, starting at the lower left corner and going roughly diagonally upwards and rightwards until it finishes at the top right corner. Because the beginning and end of the two signals should always correspond to one another, the path always begins at (1,1). The beginning of the test ought to correspond to the beginning of the reference, otherwise why are we comparing the test with the reference? Likewise, we want the end of the test to correspond to the end of the reference so that there is no material left over once we have finished matching the signals. For example, the test word 'six' will (or at least *ought to*) match the stored reference 'sixty', except that the latter part of the reference pattern is not matched by any part of the test word: the '-ty' part is left over. Such incomplete matches are avoided by the requirement that the endpoints of the test and reference signals should preferably correspond to one another, that is, the path through the matrix ends at whatever the coordinate of the upper-right cell happens to be: in this example (6,7).

We can also think of the path as a sequence of moves, upwards, rightwards or diagonally up and to the right, from the bottom left to the upper right. Leftward and downward moves, however, are prohibited because time moves forwards: a leftward move would mean a reversal of time on the *x* axis, and a downward move would be going backwards in time on the *y* axis, according to the orientation convention we have chosen. This constraint can be satisfied by allowing just three kinds of move: up, right, or up-and-right. This means that there are only three ways of arriving at a particular cell: from below, from the left or from below-left.

Since the best path generally lies *near* to the diagonal, a diagonal move going upwards and to the right should be favoured over simple upward or rightward moves. Since a combination of an upward and rightward move is two steps and a diagonal one step, diagonal moves are, in a sense, usually 'cheaper' than a sequence of two moves.

The way in which we find the *closest* correspondence between successive frames in the test and reference is to work out the costs of following *every* reasonable path through the matrix, and choosing the cheapest. How much a path costs is determined by the distance measure of each correspondence. If we drift too far away from the track of closest correspondences, we will add higher and higher costs, reflecting more and more distant matches between parts of the two signals. But the closer we stick to the diagonal, where the distances are lower, the less the difference between the two signals will be.

Now I have described the method that we will follow, the second step of the dynamic time warping algorithm can be stated as follows:

For each cell in the matrix, calculate the cost of arriving from (a) below, (b) left and (c) below-left, by adding the cell distance value to the lowest-cost way of arriving at the cell from below, left, or below-left, respectively.

Thus, we shall also calculate the costs of arriving at that cell from below, left and below-left. We shall use two other matrices, *accdist* and *move*, to store (a) the cheapest cost of arriving at each cell (accumulated distance), and (b) the move that takes us to that cell by the cheapest route. If the cheapest move to a cell is upwards (from below), *move*(x,y) = 1. If the cheapest move is diagonally (from below-left), $move(x,y) = 2$, and if the cheapest arrival route is from the cell to the left, $move(x,y) = 3$. For cell (1,1), the start of the alignment, a move of 0 can be recorded, so that there are no missing values in the *move* matrix.

This step can be considered in two parts: initialization and recursion. Initialization works out the costs of cells in the leftmost column and in the bottom row of the matrix. The recursion step fills in the costs of all the remaining cells.

1. **Initialization.** The only way of arriving at cells in the leftmost column is from below, and the only way of arriving at cells in the lowest row is from the left. Thus, the cost of getting to cell (1,y) in the leftmost column of *accdist* is given by:

$$accdist(1,y) = accdist(1,y-1) + d(1,y)$$

The cost of getting to cell (x,1) in the bottom row of *accdist* is given by:

$$accdist(x,1) = accdist(x-1,1) + d(x,1)$$

The only possible moves to cells on the bottom row are rightward moves (move 3), and the only possible moves to cells in the leftmost row are upward moves (move 1).

After initialization, *accdist* and *move* are as in table 6.4:

Table 6.4.

accdist:

y	7	5					
coordinates	6	5					
	5	4					
	4	2					
	3	1					
	2	1					
	1	1	2	4	7	9	9
		1	2	3	4	5	6	x coordinates

move:

y	7	1					
coordinates	6	1					
	5	1					
	4	1					
	3	1					
	2	1					
	1	0	3	3	3	3	3
		1	2	3	4	5	6	x coordinates

Table 6.5.

accdist:					
y					
coordinates	⋮	⋮	⋮		
	2	**1**	**1**	...	
	1	**1**	**2**	...	
		1	2	...	*x* coordinates
move:					
y					
coordinates	⋮	⋮	⋮		
	2	**1**	**2**	...	
	1	**0**	**3**	...	
		1	2	...	*x* coordinates

2. **Recursion**. Now consider the task of filling in the remainder of these matrices, especially *accdist*. The cost of arriving at cell (x,y) from below is the cost of the cheapest route to the cell below, *accdist*(x,y−1), plus the distance associated with the arrival cell, *d*(x,y). The cost of arriving at cell (x,y) from the cell to the left is the cost of the cheapest route to the cell on the left, *accdist*(x−1,y), plus the distance *d*(x,y). The cost of arriving at cell (x,y) from the cell that is immediately below and to the left is the cost of the cheapest route to the cell diagonally below, *accdist*(x−1,y−1), plus the distance *d*(x,y). Whichever of these three costs is the cheapest is recorded as *accdist*(x,y), and the appropriate move number is recorded in *move*(x,y). If the cost of a diagonal move turns out to be the same as a move upwards or to the right, the diagonal move is always preferred. (If an upward and rightward move are equally cheap and cheaper than the diagonal move, we shall arbitrarily choose the rightward move.) For example, the cost of arriving at (2,2) is the cheapest cost to (2,2), 1 (the cost of getting to the below-left cell), plus the distance *d*(2,2), 0, making a total of 1 for a best move from below-left.

So, for each empty cell, the algorithm considers the three moves that could be followed in order to reach that cell. In this example, only three possible moves are allowed: a move one step upwards, rightwards or diagonally. When all the lowest-cost accumulated distances and associated moves have been tabulated, the *accdist* and *move* matrices for this example are as in table 6.6.

By the time we have finished filling in the matrix, there will be many paths through the matrix, representing a variety of possible alignments between one signal and the other, a variety of ways of lining up frames in one signal with frames in another signal. Each path will have a specific cost associated with it. So the coloured path in table 6.6, for instance, in which *all* of the frames of the *x* signal are lined up with just the first frame

Table 6.6.

accdist:

y							
	7	5	5	3	4	2	2
coordinates	6	5	5	2	2	1	3
	5	4	4	2	1	2	5
	4	2	2	1	2	2	4
	3	1	1	2	4	5	6
	2	1	1	2	4	5	6
	1	1	2	4	7	9	9
		1	2	3	4	5	6	x coordinates

move:

y							
	7	1	2	1	2	1	2
coordinates	6	1	2	1	1	2	3
	5	1	2	1	2	3	2
	4	1	2	2	3	3	3
	3	1	2	2	2	2	2
	2	1	2	3	3	3	3
	1	0	3	3	3	3	3
		1	2	3	4	5	6	x coordinates

Table 6.7.

move:

y							
	7	1	2	1	2	1	2
coordinates	6	1	2	1	1	2	3
	5	1	2	1	2	3	2
	4	1	2	2	3	3	3
	3	1	2	2	2	2	2
	2	1	2	3	3	3	3
	1	0	3	3	3	3	3
		1	2	3	4	5	6	x coordinates

of the y signal, is considered possible by the algorithm. However, it is an extremely high cost solution ($accdist(6,1) = 9$), which means that it is a very poor way of matching the two signals. It is also inadequate as a solution because it does not align the endpoints of the two signals. Paths that end near to the top right-hand corner characteristically turn out to have a lower cost, because they represent a closer match between the test signal and the reference signal. In this example, *accdist*(6,7) is only 2.

Step 3. Completion

To conclude the process, we must now select the *best* path through *move*. We work backwards from the top-right corner, repeatedly tracing back the move indicating the cheapest route to that point. This gives us a path through the matrix along which the test and reference signals are most similar to each other (table 6.7).

Exercise 6.1

Complete the *d*, *accdist* and *move* matrices for the following pair of signals:

$x[t]$ = 6 6 5 -3 -3 6 6
$y[t]$ = 1 1 5 5 4 3 2 1

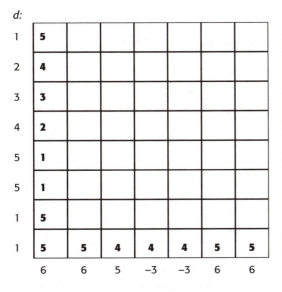

d:

1	5						
2	4						
3	3						
4	2						
5	1						
5	1						
1	5						
1	5	5	4	4	4	5	5
	6	6	5	-3	-3	6	6

accdist:

26						
21						
17						
14						
12						
11						
10						
5	10	14	18	22	27	32

move:

1						
1						
1						
1						
1						
1						
1						
0	3	3	3	3	3	3

Warp paths and alignment

What does the path through the matrix tell us about the correspondence between the test and reference signals? It tells us which samples of the test signal are most similar to which samples of the reference. It also tells us by how much the two signals differ, when best aligned. (This can be derived from the sum of the distances along the warp path.)

A warp path that follows coordinates (1,1), (2,2), (2,3), (3,4), (4,5), (5,6), and (6,7) means:

Frame 1 of $x[t]$ maps onto frame 1 of $y[t]$
Frame 2 of $x[t]$ maps onto frame 2 of $y[t]$
Frame 2 of $x[t]$ also maps onto frame 3 of $y[t]$
Frame 3 of $x[t]$ maps onto frame 4 of $y[t]$
Frame 4 of $x[t]$ maps onto frame 5 of $y[t]$
Frame 5 of $x[t]$ maps onto frame 6 of $y[t]$
Frame 6 of $x[t]$ maps onto frame 7 of $y[t]$

This warp path can be depicted graphically as in figure 6.8.

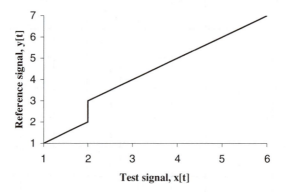

FIGURE 6.8
A warp path

Illustration of DTW using speech parameters

Although DTW may be used in automatic speech recognition to compare a spoken word to a stored reference pattern, it can also be used to compare and contrast a pair of spoken inputs, such as two variant renditions of the same word, or even two somewhat different words, to discover where and in what ways they differ. For example, we can use this technique to get a more detailed understanding of minimal pairs, in order to find out more about phonological distinctions between utterances. (A full-scale study of this kind is described in Coleman 2003.) Suppose we look at a single parameter. In the following example, we will look at the first formant of the words 'coming' and 'cunning'. These words (and their F1 contours) are fairly similar (figure 6.9), but their details are different. Not surprisingly, the overall durations of the two signals in this example are also different: 'coming' has 70 frames and 'cunning' has 74 frames. So each of them is about three-quarters of a second of speech, but they are not exactly the same length. I shall assume that there is no linguistic significance to their different durations at the moment, but it does mean that we

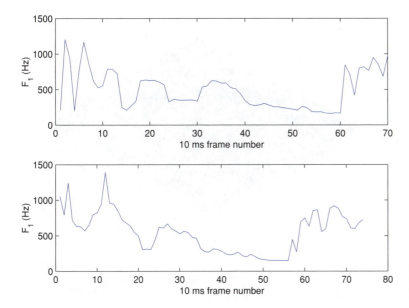

FIGURE 6.9
First formant frequencies of 'coming' (above) and 'cunning' (below)

can't simply compare them by computing the sample-by-sample differences between the two signals. There is no reason to expect the peaks of one to line up exactly with the peaks of the other, nor the troughs. So the axes of the matrix d will be F1 of 'coming', the x-axis, and F1 of 'cunning' on the y-axis. As there are about 5000 cells in this matrix, it would be impractical to print them out. However, in figure 6.10 I have plotted matrix d in three dimensions. The distances in each cell are shown in two ways: along the vertical dimension, and also through shading. Large differences between the F1 traces are shown as high, mountainous peaks in a lighter shade; smaller differences are lower (on the vertical axis) and darker. The dark rectangular patches indicate regions where the F1 traces are similar; the sharp mountain ridges lie where the F1 traces are different.

6.4 Applications

DTW pattern matching may be used for speech recognition applications with a small vocabulary of stored 'prototype' pronunciations. For example, given the task of recognizing which of ten digits (0–9) was spoken, a spoken input can be compared to a library of ten recordings, and the closest-matching word identified. Other words than digits, in any language, could be used instead, without altering the method.

Exercise 6.2
Think of as many pitfalls for this method as you can. For example, will it work with a large vocabulary, or if it is used by someone with a heavy foreign accent? What would happen if you coughed into it?

Another practical application uses DTW to time-align multiple repetitions of the same parameter so that they are precisely synchronized in time. The

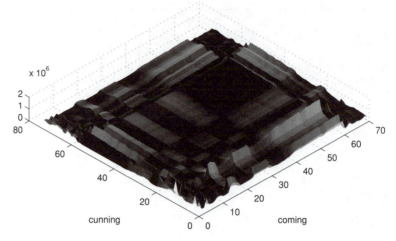

FIGURE 6.10
A contour plot of the
differences between
'coming' and 'cunning'

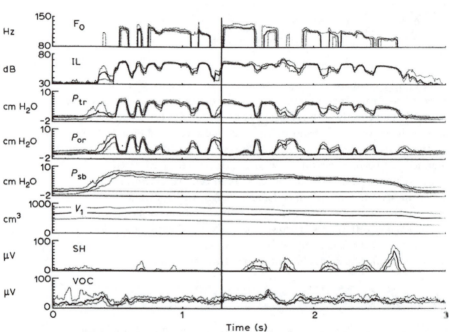

FIGURE 6.11
Median signals for eight physiological signals, time-aligned using dynamic time warping
(from Strik and Boves 1991)

parameter could be an acoustic parameter, but it could equally well be an articulatory parameter, or any other physiological measurement. Strik and Boves (1991) describe how various articulatory parameters, taken from multiple repetitions of the same utterance, can be massaged using DTW so as to be made precisely aligned in time. This then enables the multiple repetitions to be averaged (frame-by-frame), to produce what is in a sense a prototype representation of some properties of a word. For example, figure 6.11 shows the median signals for f_0, intensity (IL), transglottal pressure (P_{tr}), oral pressure (P_{or}), subglottal pressure (P_{sb}), lung volume (V_1), and electromyographic activity of the sternohyoid and vocalis muscles (SH and VOC). The traces were derived from 29 repetitions of the same utterance, time-aligned using DTW. The dotted lines are a measure of the degree of variation (the range of the middle 20 values at each time instant).

Vector Quantization

In many applications, we may want to compare two or more parameters extracted from an utterance, such as *all* the LPC coefficients or *many* formant frequencies. In that case, the distance metric has to be not one-dimensional (e.g. $|x[t] - y[t]|$), but a *multidimensional* difference between all the parameters of one signal and the corresponding parameters of another signal at other frames. Probably the most common method of calculating the distance between two *sets* of parameters (two vectors), is the *sum of the squared differences*. For instance, we can compute the distance between the first three formant frequencies of two vowels as follows:

Parameter	Vowel 1	Vowel 2	Squared difference
F1	400 Hz	550 Hz	22500
F2	1900 Hz	1700 Hz	40000
F3	2600 Hz	2550 Hz	2500
			Sum = 65000

Now consider the distance between vowel 1 and another vowel:

Parameter	Vowel 1	Vowel 3	Squared difference
F1	400 Hz	280 Hz	14400
F2	1900 Hz	2250 Hz	122500
F3	2600 Hz	2750 Hz	22500
			Sum = 159400

The sum of the squared differences between vowels 1 and 2 is 65000 Hz^2, and between vowels 1 and 3 it is 159400 Hz^2. Therefore, vowel 1 is more similar to vowel 2 than to vowel 3. (In case you are wondering, vowel 1 is an American English /ɪ/, vowel 2 is /e/, and vowel 3 is /i/. Therefore, /ɪ/ is acoustically closer to /e/ than to /i/!)

In the next example, we compute the distance between one set of LPC coefficients and another:

Vector 1	Vector 2	Squared difference
1.001708	0.629627	0.138444
−0.201289	0.167945	0.136334
0.068966	−0.015374	0.007113
0.016894	−0.050550	0.004549
0.135456	−0.087576	0.049743
−0.093006	−0.008318	0.007172
−0.056108	0.165056	0.048914
−0.045149	0.069519	0.013149
0.044609	0.110669	0.004364
0.019852	0.034234	0.000207
0.011160	0.024627	0.000181
0.140104	0.050056	0.008109
−0.103086	−0.032632	0.004964
0.025018	−0.064510	0.008015
		Sum = 0.008015

Table 6.8						
	1024					
Code of	⋮					
spectrum 1						
	885					
	884	...	...	**0.008015**		
	883	...	...	...		
	⋮	...	...	...		
	1	...	...	...		
		1	...	434	...	Code of spectrum 2

In speech recognition systems, a major component of the computational load is the repeated calculation of the distances between spectral vectors. Imagine, for example, the number of calculations that would have to be completed if the DTW algorithm were repeated over and over again in order to compare a single word input against a lexicon of only 1000 words! To reduce this considerable processing load, and make the representations of speech more compact, we can compile a codebook (i.e. a look-up table) of spectral vectors, a scheme for numbering n distinct, typical spectral vectors. For example, we might make a codebook with 1024 distinct spectral templates, in which vector 1 (above) is (say) number 435, and vector 2 is (say) number 884. We could even draw up a 1024 × 1024 table, as in table 6.8, giving the spectral distance between every pair of spectra in the codebook. Although it would have over one million cells, it would only have to be calculated once. After that, calculating spectral distances would boil down to (a) working out the code numbers of the two spectra to be compared, and then (b) looking up the distance between them in the table. Likewise, comparing one utterance with another boils down to comparing the sequence of code-numbers for one utterance with those of the other.

6.5 Sources of variability in speech

The main difficulty faced by the pattern-matching approach to speech recognition is that the spoken input is almost guaranteed to differ from all stored examples, even examples of the same word(s), because of the extensive, naturally occurring variability in pronunciation. Dynamic time warping provides a way of overcoming natural variations in the timing of words and parts of words, and of finding the *closest* match, in the absence of an *exact* match. Here, I shall briefly review some other important causes of variability.

Dialect/accent: Pronunciation differences between speakers due to dialect are common in most languages. In English, a global language, there are differences between speakers from different countries, and within countries. In the British Isles there are many distinct dialects, and even in North America, where the dialect differences are less extensive, there are still many notable patterns of pronunciation differences (see Olive et al. 1993 chapter 9). The pronunciation of non-native speakers of a language is usually different in many ways from that of native speakers. 'Dialect' is a difficult construct to model, because many speakers may use more than one dialect at a time. Greater social and geographical mobility nowadays means that most people command many different ways of speaking, and can use them to different effect in different circumstances.

Male/female differences: The speech of men and women is often different, for a variety of reasons. There may be differences in the physical size of the speakers, including differences in the length of their vocal tracts. The larynxes of men and women mature in different ways (male voices 'break' at puberty). In many societies there are other socially influenced differences in the ways of speaking. Women may have breathier voices than men, for instance, which obviously affects the acoustic details of a word's pronunciation.

Speaker: Differences can occur between individual speakers of the same dialect and sex. These may in part be physical, due to, for example, size differences or state of health.

The preceding sources of variability are usually dealt with by requiring the user of a speech recognition system to *train* the system on their particular speech characteristics. For a large-vocabulary system, such a step is presently almost obligatory, as we have no complete, accurate models of these kinds of variability. In some applications – speech recognition via telephone, for example – it may not be feasible to train the system. In such a case, the system must be robust even when used by numerous different speakers. The price of such robustness is that the system will not be able to accept continuous speech input, and will have a small vocabulary (a few words, such as the digits, or 'yes' and 'no'), that can be used in conjunction with a menu-based dialogue.

A second important strategy in dealing with variation in the pronunciation of words is to move away from a single stored pattern for each word, and build statistical models of the normal range of variability of pronunciations. That topic will be examined in the next chapter.

Variation at the edges of words: The pronunciation of words when spoken one at a time is often different from their pronunciation during continuous speech. In particular the way in which one word ends may vary according to the sound at the start of the next word. For example, the isolation pronunciation of 'ten' is [tɛn], but in connected speech it has many other variants, such as [tɛ̃], or any of the following:

ten pence	[tɛm]
ten windows	[tɛmʷ]
ten fish	[tɛɱ]
ten things	[tɛṇ]
ten toes	[tɛn]
ten chairs	[tɛn]
ten useless things	[tɛɲ]
ten cars	[tɛŋ]

One way of dealing with this would be to store eight different variant pronunciations of the word 'ten'. By that strategy, though, we ought to store eight variants of every word that ends in /n/. There are 4523 words ending in /n/ in the 70000-word Oxford Advanced Learner's Dictionary. To store eight variants of each word would clearly enlarge the stored lexicon substantially! Nevertheless, in such a case, mass storage of multiple variant forms may be more straightforward than debugging a more elaborate, rule-based system.

Chapter summary

In this chapter, we surveyed the two most important approaches to automatic speech recognition: the knowledge-based and pattern-matching approaches. The knowledge-based approach uses feature detectors to classify sounds, and then may use other sources of knowledge, such as a lexicon and/or rules, to work out what words are being spoken. The pattern-matching approach was illustrated with the method of Dynamic Time Warping, in which a test signal is compared to a stored reference signal, in order to determine how similar they are, as well as where and in what ways they differ. Finally, we briefly surveyed the main causes of variability in speech.

Further reading

The accounts given here of the knowledge-based and pattern-recognition approaches to automatic speech recognition are based on Rabiner and Juang 1993, which is almost a standard manual of speech recognition techniques. The papers collected in Waibel and Lee 1990 are also very useful and informative. The account of dynamic time warping is completely standard: Sakoe and Chiba 1978 is a key reference. Most accounts of classification tend to be mathematically fairly advanced: for a somewhat more digestible survey, see Harrington and Cassidy 1999, chapter 10.

CHAPTER PREVIEW

In this chapter we draw together the two main themes of the book – acoustic analysis and finite-state machines – in a presentation of probabilistic finite-state models, as they are applied in speech recognition systems. We examine two main successes of such probabilistic models: part-of-speech tagging and acoustic modelling.

KEY TERMS

Markov models
n-grams
part-of-speech tagging
probability
back-off
HMMs
Viterbi decoding
speech recognition

7.1 Introduction

The most significant development in computational linguistics during the 1990s was the return to centre-stage of probabilistic and finite-state models, in a variety of applications (see, e.g., Klavans and Resnik 1996; Bod et al. 2003). Statistical and finite-state models of language (such as Markov models) were roundly criticized during the early years of generative linguistics, notably by Chomsky (1957, 1965) and Miller and Chomsky (1963). These criticisms won general acceptance by linguists and have been promoted on linguistics courses ever since. The fact that statistical and finite-state models have recently won a renewed lease of life in speech and language technology makes it worthwhile returning to the original criticisms, as I shall do in section 7.9. We shall see that, though some of the earlier criticisms are technically valid, they are often not relevant to some practical applications. More seriously, however, some of the arguments against probabilistic and finite-state models rest on factual errors that deserve to be exposed and understood. Now that we understand much more about probabilistic and finite-state models, we can see ways of addressing a number of the former problems. The upshot of this chapter will be that statistical models of language have much to commend them, which explains their recent widespread uptake in almost all areas of speech and language processing.

We shall begin by looking at Markov models: nondeterministic finite-state automata in which a probability is associated with each transition. We will then move on to several examples of Hidden Markov Models (HMMs). HMMs were originally developed for use in automatic speech recognition, and in recent years have also been widely used in statistical natural language processing, for tasks as diverse as part-of-speech tagging and machine translation. They are arguably the single most important technique in speech and language processing. Unfortunately, most published explanations of HMMs assume a fairly high level of technical training, and are quite impenetrable to beginners. I shall explain what HMMs are and how they can be used in two kinds of application, beginning with statistical models of word sequences (a rudimentary 'language model'). My presentation of this topic is closely based on that of Charniak (1993). Later in the chapter, I present a more general account of HMMs and their use in speech recognition.

Probabilistic methods are particularly useful in situations of uncertainty. Uncertainty arises in several circumstances in speech and language processing:

- A single acoustic parameter vector might correspond to more than one different phonological unit.
- A word may be of more than one possible category, so we have to decide which is correct in some context. If there is more than one correct answer, we may need to work out which part of speech is most likely, given the context.
- There may be more than one possible structural analysis of a sentence (ambiguity).

- Homophony: a spoken word may be spelled in different ways, according to its meaning or syntactic category. For example, rose, rows, row's, roes, roe's or *rho*s (plural of the Greek letter *rho*).

Probabilities are also indispensable when there is more than one *source* of uncertainty. For example, in the spoken expression [ɹəʊzɪzəɹɛd], we encounter the problems of homophony, word division and part of speech assignment:

- [ɹəʊ] could be 'row', 'roe' or the Greek letter '*rho*'.
- [ɹəʊz] could be 'rose', 'rows', 'row's', 'roes', 'roe's' or '*rho*s'. Also, 'rose' could be a common noun, a personal name or a verb.
- [ɹəʊzɪz] could be 'rose is', 'roses' or (for some speakers) 'Rosie's'.
- [ə] could be 'a' or 'are'.
- [ɹɛd] could be 'read' or 'red'.

When we have many interacting sources of uncertainty, probability theory gives us a mathematically sound basis for working out which combination of decisions is most likely to be correct.

7.2 Indeterminacy: *n*-gram models for part-of-speech tagging

The particular examples that I want to begin with relate to Markov models of word sequences, rather than problems relating to speech recognition. We shall examine the use of Markov models to tag strings of words with part-of-speech labels. Historically, this was not the first application of HMMs at all, but one that was developed more recently. It is an adaptation of what was originally a speech recognition technology to a language-processing problem. The kind of Markov model we shall use is an *n*-gram model of word sequences.

The problem that this model is designed to address is the fact that many, if not most, words in English are of several syntactic categories. Because of that, most sentences are syntactically ambiguous. Consider the widely repeated textbook example of the sequence of words 'time flies like an arrow'. This has several interpretations, and several possible syntactic structures, depending in part on how you group words into phrases, but also in part on the categories of the words:

(7.1)
(a) [Time [flies [like an   arrow]]] (The normal 'simile' interpretation)
    N   V   ADJ DET N
(b) [[Time flies] [like an   arrow]] (A curious command)
    V   N   ADJ DET N
(c) [[Time flies] [like an   arrow]] (A strange species of insect)
    N   N   V   DET N

If 'time' is a noun, 'flies' is a verb, 'like' is an adjective, 'an' is a determiner and 'arrow' a noun, the parse given in example 7.1(a) is appropriate, and gives the normal, idiomatic interpretation of that expression. Alternatively, there is a curious imperative reading 7.1(b), an order to someone to 'time flies, like an arrow!' The imperative 'time flies!' would be meant if you decided that 'time' was a verb, 'flies' was the object noun, the plural of 'fly', and 'like' was an adjective. 7.1(c) is a third reading in which 'time flies' is a noun-noun compound, the name of a strange species of insect, 'like' is a verb, and 'an arrow' is what time flies are attracted to. So, working out the part of speech of each of these words is an important part of grammatical analysis. The sequence of words is syntactically ambiguous, and which structure it is assigned to depends on which parts of speech we assign to the words. That is the first point.

The second point is a notion that is usually disregarded in generative approaches to syntax, which is that we know that some parses are more probable, more *plausible* than the others. Even though we don't want to say that the readings 7.1(b) or (c) are impossible or ungrammatical, we might want to capture the idea that they are a less *likely* interpretation of that particular sequence of words. So even if we had a very good grammar, a complete-enough generative grammar of English, and a great parsing algorithm that will give us all three parses as possibilities, we won't be able to distinguish the more likely from the less likely parses without some other component. Neither the grammar nor the parser provides us with probabilities, only possibilities.

In many ambiguous sentences, it is not necessary to obtain full parses in order to resolve the most likely part of speech of a word. For example, words ending in '-ing' may be verbs (e.g. 'was swinging'), adjectives derived from verbs ('low swinging branches') or nouns derived from verbs ('swinging of the branches'). In such cases, it may be sufficient to look at a few adjacent words in order to settle the part of speech:

(7.2)

(a)   was X-ing: 'X-ing' is probably a verb
(b)   ADJ X-ing N: 'X-ing' is probably an adjective
(c)   the X-ing of: 'X-ing' is probably a noun.

Not only is syntactic structural ambiguity very common, lexical category ambiguities are also very common and present a problem for parsing. A pure computational-linguistic approach to the problem of ambiguity is simply to generate all possible parses without adjudicating between them, on the grounds that they are all in various ways correct. However, in realistic applications of speech and language technology we usually want to find the *most likely* parse and its associated interpretation. One way of doing that is to build, as the front end to our parser, an *n-gram language model*, specifically, an *n-gram part-of-speech tagger*. In an *n*-gram model the idea is that we can determine the most likely part-of-speech label for a given word by inspecting a few adjacent words. For instance, if we consider sequences of just three words, a trigram model, we might be able to score the examples in 7.2 according to table 7.1.

For instance we can say that 'swinging' in the trigram 'branch was swinging', is a verb with probability 0.8, that is, very likely to be a verb. It could be an adjective, but the associated probability of 0.2 means that 'swinging'

Table 7.1. Part of a table of trigrams, parts of speech and probabilities		
Trigrams	Category	Probability
branch was swinging	Verb	0.8
branch was swinging	Adjective	0.2
branch was swinging	Noun	0
the low swinging	Verb	0
the low swinging	Adjective	0.8
the low swinging	Noun	0.2
under the swinging	Verb	0
under the swinging	Adjective	0.7
under the swinging	Noun	0.3

is much less likely to be an adjective in that context. As a noun it perhaps has a probability of zero in that context, meaning it cannot be a noun in that position. This is in contrast to the context 'the low swinging', where 'swinging' is definitely not a verb, as we give that a zero score. How we get these scores is a question we will come to in a moment. Anyway, in 'the low swinging', 'swinging' is probably an adjective, as we have given it a score of 0.8, say, or thereabouts, as in 'the low swinging branches'. It could feasibly be the -ing form of a noun, as in 'low swinging of the swing', so we will say it could be a noun but with a fairly low probability, 0.2.

Probabilities

In probability theory, the probability of an event is usually expressed as a decimal number between 0 and 1. In general, the probability P of an event e can be found by making multiple, repeated observations and calculating:

(7.3)

$$P = \frac{\text{no. of times } e \text{ occurred}}{\text{total no. of observations}} \text{ (whether or not } e \text{ occurred)}$$

Events that never occur at all, including impossible events, have a probability of 0. Events that always occur, or that are certain to occur, have a probability of 1. An event that is just as likely to occur as not has a probability of 0.5 ('evens' or 'chance'). Probabilities below 0.5, or close to 0, are unlikely; probabilities closer to 1 are more likely. Note that we can also write probabilities as percentages: certainty ($P = 1$) is 100%, an evens chance ($P = 0.5$) is 50%, $P = 0.1$ is 10%, and so on.

To work out the probability of a particular word occurring as the third word of a trigram, or the probability of its being a particular part of speech, we count the number of instances of every word in a corpus (i.e. a body of text), and calculate the proportion in which word *w* occurs as part of speech *x* as the third word of trigram *t*. We look at the contexts in which a word occurs (with 'context' defined as just 'preceding two words'), and find out which categorizations are more frequent, and which are less frequent.

> **Notation:** by $C(w_i)$ we mean the total **count** of how many times word w_i occurs in the corpus.

A third example in which a probabilistic *n*-gram model may be useful is the following. Suppose that you are taking dictation, and you are given sentence 7.4 to write down:

(7.4)   I saw a [lɑmə].

The final word, in many varieties of English, can be spelled in two ways, depending on the meaning: 'lama', a kind of Tibetan Buddhist monk, and 'llama', a South American animal. In 7.4, either of these could be correct. Imagine the difficulty that an automatic speech recognition program would face if presented with this sentence.

In other contexts, however, it becomes possible to estimate which spelling is more likely. Consider:

(7.5)   (a)   I saw a Tibetan [lɑmə].
       (b)   I saw a Bolivian [lɑmə].

As with 7.4, we cannot be *certain* which spelling is correct in either of these sentences. However, in 7.5(a), the spelling 'lama' is more likely than 'llama', and vice-versa for 7.5(b). Note that syntactic analysis is of no help here. But we do not need to go as far as finding a semantic interpretation, as it is sufficient to collect some reasonable statistics concerning the frequency of bigrams in English to determine that 'lama' is more likely to follow 'Tibetan' than 'Bolivian'. Expressed mathematically:

(7.6) P(Tibetan lama) $> P$(Bolivian lama)
       P(Bolivian llama) $> P$(Tibetan llama)
       P(Tibetan lama) $> P$(Tibetan llama)
       P(Bolivian llama) $> P$(Bolivian lama)

It is clear that since we would like to calculate the relative likelihoods of various word-sequences, we shall need a little probability theory.

7.3 Some probability theory for language modelling

Suppose that we have a large body of texts (a corpus), which we can use for estimating various statistical properties. We hope that the statistics we calculate from the corpus reflect statistics of the language in general, that is, that the corpus is representative of the language. Whether or not this is true can be determined by statistical tests we shall not go into here: we shall take it that, provided the corpus is reasonably large, it will be representative of the language in general, up to some margin of error.

Naturally, there will be some words that occur more than once in the corpus, some that occur many times (e.g. 'the'), some that occur exactly once, and some words that exist but happen not to be in the corpus. In a text corpus that is m words long, there will be n different words. Generally, $n < m$. For clarity, we say there are m word **tokens** and n word **types.**

According to equation 7.3, the **(independent) probability** of picking a particular word, w_i, out of a corpus containing n different words (or m word tokens), is:

(7.7)
$$P(w_i) = C(w_i)/m$$
$$= C(w_i)/\Sigma_{j=1}^{n} C(w_j)$$

that is, the number of times word i occurs in the corpus divided by the total number of word-tokens in the corpus. For example, the British National Corpus (BNC: Burnard 2000) contains just over 100 million word tokens. 'Lama' occurs 132 times and 'llama' occurs 33 times. 33 divided by 100 million is a rather small number, and once we begin to multiply such fractions, as in equation 7.9 below, the results are even smaller. Consequently, it is often helpful when working with very small fractions to take their logarithms, and then use addition of logarithms instead of multiplication.

Exercise 7.1

Using the numbers just given, calculate the probability of picking 'lama' from the British National Corpus. And likewise, the probability of picking 'llama'.

The **conditional probability** that w_j (e.g. 'lama') occurs after w_i (e.g. 'Tibetan') is:

(7.8)
$$P(w_j \mid w_i) = C(w_i\ w_j)/C(w_i)$$

that is, the number of times that the bigram $w_i\ w_j$ occurs divided by the number of times w_i occurs (everywhere, including before w_j). For example, $P(\text{'lama'} \mid \text{'Tibetan'}) = C(\text{'Tibetan lama'})/C(\text{'Tibetan'})$.

Here are the relevant counts from the British National Corpus:

$C(\text{'Tibetan lama'}) = 1$
$C(\text{'Tibetan'}) = 217$

Exercise 7.2

Calculate $P(\text{'lama'} \mid \text{'Tibetan'})$. How does this figure compare with the *independent* probability $P(\text{'lama'})$?

Notation: we denote the sequence of words from w_1 to w_n as $w_{1,n}$

The **probability of a sequence** of words from w_1 to w_n is:

(7.9)
$$P(w_{1,n}) = P(w_1) \times P(w_2 \mid w_1) \times P(w_3 \mid w_{1,2}) \times P(w_4 \mid w_{1,3}) \times \cdots \times P(w_n \mid w_{1,n-1})$$

For example, the probability of 'I saw a lama' is $P(\text{'I'}) \mid P(\text{'saw'} \mid \text{'I'}) \times P(\text{'a'} \mid \text{'I saw'}) \times P(\text{'lama'} \mid \text{'I saw a'})$. Let's work these out:

$P(\text{'I'}) = C(\text{'I'}) / m$ (For the BNC, $m = 100{,}106{,}029$)
$P(\text{'saw'} \mid \text{'I'}) = C(\text{'I saw'}) / C(\text{'I'})$
$P(\text{'a'} \mid \text{'I saw'}) = C(\text{'I saw a'}) / C(\text{'I saw'})$
$P(\text{'lama'} \mid \text{'I saw a'}) = C(\text{'I saw a lama'}) / C(\text{'I saw a'})$

Here are the relevant counts from the British National Corpus:

$C(\text{'I'}) = 869460$
$C(\text{'I saw'}) = 4391$
$C(\text{'I saw a'}) = 408$
$C(\text{'I saw a lama'}) = 0$

Exercise 7.3

Calculate $P(\text{'lama'} \mid \text{'I saw a'})$. What's the problem with the answer?
Hint: a probability of zero means the event *never* happens.

7.4 Markov models

Each term in equation 7.9 is of the form $P(w_n \mid w_{1,n})$, that is, the probability of a word's occurrence given the occurrence of *all* the previous words from w_1 to w_n. Although this is technically accurate, for long enough strings we soon run into the problem of exercise 7.3, in which the prior context of a string is not in the training corpus, and hence we apparently have no basis on which to estimate the probability of the word sequence. In many language models it is often adequate to take into account not *all* the previous words, only the previous one or two words. When only the single previous word is taken into account, we have a bigram model, in which the probability of a word sequence is estimated by:

(7.10)
$$P(w_{1,n}) = P(w_1) \times P(w_2 \mid w_1) \times P(w_3 \mid w_2) \times P(w_4 \mid w_3) \times \cdots \times P(w_n \mid w_{n-1})$$

The assumption that it is more-or-less sufficient to take into account only the previous item in the sequence is know as the Markov assumption, after pioneering work on the statistics of letter sequences by Markov (1913) (see Miller and Chomsky 1963). A Markov model is a probabilistic, nondeterministic finite-state automaton. Because it is finite-state, the transition from state n to state $n+1$ is independent of the previous transition, from state $n-1$ to state n. For example, from state 3 in figure 7.1 we can move either to state 4 or 5: hence, this finite-state automaton is nondeterministic. Furthermore, which path we follow out of state 3 is independent of how we arrived at state 3, whether it was from state 1 or state 2.

Figure 7.1 shows (part of) a finite-state automaton, something that is already familiar to us from chapter 5. There are a number of states and transitions, and probabilities assigned to each transition. These indicate the probability of changing from one state to another. From state 3 we can choose whether to move to state 4 or 5, but those choices are not necessarily equally likely. p_1 is the probability of moving to state 4 and p_2 is the probability of going to state 5.

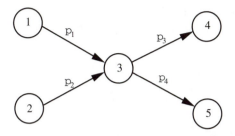

FIGURE 7.1
Part of a probabilistic
finite-state automaton

If we accept the Markov assumption, we can calculate the probability of the sentence 'I saw a Tibetan lama' as follows:

(7.11)
P('I saw a Tibetan lama')
$$= P(\text{‘I’}) \times P(\text{‘saw’} \mid \text{‘I’}) \times P(\text{‘a’} \mid \text{‘saw’}) \times P(\text{‘Tibetan’} \mid \text{‘a’})$$
$$\times P(\text{‘lama’} \mid \text{‘Tibetan’})$$

Recall from (7.8) that:

P('a' | 'saw') = C('saw a') / C('saw')
P('Tibetan' | 'a') = C('a Tibetan') / C('a')
P('lama' | 'Tibetan') = C('Tibetan lama') / C('Tibetan')

From the BNC we can find:

C('saw') = 26,737

(N.B. this includes occurrences of both the past tense form of the verb 'see' and the noun '(a) saw'. Lumping them all together doesn't matter much, as the verb is much more frequent than the noun. 98% of instances are of the verb.)

C('a') = 2,150,885
C('Tibetan') = 216

C('saw a') = 1841
C('a Tibetan') = 25
C('Tibetan lama') = 1

Exercise 7.4
According to these bigram counts, what is the probability of the sentence 'I saw a Tibetan lama'?

Markov models are very simple, but when used to model sequences of words they can seem rather complex at first. Therefore, let's first examine a number of very simple cases of how they can be used to model sequences of events in general, not just sequences of words.

The Markov assumption and the analogy of the drunken man

To show the thinking behind the Markov assumption, consider the following analogy. A drunken man is crossing a road, erratically swaying as he goes from left to right. However, it is not the case that he steps towards the left as frequently as towards the right: $x\%$ of the time he goes to the right, and *y*% of the time to the left. If the road is only five steps wide, we can construct a model of his progress across the road as in figure 7.2.

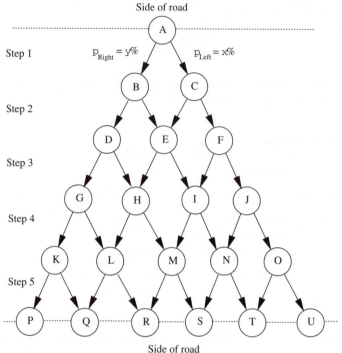

FIGURE 7.2
Markov model of a drunken man's swaying path

Suppose that after step 3 he is at point I. He could go forwards in one direction or another, to point M or N. Whichever way he lurches, however, does not depend on how he got to point I. He could have got there via point B or C, and then via E or F. But that makes no difference to what happens subsequently.

This is an example of a **first-order** Markov model: one in which the probability of the next state depends only on the current state, not on any previous states. In a **second-order** Markov model, the probability of the next state depends on the current state and on the previous state (but no earlier ones).

Markov model of the weather

Another non-linguistic example, a Markov model of the weather, is given in figure 7.3.

In this model each state denotes the weather on a particular day: sunny, cloudy or precipitation (e.g. rain or snow). If we are in the precipitation state it will probably still be precipitating the next day too, so the probability of the transition from this state back to itself is 0.4. But the next day might be sunny or it might be cloudy. These are less likely than a continued downpour, but they are as likely as each other, 0.3. If we are in

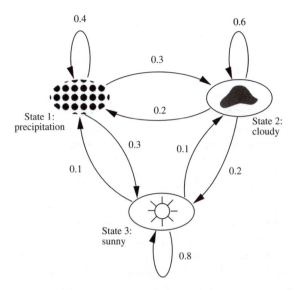

FIGURE 7.3
A Markov model of the
weather model (after
Rabiner and Juang 1993)

the 'sunny' state then thankfully the probability that tomorrow will be sunny is quite high, though there is a slight chance of precipitation or of cloud. Now, given this model, there are certain questions we can ask about the way in which weather patterns unfold over time. For instance, we might like to know the probability that the weather over eight consecutive days is sun, sun, sun, rain, rain, sun, cloudy, sun. (We might stake a large bet on it, for instance. Or if we work in a weather station, our professional standing may depend on the accuracy of our forecasts!) The **observation sequence O** = 'sunny, sunny, sunny, rain, rain, sunny, cloudy, sunny' in this model corresponds to a sequence of transitions through states 3, 3, 3, 1, 1, 2 and 3. We want to work out the probability of that observation sequence given this model. This is a simple case of conditional probability over sequences, as in 7.10 above. Assuming that the initial state probability (of sunshine) is 0.7, the calculation is given step-by-step in 7.12:

(7.12)
$$P(O|\text{Model}) = P(3, 3, 3, 1, 1, 2, 3|\text{Model})$$
$$= P(3) \times P(3|3) \times P(3|3) \times P(1|3) \times P(1|1)$$
$$\times P(3|1) \times P(2|3) \times P(3|2)$$
$$= 0.7 \times 0.8 \times 0.8 \times 0.1 \times 0.4 \times 0.3 \times 0.1 \times 0.2$$
$$= 0.00010752$$

The probability of the sequence is the probability of the first step in the sequence, that is, the probability that you are in state 3 to begin with, $P(3)$, times the probability that the weather changes from state 3 to state 3 (i.e. it does not change), times the probability of staying in state 3 again, times the probability that we move to state 1 from state 3, times the probability that we remain in state one, and so on and so forth. For each move, we calculate the probability of being in a given state given the previous state, and then we multiply all of those transitions' probabilities. Now we know the probability of each transition because it is given in the figure, so we

can just read them off the figure and work out that the sequence probability is 0.00010752, a very low probability.

Exercise 7.5
Is this a first order or a second order model?

The thing to bear in mind is that at the outcome of this process we are not
very concerned what the precise probability is. What we are concerned
with is: for two or more *alternative* hypotheses, which of them is the more
probable? So in example 7.5 we were trying to work out what the most
likely final word is, given the previous words. In example 7.1 we wanted to
find out which of the many possible ways of assigning part-of-speech
labels to a string of words is the most probable.

Note that in the weather model the calculation of the probability at each
point in the observation sequence was dependent only on the current state
and the previous state. It wasn't dependent upon all of the previous states,
which is what makes this a Markov model. So the weather model is a probabilistic finite-state model in which the transition probabilities only
depend on the previous state and the state that the transition goes to. It is
not a *hidden* Markov model because the state transitions are all explicit: we
will go on to look at what is meant by 'hidden' Markov models shortly.

Coin-Toss Models
My presentation of this example closely follows that of Rabiner and Juang
(1993, 326–7):

Assume the following scenario. You are in a room with a curtain
through which you cannot see what is happening. On the other side of
the curtain is another person who is performing a coin-tossing experiment, using one or more coins. The coins may be biased. The person will
not tell you which coin he selects at any time; he will only tell you the
result of each coin flip, by calling 'heads' or 'tails' through the curtain.
Thus, a sequence of *hidden* coin-tossing experiments is performed, with
your observation sequence consisting of a series of heads and tails. A
typical observation sequence would be:

$$O = (o_1 \ o_2 \ o_3 \ o_4 \ o_5 \dots o_n)$$
$$\quad = (H \ H \ T \ T \ T \ H \ T \dots H)$$

where H stands for heads and T stands for tails.

Given the above scenario, the question is: how do we build a Markov model
to explain (model) the observed sequence of heads and tails? The first problem
we face is deciding what the states in the model correspond to, and then deciding how many states should be in the model. One possible choice would be to
assume that only a single biased coin was being tossed. In this case, we could
model the situation with a two-state model in which each state corresponds to
the outcome of the previous toss (i.e. heads or tails). This model is depicted in
figure 7.4. In this case, the Markov model is *observable*, and the only issue for
complete specification of the model would be to decide on the best value for
the single parameter of the model (i.e. the probability of, say, heads).

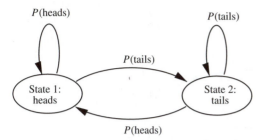

FIGURE 7.4
Observable Markov
model of tossing a biased
coin (after Rabiner and
Juang 1993)

An equivalent model to figure 7.4 would be a one-state model in which the state corresponds to the single biased coin, and the unknown parameter is the bias of the coin (e.g. P(heads)). In figure 7.4, states correspond to 'heads and tails', so the state of the machine at any moment encodes the outcome of the previous toss of the coin. In figure 7.5, however, the single state does not encode the outcome of the previous coin-toss. If you just examine the state of the machine at any moment, you cannot tell what the outcome of the previous coin-toss was. That information is inaccessible. Therefore, this is called a *Hidden* Markov Model.

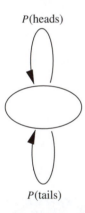

P(heads)

P(tails)

FIGURE 7.5
A one-state Markov
model of tossing a biased
coin (after Rabiner and
Juang 1993)

A second Hidden Markov Model for explaining the observed sequence of coin toss outcomes is given in figure 7.6. In this case, there are two states in the model, and each state corresponds to a different, biased coin being tossed. Each state is associated with a probability distribution of heads and tails, and transitions between states are characterized by a separate set of probabilities, the probability of whether the experimenter continues with the same coin or changes to the other coin.

A third possible HMM of the same situation is given in figure 7.7, in which we hypothesize that three coins are being tossed.

These examples illustrate the fact that, because of uncertainty regarding the underlying mechanism of a process, there may be many different possible models, all capable of simulating the sequence of observations. Such uncertainty is a commonplace of speech and language processing: our knowledge of the underlying mechanisms is certainly incomplete! This makes probabilistic models such as HMMs very appropriate in conditions of ignorance.

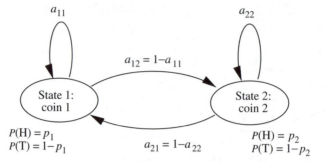

FIGURE 7.6
A Hidden Markov Model, supposing that two coins are being tossed (after Rabiner and Juang 1993)

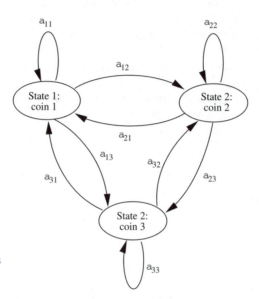

FIGURE 7.7
A Hidden Markov Model, supposing that three coins are being tossed (after Rabiner and Juang 1993)

7.5 Trigram models

Now that we have seen several examples of Markov models, from linguistic and non-linguistic applications, let us return to the problem with which I started, that of assigning part-of-speech labels to sequences of words. In order to apply this approach to the *tagging* problem, we need some idea of the likelihood of a word being a particular part of speech, given the previous words. But where are we going to get those probabilities from? The answer is that we get them from a *tagged corpus*, to begin with. (When the model has been trained with the statistics of the corpus, they are derived from the model, though.) So we are going to build our model on the basis of an obviously limited, but hopefully quite large, text that is representative of the kind of language that we are going to encounter when we use the model for processing. There are various large-scale tagged text corpora that we can draw upon, which are publicly available or for sale commercially: the companion website to this book has some links to a number of such corpora. They are a valuable resource when building models of this sort.

In order to estimate the probabilities of particular word sequences, we must count the number of occurrences of particular kinds of word sequences. Roughly speaking, the bigger the corpus, the more accurate our counts will be as an estimate of the probability of a particular word having a particular category in a particular context. Let's take an example. Suppose our corpus is the entire text of the novel *Rebecca* (du Maurier 1938), which opens with the sentence 'Last night I dreamt I went to Manderley again.' We can take that text and break it up into trigrams, that is, we group every three adjacent words together. So the first trigram is 'Last night I', and the second trigram is 'night I dreamt', and the third trigram is 'I dreamt I'. We count how often each of those trigrams occurs in the corpus. As well as counting how often each trigram occurs, the crucial thing we also need for a tagging model is also to record the category of the third word in each trigram. So we actually count not just the trigrams, but the (trigram, category) pairs. As we start to analyse the corpus, each of the trigrams is unique to the first few lines of the text, so the count of each trigram will be exactly one to begin with. For many if not most of the trigrams the count will be very low. We expect trigram counts to be low even in a very large corpus, but for some trigrams, for instance 'I went to', might occur many times in the novel. 'I dreamt I' or 'night I dreamt' might occur only once or a few times. By the time you get to the end of the novel, having counted all these darned things, you will have a huge table of statistics of a very simple kind: a list of trigrams, the category of the third word of each trigram, and a count of how many times each of those (trigram, category) pairs occurred. It is a boring task to gather these statistics (which is why we use a computer program to do it), but it is quite useful if we want to find the most likely word tag for the third word of a given trigram. Now if we had a table of this sort, it would be very easy, given a string that actually occurs in the corpus, to work out what the most likely category was of every word in the sequence because we could just look up the trigrams in the table. For example, in the trigram 'I went to', the third word, 'to', could be a preposition, as in 'I went to Manderley', or the infinitival marker, as in 'I went to buy something'. So, without looking at the word after 'to', we can work out what part of speech 'to' is most likely to be. In the British National Corpus, for instance, 'to' is a preposition in 76% of instances of 'I went to' and is infinitival 'to' in the other 24% of instances. In most cases this will give the most likely part of speech for each word in the text. The problem, however, is that in order for this technique to be useful we want to be able to tag the words of *any* sentence, not just those that happen to be in the corpus. The point of building a model of this kind is that we want to build a tagging algorithm that will work on any phrase in the language, not just for the specific sentences that occur in the corpus. We want to be able to work out in a phrase like 'I went to Twickenham' that 'Twickenham' is probably a proper noun because it follows 'went to', the same context in which 'Manderley' occurs. The algorithm has the information that Manderley is a proper noun, because it was labelled as such in the corpus, and it follows 'went to'. 'Twickenham' may occur in a dictionary, but even if it does, that doesn't tell us anything about its distribution with respect to 'went to'. So let's look at how we take this idea and turn it into a usable model.

Recall how we worked out the probability of a sequence of words in equation 7.8. In a trigram model we assume that the probability of each word's occurrence is affected only by the two previous words: this is an instance of the Markov assumption. In the Markov model of the weather we only looked at one previous state, but in the trigram model the preceding context is slightly larger than that: we look at the *two* previous words.

Trigram model calculations

The equation for the probability of a sequence of words was given in 7.9, repeated here for convenience:

(7.9)
$$P(w_{1,n}) = P(w_1) \times P(w_2 \mid w_1) \times P(w_3 \mid w_{1,2}) \times P(w_4 \mid w_{1,3}) \times \cdots \times P(w_n \mid w_{1,n-1})$$

In equation 7.10 this was revised so that the prior context was limited to a single word. In a trigram model we take *two* previous words into account, except that the first word has no previous words and the second word has only one previous word:

(7.13)
$$P(w_{1,n}) = P(w_1) \times P(w_2 \mid w_1) \times P(w_3 \mid w_{1,2}) \times P(w_4 \mid w_{2,3}) \times \cdots \times P(w_n \mid w_{n-2,n-1})$$

This says that the probability of a sequence of words from w_1 to w_n is equal to the probability of the first word, times the probability of the second word given the first word, times the probability of the third word given the first two words, times the probability of the fourth word given the two words previous to that, and so on to the end of the sequence where we have got the probability of the last word given the previous two words. The first two terms in this equation are different from the remaining terms: all the remaining terms from the third to the end are the probabilities of a word given the two previous ones. We can tidy this up a bit and simplify things by imagining that there are two *empty* words at the beginning of the string, which we will call word zero (w_0) and word minus one (w_{-1}). Both of these empty words are the string ' ', i.e. nothing at all. If we postulate the existence of these empty words, we can tidy up 7.13 and derive from it 7.14, in which the first term is the probability of the first (non-empty) word given the previous two (empty) words, and the probability of the second word is conditional on the previous two words, even though words 0 and −1 are empty words. That means that the first trigram of 'Rebecca' will be '(empty) (empty) Last' and '(empty) Last night'.

(7.14)
$$P(w_{1,n}) = P(w_1 \mid w_{-1,0}) \times P(w_2 \mid w_{0,1}) \times P(w_3 \mid w_{1,2})$$
$$\times P(w_4 \mid w_{2,3}) \ldots \times P(w_n \mid w_{n-2,n-1})$$

This makes every term in the equation the same: the probability of a sequence is the product of its trigrams. That is what equation 7.15 states more concisely: the probability of a sequence of words from 1 to n is the *product* (Π) of the probabilities of the ith word given word $i-2$ and word

$i-1$, where i takes values from 1 to n. So if we have a table of the trigram probabilities, we can easily work out the probability of a sequence of words of any length, just by multiplying the trigram probabilities. That is how, once we have a list of the trigram probabilities, we work out the most plausible part of speech labelling for any given string.

(7.15)

$$P(w_{1,n}) = \prod_{i=1}^{n} P(w_i | w_{i-2, i-1})$$

So now we need get the trigram probabilities, and where do we get them from? From counts of the trigrams in the text, as I have already said. From 7.8 we can work out:

(7.16)
$$P(w_i | w_{i-2,i-1}) = C(w_{i-2,i}) / C(w_{i-2,i-1})$$

This says that the estimated probability of word i given the previous two words is the count of the trigram from $i-2$ to i, divided by the count of the previous bigram. For example:

(7.17)
$$P(\text{'such'} | \text{'to create'}) = C(\text{'to create such'}) / C(\text{'to create'})$$

The estimated probability of the word 'such' occurring, given that the previous two words were 'to create', is the count of how many times 'to create such' occurs in the corpus, divided by how many times the bigram 'to create' occurs in all contexts (including before 'such' but also before any other words).

Exercise 7.6
In the BNC, 'to create' occurs 4632 times and 'to create such' occurs 16 times. Calculate $P(\text{'such'} | \text{'to create'})$.

To recap, we estimate trigram probabilities by counting how often they occur in the text, and then we will be able to compute an estimate of the probability of a sequence of words of any length, using equation 7.15.

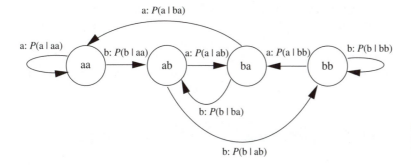

FIGURE 7.8
A Markov model for trigrams (after Charniak 1993)

We can relate the method of estimating trigram probabilities to finite-state models as in figure 7.8. We encode the current word as a transition label, and the pair of previous words is encoded as one previous state, so we use word *pairs* as the state labels. Figure 7.8 is an example of a trigram model where the words are just letters, either 'a' or 'b'. This is a very simple model that is only capable of generating or accepting strings of 'a's and 'b's, of any length, in any order. The four states correspond to all four possible bigrams, every possible combination of the two previous words. The previous two words could be 'aa', 'ab', 'ba' or 'bb'. (I have deliberately omitted the empty words that must be added at the beginning from this model for simplicity.) The transition arcs are also labelled with 'a's and 'b's, and each is associated with a conditional probability. The transition probabilities P are trigram probabilities. Each state has two arcs leading from it: one for where the third word of the trigram is 'a', the other for where the third word of the trigram is 'b'. If the observation sequence is 'bab', the third word is 'b' and the previous two words were 'ba', so, we start in the state labelled 'ba' and follow the arc labelled 'b'. The transition probability associated with this arc is the conditional probability that the third word is 'b' given that the previous two words were 'ba', $P('b'|'ba')$. That transition takes us to state 'ab', the last two symbols of 'bab'. If a fourth symbol is read into this automaton, and it is 'a', the transition probability is $P('a'|'ab')$, the probability that the current word is 'a', given that the previous two words were 'ab'. If the input string is 'baa', the third word is 'a' and the previous bigram is 'ba', and the next state will be 'aa'. That shows how we can still use Markov models while working with trigrams, where we take account of not just one but two previous words. We bundle the previous two words together into one bigram, and have a separate state for each bigram.

> *Student: Does anybody use bigger n-grams than trigrams?*
> Yes, sometimes. But whatever method you use, whether trigrams, bigrams or larger units, is only going to be an approximation to the language. Is there anything to be gained by using a larger context than just the previous two words? That is largely an empirical question. If we use *n*-grams that are larger than trigrams, tetragrams, for example, there is even more likelihood of a given tetragram not occurring in a corpus of, say, ten million words. Also, a larger number of tetragrams than trigrams only will occur once, so estimating probabilities will be more difficult. The size of the units you can work with is related to the size of the training corpus. On the other hand, experience has shown that bigram models aren't usually as good as trigram models. If the trigram model is good enough then moving up to tetragrams doesn't buy you very much.

7.6 Incompleteness of the training corpus

A problem with equation 7.15 is that we will not be able to calculate the probability of a word sequence if any of the trigrams in the sequence are missing from the corpus. For example, if we want to work out the probability of a sentence containing 'went to Twickenham' but 'Twickenham' doesn't occur in the corpus, then obviously the trigram 'went to Twickenham' won't be in the corpus either, so we will be a bit stuck. The probability estimate for 'went to Twickenham' will be zero, according to 7.16, because $C(w_{i-2,i}) = 0$, which means that the probability estimate of the whole string will also be zero, which is wrong, not what we want at all. Provided that all of the relevant trigrams are in the corpus, equation 7.16 will be fine, but if any word is missing from the corpus, it is going to have a disastrous effect. Remember that a probability of zero means 'completely impossible', or 'wholly ill-formed', whereas if a sentence contains some word that doesn't occur in the corpus, we don't want to say that it is *impossible*. We may regard it as rare or novel, but not entirely illegal. In cases like this it would be much better to say 'well, if we don't have counts for trigrams, let's see if there are any bigrams containing the words in question, or even just the unigram counts'. Bigram and unigram models are not as good for estimating probabilities as trigram models, but if the word that is causing problems occurs in the corpus in *some* context, we would like to be able to use that information.

> *Student: But if it never occurs in the corpus we are stuck?*
> Yes, we are still stuck if it never occurs at all.
> *Student: So 'I wrote to my sister in Twickenham' would get Twickenham in there.*
> Yes, even if 'Twickenham' never occurred in the context 'went to Twickenham'.
> *Student: So that is an important point.*
> Yes, that is an important point.

In short, we must take account of two ways in which the corpus may be incomplete:

1. A trigram we are interested in might not be in the corpus. Provided that all of the words of the trigram are in the corpus, there is a fall-back position we can adopt: we can look at the probabilities of its constituent words (or preferably, bigrams). But . . .
2. A word we are interested in might not be in the corpus. If this is the case, we must try to estimate the probability of the missing ('unseen') word. Let's look at the solution to this problem first.

Smoothing

Just because a word is missing from a corpus does not mean that its probability is 0. In fact, it would be a mistake to think so, as that would amount to a claim that the only words in the language are those in the training set (whose observed probabilities sum to 1). That would be manifestly untrue if we ever encounter 'out-of-vocabulary' items, that is, previously unseen words.

A better approach would be to assign a small but nonzero probability to unseen words, smaller than the probability of the least frequently seen words. In every corpus, the least frequent words are those that occur exactly once. In the 100-million-word British National Corpus, words that occur only once have a probability of 10^{-8} (or 0.00000001). Therefore, we could estimate the probability of unseen words as something less than

10^{-8}. In order to do so, however, we ought to reduce the probabilities of all the observed words in some systematic way, otherwise the sum of all the word probabilities (including the previously unseen words) will be greater than 1, which is not permitted.

The process of estimating small probabilities for unseens and for adjusting the probabilities of seen words is known as smoothing. There are many techniques for smoothing (see, e.g., Jurafsky and Martin 2000: 206–16), the details of which need not divert us here.

Back-off to bigrams and unigrams

Now that we can estimate probabilities even for unigrams that aren't in the corpus, we can deal with the problem of missing trigrams thus: we define trigram probabilities by equation 7.18, not just by 7.16:

(7.18)

$$
\begin{aligned}
P(w_i \mid w_{i-2,i-1}) \quad &= \lambda_1\, P(w_i \mid w_{i-2,i-1}) \quad &&\text{(trigram probability)} \\
&+ \lambda_2\, P(w_i \mid w_{i-1}) \quad &&\text{(bigram probability)} \\
&+ \lambda_3\, P(w_i) \quad &&\text{(unigram probability)}
\end{aligned}
$$

This says that the probability of a word given the previous two words is the sum of *three* separate probabilities: the estimated trigram probability, as defined previously, the estimated bigram probability of the last two words of the trigram, and the estimated unigram probability of the third word of the trigram. We scale or weight each of these three parts by a multiplier, λ_1, λ_2 and λ_3. We can estimate λ_1, λ_2 and λ_3 by the following logic. First, they must add up to one (certainty). Second, if we *have* a trigram count, we want that to figure much more prominently in the calculation than if we don't. Likewise, if we don't have a trigram count but we do have the final bigram in the corpus, we want the bigrams to figure more prominently than the unigrams in the calculation. In short we want λ_1 to be greater than λ_2, and λ_2 to be greater than λ_3, so that trigrams are 'worth' more than bigrams and bigrams more than unigrams. Something like λ_1 as 0.6, λ_2 of 0.3, and λ_3 of 0.1 are the sort of weights we are looking for.

Although those values for λ_1 to λ_3 are more or less OK, we might question whether those particular numbers are the best numbers. Is there any way of improving those numbers, rather than just picking them out of the air so that they look more or less right? This is part of the task of choosing the best parameters of a Hidden Markov Model, but before we go on to that, let's have a look at what part of the finite-state trigram model looks like once we have added this notion of weights. Let's consider just the part of the network involving the states labelled 'ab', 'ba' and 'bb'. In figure 7.9 we have added three extra states labelled λ_1, λ_2 or λ_3. It is possible to move from state 'ab' to any of these three by reading in the empty symbol ". Since the empty symbol occurs everywhere in all strings, that effectively means that it is possible to move to one of the lambda states without reading any letter off the start of the string. The introduction of the lambda states create multiple routes through the graph, depending upon whether λ_1, λ_2 or λ_3 is used, that is, whether trigrams, bigrams or unigrams are employed in estimating the probability of 'aba' or 'abb'.

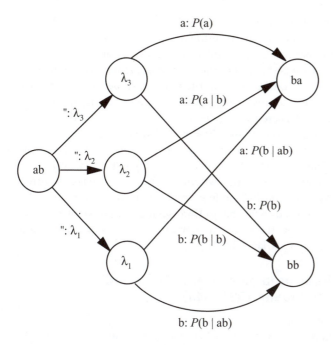

a: P(a)

": λ₃

a: P(a | b)

": λ₂

a: P(b | ab)

b: P(b)

": λ₁

b: P(b | b)

b: P(b | ab)

λ₃

λ₂

λ₁

ab

ba

bb

FIGURE 7.9
An HMM for the trigram
model, with back-off
routes (after Charniak
1993)

Consider, for instance, how we estimate the probability of a 'b' occurring after 'ab'. In other words, what is the best estimate of the probability of the sequence 'abb'? So, we start in state 'ab', and if a 'b' occurs next, we must end up in state 'bb', the final bigram of 'abb'. But there are three ways that we can get there: we can either go via λ_1, λ_2 or λ_3. If we go via λ_3, the probability of a 'b' occurring next is just the unigram probability $P(b)$. If we go via λ_2, the probability of a 'b' occurring next is the bigram probability $P(b|b)$, the probability of a 'b' given that the previous word was a 'b', whereas if we go via λ_1, the probability that a 'b' occurs next is the trigram probability $P(b|ab)$. The probability of arriving at state 'bb' depends on which of the three routes we follow. Since λ_1 is greater than λ_2 and λ_3, if the trigram 'abb' does occur in the corpus, the route via λ_1 will be the most probable. If 'abb' isn't in the training corpus but 'bb' is, the bigram route via λ_2 will yield the highest probability result. If 'b' didn't occur after a 'b' anywhere in the corpus, we must fall back on the unigram probability of 'b'. In that case, the two routes via λ_1 and λ_2 will score very low because the trigram and bigram are not in the corpus ($P = 0$), so the route via λ_3 will have a comparatively high probability, since any small probability is greater than 0! If you know whether the trigram or the bigram occurred in the corpus, you could work out which route yields the highest probability estimate. But, as equation 7.18 shows, we do not need to find the route with the highest probability: it is sufficient to take the *sum* of the probabilities by all three routes, and let the lambda coefficients give greater weight to the trigram route, if the trigram is in the corpus, or **back-off** to bigrams, if they exist.

When we use such a model for analysis, we don't know and we don't even care which routes it uses to figure out the most likely probability of each trigram. We want it to use the trigram counts if it has them in its corpus, but we don't really mind whether it has that information or not. We just want the model to give us the *best* estimate of the probability of the third word occurring that it can, given the data that it was trained on. Since we don't know or care whether or not the trigram or bigram probabilities are in the training corpus, when we give the model a sequence like 'abb' and ask for the likelihood of this string, it will return a result that will depend on one of these three routes. But we don't know which, it is hidden from us: that is why these models are called *Hidden* Markov Models.

We would like to have a way of setting the weights λ_1 to λ_3 automatically, and to find the best values for these weights. (By 'best' values we mean whatever values make the system work best, i.e. make it correct most often.) We also want to be able to compute the best route through a network, since we need to be able to find the highest probability for any particular observation sequence. In short, we have to solve three basic problems for Hidden Markov Models.

The three basic problems for HMMs (according to Rabiner and Juang 1993: 333)

Problem 1: Evaluation

Given an observation sequence O and a model M_i, how do we efficiently compute $P(O \mid M_i)$, the probability of the observation sequence, given the model?

We can also view this problem as one of scoring how well a given model matches an observation sequence. This is done by working out the probability of the observation sequence according to some particular model. If we are trying to choose among several competing models, the solution to this problem allows us to choose the model that best matches the observations.

Because there may be many different state sequences for a given observation sequence, in order to solve problem 1 we must find which state sequence (route through the model) is the best (most likely). This is problem 2:

Problem 2: Decoding

Given the observation sequence O and the model M_i, how do we choose a corresponding state sequence X that is optimal in some sense (i.e. best 'explains' the observations)?

In this problem, we attempt to uncover the hidden part of the model – the unknown state sequence. In most cases, there is no 'correct' state sequence to be found, and in many cases it is computationally infeasible to actually consider all possible state sequences. In any event, some possible state sequences are so unlikely that it is not worth spending time considering them. All we require is to find the best state sequence we can for the task at hand, or even a sub-optimal one, provided that it works well enough for the purpose in question.

Problem 3: Training

How do we set or adjust the parameters of each model so that the probability of an observation sequence will be highest? That is, how do we maximize $P(O \mid M_i)$? In other words, how do we train each model so that it works as well as it can?

In order to be able to employ models like this in useful real world applications, we need to have solutions to these three problems. At first, we merely guess values for the model parameters. Then we use the solution to problem 3 to improve the estimates of the model parameters.

Problem 1 is the problem of calculation of how well the model accounts for a given observation sequence. That is fairly simple to solve: we already have most of the technical machinery in place for solving any instance of problem 1. In brief, we calculate the sum of the probabilities of all routes through the model. The solutions to problem 2 and problem 3 are harder to implement. However, having said that, there is an algorithm for working out the optimal solutions to problem 2 given any one of several fairly reasonable optimality criteria.

The algorithms that are customarily used to solve each of these three problems are:

Solution to problem 1: the Forward-Backward algorithm.
Solution to problem 2: the Viterbi algorithm.
Solution to problem 3: the Baum-Welch re-estimation algorithm, also
    known as the EM (expectation maximization) algorithm.

The details of these are too complicated to present in detail in a book of this (introductory) level, though Jurafsky and Martin 2000, Rabiner and Juang 1993 and Huang et al. 2001 provide full details. The solutions to all three problems are interrelated, and build upon the technique of **dynamic programming,** which was illustrated in the previous chapter (the dynamic time warping method). In this case, however, instead of listing acoustic analysis *frames* along the two dimensions of the distance matrix, we can list *states* (or state numbers) along the vertical axis and *observations* along the horizontal axes. Each cell (x, y) represents an observation x made in state y, as in table 5.2, in chapter 5. The numbers in each cell is not acoustic distance (as in the previous chapter), but the probability of the transition from observation x made in state y to observation x' made in state y'. Just as we used dynamic time warping to find the best route through the distance matrix, we can use a similar recursive procedure in this case to find the sum of all transition probabilities for a sequence of observations.

To find the optimal (most likely) state sequence for a given observation sequence, the Viterbi algorithm uses dynamic programming. It uses backtracking through the observation-state space to find the most likely sequence of transition probabilities, just as we used backtracking in DTW to find the lowest-cost path through the distance matrix.

Jurafsky and Martin (2000) give the following simple example. Suppose we have a system with a vocabulary of four words, *knee, new, need* and *neat*, with (possible) transcriptions /ni/, /niu/, /nid/ and /nit/. If the utterance [ni] is input to the system, what word is it most likely to represent? On the one hand, simplicity suggests that it should be /ni/, *knee*, but that is not a particularly frequent word: perhaps it is more likely to be a 'defective' version of a more frequent word.

Table 7.2. Calculating the most likely sequence of symbols in a sequence, using dynamic programming (after Jurafsky and Martin 2000)

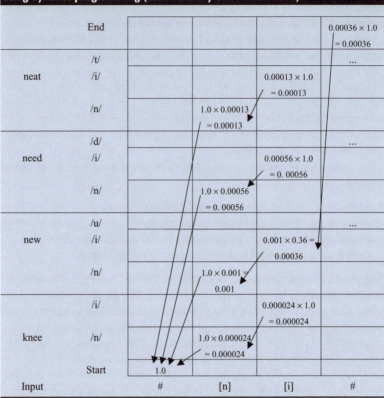

		#	[n]	[i]	#
	End				0.00036×1.0 = 0.00036
neat	/t/				...
	/i/			0.00013×1.0 = 0.00013	
	/n/		1.0×0.00013 = 0.00013		
need	/d/				...
	/i/			0.00056×1.0 = 0.00056	
	/n/		1.0×0.00056 = 0.00056		
new	/u/				...
	/i/			0.001×0.36 = 0.00036	
	/n/		1.0×0.001 = 0.001		
knee	/i/			0.000024×1.0 = 0.000024	
	/n/		1.0×0.000024 = 0.000024		
	Start	1.0			
Input		#	[n]	[i]	#

(Jurafsky, Daniel; Martin, James H., *Speech and Language Processing: An Introduction to Natural Language Processing, Computational Linguistics and Speech Recognition*, 1st edition, © 2000. Reprinted by permission of Pearson Education, Inc., Upper Saddle River, NJ.)

Table 7.2 (based on Jurafsky and Martin's figure 5.20) shows how the cells of the dynamic programming matrix contain (a) the accumulated probabilities of the sequence of symbols, and (b) a pointer back to the previous state. Having tabulated the probabilities and 'moves' during training, a 'most likely route' for a given input (e.g. [ni]) can be calculated by working backwards from the end state. (Only a few of the possible transitions from one state to another are shown.) For the calculation of the probabilities of the initial [n], we assume that the words in question have probabilities 0.000024 (*knee*), 0.001 (*new*), 0.00056 (*need*), and 0.00013 (*neat*).

Baum-Welch re-estimation can be used to adjust the parameters of a Hidden Markov Model. First, an initial estimate is made of the model parameters. Then, they are repeatedly adjusted a little by a version of the Forward-Backward algorithm that incorporates equations for replacing the old parameter estimates by new, improved estimates of the state transition probabilities. The algorithm is closely related to the previous two, but the equations for parameter re-estimation are beyond the level of this textbook. As I said, the full details may be found in the technical manuals cited above.

7.7 Part-of-speech model calculations

We have now surveyed the main methods used in building a Hidden Markov Model, such as a trigram model of word sequences. We have seen how to deal with unseen words (by estimating a small, positive probability), and unseen trigrams (by backing-off to bigrams and unigrams). We can now adapt this approach to deal with part-of-speech sequence probabilities, essentially by treating each (word, tag) pair $w_i\, t_i$ as a single symbol. Since there are several slightly different ways of doing this, for concreteness I shall follow the approach used by Jurafsky and Martin (2000).

In section 7.2 I introduced the idea of finding the most probable tag for a word by examining the previous word or two, and then looking that bigram or trigram up in a table of correspondences between *n*-grams and tags. In fact, in an HMM-based probabilistic tagger we try to find the most probable *sequence* of tags *T* for a sequence of words *W*. That is, we want to find argmax$_T$ $P(T|W)$. That expression means 'the value of *T* for which $P(T|W)$ is greatest'.

By Bayes' rule:

(7.19)

$$P(T|W) = \frac{P(T)\, P(W|T)}{P(W)}$$

Since the sequence of words is given, that is, fixed whatever sequences of tags we may consider, $P(W)$ is always the same and can be ignored. Therefore, we want to find argmax$_T$ $P(T)\, P(W \mid T)$.

From the chain rule, (7.9):

(7.20)

$$P(T)\, P(W|T) = \prod_{i=1}^{n} P(w_i|w_1 t_1 \ldots w_{i-1}\, t_{i-1} t_i)\, P(t_i \mid w_1 t_1 \ldots w_{i-1}\, t_{i-1} t_{i-1})$$

For simplicity, we suppose that the probability of a word is mostly dependent on its tag, not on those of previous words:

(7.21)

$$P(w_i \mid w_1\, t_1 \ldots w_{i-1}\, t_{i-1}) \approx P(w_i \mid t_i)$$

Also, we adopt the Markov assumption that the probability of the sequence of tags from the beginning of the sequence to the current word is mostly determined by the two most recent tags:

(7.22)

$$P(t_i \mid w_1\, t_1 \ldots w_{i-1}\, t_{i-1}\, t_{i-1}) \approx P(t_i \mid t_{i-2,i-1})$$

Therefore, we choose the tag sequence that maximizes:

(7.23)

$$P(t_1) \times P(t_2|t_1) \times \prod_{i=3}^{n} \left[P(t_i|t_{i-2,i-1}) \prod_{i=1}^{n} P(w_i|t_i) \right]$$

The main thing to notice about this is that it is an extension of the word sequence probability equation 7.15 to include tags.

7.8 Using HMMs for speech recognition

The examples discussed so far illustrate the general characteristics of an HMM, and their specific application to the trigram model of word sequences. Now, instead of generating strings of letters or words, consider a model that generates acoustic parameter vectors. To make the explanation simpler, assume that the acoustic parameter vectors are represented as codebook numbers. That is, the alphabet of the model output is a (smallish) set of numbers.

There is one acoustic vector per frame (e.g. each 10 ms interval of a signal), and transitions between states correspond to transitions from one frame to the next. If the acoustic vector does not change from one frame to the next, it is possible to remain in a state. Also, if the acoustic vector does change, it is still possible to remain in a state. But it is also possible, under either condition, to change state.

In the coin-tossing models and in the weather model, state transitions were permitted from each state to every other state. Such fully connected models are called ergodic. When each state transition corresponds to a change from one frame to the next, we are constrained by the laws of time as to which transitions are possible. The model in figure 7.10 exemplifies the subset of HMMs called 'left-to-right' or Bakis models.

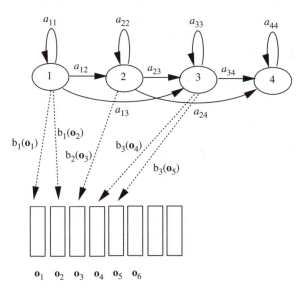

FIGURE 7.10
An HMM for generating acoustic parameter vectors (after Young et al. 1997)

Observed acoustic parameter vectors

Training the model

We estimate the hidden parameters (the transition probabilities and the output probabilities) by training the model on a corpus of training examples: that is, recordings of multiple pronunciations of each word. This is where HMMs improve on, say, DTW-based pattern matching. By virtue of being trained on multiple examples of each word, naturally occurring variations in the pronunciation of each word can be incorporated.

The general scheme of training and recognition is shown in figure 7.11. For isolated word recognition, a separate HMM is built and trained for each word. Recognition, then, is the task of identifying, for a given sequence of input vectors (the observation sequence), which HMM best explains that sequence. So, how does that work?

(a) Training

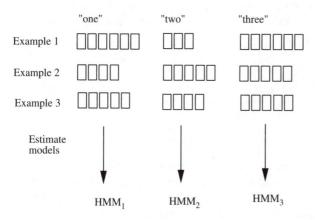

(b) Recognition

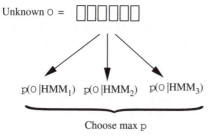

FIGURE 7.11
General scheme for training and using an HMM-based isolated word speech recognition system (after Young et al. 1997)

A few technicalities (after Young et al. 1997)

Let's represent each spoken word by a sequence of acoustic vectors, as in chapter 6. Each observation sequence O is defined as:

(7.24)

$$O = (o_1 \, o_2 \, o_3 \, o_4 \, o_5 \dots o_n)$$

where o_t is the speech vector observed at time t. The isolated word recognition problem can then be regarded as that of computing $\text{argmax}_i \, P(w_i \mid O)$, the most probable word w_i given the observation sequence. So, w_i is the ith word in the dictionary, and $P(w_i \mid O)$ is the probability of w_i being the right word, given O. This probability is not computable directly, but, according to Bayes' Rule, we have:

(7.25)
$$P(w_i \mid O) = P(O \mid w_i)\, P(w_i)/P(O).$$

$P(w_i)$ is referred to as the *prior probability* of word w_i's occurrence. It is related to that word's frequency of occurrence in some domain. $P(O)$, the observation probability, is 1, because the observation sequence is known. Hence, $P(w_i \mid O)$ depends only on $P(O \mid w_i)$. That is why we use an HMM which is a *generator* of speech vectors, as in figure 7.10, to estimate $P(O \mid w_i)$. Given a set of models M_i, corresponding to words w_i, we assume that:

(7.26)
$$P(O \mid w_i) = P(O \mid M_i).$$

For a particular state sequence X in figure 7.10:

(7.27)
$$P(O, X \mid M_i) = a_{01}b_1(o_1) \times a_{11}b_1(o_2) \times a_{12}b_2(o_3) \ldots$$

However, only the observation sequence is known: the underlying state sequence X is hidden. That is why it is called a *Hidden* Markov Model. Given that X is unknown, the required likelihood is computed by summing over all possible state sequences. Alternatively, the likelihood can be approximated by considering only the most likely state sequence.

All this, of course, assumes that the state transition probabilities a_{ij} and the observation probabilities $b_j(o_t)$ are known for each model. One of the most attractive features of the HMM framework is that the parameters of a model can be determined automatically from an appropriate set of training examples (i.e. recordings) of the word in question.

We saw in the previous chapter that some early word recognition algorithms were based on simple pattern matching against stored templates, using dynamic time warping to align the test word to a stored reference. For a small vocabulary, we could use such an approach to generate a hypothesis about the sequence of words in the input. It is then possible to use one of these probabilistic word sequence models to work out what were the most likely parts of speech of those words. These part-of-speech tags could then be passed upwards to a linguistic parser or something more sophisticated than that, such as a database query system.

However, since this is an extension of finite-state approaches, as well as modelling probabilities of sequences on one level, or alignments between sequences on two levels, such as words and tags, we can use the same general approach to estimate the probability of correspondences between various kinds of units, on various levels. For instance, we could use this approach with observation sequences consisting of pairings of words and acoustic analysis vectors to figure out the relationship between words and portions of the speech signal. Or alternatively, between sub-word units of some kind, such as phonemes or diphones on one level, and analysis vectors on the other level. You can use this technology for many problems that involve aligning or matching symbols on one level with different units on another level.

There have been one or two attempts recently to have independent HMMs for independent phonetic parameters, and in that way build an HMM analogue to non-linear phonology (Huckvale 1992; Deng and Sun 1994).

The structure of an isolated word recognition system built using objects of this kind is shown in figure 7.11(b). In an initial pre-processing stage (not shown in the figure), the raw speech signal S is analysed into acoustic features, such LPC vectors. Those vectors might then be pooled into clusters of similar vectors that are deemed to be equivalent by vector quantization. That step yields an observation sequence O, which might simply be a sequence of numbers such as spectral vector 186, spectral vector 23, spectral vector 63, spectral vector 10 and so on. A Hidden Markov Model is needed for each of the words in the vocabulary of maybe ten, maybe a hundred words, a fairly small vocabulary. Each of these models computes the probability that the observation sequence is a particular word in the vocabulary. So we submit the observation sequence to all of the word models, and then we arbitrate between them by picking the HMM that assigns the greatest output probability to the given observation sequence. That tells us which of the words in the vocabulary is the most probable word given the observation sequence.

Sub-word units

In large-vocabulary speech recognition systems, sub-word units (such as diphones or phonemes) may be used, rather than whole-word models. Whole-word models are still used for small vocabulary tasks, but for large vocabulary tasks sub-word models are preferable. They are trained on very large speech corpora though: they are typically trained on speech from many different speakers in order to improve the robustness. The model of word sequences (the language model) is also trained on very large corpora: tens of millions of words would not be unreasonable.

7.9 Chomsky's objections to Markov models and some rejoinders

I mentioned at the start of this chapter that statistical and finite-state models of language (such as Markov models) were heavily criticized by Chomsky (1957, 1965) and Miller and Chomsky (1963). Although these criticisms were important and influential in moving syntactic studies away from finite-state approaches, they deserve reconsideration in the light of the technical developments reviewed in this chapter.

Chomsky presents two kinds of objections to Markov models. One line of argument focuses on limitations of *all* finite-state machines, not just probabilistic ones. This argument concerns constructions with the unbounded, recursive embedding of one phrase within another. In addition, Chomsky also offered some independent arguments against probabilistic approaches. Given the recent successes of finite-state and probabilistic approaches, it is important to try to determine whether (a) Chomsky had it right all along, so that the current speech and language technology using, for example, HMMs is inherently misguided; or (b) the objections that he raised are not particularly problematic for the practical purposes in which these techniques are used. I shall deconstruct and reflect on each of his objections in turn.

An objection to finite-state models

At the end of chapter 5 we considered the argument by Chomsky (1957: 22) concerning constructions involving *unbounded centre-embedding*, as in (7.28):

(7.28)
If [either [the man who said that S5 is arriving today], or S4], then S2

Chomsky claims that such examples demonstrate 'that there are processes of sentence formation that finite state grammars are intrinsically not equipped to handle ... If these processes have no finite limit, we can prove the literal inapplicability of this elementary theory.' In chapter 5 we noted that the antecedent of the latter statement is false, because centre embedding *does* have a finite limit. Chomsky has a second argument, though:

> If the processes have a limit, then the construction of a finite state grammar will not be literally out of the question, since it will be possible to list the sentences, and a list is essentially a trivial finite state grammar ... But this grammar will be so complex that it will be of little use or interest.

There are three prongs to this objection, then: complexity, utility and interest. Regarding complexity, a finite-state grammar of English or any other natural language will certainly be *large*, but by definition, finite-state grammars are the simplest kind of grammar. The structure of a machine required to process constructions with centre embedding is not particularly complex, as figure 5.19 illustrates. In general, finite-state automata are simpler than the kinds of automata needed to process more powerful phrase-structure grammars of the kind preferred by Chomsky. Thus, the argument from complexity does not stand up very well to scrutiny.

The statement that finite-state grammars are of 'little use' is easily dispensed with, since the simplicity and efficiency of these grammars has made them very attractive and popular in natural language engineering.

As for 'little interest' ... Interest is in the mind of the reader! For linguists, the fact that finite-state methods turn out not to suffer from the problems alleged for them is surely of importance and interest. From a cognitive science perspective, we note that with the finite-state model of centre embedding of figure 5.19, it is the necessity to travel through a larger and larger portion of the network in order to process more and more deeply embedded sentences. This seems to fit in with the discovery from brain imaging experiments that in processing sentences with more embedded clauses, a larger and larger area of cortex is recruited (Just et al. 1996). This fact also points at an explanation of why embedding is finitely bounded: we only have a finite amount of grey matter to employ for such purposes!

Objections to probabilistic models

Chomsky gives two different lines of argument against probabilistic approaches. The first of these centres on the idea that we can create new sentences that have never been spoken or heard before, and which there-fore have an observed frequency of 0, and hence a probability of 0.

For example, Chomsky (1957: 15–17) writes:

the notion 'grammatical in English' cannot be identified in any way with the notion 'high order of statistical approximation to English'. It is fair to assume that neither sentence (1) nor (2) (nor indeed any part of these sentences) has ever occurred in an English discourse.

(1) Colorless green ideas sleep furiously.
(2) Furiously sleep ideas green colorless.

Hence, in any statistical model for grammaticalness, these sentences will be ruled out on identical grounds, as equally remote from English. Yet (1), though nonsensical, is grammatical, while (2) is not. . . . a speaker of English . . . may never have heard or seen any pair of words from these sentences joined in actual discourse.

In short, Chomsky claims that since neither of these strings of words (nor their constituent bigrams) will ever have been encountered before, they are equally improbable. There are two problems with this argument. First, we have already shown how an *n*-gram model may take into account the probabilities not just of word sequences, but also the probabilities of the sequences of the *parts of speech* of those words. In Chomsky's pair of examples, for instance, note that sentence (1) is of the form adjective-adjective-noun-verb-adverb, whereas (2) is of the form adverb-verb-noun-adjective-adjective. The tag sequence of (2) is much less likely than that of (1) because (a) adjectives normally come before nouns, and (b) in a sentence with only one noun and one verb, the noun is most frequently *before* the verb, not after it. These are facts about the frequency of part-of-speech tags that even a relatively simple statistical tagger could calculate. (This rejoin-der begs the question of where part-of-speech tags come from, but it has been shown that they too can be learned by statistical methods related to those presented above (Brown et al. 1992).)

The second way in which the argument is false is in the claim that the bigrams of these sentences are equally improbable. Recall that in a bigram model it is possible (and customary) to regard the first word of a sentence as the second word of a bigram (w_0, w_1) in which w_0 is the empty string, or some other 'start of sentence' boundary symbol. In this way, we can esti-mate the probability of w_1's occurrence *as the first word of a sentence*. The first bigram of (1), then, is (' ', 'colorless') and of (2), (' ', 'furiously') – and these do *not* have the same probability. Likewise, we could postulate an empty word at the end of the sentence – or even take the final full stop as the last word – so that the final bigram of (1) is ('furiously', '.') and the final bigram of (2) is ('colorless', ' '), again with different probabilities. Thus (1) and (2) are not *equiprobable*, as Chomsky claims, anyway.

Chomsky (1957) gives a second example of the same type of argument:

in the context 'I saw a fragile —,' the words 'whale' and 'of' may have equal (i.e. zero) frequency in the past linguistic experience of a speaker who will immediately recognise that one of these substitutions, but not the other, gives a grammatical sentence.

The rejoinder to this is the same: it is easy to infer statistically that 'a fragile of' is less probable than 'a fragile whale' in an *n*-gram model that takes note of the parts of speech of the two sentences and if we treat the beginning and end of the sentence as empty words. 'Adjective-noun-END' is far more likely than 'adjective-preposition-END'!

Chomsky (1965: 11 and n.5, and again in Chomsky 1966: 35–6) argues against the use of sentence probabilities as a characterization of sentence acceptability:

The more acceptable sentences are those that are more likely to be produced, more easily understood, less clumsy, and in some sence more natural ... These characterisations are equally vague, and the concepts involved are equally obscure. The notion 'likely to be produced' or 'probable' is sometimes thought to be more 'objective' and antecedently better defined than the others, on the assumption that there is some clear meaning to the notion 'probability of a sentence' or 'probability of a sentence type.' Actually, the latter notions are objective and antecedently clear only if probability is based on an estimate of relative frequency and if sentence type means something like 'sequence of word or morpheme classes.' ... But in this case, though 'probability of a sentence (type)' is clear and well-defined, it is an utterly useless notion, since all highly acceptable sentences (in the intuitive sense) will have probabilities empirically indistinguishable from zero and will belong to sentence types with probabilities empirically indistinguishable from zero. Thus the acceptable or grammatical sentences (or sentence types) are no more likely, in any objective sense of this word, than the others.

The nub of the argument is that even grammatical sentences have very low probabilities. We have seen that the probabilities of sentences and sentence types are indeed very small numbers. But there are ways of working with and comparing even very small quantities: for instance, we can use scientific (exponential) notation, as above, or use log probabilities, to make the numbers more manageable. Furthermore, any probabilistic model must have a method for estimating probabilities of previously unseen events. In a bigram model, for instance, the difference in the likelihoods of 'I saw a fragile whale' and 'I saw a fragile of' hinges entirely on the difference in the likelihoods of the final bigrams. Even if neither 'fragile whale' nor 'fragile of' occur in a corpus (or in a speaker's experience), we note that the frequency of 'fragile Noun' is much greater than that of 'fragile Preposition' (in the BNC, for example, C('fragile Noun') = 323, whereas C('fragile Preposition') = 19. (An example of 'fragile Preposition' occurs in the phrase 'fragile in defence'.) We can easily predict, therefore, that the word following 'fragile' is much more likely to be a noun than a preposition, which could explain why 'fragile of' is far less acceptable than 'fragile whale'. In addition, since the word 'whale' is sometimes preceded by adjectives (in 17.9% of instances in the BNC), whereas 'of' is rarely preceded by adjectives (2.5% of instances in the BNC), we can explain the greater acceptability of 'I saw a fragile whale' by using a bigram model that is sensitive to parts of speech, a modest requirement that it is possible to meet using contemporary statistical language models.

A quite different objection to probabilistic finite-state models of language is given by Miller and Chomsky (1963: 427,430):

If there are D symbols in the alphabet, then a k-limited stochastic source will have (potentially) D^k different states . . . when we examine this model . . . as a serious proposal for the way people create and interpret their communicative utterances, it is all too easy to find objections. We shall mention only one but one that seems particularly serious: the k-limited Markov source has far too many parameters . . . there can be as many as D^k probabilities to be estimated. By the time k grows large enough to give a reasonable fit to ordinary usage the number of parameters that must be estimated will have exploded; a staggering amount of text would have to be scanned and tabulated in order to make reliable estimates.

Just how large must k and D be in order to give a satisfactory model? Consider a perfectly ordinary sentence: *The people who called and wanted to rent your house when you go away next year are from California*. In this sentence there is a grammatical dependency extending from the second word (the plural subject *people*) to the seventeenth word (the plural verb *are*). In order to reflect this particular dependency, therefore, k must be at least 15 words . . . and the vocabulary must have at least 1000 words. Taking these conservative values of k and D, therefore, we have $D^k = 10^{45}$ parameters to cope with, far more than we could estimate even with the fastest digital computers.

Even by the standards of today's fastest computers, 10^{45} is still an inconceivably large number of parameters to estimate. But the scale of the problem is not as great as this argument makes out, for two reasons. First, the research of the 1960s and 1970s into the estimation of Markov model parameters led to the discovery of techniques such as Baum-Welch re-estimation. As we have already noted, the use of dynamic programming reduces the problem of parameter estimation from an exponential search to a more tractable polynomial-time algorithm. In part, therefore, this argument of Miller and Chomsky's has been overtaken by improvements in our understanding of how to train such models.

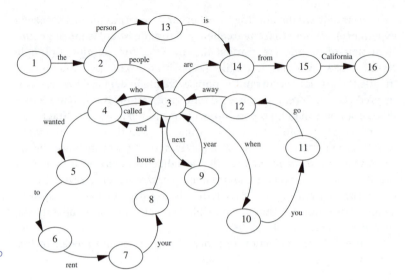

FIGURE 7.12
Finite-state automata for a subset of English involving a long-distance dependency (subject-verb agreement)

A second rejoinder is that although 'people' and 'are' are indeed separated by fourteen intervening words in this example, that makes it a poor example from which to learn subject-verb agreement in English. In fact, this kind of dependency can *easily* be handled in a finite-state architecture. Figure 7.12 presents a finite-state automaton that will accept Miller and Chomsky's long sentence, as well as several grammatical shorter ones:

The people (who called) (and wanted to rent your house) (when you go away) (next year) are from California.

The parenthesized phrases may be placed in other orders, while remaining grammatical (although perhaps with an altered meaning) and acceptable by the automaton, e.g.

The people who called next year when you go away and wanted to rent your house are from California.

Whatever phrases lie between 'people' and 'are', the grammatical dependency between those two words is captured by the fact that any path through the automaton via states 2 and 3 ('people') must subsequently go through state 14 ('are'). Thus, the probability of 'are', given the earlier plural subject, is 1. Alternatively, generation or recognition of the singular subject 'person' demands a route via state 13, and subsequently selection of the singular verb form 'is'. Thus, the agreement facts can be represented and enforced in a finite-state architecture. The strength of the dependency between 'people' and 'are' is best estimated by the (strictly local) bigram probability, P('are' | 'people'), estimated from shorter phrases, such as *the people are from California*. Developers of *connectionist* models of language acquisition, who have also attempted to deal with long-distance grammatical dependencies in a finite-context architecture, have referred to this as 'the importance of starting small' (Elman 1993, 1999; Allen and Seidenberg 1999). From this we can see that the flaw in Miller and

Chomsky's argument is their assumption that all the model parameters must be learned at once. In fact, the parameters might be better inferred from simple sentences first, before moving on to elaborations of the model that enable it to process longer sentences. We conclude that Miller and Chomsky's estimate of $k = 15$ is much larger than necessary. Practical experience with n-gram models in the last fifteen years or so has taught us that a value of 2 or 3 for k is more realistic.

To conclude this section, I would like to make it clear that I am not claiming that finite-state models are ideal models of language: they certainly suffer from some shortcomings. My purpose in the foregoing discussion has been to try to explain why probabilistic finite-state models are not as bad as was formerly believed. In part, this is because earlier objections contained various faults; in part, because more sophisticated models (such as phrase-structure grammars) bring a new set of hard problems; in part, because scientific progress arising from practical experience (such as the development of methods for back-off and smoothing, in order to deal with very rare events) has improved the finite-state toolkit enormously.

Chapter summary

In this chapter we examined how finite-state models are used for two purposes in current speech recognition programs. Firstly, probabilistic finite-state language models are useful for estimating what word is likely to occur next in a sequence. They can also be used to estimate the most likely part-of-speech label to assign to an ambiguous word. One variety of such devices, Hidden Markov Models, is also used for working out what word a given piece of a speech signal is most likely to be.

Further reading
The account of Hidden Markov Models given in this chapter closely follows — in some paragraphs very closely — Rabiner and Juang 1993 and Young et al. 1997. For more on probabilistic language modelling, see Charniak 1993 or Jurafsky and Martin 2000: 191–200. There has been an explosion of work in this area in the last decade, leading to extensive re-examination of Chomsky's early critique of probabilistic and finite-state methods. For a recent discussion, see Pereira 2000.

Reading in preparation for the next chapter
Clocksin and Mellish 2003: 213–23.

8 Parsing

CHAPTER PREVIEW

KEY TERMS

parser
Definite Clause Grammar
recursive descent
syllabification
chart parsing

In this chapter we examine parsing: computer programs that work out the syntactic structure of a sentence (or any sequence of symbols), according to a given grammar. We examine one method, recursive descent parsing using Definite Clause Grammars, in some detail, before surveying a number of more sophisticated alternative approaches.

8.1 Introduction

We started this book by looking at speech and signals and so on, and we have gradually been considering linguistically richer models. With this topic, parsing, we reach a technique that is more commonly used in language analysis than in speech analysis, although it does have applications to speech analysis, some of which I will get on to later. The examples that I will present to begin with are examples of parsing in natural language processing. By parsing is meant the computation of phrase structure given a string of words. The structure is typically computed according to a grammar of the language, which specifies the rules of syntactic structure. But not always: it is possible to parse with a less explicit theory about what the syntactic structures are in the grammar, but I am not going to consider those in detail (see section 9.7).

The first example we shall consider illustrates how grammar rules can be implemented in Prolog. Using this method, it turns out that a specification of the phrase-structure grammar of the language is in itself a program that can be executed and run as a parser. The distinction between parser and grammar is thus not at all clear-cut, but that makes it quite a useful starting point. Later, we will look at systems in which the grammar and parser are kept more separate from one another.

8.2 A demo

Our first example is based on Clocksin and Mellish 2003, chapter 9: the grammar in listing 8.1 (which is also in the file sentence_grammar.pl, on the CD-ROM).

Listing 8.1

```
/* SENTENCE_GRAMMAR.PL                                        */
/* Simple syntactic DCG, after Clocksin & Mellish ch.9        */

sentence --> noun_phrase, verb_phrase.
                                                              5
noun_phrase --> determiner, noun.

verb_phrase --> verb, noun_phrase.
verb_phrase --> verb.
                                                             10
determiner --> [the].

noun --> [apple].
noun --> [man].
                                                             15
verb --> [eats].
verb --> [sings].

/* Generate all sentences */
                                                             20
loop:- sentence(S,[]), write(S), nl, fail.
```

This is not a great grammar or parser but it is worth having a look at it in order to get a feel for the potentialities of parsing. In order to use it you need to pay attention to the vocabulary of words that the demo recognizes, since you can't just type in any words of English. It has a restricted vocabulary: *the*, *apple*, *man*, *eats*, *sings*. (You can add more words to the listing if you want to, of course.) First, the Prolog interpreter has to load the program. You can do this by typing

```
consult('sentence_grammar.pl').
```

after the Prolog ?- prompt. Then, you can use it in two main ways. You can either type in a string of words for it to parse, in which case Prolog will report whether or not the string is grammatical (i.e. in accordance with the grammar). For example:

```
?- sentence([the, apple, eats, the, man],[]).
Yes
?- sentence([the, apple, man, sings],[]).
No
```

Alternatively, I have provided a `loop` predicate to generate all the grammatical sentences. There are only twelve of them, because of the extremely limited grammar and vocabulary of this example, of which only three make sense!

8.3 'Intuitive' parsing

Before we get involved in the details of computational parsing, let's look at parsing from an intuitive point of view. Then, I'll look at how parsing works using Definite Clause Grammars. Later, I'll go into some other issues.

If you don't know very much about computing or the theory of parsing, figure 8.1 shows one way in which you could intuitively assign a syntactic structure to a sentence like 'the quick brown fox jumped over the lazy dogs'. I'll assume you know something about syntactic theory: more than me, probably. You have a theory of grammar, but not necessarily of parsing, so how would you assign an analysis? The steps that I might take would be as follows. (This is how I learned to parse as an undergraduate.) First you tag the words, that is, you have to categorize them with some part of speech or another, as in 8.1. This is step 1 in figure 8.1, note.

(8.1)

String:	the	quick	brown	fox	jumped	over	the	lazy	dogs
Tags:	DET	ADJ	ADJ	N	V	P	DET	ADJ	N

We saw in the previous chapter that this is actually a fairly tricky thing to do. For instance, although in this particular case 'dogs' is a plural noun, it can also be a verb. But I will gloss over that and assume that in this particular case the tagging is not particularly controversial. I will assume that you can get the tagging right, without going into the mysteries of how you might do that.

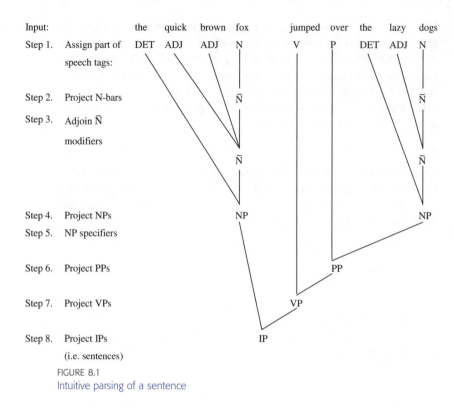

FIGURE 8.1

Intuitive parsing of a sentence

That is the easy bit (at least it feels like the easy bit). The hard bit is to work out how to group the words together into phrases. One way of doing that is if you are using a fairly restrictive theory of syntactic structure, like X-bar syntax, you find the lexical heads first (N, V, A, P), and then their complements and specifiers and adjuncts. Let's take the nouns first. They are going to be the heads of noun phrases, so there are likely to be some other words that go together with those nouns to make a phrase. The verb and the preposition are also going to be lexical heads that will combine with certain kinds of other words. In this example there are two nouns: one towards the middle of the sentence ('fox'), and one towards the end ('dogs'). They have some modifiers (adjectives and determiners) before them, so we can build N-bars and NPs (figure 8.1, steps 2–5). That gives us two noun phrases 'the quick brown fox' and 'the lazy dogs', plus 'jumped over' in the middle that has to be included somehow. We might then build the prepositional phrase (step 6), since we recognize that a preposition and a following noun phrase can be a prepositional phrase. Then we could build a verb phrase (step 7), so we have a noun phrase and a verb phrase. That is enough to build a sentence with step 8.

By this method, we start with a string of words and build the tree upwards. (I have drawn figure 8.1 downwards actually, because it is arranged step by step, from the frontier to the root of the tree. But the conventional orientation of syntax trees has the tree going the other way round, as in figure 8.2, grouping collections of words together into larger

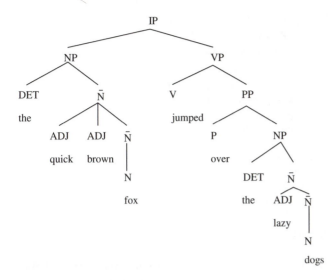

FIGURE 8.2
Conventional orientation
of the parse tree in fig-
ure 8.1.

and larger units, until eventually you have got one unit which spans the whole string, and that unit is the sentence.) So, that is a naive, intuitive theory of how you might do parsing. It is called **bottom-up**, because you move from small constituents 'up' the tree to larger and larger constituents. It does not proceed exclusively from left to right, but starts with the fourth and ninth words, and then moves to earlier and later bits of the sentence, leaving the middle until last. The strategy focuses on lexical heads rather than going rigidly from left to right or right to left. Starting with the most deeply embedded words, it is goes up the tree from the smaller to the larger units.

8.4 Recursive descent parsing

In contrast, the next example of 'proper' (i.e. computational) parsing uses the same approach that is exemplified in section 8.2. This method, **top-down recursive descent parsing**, is quite different from the intuitive approach. Instead of starting from the words in the input, we start from the top of the tree with the start symbol IP (i.e. sentence). The technique is to repeatedly consider the problem 'how can we build the tree downwards, so as to generate the input string?' In other words: 'Can we build a tree between IP and the words, so that when we have built the tree every word is included in the tree?'

Consequently, we need a theory about the structures of the language — in other words, a **grammar**. In 8.2 is a set of rules illustrating what I mean here by a grammar. We also need some information about the categories of words: we will express those as grammar rules too, as in rules 5–9.

(8.2)

Rule 1	IP → NP VP
Rule 2	NP → (DET) ADJ* N

Rule 3	VP → V NP
Rule 4	VP → V PP
Rule 5	DET → the; a; an . . .
Rule 6	N → dogs; fox; jumps . . .
Rule 7	ADJ → quick; brown; lazy . . .
Rule 8	V → jumped; runs . . .
Rule 9	P → over; onto; in ; under . . .
Rule 10	PP → P NP

Start symbol:

FIGURE 8.3
Initial state of the parser

Input string: the quick brown ...

In the initial state of the parser (figure 8.3), we have the start symbol IP, the input string and the grammar. The algorithm works by considering how we might *generate* the string. It computes an analysis by trying to generate the string and the tree that fits that string. According to the grammar, the only way of getting from IP closer to the string is to expand IP as an NP and a VP. There is only one rule that enables you to get nearer to the string given IP, so that is the rule that you apply first. That gives us the state of play in figure 8.4, where we have expanded the IP to an NP and a VP. You could say that we have hung an NP and a VP below the root node. The question is now: how can we expand each of these symbols, in order to get down to the string?

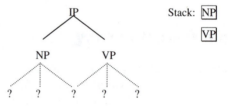

FIGURE 8.4
Second state of the parser

Input string: the quick brown ...

As we expand the tree further, we shall generate more non-terminal nodes at the lower edge of the tree, so we also need a mechanism for keeping track of what phrases remain to be completed. The mechanism for doing this is called the **stack**, shown schematically at the right-hand side of figure 8.4 as a stack of 'cards', one for each category remaining to be dealt with. We use the stack to keep a note of what symbols remain to be expanded. In figure 8.4, the stack tells us that in order to complete the sentence we have still to find an NP and then a VP. As well as the stack, we shall refer to what remains of the string, what is left to be parsed, as the **remainder** of the string. At this stage, all of the string remains to be parsed. Later, when we have parsed a bit at the beginning of the string, the remainder of the string will be a certain number of words at the end of the string.

So the algorithm needs three things: (1) some kind of storage to build a tree in, including the words from the part of the string that have been parsed; (2) some storage for the remainder of the string, and (3) a stack: a store of notes about what remains to be done.

There is only one way of expanding the initial symbol IP, but the next step is one that we are going to use over and over again in order to complete the parse. This is where the notion of recursive descent comes in: we repeatedly expand the *leftmost unexpanded daughter*. In this particular case, the leftmost unexpanded daughter is the NP. To expand it, we look at the grammar and find the first rule that allows us to expand the NP. It is rule 2, which says that a noun phrase can have an optional determiner, zero or more adjectives, and a noun. There are two ways of finding the leftmost unexpanded daughter. One is that you might have a technique that finds that symbol on the frontier of the tree you are building, as you go along. But preferably – this is where the stack comes into play – the leftmost unexpanded daughter is the symbol on the top of the stack. When we expand the leftmost unexpanded daughter, we remove its symbol from the top of the stack. In this case, we take the NP off the top of the stack, expand it (that is, replace it by (DET) ADJ* and N), and we put those three symbols on the top of the stack. We must put them on the stack in reverse order, so N goes on first, above VP, then ADJ* goes on top of N, and finally (DET) goes on top of ADJ*, as in figure 8.5.

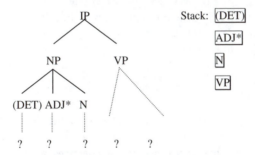

Remainder: the quick brown fox jumped over the lazy dogs

FIGURE 8.5
Third state of the parser

Now we have expanded NP as (DET) ADJ* and N, you can see from the tree and the stack in figure 8.5 that we now have to look for an optional determiner, zero or more adjectives, a noun, and a VP. The remainder is still the whole of the input string.

Now the leftmost unexpanded daughter — the symbol on top of the stack in other words — is the optional determiner. The grammar has a rule for a determiner, rule 5. (Actually, this could be regarded as shorthand for a set of rules, each of which introduces one determiner. That doesn't really matter, though.) We have a statement to the effect that a determiner can be 'the'. Since 'the' is in fact the first word of the remainder of the string, we can take that word off the beginning of the remainder and attach it to the tree under the (DET) node. Since we have now expanded the (DET) node, we can take the (DET) symbol off the top of the stack, since it is no longer on our schedule, and we have successfully parsed the first word of the sentence (figure 8.6).

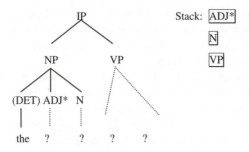

Stack: ADJ*
      N
      VP

FIGURE 8.6
Fourth state of the parser

Remainder: quick brown fox jumped over the lazy dogs

Student: Suppose there is no determiner?
Well, that is OK: determiners are optional.
Student: If the first word is not a determiner, does the (DET) node just vanish?

You can treat optional symbols in various ways. One way of doing it is to interpret an optional symbol such as (DET) as meaning 'a DET or the empty string'. So the (DET) node can be checked off the stack whether or not the remainder begins with a determiner, in the way you hinted at. Another way of doing it is to say that the determiner is actually compulsory in the noun phrase rule, but that one of the lexical possibilities for a determiner is the empty string. That is, we amend rules 2 and 5 as in (8.2):

(8.2)
Rule 2   NP → DET ADJ* N
Rule 5   DET → "; the; a; an . . .

You can do it either way; it doesn't make much difference. The same considerations apply to the 'ADJ*' notation, for a sequence of zero or more adjectives. Obviously, it means 'no adjectives, or one adjective, or two adjectives . . .'. There are various ways of expanding an ADJ* node: technically, an infinite number of ways. In the Prolog implementation of this grammar (`dog_grammar.pl`), which we shall examine in the next section, you will see that instead of there being one rule for noun phrases there are several. In writing the Prolog implementation, I limited Rule 2 to a maximum of two adjectives, giving three possible ways of spelling out the ADJ* symbol (0, 1 or 2 ADJ nodes). With an optional initial determiner (i.e. 0 or 1 DET nodes), there are six specific variants of rule 2. So in `dog_grammar.pl`, I just have six similar rules but with different numbers of ADJs and presence or absence of DET.

Student: I get the feeling that you will quickly get into a combinatorial explosion in the number of rules.

Well, only if you adopt the brute force solution of actually trying to spell out all of the possible sequences. That perhaps isn't always the most sensible way of doing it for a large grammar, but for a simple application or a small demonstration it is fine. But I am presenting the theory at the moment rather than an implementation.

Now what remains to be parsed? Well, the ADJ* node of rule 2, the N node of rule 2, and the VP node of rule 1 still remain on the stack, and the remainder of the string is 'quick brown fox jumped over the lazy dogs'. The leftmost unexpanded daughter is the ADJ* node, and 'quick' and 'brown' are both ADJs, so they can be included in the tree, leaving 'fox jumped over the lazy dogs' as the remainder. Since 'fox' is not an ADJ, we can take the ADJ* off the stack, which just leaves an N and a VP on the stack (figure 8.7).

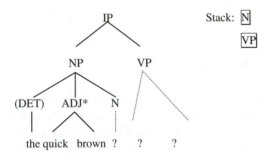

Remainder: fox jumped over the lazy dogs

FIGURE 8.7
Fifth state of the parser

We do this over and over again. The next thing we expand is the N. 'Fox' is an N, so we can include it; then the VP node is on top of the stack. The VP can be expanded just as we did for the NP earlier. The first rule for VP is rule 3: VP expands to V NP. We deal with the V first. 'Jumped' is a V, so that is OK. Then we expand the NP node according to rule 2, as we did for the first NP (figure 8.8).

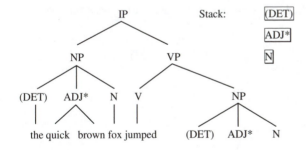

Remainder: over the lazy dogs

FIGURE 8.8
Ninth state of the parser

At this point we run into a problem because the first word of the remainder is 'over' and the leftmost unexpanded symbol is DET, and 'over' is not listed among all of the possibilities for rewriting DET. What happens now? The (DET) is optional, though, so the parser must infer that the (DET) node remains empty. Now we still have the same problem with ADJ*, since 'over' is not an ADJ either. So ADJ* must be empty (figure 8.9).

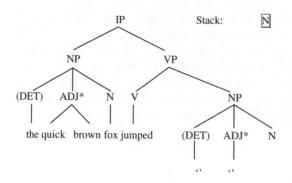

FIGURE 8.9
Eleventh state of the
parser

But 'over' is not an N either: now we are really stuck. With this parsing technique (which is nondeterministic) we must **backtrack**. We have reached a point where we are stuck. We can't expand the remaining symbols in the tree, and the string is not all analysed yet. We can't just finish: either (a) the string is in fact ungrammatical, or (b) we must have done something wrong earlier on. (a) is a serious possibility, of course: we would arrive at this same point given the input 'the quick brown fox jumped the lazy over'. But we can't conclude that the string is ungrammatical until we have ruled out possibility (b).

So, we backtrack – just as we did with finite-state parsing in chapter 5 (section 5.2) – and consider whether we might get further with the parse by using some other rules instead. We backtrack to the recently introduced NP node, and consider whether we got it wrong. Is 'over the lazy dogs' some different kind of NP? But according to this grammar it can't be: there are no other rules for NPs, so we are stuck again. What do we do? Well, we have to backtrack again, which takes us back to the VP node (figure 8.10).

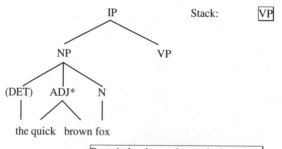

FIGURE 8.10
Thirteenth state of the
parser

Note that when we backtrack, as well as removing previously constructed parts of the parse tree and amending the stack, we also have to amend the remainder list, by putting any of the previously parsed words back onto the beginning of the list.

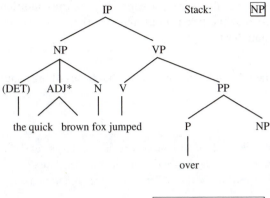

FIGURE 8.11
Fifteenth state of the parser

There is another rule for VPs: the rule we used before was rule 3 (VP expands to V NP) whereas the alternative VP rule is rule 4 (VP expands to V PP), with a prepositional phrase complement to the verb. So we try that one instead, attaching 'jumped' as a V, and expanding the PP as a P and an NP. Now 'over' can be parsed as a P, so we are OK now, we have overcome the problem of 'over'.

That leaves an NP to be parsed. 'The lazy dogs' will be parsed as an NP, no problem, just as we did for 'the quick brown fox'. So all of the string can be parsed, and we end up with a state at which the tree is complete, there are no dangling nodes without any terminal symbols attached to them, and also importantly there are no words left over in the string (figure 8.12).

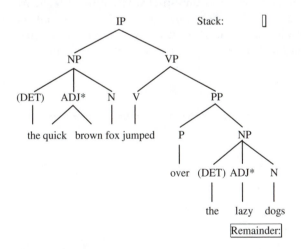

FIGURE 8.12
Final state of the parser

The requirement that the remainder list is empty is important, because we frequently encounter sentences that start with a sentence. For example, sentence (8.3) starts with the sentence 'I did not consider the fact that John doesn't know what he is talking about.' You could reach 'very distressing' with a complete parse tree, but that would not be the *correct* parse, because the words 'very distressing' are left over. So, the condition for finishing is not just that the tree is built, but also that there are no more words in the remainder list.

(8.3)
I did not consider the fact that John doesn't know what he is talking about very distressing.

> *Student: When you were talking about backtracking because of the preposition 'over', and it backtracks to the verb phrase, and there are two verb phrase rules, does the parse never re-do a rule it has done before? Is that how it gets to the 'the'?*
>
> Yes, it goes to each rule in turn; it keeps track of what rules it has already tried.
>
> *Student: And it doesn't try what it has already done again?*
>
> No, otherwise it would only ever try that one rule and never consider any others.

8.5 The simplest parsing program

The file `dog_grammar.pl` (listing 8.2) implements grammar 8.2 as a Prolog definite clause grammar (DCG), which is notationally similar to a context-free grammar. (This grammar *is* context-free, in fact, though in general the DCG formalism includes various powerful additional mechanisms, making them as powerful as unrestricted rewriting systems. We shall not exploit that excessive power, however: in this chapter and the next, the DCGs are all context-free.) This is a 'toy' grammar, rather like that of listing 8.1, but with different rules and a different vocabulary.

Listing 8.2

```
/* DOG_GRAMMAR.PL*/

ip -> np, vp.

np --> n.                                          5
np --> adj, n.
np --> adj, adj, n.
np --> det, n.
np --> det, adj, n.
np --> det, adj, adj, n.                          10

vp --> v, np.
vp --> v, pp.

pp --> p, np.                                      15
```

```
det --> [the].
det --> [a].
det --> [an].

n --> [dogs].                                                    20
n --> [runs].
n --> [fox].

adj --> [quick].                                                 25
adj --> [brown].
adj --> [lazy].

v --> [jumped].
v --> [runs].                                                    30
v --> [dogs].

p --> [over].
p --> [onto].
p --> [in].                                                      35
p --> [under].

/* Generate all sentences   */

loop:- ip(S,[]), write(S), nl, fail.                            40
```

To see how it works you could try starting Prolog, consulting the file and, at the Prolog prompt, try out query 8.4.

(8.4)
```
ip([the,quick,brown,fox,jumped,over,the,lazy,dogs],[]).
```

8.6 Difference lists

Note that in a definite clause grammar, a string is represented as a pair of lists called a difference list. For example, the string `[a,b,c,d]` could be considered to be the difference between `[a,b,c,d,e]` and `[e]`, or between `[a,b,c,d,e,f]` and `[e,f]`, or an infinite number of other *pairs* of strings of the general form '`[a,b,c,d|Rest], Rest`'. This means that for any given string there is a very large number of different representations of that string. However, there are only a few cases that we usually use in a parser:

1. For the representation of an entire string, all of the words are included and nothing is left over. For example, the string `[time,flies]` can be represented by the pair of lists '`[time,flies], []`'.
2. The representation of single words of a given string will consist of a pair of strings differing only in the presence or absence of the first word. For example, given the input string `[the,quick,brown, fox,jumped,over,the, lazy, dogs]`, the first word is represented

as the pair of lists '[the,quick,brown,fox,jumped, over,the,lazy,dogs],[quick,brown,fox,jumped,over,the, lazy,dogs]'.

3. At intermediate stages in a parse, where we are parsing only remainders of the input string, single words will be represented likewise as the difference between the remainder and the remainder minus the first word. For example, in this example, 'fox' is represented as '[fox,jumped,over,the,lazy,dogs],[jumped,over,the,lazy, dogs]'.

4. The last word in a string, e.g. 'dogs' is represented as the difference between that word and the empty string (i.e. nothing left over): '[dogs],[]'.

So, we can represent strings in terms of differences of lists of words. Because of this notation, it is possible to put different parsing questions to a system of this kind rather than simply give a string, and return or compute the parse.

I suggest a number of other queries that you might put. 8.4 is a question that can be paraphrased roughly as 'Is "the quick brown fox jumps over the lazy dogs" a well formed sentence?' Another question that you might ask is 8.5, which means 'What string X is a well-formed IP (i.e. sentence)?'

(8.5)
ip(X,[]).

If you put that question to Prolog, it will follow the rules as before, using the top-down recursive descent method. But instead of having to find the analysis of a particular input string, it is trying to find the analysis of a variable. As anything will match a variable, the first word that it comes up with in each category will do. So the first string that it will generate is determined by which rule in each group is listed first, and by which word in each category is listed first in the lexicon. The first sentence it will generate is, in fact, '[dogs,jumped,dogs]'.

If you don't want the first sentence that it returns, or if you want to see what other sentences it would non-deterministically compute, you can enter a semicolon after the first answer, and it will backtrack and get another answer. If you enter a semicolon again, it will generate the next answer, and so on. It does that by backtracking: entering a semicolon tells Prolog to backtrack, so it undoes the last rule that it applied and applies some other rule that could have applied at that time. It will work its way back through all of the choices of lexical entries and all of the choices of rules, for as long as you keep entering semicolons. It will generate the yield of the grammar one sentence at a time, should you wish to do that. (If you really want to generate all of the strings defined by the grammar, you can just type 'loop.', though, because I included a loop predicate in the program that will generate all of the strings. As there are 243360 sentences in the language of dog_grammar.pl, from 'dogs jumped dogs' to the quite un-English 'an lazy, lazy fox runs under an lazy, lazy fox', this is a preferable way to generate them.)

You can try even more imaginative queries if you want, such as 'generate a sentence of the form "the X jumps over the Y" ':

(8.6)
```
ip([the,X,jumped,over,the,Y],[]).
```

A well-known problem with top-down parsing is left recursion, which can occur with rules in which the leftmost daughter is of the same category as the mother, e.g.

(8.7)   NP → NP PP   e.g. '[[the tree][in the park]]'
(8.8)   NP → NP CP   e.g. '[[the dog][that chased me]]'
(8.9)   VP → VP PP   e.g. '[[saw the dog][with a telescope]]'

A top-down parser that repeatedly tries to expand an NP node using rules 8.7 or 8.8 will get into an endless loop that makes the tree deeper and deeper without ever getting down to the words of the string. A simple strategy for avoiding this is to order the rules, such that non-recursive rules are always attempted before recursive rules. However, this will not prevent cases of left-recursion that span several rules, for example

(8.10)   A → B C
(8.11)   B → D E
(8.12)   D → A F

in which there is left recursion of A in the sub-tree:

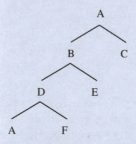

If encountered, this kind of left-recursion can be eliminated by either (a) ordering 8.10 after non-recursive expansions of A, or (b) collapsing rules 8.10–8.12 into a single rule, A → A F E C, which can be ordered after non-recursive expansions of A. This alters the syntactic structures that the parser computes, but it does at least get rid of the left-recursion.

8.7 Generating a parse tree

This very simple parsing algorithm doesn't give you back a parse tree. It computes a parse, that is, it follows a certain line of reasoning in order to compute the analysis of a string, but it doesn't tell you at the end what the analysis is. If you want to get it to tell you what the analysis was, you have to extend the grammar in order to build and store the parse tree as it goes along.

> *Student: So when it parses it just provides the answer 'yes', if it thinks it is well formed, or 'no' if it isn't.*
> Yes, that is right. It can also fill in any variables in the input string, or generate strings, as we saw.

To get back a parse tree, we have to add an extra argument to each predicate in the grammar, in which to store the piece of the parse tree dominated by that node. For the daughter categories in a rule (i.e. those on the right of the arrow), use variables for this extra argument. For the mother category (i.e. the one before the arrow), add a structure that shows how the daughters are joined together into a tree fragment. There is more than one way of doing this, though the following two methods are the main ones often used.

Method 1. Mother categories are of the form:

```
mothercategory(Daughter1Variable,
    Daughter2Variable ... LastDaughterVariable).
```

We replace rules of the form:

```
a --> [word].      by  a(a(word)) --> [word].
```

and

```
a --> b.           by  a(a(B)) --> b(B).
a --> b, c.        by  a(a(B,C)) --> b(B),
c(C).
a --> b,...,z.     by  a(a(B,C,...Z)) -->
b(B),...z(Z).
```

The file `dog_grammar2.pl` is a re-coding of `dog_grammar.pl` that uses this method. Instead of 8.4, 8.5 and 8.6, we must give queries with an extra variable as the first argument, such as those in 8.13 – 8.15, respectively:

(8.13)
```
ip(Tree, [the,quick,brown,fox,jumped,over,
         the,lazy,dogs],[]).
```

(8.14)
```
ip(Tree,X,[]).
```

(8.15)
```
ip(Tree,[the,X,jumped,over,the,Y],[]).
```

Prolog's responses to these queries are given in 8.16–8.18, respectively:

(8.16)
```
Tree = ip(np(det(the), adj(quick), adj(brown), n(fox)),
vp(v(jumped), pp(p(over), np(det(the), adj(lazy),
n(dogs))))))
```

(8.17)
```
Tree = ip(np(n(dogs)), vp(v(jumped), np(n(dogs))))
X = [dogs, jumped, dogs]
```

(8.18)
```
Tree = ip(np(det(the), n(dogs)), vp(v(jumped),
pp(p(over), np(det(the), n(dogs)))))
X = dogs
Y = dogs.
```

Method 2. Mother categories are of the form:

```
mothercategory: [Daughter1Variable,
Daughter2Variable ... LastDaughterVariable].
```

That is, the tree is an attribute:value structure. A common variant on this allows other features of the construction to be included in the tree too (for example, agreement features etc.).

```
[category: mothercat,
daughters: [Daughter1Variable,
Daughter2Variable ...
    LastDaughterVariable],
... other features of the construction ...
].
```

We can replace rules of the form:

```
a --> [word].      by  a(a:[word]) --> [word].
```

and

```
a --> b.           by  a(a:[B]) --> b(B).
a --> b, c.        by  a(a:[B,C]) --> b(B), c(C).
a --> b,...,z.     by  a(a:[B,C,...Z])-->
                           b(B),...z(Z).
```

The file `dog_grammar3.pl` is a re-coding of `dog_grammar.pl` that uses this method. Once again, we must give queries with an extra variable as the first argument, such as those in 8.13–8.15. Prolog's answers to these queries are:

(8.19)
```
Tree = ip:[np:[det:[the], adj:[quick],
adj:[brown], n:[fox]], vp:[v:[jumped],
pp:[p:[...],...:...]]]
```

(8.20)
```
Tree = ip:[np:[n:[dogs]],vp:[v:[jumped],
np:[n:[...]]]]   X = [dogs, jumped, dogs]
```

(8.21)
```
Tree = ip:[np:[det:[the], n:[dogs]],
vp:[v:[jumped], pp:[p:[...], ... :...]]]
X = dogs
Y = dogs
```

With either of these methods, it is possible to add other features to the mother category, or to re-code the lexical entries in various ways. For example, instead of:

(8.22)
```
n(n:[dogs]) --> [dogs].
```

we might have:

(8.23)
```
n(n:[lemma: dog, form: plural]) --> [dogs].
```

or, in an English–French machine translation application:

(8.24)
```
n(n:[lemma: chien, forme: pluriel]) -->[dogs].
```

8.8 Syllabification

Parsing is not restricted to syntax, of course: morphological and phonological analysis can also employ these same techniques. Listing 8.3 presents a context-free grammar of English syllable structure. (It uses the same ASCII encoding of IPA symbols as in chapter 5, though this grammar is certainly not equivalent to the finite-state analyses of syllable structure presented in that chapter.)

Listing 8.3

```
/* SYLLABLE_GRAMMAR.PL                                    */
/* Simple grammar of syllable structure                  */

syllable_sequence --> syllable.
syllable_sequence --> syllable, syllable_sequence.          5


syllable --> onset, rime.
rime --> nucleus, coda.


                                                           10
onset --> inner_onset, sonorant. /* maximal Onset hypothesis */
onset --> inner_onset.
onset --> [h].
```

```
inner_onset --> [s], obstruent.                                        15
inner_onset --> obstruent.
inner_onset --> [].
nucleus --> long_vowel.

nucleus --> diphthong.                                                 20
nucleus --> short_vowel.

coda --> [].
coda --> sonorant.
coda --> obstruent.                                                    25
coda --> sonorant, sonorant.
coda --> sonorant, obstruent.
coda --> obstruent, obstruent.

obstruent --> [p].    obstruent --> [t].     obstruent --> [k].        30
obstruent --> [b].    obstruent --> [d].     obstruent --> [g].
obstruent --> ['C'].  obstruent --> ['J'].
obstruent --> [f].    obstruent --> ['T'].
obstruent --> [s].    obstruent --> ['S'].
obstruent --> [v].    obstruent --> ['D'].   obstruent --> [z].        35

sonorant --> [r].     sonorant --> [l].
sonorant --> [w].     sonorant --> [j].
sonorant --> [m].     sonorant --> [n].

                                                                       40
short_vowel --> ['I'].
short_vowel --> [e].
short_vowel --> ['&'].
short_vowel --> [0].
short_vowel --> ['U']                                                  45
short_vowel --> ['@'].
short_vowel --> ['V'].

long_vowel --> [i].
long_vowel --> ['A'].                                                  50
long_vowel --> ['O'].
long_vowel --> [u].
long_vowel --> [3].

diphthong --> [e,'I']                                                  55
diphthong --> [a,'I'].
diphthong --> [o,'I'].
diphthong --> ['@','U'].
diphthong --> [a,'U'].
diphthong --> ['I','@'].                                               60
diphthong --> [e,'@'].
diphthong --> ['U','@'].
diphthong --> [j,u].

loop:- syllable(S,[]), write(S), nl, fail.                             65
```

Try:

```
syllable_sequence(['D','@',k,w,'I',k,b,r,a,'U',n,f,0,k,
s,'J','V',m,p,t,'@','U',v,'@','D','@',l,e,'I',z,i,d,0,
g,z],[]).
```

According to listing 8.3 (and in line with phonological theory) a syllable consists of an onset and a rime, a rime has a nucleus and a coda, and each of those units in turn can consist of various things, obstruents, sonorants and vowels. Some syllable constituents (the onset and the coda) can be empty, indicating that they are optional elements.

At the beginning of the program there are two rules for syllable sequences. The first rule says that a syllable sequence can be a single syllable, and the second rule says that a syllable sequence can be a syllable followed by a syllable sequence. Taken together, those two rules allow us to generate arbitrarily long sequences of syllables with a right-branching structure as shown in figure 8.13, until eventually we get to the rule that expands a sequence as a single syllable, and then that finishes the bottom of the structure.

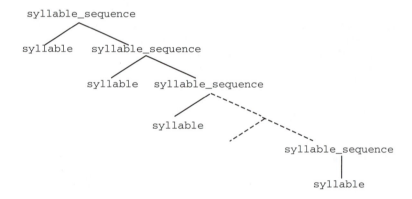

FIGURE 8.13
Right-branching structure of an arbitrarily long sequence

So an easy way of generating arbitrarily long sequences in Prolog is to have a recursive structure like figure 8.13. (We could have analysed the adjective sequences of section 8.4 in a similar way, if we had wanted. We would have needed a category adj_sequence, which expands as adj followed by adj_sequence. This is clearly a category being motivated solely by computational considerations, rather than by considerations of syntactic theory.)

Now the analogue of parsing with a phonological grammar is syllabification: the division of a string into syllables. Although this grammar does not build and give us a syllabified string as output, we can make the syllabifications visible by using the following definitions of syllable_sequence instead. (Since these are in the file syllabifications.pl, they can be loaded into Prolog just by consulting that file.)

```
syllable_sequence([S],In,Out):-
        syllable(In,Out),
        append(S,Out,In).
```

```
syllable_sequence(Sylls,In,Out):-
       syllable(In,Mid),
       syllable_sequence(Rest,Mid,Out),
       append(S1,Mid,In),
       append([S1],[Rest],Sylls).
```

Now the query:

```
syllable_sequence(X,['D','@',k,w,'I',k,b,r,a,'U',n,f,0,
k,s,'J','V',m,p,t,'@','U',v,'@','D','@',l,e,'I',z,i,d,
0,g,z],[]), write(X).
```

gives the result:

```
[[D,@],[[k,w,I,k],[[b,r,a,U,n],[[f,0,k],[[s,J,V,m,p],
[[t,@,U],[[v,@],[[D,@],[[l,e,I],[[z,i],[[d,0,g,
z]]]]]]]]]]]]
```

```
X=[['D',@],[[k,w,'I',k],[[b,r,a,'U'|...],[[f,0|...],
[[...|...]|...]]]]]
```

(I added the predicate `write` to this query in order to get Prolog to print out all the syllables in the list. In SWI-Prolog, at least, large structures are abbreviated, as in the last line of the output, using ellipses.) From this output, we can see that the assigned syllabification is 'D@ kwIk braUn f0k sJVmp t@U v@ D@ leI zi d0gz'. Although this contains the oddity of a sJ at the start of the fifth syllable, it is otherwise not bad, considering that the input string was just an undivided sequence of phoneme symbols.

(Note that the language of syllables that is expressed in this grammar is not entirely English, but it is English-like. You might wish to run the 'loop.' predicate to see what syllables the grammar includes. For one instance, [s,p,w,a,'U',p] is OK as a syllable of this language, even though it is not phonotactically acceptable in English. 'pmip' is also OK, though 'mpip' is not OK. And because codas are no longer than two phonemes long in this grammar, many English words, such as 'tempts', or 'sixths' cannot be parsed and will be declared as ill-formed according to this grammar, even though they are actual English words.

Church 1983 or 1988 is perhaps the most influential work on phonological parsing. Not that there is anything particularly exciting about the parsing method that he used: the originality of that work is that he looked into the possibility of using an explicit grammar of syllable structure, and a parser for syllable structure, in order to constrain word analyses in a speech recognition system. He observed, for instance, that stops have slightly different degrees of aspiration in different environments in a syllable. This was then regarded in main-line speech recognition research as being a problem, on the view that variability is 'noise' that makes recognition more difficult. Church argued that pronunciation variability in different contexts is not noise at all: it is information. The fact that syllable initial /t/s are strongly aspirated and syllable final /t/s aren't actually tells you something about syllable structure, and so if we employ that information we can actually use that to refine our hypothesis about the sequence of words that our speech recognition system thinks it is looking at. For subsequent work on phonological parsing, see Dirksen 1993 and Coleman 1992, 1998 and 2000b.

8.9 Other parsing algorithms

I want to mention a couple of other issues that really deserve better coverage than I have space for here. We have looked at one technique for parsing: top-down, recursive descent parsing. We also looked at an intuitive technique, which was a kind of bottom-up technique. I don't want to give the impression that the top-down left to right recursive descent parsing is the only respectable parsing method. Far from it: there are various other, reliable, well-established parsing algorithms:

The CKY (Cocke–Kasami–Younger) parser (Younger 1967; Kasami and Torii 1969) is a bottom-up parsing algorithm. It requires the grammar to be written in a particular way, with at most binary branching rules.

Earley's algorithm (Earley 1970; Jurafsky and Martin 2000, section 10.4) is a refinement of the top-down technique that we looked at above. DCGs, definite clause grammars, employ an Earley-like parsing strategy.

Generalized LR parsing (Tomita 1991) is the most efficient parsing algorithm of all for context-free grammars.

8.10 Chart parsing

Consider sentence 8.3 again:

(8.3)
I did not consider the fact that John doesn't know what he is talking about very distressing.

The verb 'consider', like most verbs, has more than one pattern of complementation or at least on the surface it appears to. It is found in VPs like 'consider NP ADJ' (e.g. consider it distressing, consider it done, consider him boring etc.), or 'consider NP' alone (e.g. 'consider this example', 'consider the lilies of the field' etc.), and 'consider NP NP' (e.g. 'consider him an idiot'). In example 8.3, 'that' could be an NP, the complement of 'consider', by itself, as in the sentence 'I did not consider that.' Or, 'consider the fact' could be the NP complement, as might 'the fact that John doesn't know', or 'the fact that John doesn't know what he is talking about'. But in order to include 'very distressing' in the sentence, we need to use the 'V NP ADJ' expansion of VP.

(8.25)   VP → V NP

(8.26)   VP → V NP ADJ

(8.27)   VP → V NP NP

Let's think about how the top-down, recursive descent parsing algorithm with backtracking would fare given this sentence. How much work the algorithm does depends very much on which rule you happen to look at first. Suppose that you happen to pick rule 8.25 first, to expand the VP. In

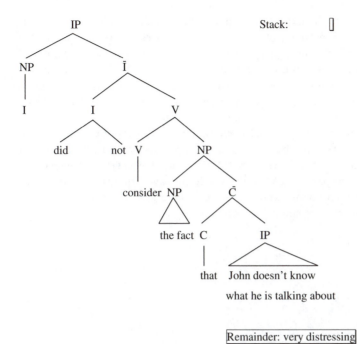

Stack: []

Remainder: very distressing

FIGURE 8.14
A false ending

that case, you will get to the state in figure 8.14, with a complete tree, but with some material left over.

So at this point the parser is forced to backtrack. It will have to undo all of the structure that it erected over the long noun phrase 'the fact that John doesn't know what he is talking about', and go back to before 'consider'. Then it can try the other expansion of VP 8.26 for which it will parse the long noun phrase 'the fact that John doesn't know what he is talking about' all over again. In backtracking (tracking back?), the parser threw away lots of structure: the analysis it computed of the long noun phrase. But it is a waste to discard that structure, because although the parse was wrong at this point, it was not wrong because of any fact about the long noun phrase. It was a perfectly formed noun phrase. It was only the selection of the verb phrase rule that was wrong. The noun phrase is fine regardless of whether 'very distressing' is there or not. Backtracking parsing may re-do a lot of work, and parse certain parts of a sentence several times over. It shouldn't need to do that.

The order of the rules is not at fault, either. Suppose we alter the grammar so that rule 8.26 is always considered before rule 8.25. Now the same problem will arise if the parser is given the shorter sentence:

(8.28)
I did not consider the fact that John doesn't know what he is talking about.

Now, if the parser tries rule 8.26 first, it will get to the end of the sentence but still be looking for an adjective phrase. Since it will not find it, it will then backtrack, undoing the tree over 'the fact that John doesn't

know what he is talking about', only to build it all again in order to satisfy
the second rule. So one of the problems with backtracking parsing is that
the parser often destroys or throws away structure that it has computed
once, only to build it up again later on. In a reasonably long sentence, the
parser may go down several blind alleys again and again. So it could build
the same structure over and over again many times, only to tear it down,
rebuild it, tear it down, and build it yet again.

So, we should keep a store of the well-formed parts of the strings that
we find. Every time the parser finishes a part of a tree, it should store it
away somewhere and keep a record of the fact that a certain stretch of the
string can be parsed in a certain way, for instance, that the substring 'the
fact that John doesn't know what he is talking about' is a noun phrase,
with the structure shown in figure 8.15.

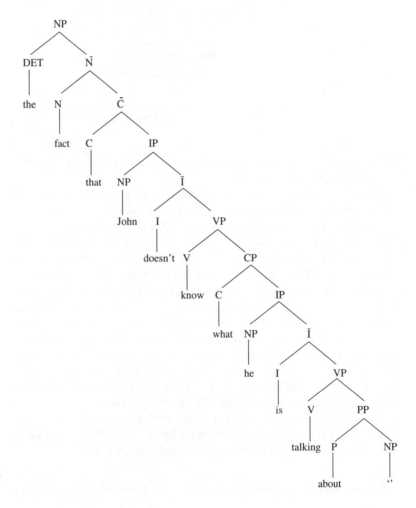

FIGURE 8.15
A well-formed parse fragment

The data structure that is usually used to store such information is a
structure called the **chart**. I am not going to give details of that now,
except for a short discussion of an example (figure 8.16).

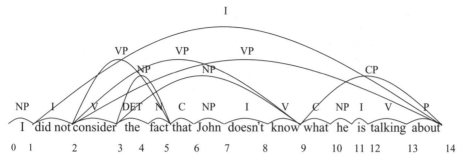

FIGURE 8.16
Storage of well-formed substrings in a chart

Figure 8.16 is a graphical representation of a chart. To build it, we label each word boundary with a position number (see the bottom line of figure 8.16). Whenever a constituent is found during the course of a parse: the following information is added to the chart: (1) the position at which the constituent starts; (2) the position at which it ends, and (3) its category. For example, (3, 5, NP) or (9, 14, CP). These triples are shown in the figure as labelled arcs, though that is just a useful pictorial notation. Constituents are entered before the final parse is actually known. This means that structures are not removed and do not have to be reconstructed over and over again. For example, if we add 'very disturbing' at the end of the sentence in figure 8.16, there is no need to delete the finding that 'the fact that John doesn't know what he is talking about' is an NP. That fact, already worked out, is represented in the chart as the arc labelled NP that goes from position 3 to position 14. The technique of parsing using a chart is (unsurprisingly) called **chart parsing**. It enables us to minimize the amount of time the parser spends thrashing about computing the same partial analyses over and over again.

8.11 Depth-first vs. breadth-first search

Recursive descent parsing is called **'depth-first'** because it goes ever deeper down the leftmost unexpanded branch of the tree, and only later broadens the tree by completing the unexpanded sisters to the right. The parser may be led to backtrack because it takes a very narrow view of the string it is analysing. For instance, it would be possible to work out at an early stage (or at least guess) which of 8.25 or 8.26 is applicable, by looking ahead to see whether there is an ADJ at the end of the string. But a depth-first parser does not do that. It is only when the parse tree broadens out that the parser may discover that it must revise its analysis. So, not surprisingly, it has occurred to some people to try **breadth-first** parsing, instead. In breadth-first parsing, we begin by expanding the start symbol (e.g. IP). We then repeatedly expand *all* the non-terminal symbols in the frontier of the parse tree, until the frontier consists of pre-terminals. We then check whether the frontier fits the entire string. If it does not, we can backtrack and try other expansions instead, until eventually we may find an analysis that fits the string.

As an example, let's parse 'the quick brown fox jumped over the lazy dogs' using the rules of listing 8.2. The derivation is as follows:

Step 1.   IP
Step 2.   NP   VP
Step 3.   N   V   NP
Step 4.   N   V   N
Step 5.   Does 'the quick brown fox jumped over the lazy dogs' match the frontier N V N? No, so backtrack.
Step 7.   Reconsider step 4.
           N   V   ADJ   N?   Still not right.
Step 8.   Reconsider step 3.
           N   V   ADJ   N?   Still not right.
Step 9.   Reconsider step 2.
           N   V   PP
Step 10.   N   V   P   NP
Step 11.   N   V   P   N?   Still not right.
           . . .

In step 1, there is only one way in which we can expand IP. In step 2, rather than just expanding the leftmost symbol, we expand both non-terminals together. We are trying to reach out across the whole breadth of the string, and eventually build a parse tree that goes down to the string. This is a technique that sort of works in certain circumstances, but not in natural language processing. You have to keep generating complete trees over and over again until you've got one that's exactly right.

Needless to say, although it sounds intuitively appealing to begin with, it turns out to be completely useless for most applications. Although a depth-first parser often has to re-build parts of its analysis, it can at least retain well-formed parts of the parse tree.

> *Student: Has anyone looked at the possibility of a combination of depth-first and breadth-first?*
>
> Not that I know of: that would be contradictory, wouldn't it?

8.12 Deterministic parsing, Marcus parsing and minimal commitment parsing

That leads me to mention a final approach, deterministic parsing, a theory of parsing that considers whether we can get rid of backtracking. For example, Marcus (1980) argues that backtracking parsers are not appropriate for human language, because in human language parsing (as examined in psycholinguistics experiments, for instance), people rarely seem to rethink their parsing hypotheses. It appears as if people can parse what they hear as the sentence goes along in real time, without having to backtrack.

Or rather, that we do occasionally do see people having to backtrack, but that when they do it is very visible. The example that illustrates this most clearly is processing of 'garden path' sentences, such as 8.29.

(8.29)
The horse raced past the barn fell.

If you have not seen this kind of sentence before, you may, like many people, find it to be very puzzling at first. It seems to be ungrammatical. 'The horse raced past the barn' is just fine, and then comes another word, 'fell'. What's that doing there? The intended analysis is synonymous with: 'the horse *that was raced past the barn* fell'. But by the time you hear 'the horse raced past the barn', it seems that you have already come up with an analysis. You immediately become committed to this analysis, so that when 'fell' comes along, you may be reluctant to reconsider your analysis and work out that 'the horse raced past the barn' is not a sentence, but a noun phrase containing a relative clause. Although backtracking would quickly resolve the problem, it seems that people are unwilling to do it. Or if they do, they perceive the sentence as curious or unusual in requiring them to backtrack in order to get 'fell' into the analysis. That may tell us something about the psycholinguistic (un)reality of backtracking.

The idea behind deterministic parsing (and one variety of it, *minimal commitment* parsing) is that when you are parsing you don't form any hypotheses or build any structures that you might have to undo at a later stage. As you work through the string, you build a parse tree with the minimal commitment: that is, you only build a structure that you are confident is correct, and you only make categorizations that you are confident are correct. What enables you to have the confidence that your hypotheses are correct is that we allow a certain degree of *look-ahead*. In the top-down parser we had no look-ahead. The only word that the parser could 'see' was the first word of the string that remained to be processed.

To illustrate deterministic parsing, consider a string that begins 'the angel falls . . .'. In this string, 'falls' could be a verb, but it could be a plural noun. In one case 'angel falls' would be a noun–noun compound; in the other, 'the angel' is a noun phrase and 'falls' would be the beginning of a verb phrase. In minimal commitment parsing we can parse 'the angel' as an NP: 'the' can only be a determiner and 'angel' is always a noun, so 'the angel' is either a noun phrase or possibly the beginning of a noun phrase: we are not sure (figure 8.17).

At that point a nondeterministic parser would plough ahead with one or another of those analyses and see how far it gets. In deterministic parsing, however, we cannot start to build any more structure than what we have here. In order to incorporate 'falls' into the rest of the structure we have to look at the next word in the input. If it is a verb, such as 'tumble', we can work out that 'falls' is not a verb, because you can't have two main

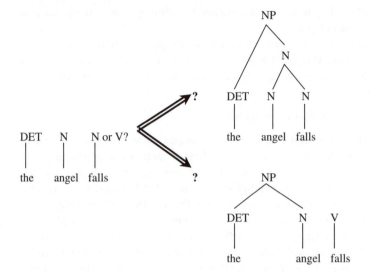

FIGURE 8.17
A choice in the categorization of a single word leads to two different possible analyses of a string

verbs, for example, 'falls tumble', at the start of a verb phrase. So 'angel falls' must be a noun–noun compound, and 'tumble' the start of a verb phrase (figure 8.18).

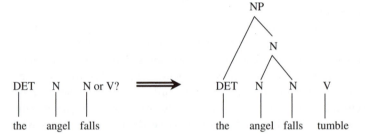

FIGURE 8.18
Looking ahead to the next word resolves the ambiguity

Marcus (1980) designed a deterministic parser of this kind, having a number of quite specific rules about what to do in particular cases of uncertainty about how the analysis should proceed. Those rules must be quite carefully tailored to the language in question. Whereas the nondeterministic parsing methods we looked at earlier work with any context-free grammars, for any language (human and non-human languages), or any sets of strings that can be specified using a context-free grammar, such as syllables, in a deterministic parser, the rules are closely tailored to the possible vaguenesses or ambiguity of the particular language. Ambiguity is resolved by looking ahead, further along the input string. No hard and fast decisions are made about the category of a word, or where it fits into the syntactic structure, until the parser has sufficient information to be sure. According to this approach, the reason that garden path sentences cause a problem is because all the way through the string there seems to be sufficient information to be confident that, for example, 'the horse raced past the barn' is a sentence. It is only when you then get 'fell' that the analysis falls to bits. Advocates of deterministic parsing could say 'Of course garden path sentences cause problems for people. That's what you would expect, because people parse deterministically.'

Marcus's deterministic parser is a particular instance of a class of parsers that are commonly used in computer science: LL(k) parsers. These are recursive descent parsers with a limited degree of look-ahead. 'LL' refers to the fact that they analyse the string from *Left* to right, with look-ahead which is also from *Left* to right. *k* is a number (usually one or two), indicating how many words of look-ahead are allowed, how far ahead the parser can peek. The idea is that with the ability to look ahead even by only a few words, it is often possible to resolve ambiguities in most cases. Not all the context-free languages can be parsed by these limited look-ahead parsers, only subsets of the context-free languages. Furthermore, parsers with limited look-ahead can be very efficient.

Student: Is there any evidence as to how much look-ahead humans normally use?

All I know on this subject is the indirect evidence that Marcus's parser had a look-ahead of about three words, and worked about as well as anyone else's parser. But he later relaxed the amount of look-ahead from two or three words to two or three constituents, which may contain more than two or three words.

8.13 Parallel parsing

Student: Can you avoid backtracking by using parallel processing, to check out more than one analysis at a time?

If there is more than one rule for each symbol, more than one way of expanding each symbol, the number of possible analyses to be considered grows exponentially. No amount of parallelism will help here. Parallel processing can only give a linear speed-up in the time taken to complete a process.

The number of processors you have got is always a finite number, so by adding more processors you are linearly increasing the computing resources that you are applying to a problem. But the real problems for a single processor are those where there is a combinatorial explosion — an exponential increase — in the amount of work that remains to be done. So even if you had a thousand processors, if the string is longer than a certain length, you may still just run out of processors.

Chapter summary

In this chapter we looked in detail at one method of parsing: that is, of working out the structure of a sentence (or of a word) according to the rules of a grammar. We used Definite Clause Grammars, a notation for grammar rules provided in Prolog. We also surveyed a variety of other parsing methods, touching upon all the main approaches.

Further reading

The literature on syntactic parsing is huge, so I can only give you a few pointers to enable you to get into it, if you want. The textbooks contain more extensive bibliographies and discussions of specific topics. To begin with, I suggest you take a look at Jurafsky and Martin 2000, chapter 10. For more on natural language processing techniques in Prolog, see Pereira and Shieber 1987, sections 2.7 (pp. 29–36), 3.4.2 (p. 612), and 3.7 (pp. 70–9).

9 Using probabilistic grammars

CHAPTER PREVIEW

In this chapter we examine three kinds of probabilistic grammars: generative grammars designed to model differences in the likelihood of different sentences or their structural analyses. We begin with the simplest case, probabilistic context-free grammars, which we shall illustrate by adding probabilities to a simple Prolog DCG. Then to conclude the book we examine two more recent developments: Tree Adjoining Grammar and Data Oriented Parsing.

9.1 Motivations

A probabilistic (or stochastic) generative grammar is like a standard, non-probabilistic grammar, such as a context-free grammar, except that a probability is assigned to each rule. Probabilistic grammars, therefore, are not alternatives to standard generative grammars, but a refinement or extension of generative grammars designed to model differences in the likelihood of different sentences or their structural analyses.

In chapter 6 I discussed one of the reasons for using probabilistic grammars: the need to determine which of several *possible* analyses is the most *likely*. There are many other reasons for using probabilistic grammars in computational linguistics. Here are five:

1. Human grammaticality judgements are gradient

According to the standard, non-probabilistic definition of grammaticality, a given string of words either is or is not grammatical, according to a given grammar. Put another way, the string either is or is not in the language defined by the grammar. When people judge the grammaticality of a string of words, however, they do not seem to operate with a simple clear-cut binary division between grammatical and ungrammatical sentences. Some sentences seem definitely grammatical, and some seem definitely ungrammatical – though judgements of ungrammaticality can be overturned if a suitable explanation or contextualization is given. For instance, 9.1 and 9.2 seem definitely ungrammatical to many people the first time they are encountered:

(9.1)   Buffalo buffalo buffalo Buffalo buffalo. (Barton et al. 1987: 99–100)

(9.2)   Rose rose rose.

These are likely to be regarded as mere repetitions of a single word upon first encountering them, not as grammatical sentences. In order to parse 9.1, note that 'buffalo' can be a common noun (the animal), a place name (Buffalo, in New York state) and (in American English, anyway) a verb meaning 'to fool'. Thus, 'Buffalo buffalo' are North American bison from Buffalo, NY. When one group of such bison fools another such group, we can say 9.1. Sentence 9.2 concerns a character that might appear in a children's story, a rose called Rose: Rose rose. One morning, after awaking, Rose rose rose. (Neither of these examples illustrate probabilistic grammaticality judgements, however: they merely show that grammaticality judgements can be overturned.)

Even in mainstream works on syntax it is recognized that a sentence may be completely ungrammatical, somewhat questionable, very questionable and so on (see, e.g., Bard et al. 1996). In recognition of this fact, Chomsky proposed a different term, 'acceptability'. His idea is that every string either is or is not grammatical, with no middle ground, but that our ability to determine the grammaticality of strings is imperfect and subject to extraneous factors, causing us to be uncertain. Although this is a reasonable proposal, it has the disadvantage of pushing grammaticality into the realm of the unobservable, since all we can ever directly obtain are (listener's reports of) acceptability judgements. Now, science is not happy with unobservables. Although they are sometimes unavoidable, the purpose of any branch of science is to explain what *can* be observed (in this case, acceptability ratings) with as little invocation of unobservables (as few laws or as few hidden factors) as possible.

One application of probabilistic grammars is to use sentence probabilities to model degrees of acceptability. For example, conjoining a possessive phrase and a possessive proper noun seems to be questionable in English, whatever the order of conjuncts:

(9.3)
(a) ?My friend and Alf's is coming.
(b) ??Alf's and my friend is coming.

Another compelling example comes from phonology. Again, according to the classical conception of grammaticality, some strings of phonemes in a language are grammatical (e.g. the actual English word /brɪk/ and the possible English word /blɪk/), whereas others are ungrammatical (e.g. the form /bnɪk/, which, by general agreement, could not be a word of English, because /bn/ is an ungrammatical syllable onset). Several empirical studies of such judgements, however, have shown that the situation is not so clear-cut (Greenberg and Jenkins 1964; Ohala and Ohala 1986; Dankovičová et al. 1998; Frisch et al. 2000; Bailey and Hahn 2001), and that such nonsense words may be *more or less* acceptable, to different degrees. For example, Dankovičová et al. (1998) found that allegedly 'impossible' words (such as /ngrɛlin/) and 'possible' words alike were judged acceptable to different degrees (table 9.1). Dankovičová et al. conducted two experiments in which subjects were required to judge the grammaticality of supposedly grammatical and ungrammatical nonsense words. In the first experiment, subjects were given a forced choice between the two possibilities, and in the second they were asked to rate the acceptability of the words on a scale from 1 to 6. Since there were several subjects, the responses in the first experiment can be considered as votes for or against grammaticality. The results from both experiments are similar in showing that, far from being a simple binary category, the acceptability of the words is a gradient variable, whether judged in terms of the number of votes in favour of the grammaticality of a word or higher ratings for those words. Across the set of words used in the experiment, there is a cline or scale of acceptability from X (most acceptable) to Y (least acceptable) (table 9.1).

In a modelling study of the results of these experiments, Coleman and Pierrehumbert (1997) found that the *acceptability ratings are significantly correlated with the (log) probability of the nonsense words*. To get this result, we wrote a simple grammar of bisyllabic words and then estimated the probability of the rules for feet, syllable structure and the frequency of every onset and rime, by counting the frequencies with which those units occur

Table 9.1.

'Ill-formed' items	'Well-formed' items	Mean rating (on a scale from 1–6)
dʒlɔpən		1.333 (the least acceptable ill-formed word)
θʌŋf	ʃələnð	1.958
sŋwɪlpət	splɛtɪsɑk	2
dʒakəmv	ɪŋsmal	2.25
silθslɒt	skwamɒn	2.5
dʒwɒnli	dɪtɔtθ	2.708
mlɪsəri	rɪdɛŋk	3
frɒŋdʒ	skwɪlpət	3.333
wɛbəlg	slɒntʃ	3.5
kilp	sinɪkɔ	3.917
plalsɪti		4.792 (the most acceptable 'ill-formed' word)
	plasɪti	5.708 (the most acceptable 'well-formed word)

in the dictionary. In short, we trained a phonological grammar with probabilities estimated from the dictionary, and found that it can be used to explain the relative acceptability of nonsense words. In additional statistical tests, we also showed that the probabilistic grammar fits the acceptability ratings better than both classical generative grammar and Optimality Theory (see the paper for details).

2. Grammaticality judgements may be uncertain

Even among (supposedly) grammatical words and sentences, a speaker's judgement may be uncertain. For example, most grammatical theories follow Chomsky (1957) in considering 9.4 to be grammatical:

(9.4)   If S1, then S2.

where S1 and S2 are any sentences. Reich (1969) observes that if 9.4 is substituted into itself, the result is decidedly odd:

(9.5)   If if S1, then S2, then S3.

(9.6)   If if if S1, then S2, then S3, then S4.

Are these grammatical? Many people think not, or are not sure. Another example, this time from phonology, is the question of the well-formedness of words such as 'phthistic'. This word starts with a consonant cluster, /fθ/, that is not found in other words. Normally we would say that /fθ/

is not an acceptable word-initial cluster, except for the fact that this word exemplifies it.

What about the following: knish, schmuck, fnug (a brand of quilt), fnac (a French restaurant chain), Khmer Rouge? These all exhibit combinations of phonemes that are essentially limited to these single words. By adding probabilities to a phonological grammar, we would be able to capture the observation to the effect that 'well, /km/ can occur, but it is very rare (whereas /kl/ and /kr/ occur quite frequently)'.

3. Predictability of unfinished sentences

Another fact about language upon which probabilistic grammars may cast some light is our ability to (sometimes) predict what the next word is likely to be. For example:

(9.7)   It was raining cats and . . . [dogs]

(9.8)   I must put some dry clothes . . . [on]

(9.9)   What kind of fool do you take me . . . [for]

(9.10)   What kind of fool do you think I . . . [am]

The predictability of words in certain circumstances, and the fact that people make such predictions during normal conversations, is demonstrated by the frequency of exchanges such as 9.11, in which the two participants, J and R, conclude J's sentence together, at the same time and with the same words (from Local 2003).

(9.11)   J: we're not going to get back till like *(pause)*   Monday morning
         R: *(simultaneously)*   Monday morning

There may, of course, be more than one possible way of finishing an unfinished sentence. For example, 9.10 *could* be concluded:

(9.12)   What kind of fool do you think I resemble?

The point, however, is that we have an ability to estimate, under certain conditions, which word is most likely to occur next *in the mouth of another speaker*. Our ability to make such predictions is an important part of our linguistic competence.

4. Collocations

Collocations (Firth 1951) – 'the company a word keeps' – represent another kind of statistical dependency between words. For example, we say 'put the light *off*' but 'put a candle *out*'.

5. Learnability of grammars

Finally, probabilistic grammars cast light on how rules of grammar (and exceptions, equally) might be learned.

For example, consider the following pairs of rules, that define the structure of some noun phrases, in a number of languages:

(9.13)   (a)   NP → Det N1   (b)   NP → N1 Det

(9.14)   (a)   N1 → Adj N1   (b)   N1 → N1 Adj

(9.15)   (a)   N1 → PP N   (b)   N1 → N PP

Rules 9.13 (a), 9.14 (a) and 9.15 (a) define right-headed structures, whereas 9.13 (b), 9.14 (b) and 9.15 (b) define left-headed structures. In English, determiners and adjectives are on the left ('the old man'), as in 9.13 (a) and 9.14 (a), but prepositional phrases follow the noun, as in 9.15 (b) ('the old man in the park'). In other languages, the opposite orders are possible.

A language learner's task is made considerably easier if they know from the outset that the rules in 9.13–9.15 are the only possibilities to be entertained. The main thing the learner must do is count the number of times that each of the above rules seems to be applicable. For example, in English, rule 9.14 (a) will be applicable in every phrase in which an adjective precedes a noun, whereas in French, rule 9.14 (b) will be applicable where adjectives follow nouns. By counting the frequencies of these rules, the English learner can soon work out that 9.14 (a) is much more representative than 9.14 (b): for the French learner, the opposite comparison holds.

An additional benefit of this approach is that in both English and French the rarer of the pair of rules are not completely unattested, but merely less frequent. For example:

(9.16)   (a)   the president elect
        (b)   a decree absolute
        (c)   some over-the-counter medicines

(9.17)   le vieux château

In 9.16 (a), an adjective derived from a verb, 'elect', follows the noun, exemplifying structure 9.14 (b). The same structure is seen in the legal term 9.16 (b). In 9.16 (c), a prepositional phrase, 'over the counter', precedes the noun. In each case, the phrase is somewhat unusual and might be treated by the speaker as if it were a single lexical entry. This strategy is open to a learner who has inferred that, in English, 9.14 (b) and 9.15 (b) are exceptional structures, an inference that can be made on the basis of the statistics of the use of the rules. Thus, the use of rule frequencies (i.e. probabilities) enables a learner to work out which of a pair of opposite orderings of words is appropriate for the particular language in which a child is brought up.

9.2 Probabilistic context-free grammars

The grammar G1 =

1. S → NP VP
2. NP → Det N
3. VP → VT NP
4. VP → VI PP
5. PP → P NP
6. Det → a

7. N → circle
8. N → square
9. N → triangle
10. VT → touches
11. VI → is
12. P → above
13. P → below

(after Stolcke 1995) encodes some implicit probability assumptions. For example, every derivation of every grammatical sentence will certainly include the application of rule 1. In other words, the probability that rule 1 applies in any sentential derivation is 1. Likewise, the probability that rule 11 applies in the derivation of a sentence containing the word 'is' is 1. The probability that rule 11 applies in the derivation of a sentence not containing 'is' is 0. The probability that either rule 3 or 4 applies is 1, though it is not possible to apportion probabilities to each of these two rules individually. However, if a sentence contains a constituent of type X, some rule with X on the left-hand side must apply, and the probability that one or another of those rules applied is 1. That is, the probabilities of a group of rules with the same left-hand side must sum to 1. Making the null assumption that every rule has the same probability as every other rule with the same left-hand side, we can assign a specific probability to each rule in G1 as follows:

SCFG1 =

1. S → NP VP, $P = 1$
2. NP → Det N, $P = 1$
3. VP → VT NP, $P = \frac{1}{2}$
4. VP → VI PP, $P = \frac{1}{2}$
5. PP → P NP, $P = 1$
6. Det → a, $P = 1$
7. N → circle, $P = \frac{1}{3}$
8. N → square, $P = \frac{1}{3}$
9. N → triangle, $P = \frac{1}{3}$
10. VT → touches, $P = 1$
11. VI → is, $P = 1$
12. P → above, $P = \frac{1}{2}$
13. P → below, $P = \frac{1}{2}$

The probability of each step in a derivation is the probability associated with the rule applied at that step. The probability of a derivation, for example, $S_1 \Rightarrow_{P1} S_2 \Rightarrow_{P2} S_3 \ldots \Rightarrow_{Pn-1} S_n$ is the product of the rule probabilities P_i. For example, consider the following leftmost derivation:

S ⇒ 1
NP VP ⇒ 1
Det NP VP ⇒ 1
a N VP ⇒ 1/3
a circle VP ⇒ 1/2
a circle VT NP ⇒ 1
a circle touches NP ⇒ 1
a circle touches Det N ⇒ 1

Probability of this partial derivation
= P(VP → VT NP) × P(VT → touches)
= $\frac{1}{3} \times \frac{1}{2} \times 1$
= $\frac{1}{6}$

a circle touches a N $\Rightarrow \frac{1}{3}$
a circle touches a square

The probability of deriving a given string x from a particular non-terminal symbol X is the sum of the probabilities of all leftmost derivations producing x from X. For example, the string probability that 'touches a square' is a VP is

$P(\text{VP} \rightarrow \text{VT NP}) \times P(\text{VT} \rightarrow \text{touches}) \times P(\text{NP} \rightarrow \text{Det N}) \times P(\text{Det} \rightarrow \text{a})$
$\qquad \times P(\text{N} \rightarrow \text{square})$
$\qquad = \frac{1}{2} \times 1 \times 1 \times 1 \times \frac{1}{3}$
$\qquad = \frac{1}{6}$

(The sum has only one term in this case, because the string is unambiguous, hence there is only one leftmost derivation.)

The particular case of sentence probability (i.e. where $X = S$) applies to complete sentences and sentential forms alike:

Sentence probability of 'a circle touches NP' $= 1 \times 1 \times 1 \times \frac{1}{3} \times \frac{1}{2}$
$\qquad \times 1 = \frac{1}{6}$
Sentence probability of 'a circle VP' $= 1 \times 1 \times 1 \times \frac{1}{3} = \frac{1}{3}$
Sentence probability of 'a circle touches a square' $= 1 \times 1 \times 1 \times \frac{1}{3}$
$\qquad \times \frac{1}{2} \times 1 \times 1 \times 1 \times \frac{1}{3} = 1/18.$

Note that not all sentences defined by this grammar are equally probable: all 9 sentence of the form 'a N touches a N' have probability $P = 1/18$, whereas all 18 sentences of the form 'a N is P a N' have $P = 1/36$. (This grammar defines 27 sentences.) The sum of all the sentence probabilities is 1.

9.3 Estimation of rule probabilities

In order to create and use a probabilistic grammar, two questions arise: (1) What is the set of rules? (2) What probability should be given to each rule?

As with non-probabilistic grammars, there are two approaches to settling the set of rules: the rules may be written 'by hand', according to the analysis of a grammarian, or they may be inferred from a corpus. The corpus may be simply a large body of texts, or it may have been subject to a degree of prior analysis, such as bracketing of phrases, or part-of-speech tagging. Such analysis may be performed by hand, though nowadays computational linguists working on corpora usually make extensive use of software to at least assist in such marking-up of texts.

There are also automatic methods for inferring probabilistic grammars from a text corpus. If the grammar is in a restricted form, such as Chomsky Normal Form, or $\bar{\text{X}}$ form, it is even possible to include every possible rule in the grammar, and let probability estimation take care of the fact that some of the rule possibilities are unattested (Pereira and Schabes 1992). Another approach is to use all of the phrase structures found in a hand-parsed machine-readable corpus. Note that it is not problematic to include as many 'special case' low-frequency rules as may be needed.

The probability estimate associated with each rule is then determined by counting how many times the rule in question is used in a corpus and dividing the result by the number of distinct rule applications needed to parse the entire corpus.

A probabilistic grammar created in this way will be a good model of the language of the corpus on which it has been trained. In most applications, however, this is not enough: usually, we want to be able to analyse sentences that are *not* in the corpus. Since the set of sentences (and their structures) outside the corpus is actually much larger than the set of sentences and structures in the corpus, the probabilities of rules and sentence structures estimated from the corpus will in general be too high. For example, the sum of the probabilities of all the sentences in the corpus will be 1, which amounts to a claim that no other sentences are possible! Likewise, the sum of the probabilities of all the (correct) sentence structures will be 1, which amounts to a claim that no other analyses of those sentences are possible. This is also too strong a claim, as many sentences are structurally ambiguous: even though some of those other possible analyses are incorrect in the context of the corpus, they are possibly correct in some other circumstance, and are in any case certainly grammatical. It is therefore necessary to 'massage' the rule probabilities estimated from the corpus downwards, that is, to reduce them all by a small amount, in order to allow nonzero probabilities for sentences and structures not in the corpus.

In particular, the possibility of *recursion* in generative grammars means that many possible sentences can be generated that are outside a particular corpus. For example, consider a grammar appropriate for a corpus consisting of the following sentences:

The man runs.
The woman runs.
The old man runs.
The old woman runs.
The old, old man runs.
The old, old woman runs.

SCFG2 =

1. $S \rightarrow NP\ VP$, $P = 1$
2. $NP \rightarrow Det\ N$, $P = 1$
3. $VP \rightarrow V$, $P = 1$
4. $Det \rightarrow the$, $P = 1$
5. $N \rightarrow man$, $P = \frac{1}{4}$
6. $N \rightarrow woman$, $P = \frac{1}{4}$
7. $N \rightarrow Adj\ N$, $P = \frac{1}{2}$
8. $Adj \rightarrow old$, $P = 1$
9. $V \rightarrow runs$, $P = 1$

For all the rules apart from 5, 6 and 7, there is only one alternative: hence their probabilities are 1. Rules 5, 6 and 7, though, show three ways in which an N may be expanded. To estimate the probabilities of each of these rules, we count how many times each rule occurs in the structural analyses of the corpus:

Sentence	Rule 5 occurrences	Rule 6 occurrences	Rule 7 occurrences
The man runs.	1	0	0
The woman runs.	0	1	0
The old man runs.	1	0	1
The old woman runs.	0	1	1
The old, old man runs.	1	0	2
The old, old woman runs.	0	1	2
Totals	3	3	6

Even though rule 7 is not used for two of the six sentences in the corpus, the probabilities of the two rules are used an equal number of times, due to the fact that rule 7 is used twice in the fifth and sixth sentences. Therefore, the probability of rules 5 and 6 is 1/4, and the probability of rule 7 is 1/2. The probability of 'The old, old man runs', therefore, is calculated as

$$P(S \rightarrow NP\ VP) \times P(NP \rightarrow Det\ N) \times P(Det \rightarrow the) \times P(N \rightarrow Adj\ N) \times P(Adj \rightarrow old)$$
$$\times\ P(N \rightarrow Adj\ N) \times P(Adj \rightarrow old) \times P(N \rightarrow man)$$
$$\times\ P(V \rightarrow runs)$$
$$= 1 \times 1 \times 1 \times \tfrac{1}{2} \times 1 \times \tfrac{1}{2} \times 1 \times \tfrac{1}{4} \times 1 \times 1$$
$$= 1/16$$

The probabilities assigned by this grammar to the other sentences in the corpus are as follows:

Sentence	P
The man runs.	1/4
The woman runs.	1/4
The old man runs.	1/8
The old woman runs.	1/8
The old, old man runs.	1/16
The old, old woman runs.	1/16

There are two things to note about these probability estimates. First, they do not correspond to the observed probability of each sentence in the corpus, 1/6. Second, the probabilities become exponentially smaller as adjectives are repeated. Third, they sum to 7/8, not 1, which implies that some other sentences are possible given this grammar. That is indeed correct:

'the old, old, old man runs' is also grammatical (and will be assigned a computed probability of 1/32).

Just as we saw in chapter 7, on Hidden Markov Models, we can ask: are these rule probability estimates optimal? Here, 'optimal' means that for sentences in as well as outside the corpus, do the computed probabilities accurately reflect the observed likelihood of the sentences (and/or their structural analyses)?

We can account for productive rule interaction by re-estimating rule probabilities in the light of computed corpus sentence probabilities using the inside-outside algorithm (Lari and Young 1990).

9.4 A practical example

In order to develop a probabilistic context-free parser, at least the following three resources are needed:

1. A (non-probabilistic) context-free grammar
2. A lexicon, in which each word is assigned to one or more parts of speech
3. A corpus of text, from which rule probabilities may be learned

It may be helpful if, instead of a text corpus, a treebank is available. (A treebank is a hand-parsed corpus; as the name suggests, it takes the form of a set of analysis trees.) Failing that, it may be good enough to make our own database of analysis trees, by using the grammar to parse all the sentences in the corpus.

To illustrate the method of training a probabilistic context-free grammar, let's go back to the miniature grammar presented in section 9.2. This can easily be translated into a Prolog DCG, as in listing 9.1.

Listing 9.1

```
/* stolcke_grammar1.pl */
/* (after Stolcke 1995) */

s --> np, vp.
np --> det, n.                                              5
vp --> vt, np.
vp --> vi, pp.
pp --> p, np.

det --> [a].                                               10
n --> [circle].
n --> [square].
n --> [triangle].
vt --> [touches].
vi --> [is].                                               15
p --> [above].
p --> [below].
```

In section 9.3 we assumed that where there was more than one rule with the same left-hand side, the rules were equally probable. In training a grammar, however, we make no such assumption. Instead, we observe the actual frequency with which each rule is used in parsing the training corpus. Suppose, for example, that in the world of shapes described by the sentences of this language, some situations were not encountered. First, suppose that circles tend not to occur in pairs. In that case, sentences such as 'a circle touches a circle' are unlikely. Therefore, we'll leave them out of the training set. Second, suppose that when two squares occur, they tend to touch one another side-to-side. Therefore, the sentences 'a square is above/below a square' are unlikely, and we'll leave them out of the training set. The training set will therefore consist of the following 22 sentences:

```
[a, circle, touches, a, square]
[a, circle, touches, a, triangle]
[a, circle, is, above, a, square]
[a, circle, is, above, a, triangle]
[a, circle, is, below, a, square]
[a, circle, is, below, a, triangle]
[a, square, touches, a, circle]
[a, square, touches, a, square]
[a, square, touches, a, triangle]
[a, square, is, above, a, circle]
[a, square, is, above, a, square]
[a, square, is, above, a, triangle]
[a, square, is, below, a, circle]
[a, square, is, below, a, square]
[a, square, is, below, a, triangle]
[a, triangle, touches, a, circle]
[a, triangle, touches, a, square]
[a, triangle, touches, a, triangle]
[a, triangle, is, above, a, circle]
[a, triangle, is, above, a, square]
[a, triangle, is, above, a, triangle]
[a, triangle, is, below, a, circle]
[a, triangle, is, below, a, square]
[a, triangle, is, below, a, triangle]
```

These sentences are given in the format required by the DCG. To parse 'a circle touches a square', for instance, we can use the query:

```
?- s([a, circle, touches, a, square],[]).
```

In order to count the number of times each rule is used in parsing the training set, it is helpful to assign it a rule number. It is easy to modify the grammar so that when a rule is used it also assembles a list of rule numbers, consisting of its own rule number followed by the rule number lists gathered up by its daughter symbols. For example, we can recast the first rule as follows:

```
s(D1) --> np(D2), vp(D3),
     {append3([1],D2,D3,D1)}.
```

For pre-terminal rules, no appending is necessary. For example:

```
det([6]) --> [a].
```

The predicate `append3` is defined in listing 9.2:

Listing 9.2

```
append3(A,B,C,D):-
    append(A,B,X),
    append(X,C,D).

append([],X,X).
append([H|T],X,[H|T2]):- append(T,X,T2).
```

A complete version of this grammar is given in the file `stolcke_grammar2.pl`. Using it, we can present parse queries such as:

```
s(D,[a, circle, touches, a, square],[]).
```

and obtain the response:

```
D = [1, 2, 6, 7, 3, 10, 2, 6, 8]
```

which tells us which rules are used to define the sentence and its structure. Such a sequence of rule numbers is sometimes called the deriva-tional history of the sentence. If we parse the entire training set in this way, we will obtain the following set of derivational histories:

Training sentences	Derivational histories
a circle touches a square	[1, 2, 6, 7, 3, 10, 2, 6, 8]
a circle touches a triangle	[1, 2, 6, 7, 3, 10, 2, 6, 9]
a circle is above a square	[1, 2, 6, 7, 4, 11, 5, 12, 2, 6, 8]
a circle is above a triangle	[1, 2, 6, 7, 4, 11, 5, 12, 2, 6, 9]
a circle is below a square	[1, 2, 6, 7, 4, 11, 5, 13, 2, 6, 8]
a circle is below a triangle	[1, 2, 6, 7, 4, 11, 5, 13, 2, 6, 9]
a square touches a circle	[1, 2, 6, 8, 3, 10, 2, 6, 7]
a square touches a square	[1, 2, 6, 8, 3, 10, 2, 6, 8]
a square touches a triangle	[1, 2, 6, 8, 3, 10, 2, 6, 9]
a square is above a circle	[1, 2, 6, 8, 4, 11, 5, 12, 2, 6, 7]
a square is above a triangle	[1, 2, 6, 8, 4, 11, 5, 12, 2, 6, 9]
a square is below a circle	[1, 2, 6, 8, 4, 11, 5, 13, 2, 6, 7]
a square is below a triangle	[1, 2, 6, 8, 4, 11, 5, 13, 2, 6, 9]
a triangle touches a circle	[1, 2, 6, 9, 3, 10, 2, 6, 7]

Training sentences	Derivational histories
a triangle touches a square	[1, 2, 6, 9, 3, 10, 2, 6, 8]
a triangle touches a triangle	[1, 2, 6, 9, 3, 10, 2, 6, 9]
a triangle is above a circle	[1, 2, 6, 9, 4, 11, 5, 12, 2, 6, 7]
a triangle is above a square	[1, 2, 6, 9, 4, 11, 5, 12, 2, 6, 8]
a triangle is above a triangle	[1, 2, 6, 9, 4, 11, 5, 12, 2, 6, 9]
a triangle is below a circle	[1, 2, 6, 9, 4, 11, 5, 13, 2, 6, 7]
a triangle is below a square	[1, 2, 6, 9, 4, 11, 5, 13, 2, 6, 8]
a triangle is below a triangle	[1, 2, 6, 9, 4, 11, 5, 13, 2, 6, 9]

Next, we must count the number of times each rule occurs in the derivational histories. For a small grammar and training corpus, that can be done by hand, though for a more realistically sized grammar and training corpus, it will be necessary to count the rule numbers using software. In this case, the counts are as follows:

Rule number	Count
1	22
2	44
3	8
4	14
5	14
6	44
7	12
8	14
9	18
10	8
11	14
12	7
13	7

These counts must then be translated into rule probabilities. For rules 1, 2, 5, 6, 10 and 11, this is easy: since each of those rules specifies the only way a given symbol can be expanded, their probabilities are all 1, as in SCFG1, even though their counts are different:

1. $S \rightarrow NP\ VP$, $P = 22/22 = 1$
2. $NP \rightarrow Det\ N$, $P = 44/44 = 1$

5. PP → P NP,   P = 44/44 = 1
6. Det → a,   P = 44/44 = 1
10. VT → touches,   P = 8/8 = 1
11. VI → is,   P = 14/14 = 1

Rules 3 and 4, however, define two different VP structures. The number of times either 3 or 4 is used is 22, but as rule 3 is used 8 times and rule 4 is used 14 times, their probabilities are not equal:

3. VP → VT NP,   P = 8/22 ≈ 0.364
4. VP → VI PP,   P = 14/22 ≈ 0.636

This reflects the fact that there are more sentences that mention the spatial relationships 'is above/below' than those using the verb 'touches'. Note that 0.364 + 0.636 = 1, meaning that either one or the other of these rules must certainly be used (P = 1) in a sentence containing a VP.

Similarly, there are 44 instances of nouns in the training set, but the 3 different nouns are used with different usage frequencies. 'Circle' (and hence, rule 7) occurs 12 times, 'square' 14 times and 'triangle' 18 times. Thus the rule probabilities are:

7. N → circle,   P = 12/44 ≈ 0.273
8. N → square,   P = 14/44 ≈ 0.318
9. N → triangle,   P = 18/44 ≈ 0.409

This means that the word 'triangle' occurs more often than 'square', which in turn occurs more often than 'circle'. Note that the observed probabilities of rules 3, 4 and 7–9 are different from the equal probabilities assumed earlier. The two prepositions occur equally often (7 times each, 14 times in total) so their probabilities are equal:

12. P → above,   P = 7/14 = 0.5
13. P → below,   P = 7/14 = 0.5

We can now use these probabilities in a third version of the original grammar (listing 9.3).

Listing 9.3 A probabilistic DCG

```
/* stolcke_grammar3.pl */

s(P) --> np(P1), vp(P2),
     {P is 1 * P1 * P2}.
np(P) --> det(P1), n(P2),
     {P is 1 * P1 * P2}.                              5
vp(P) --> vt(P1), np(P2),
     {P is 0.364 * P1 * P2}.
vp(P) --> vi(P1), pp(P2),
     {P is 0.636 * P1 * P2}.                          10
pp(P) --> p(P1), np(P2),
     {P is 1 * P1 * P2}.
```

```
det(1) --> [a].
n(0.273) --> [circle].                                          15
n(0.318) --> [square].
n(0.409) --> [triangle].
vt(1) --> [touches].
vi(1) --> [is].
p(0.5) --> [above].                                             20
p(0.5) --> [below].
```

Here, we have dispensed with the rule numbering once again, instead adding a mechanism for calculating the running product of the probabilities associated with the use of each rule. In general, a rule of the form:

$$a \rightarrow b\ c, P$$

can be encoded as a DCG rule of the form:

```
a(P) --> b(P1), c(P2),
       {P is p * P1 * P2}.
```

where the variables P1 and P2 will in turn store the running probabilities calculated from the rules used in parsing phrases b and c.

Finally, we can use such a probabilistic grammar to determine the probabilities of its parses, using queries such as s(P,[a,circle, touches,a,circle],[]). The language defined by this grammar is small enough that we can do this for all of its sentences, even those that were not in the training set (these are marked with a question mark in the following list):

?a circle touches a circle	P = 0.027129
a circle touches a square	P = 0.0316
a circle touches a triangle	P = 0.040643
?a circle is above a circle	P = 0.0237
a circle is above a square	P = 0.027607
a circle is above a triangle	P = 0.035507
?a circle is below a circle	P = 0.0237
a circle is below a square	P = 0.027607
a circle is below a triangle	P = 0.035507
a square touches a circle	P = 0.0316
a square touches a square	P = 0.036809
a square touches a triangle	P = 0.047343
a square is above a circle	P = 0.027607
?a square is above a square	P = 0.032157
a square is above a triangle	P = 0.04136
a square is below a circle	P = 0.027607
?a square is below a square	P = 0.032157
a square is below a triangle	P = 0.04136
a triangle touches a circle	P = 0.040643
a triangle touches a square	P = 0.047343
a triangle touches a triangle	P = 0.06089
a triangle is above a circle	P = 0.035507

```
a triangle is above a square       P = 0.04136
a triangle is above a triangle     P = 0.053195
a triangle is below a circle       P = 0.035507
a triangle is below a square       P = 0.04136
a triangle is below a triangle     P = 0.053195
```

This example demonstrates one of the important and useful properties of probabilistic grammars: *the ability to estimate the probability of sentences that are not in the training database*, on the basis of the probabilities of its words and phrases, which *are* in the training set. For example, the probabilities of the three sentences:

```
a square is below a circle         P = 0.027607
a square is below a square         P = 0.032157
a square is below a triangle       P = 0.04136
```

reflects the fact that the word 'square' is less frequent than 'triangle' but more frequent than 'circle'. (Estimation of probabilities for sentences with words or structures that are not exemplified at all in the training set is a separate, more difficult, problem, but not by any means intractable.)

9.5 A limitation of probabilistic context-free grammars

The parameters of a stochastic context-free grammar do not correspond directly to a distribution over words since distributional phenomena over words that are embodied by the application of more than one context-free rule cannot be captured under the context-freeness assumption. (Schabes 1992)

For example, Bod (1998: 35) refers to sentences of the form 'DET emaciated N starved' (e.g. 'the emaciated man starved'), in which there is a statistical dependency between 'emaciated' and 'starved'. (We expect, for example, that sentences of this form will occur more frequently than 'DET emaciated N was fat'. This is a statistical fact that does not require us — or the computer — to understand the semantic relationship between the words 'emaciated' and 'starve'.) The statistical dependency is not captured in a context-free grammar; not even in a probabilistic context-free grammar. Its structure would most likely be described by rules very similar to those of SCFG2, for example:

1. S → NP VP
2. NP → Det N
3. VP → V
4. Det → the
5. N → man
6. N → Adj N
7. Adj → emaciated
8. V → starved
9. V → was fat

There is no connection in this grammar between rules 7 and 8. Consider the following derivation:

S ⇒
NP VP ⇒
Det N VP ⇒
the N VP ⇒
the Adj N VP ⇒
the emaciated N VP ⇒
the emaciated man VP ⇒
the emaciated man V ⇒

At this point in the derivation, the choice of whether to replace V by 'starved' or 'was fat' is open: the derivational mechanism of a context-free grammar cannot 'look backwards' to see what rules have been used previously.

For another example, consider the idioms 'kick the bucket' (meaning 'die') and 'bury the hatchet' (meaning 'make peace'). These have the structure shown in figure 9.1. According to a context-free grammar, 'kick the hatchet' and 'bury the bucket' are also grammatical (which is fine). However, it would be nice to capture the statistical dependencies between 'kick' and 'bucket', on the one hand, and 'bury' and 'hatchet', on the other. Note that these dependencies are also found in the modified idioms 'kick the proverbial bucket' and 'bury the proverbial hatchet'.

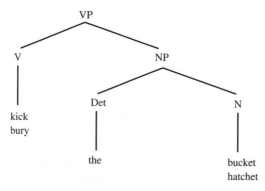

FIGURE 9.1
Structure of some idioms

9.6 Tree adjoining grammars

These and related considerations have prompted a number of computational linguists to consider grammar formalisms in which much larger chunks of sentence structure are taken as primitives. One of the most influential proposals along these lines is the tree adjoining grammar (TAG) formalism (e.g. Joshi 1985). In this approach, sentence structures are made by combining tree fragments, using two operations: *substitution* and *adjunction*. To illustrate substitution, consider an analysis of the sentence 'He kicked the bucket.' We propose a grammar of three tree fragments (figure 9.2), which can be joined together by substituting root nodes of tree fragments by non-terminal leaf nodes of other fragments.

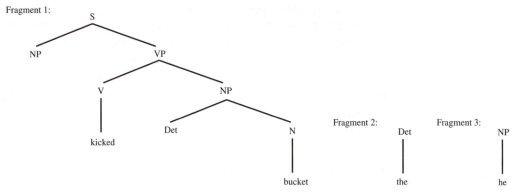

FIGURE 9.2
Fragments of the parse tree of an idiom

By substituting fragment (3) for the initial NP node of (1), and fragment (2) for the Det node, we derive the complete tree shown in figure 9.3.

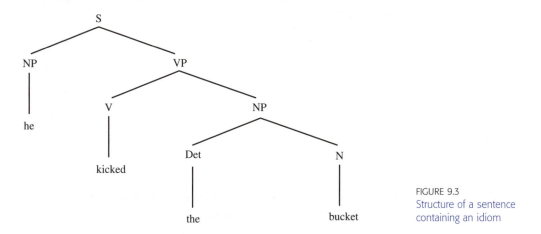

FIGURE 9.3
Structure of a sentence containing an idiom

A tree adjoining grammar that only uses substitution is weakly equivalent to a context-free grammar. To see this, note that each tree fragment can be summarized using a context-free rule in which the root node is the left-hand side of the rule and the sequence of leaf nodes are written as the right-hand side. Thus, the three tree fragments given above can be summarized with the three rules:

TAG-CFG:
1. S → NP kicked Det bucket
2. Det → the
3. NP → he

But consider the modified idiom 'kick the *proverbial* bucket' (Shieber and Schabes 1990). 'Proverbial' is an adjective that is inserted as a modifier to the noun 'bucket'. There is no easy way to do that using the grammar just given, as there is no reference to an adjective position in rule 1 of TAG-CFG.

Of course, we could break rule 1 up into five smaller pieces, as in CFG2, and add the rule 'N → Adj N', but then we would lose the dependency between 'kick' and 'bucket' that is successfully captured in rule 1, above:

CFG2:
S → NP VP
VP → V NP
V → kicked
NP → Det N
N → bucket

There is a way round this problem, which I leave as an exercise:

Exercise 9.1.
Amend rule 1 so that it contains an adjective position. How do we capture the fact that the adjective is not obligatory?

The second operation of TAGs, adjunction, breaks a tree fragment into two parts at a given node, and inserts another tree fragment between those two parts. For example, we can adjoin tree fragment 4 to fragment 1 as in figure 9.4.

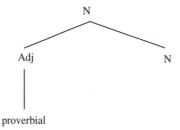

FIGURE 9.4
Fragment 4

First, we split fragment 1 into two parts either side of the N node, duplicating the N node in the process (figure 9.5).

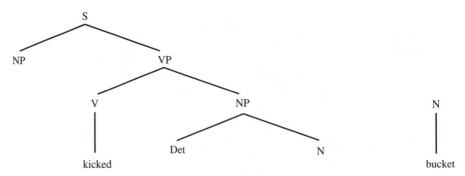

FIGURE 9.5
Left: fragment 1a; right: fragment 1b

Next, we substitute the root N of fragment 4 for the leaf N of fragment 1a, to produce the structure shown in figure 9.6.

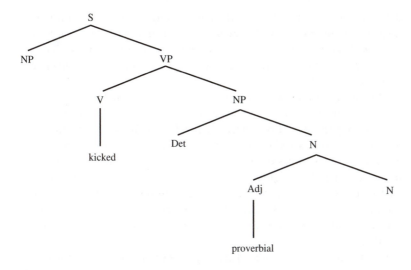

FIGURE 9.6

Finally, we substitute the root N of fragment 1b for the newly added leaf N, giving the finished structure (figure 9.7).

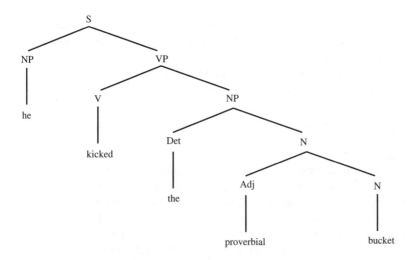

FIGURE 9.7
Structure of a modified idiomatic sentence

(The order of the two substitutions does not make any difference to the outcome.) This use of adjunction enables us to derive the 'extended' idiom from the 'basic' pattern. Although the derivation involves the insertion of material between 'kicked' and 'bucket', we do not lose the distributional (collocational) relationship between those two words, since they are linked together in fragment 1.

9.7 Data-oriented parsing

Let's finish the book with a quick look at data-oriented parsing, an extension of tree adjoining grammar proposed by Bod (1998) that completely dispenses with grammar rules. The idea is to use a corpus of syntax trees instead of grammar rules. The trees in the corpus are broken up into sub-trees, which can be put together again in the same ways as in tree adjoining grammar. These sub-trees can then be used to parse sentences that aren't in the original corpus.

Of course, a given corpus can be broken up into sub-trees in an enormous variety of ways. If every possible fragment of every tree were allowed, parsing would be extremely inefficient. To get round this, Bod examines various ways of constraining the approach. For example, it is possible to place limits on, say, how deep a tree fragment can be, or to insist that each tree fragment includes a word (i.e. it is not just a piece of structure). More importantly, though, the method is probabilistic: once the corpus has been broken up into pieces, each piece is associated with a probability of its use, according to how many times that piece appears in the corpus.

The attraction of data-oriented parsing comes from the following features:

1. Like TAG, it can cope with, e.g., idioms, and other collocational dependencies, as discussed in previous sections.
2. As it is probabilistic, it can model parsing preferences, word-frequency biases etc.
3. As it is corpus-based, it is not necessary to craft a set of rules (or basic trees) by hand. The structural inventory of a grammar is derived by chopping up the corpus.
4. Finally, and perhaps most importantly, it is not difficult to implement, and is quite an accurate and efficient parsing method.

Chapter summary

We began this chapter by considering evidence for the idea that grammaticality is gradient, that is, sentences (and words) are *more or less* grammatical, not simply grammatical or not. We showed how probabilistic grammars can be used to capture this idea, by modelling degrees of grammaticality on the basis of usage frequencies. We saw how the simple DCG parsing technique of the previous chapter can easily be extended to incorporate rule probabilities. We ended by examining two recent and sophisticated grammatical frameworks developed in computational linguistics: tree adjoining grammar and data-oriented parsing.

Conclusion and suggestions for further reading

In this book, we have examined a wide range of methods and ideas in speech and language processing. Throughout, I have provided working example programs, and I have attempted to keep the technical details to a minimum, focussing instead on key ideas. However, if you continue with this subject, it is now time to start to set your sights higher, and get to grips with some more technical works. Various references have been given throughout the book, in relation to specific topics. You should now be ready to turn to some of the following, in particular, depending on your specific needs or interest.

C programming: Kernighan and Ritchie 1988; Press et al. 1992.

Digital signal processing in C: Embree and Kimble 1991; Press et al. 1992.

The Klatt synthesiser: Klatt 1980; Klatt and Klatt 1990.

Speech recognition: Rabiner and Juang 1993; Waibel and Lee 1990; Huang et al. 2001.

Prolog programming: Clocksin and Mellish 2003; Sterling and Shapiro 1994.

Computational linguistics: Jurafsky and Martin 2000.

Probabilistic grammars: Sampson 2001; Jurafsky and Martin 2000; Charniak 1993; Bod 1998; Manning and Schütze 1999; Bod et al. 2003.

The American Standard Code for Information Interchange (ASCII)

For most purposes, you can think of the code as simply a standard assignment of some numbers to keys on the computer keyboard. Thus, when you type a capital 'A' on the keyboard, it is converted to the number 65, as far as the computer is concerned. As well as all the letters and numbers, there are 16 'control codes', that is, combinations formed by holding down the 'Control' key (often labelled 'Ctrl') and a letter key simultaneously (code numbers 0 to 15). Many of these have special meanings, according to the code. Thus, if your 'Tab' key doesn't work, 'Ctrl-I' ought to work instead!

The codes are also used for the computer's output to, for example, your monitor or a printer. For example, when the computer sends code 37 to a terminal or printer, the percent sign will be displayed or printed. Sending code 8 to a terminal makes it bleep, whereas sending code 10 moves the printer or terminal output down on to the next line.

Key	(Decimal) code number	'Official' meaning	Key	Decimal code	Key	Decimal code	Key	Decimal code
Ctrl-@	0	Null character	Space	32	@	64	`	96
Ctrl-A	1	Start of heading	!	33	A	65	a	97
Ctrl-B	2	Start of text	"	34	B	66	b	98
Ctrl-C	3	End of text	#	35	C	67	c	99
Ctrl-D	4	End of transmission	$	36	D	68	d	100
Ctrl-E	5	Enquiry	%	37	E	69	e	101
Ctrl-F	6	Acknowledge	&	38	F	70	f	102
Ctrl-G	7	Bell (beep)	'	39	G	71	g	103
Ctrl-H	8	Backspace	(	40	H	72	h	104
Ctrl-I	9	Horizontal tab	)	41	I	73	i	105
Ctrl-J	10	Line feed	*	42	J	74	j	106
Ctrl-K	11	Vertical tab	+	43	K	75	k	107
Ctrl-L	12	Form feed	,	44	L	76	l	108
Ctrl-M	13	Carriage return	-	45	M	77	m	109
Ctrl-N	14	Shift out	.	46	N	78	n	110
Ctrl-O	15	Shift in	/	47	O	79	o	111
Ctrl-P	16	Data link escape	0	48	P	80	p	112
Ctrl-Q	17	(Device control 1) Xmit ON	1	49	Q	81	q	113
Ctrl-R	18	Device control 2	2	50	R	82	r	114
Ctrl-S	19	(Device control 3) Xmit off	3	51	S	83	s	115
Ctrl-T	20	Device control 4	4	52	T	84	t	116
Ctrl-U	21	Negative acknowledge	5	53	U	85	u	117
Ctrl-V	22	Synchronous idle	6	54	V	86	v	118
Ctrl-W	23	End of transmission block	7	55	W	87	w	119
Ctrl-X	24	Cancel	8	56	X	88	x	120
Ctrl-Y	25	End of medium	9	57	Y	89	y	121
Ctrl-Z	26	Substitute	:	58	Z	90	z	122
Ctrl-[	27	Escape	;	59	[	91	{	123
Ctrl-\	28	File separator	<	60	\	92			124
Ctrl-]	29	Group separator	=	61	]	93	}	125
Ctrl-^	30	Record separator	>	62	^	94	~	126
Ctrl-_	31	Unit separator	?	63	_	95	Delete	127

Glossary

Abstract machine: A theoretical, rather than physical, computer; for example, an **automaton.**

Accept: If a sequence of symbols can be read by an automaton with the result that the automaton ends up in an end state, the automaton is said to accept the string. When a string is acceptable by an automaton, the string is grammatical or well formed, according to the automaton.

Address: A number referring to a particular cell of an **array.** In computer hardware, each memory cell also has an address. For a two-dimensional table, the address of a cell could be a two-dimensional coordinate. In C, for example, we could write a [5] [7] to refer to the cell in the sixth row and eighth column of matrix a (sixth and eighth because the first row and the first column are numbered 0).

Array: A data structure for tables or matrices. Typically, an array contains multiple instances of the same data type. Each instance is stored in one cell of the array. A one-dimensional array is good for the storage of a sequence of numbers, such as a signal.

Autocorrelation: A set of measurements showing how similar one portion of a signal is to earlier or later portions. A roughly periodic signal of frequency f (and hence period $T = 1/f$) is very similar to itself at earlier and later times T, $2T$, $3T$ etc. By calculating the degree of self-similarity at different estimates of T, it is possible to find the T corresponding to the fundamental frequency of the signal. For voiced speech signals, this corresponds to the frequency of voicing: informally called the 'pitch' of the voice.

Automaton (sg.), automata (pl.): Originally, the term 'automaton' meant a mechanical toy or a clockwork ornament that could perform a fixed sequence of actions according to a program encoded on a metal drum or disk with pins or holes in it. In computer science, an automaton is an abstract machine: a theoretical computer that can go through a series of 'moves' from one state to another, according to a program encoded in a table or written on an (imaginary) 'tape'.

Average: The average value of a signal usually means the arithmetic mean (i.e. the sum of all the samples, divided by the number of samples).

Back-off: A grammar may be unable to parse a certain sequence of symbols, because that sequence was not included in the data from which the grammar was constructed, or because it lacks appropriate rules. Rather than declaring such a string to be ungrammatical, a probabilistic grammar assigns it a very low probability, lower than the least probable observed string. In order to do this, it may employ a small number of very general 'catch-all' rules that allow any string to be parsed. In particular, in trigram-based Markov models (including Hidden Markov Models) it is customary to use bigram or unigram probabilities to estimate the probability of previously unseen trigrams.

Backtracking: A computer program is non-deterministic if, at any point in the execution of the program, there is more than one possible way of proceeding. Since actual computers are all deterministic machines, a decision must be made about which way the program should go next. However that choice is made, if it turns out to be wrong, or to lead up a blind alley, it will be necessary for the computer to go back to the point at which the choice was made, and try out the other possibilities. Returning to the choice point is called *backtracking*. Also, if both possible ways forward give different 'right answers', and we want to find all of the outcomes of a program, backtracking can be used to make sure that all the possibilities are covered.

Bakis model: Also known as a 'left-to-right' model, a Bakis model is a Markov model in which the state sequence is ordered. Although it is permitted to remain in a state, or to hop over certain states, it is prohibited from jumping backwards to an earlier state. This kind of model is most appropriate for modelling processes in which there is a definite 'flow of time', or chains of cause-and-effect between earlier and later events.

Band pass filter: See **filter.**

Bandwidth: A peak in a spectrum (e.g. the peak corresponding to a resonant frequency of the vocal tract) may be wider or narrower. In order to quantify the 'width' of a peak, it is customary to measure the range of frequencies the peak spans at an amplitude that is 6 dB below the maximum.

Big endian: When a 16-bit binary number is stored as a pair of bytes, there are two different possible conventions for ordering the bytes. In the 'big endian' convention, the higher 8 bits (i.e. bits 9–16) are stored before the lower 8 bits. In the 'little endian' convention, the lower 8 bits are stored before the higher 8 bits. (The terms 'big endian' and 'little endian' derive from Jonathan Swift's *Travels into Several Remote Nations of the World, by Lemuel Gulliver,* in which the island of Lilliput had suffered six civil rebellions against an Imperial edict concerning the correct way of breaking open a boiled egg.)

Bigram: A sequence of two symbols, e.g. words or letters, depending on the application.

Binary numbers: Whereas the decimal number system that we ordinarily use has ten digits (0 to 9) and a place notation based on powers of ten (units, tens, hundreds, thousands etc.), binary numbers are made with just two 'digits' — **bits** — (0 and 1). Its place notation employs powers of 2, so that, for example, binary 1101 means (reading from right to left) 1 unit, 0 twos, 1 four and 1 eight, i.e. $1 + 4 + 8 = 13$.

Bit: A binary 'digit', i.e. 0 or 1. The term digit is not quite appropriate, as it means 'finger' in Latin. We normally have ten fingers, of course!

Blackboard architecture: An approach to knowledge-based speech recognition in which various measurements or hypotheses concerning the content of a speech signal are stored in a data structure (the 'blackboard') that makes information from all levels of linguistic structure available to other components of the recognition process. It is an attempt to break out of the division between 'top-down' and 'bottom-up' approaches.

Bottom-up parsing: In bottom-up parsing, structures are built by successively combining symbols (words or letters) from the input into larger and larger expressions.

Breadth-first parsing: See **depth-first parsing**.

Butterworth filter: A design of filter, based upon Butterworth polynomials, named after the British engineer who invented this type of filter. Originally constructed in electronic hardware, the term is now more frequently applied to their digital implementation.

Byte: **A binary number** consisting of eight bits: 1s, 2s, 4s, 8s, 16s, 32s, 64s and 128s. The greatest binary number that can be expressed as one byte is thus 1111 1111, i.e. $1 + 2 + 4 + 8 + 16 + 32 + 64 + 128 = 255$. To represent larger numbers, it is necessary to use more bytes. The capacity of computer memories is measured in bytes (kilobytes, megabytes and gigabytes).

C pre-processor: A program that is applied as the first step in compiling a C program. The pre-processor expands any macros that the programmer may have used for brevity, and replaces any #include statements by the file to which they refer, e.g. to include a **library file** in the compilation process.

Cascade (of finite-state transducers): Suppose you have three transducers, one that translates between Chinese characters and alphabetic (e.g. roman) letters, one that maps roman letters onto Chinese phonemes, and one that maps Chinese phonemes into sounds. This *cascade* of transducers can be automatically combined into one big transducer that maps Chinese characters directly into sounds.

CELP (Code-book excited linear prediction): A method for improving the quality of **linear prediction** synthesis, in which a broad repertoire of source samples (pitch pulses and noise bursts) is stored. Each such sample is given a code number; a sequence of code numbers represents a complex, rather detailed synthetic imitation of the sound source. Instead of transmitting speech (e.g. over a telephone network), it suffices to send a sequence of source code numbers and the associated predictor coefficients in order to resynthesize a quite believable imitation of speech at the receiver's end.

Centre embedding: In centre-embedding constructions, a clause or phrase is incorporated into another. For example: 'the cat ate the rat' can be embedded in the interior of 'the rat ate the malt' to yield 'the rat [that the cat ate] ate the malt'. In contrast, 'this is the cat that chased the rat [that ate the malt]' has an embedded clause at the end. Centre-embedded structures are harder to parse than those with embedding at the end (or the beginning).

Cepstral analysis: A method for decomposing a spectrum into **harmonics** and resonant frequencies.

Cepstrum: The inverse Fourier transform of the log power spectral density (roughly, the spectrum of a spectrum). The cepstrum shows the amplitude of the signal at different time intervals (corresponding to different frequencies). The low frequency harmonics are at one end of the time scale, and the higher frequency resonances are at the other end.

Chart parsing: Chart parsing stores all well-formed substrings that are found during the parsing process in a table, so that time and effort do not have to be wasted by parsing those substrings again (for instance, because of backtracking).

CKY (Cocke-Kasami-Younger) parser:	An efficient bottom-up parser for (a certain class of) context-free grammars.
Classification:	The process of deciding the class of a certain object. For example, a certain acoustic analysis vector (such as LPC coefficients) could be labelled as one sound or another, according to a phonetic classifier, or a word (e.g. rose) could be labelled as being one part of speech or another by a part-of-speech classifier.
Classification and regression trees:	A method of automatic classification that uses an algorithm to construct a decision tree on the basis of some training data.
Clause:	In Prolog, a statement (a 'fact') or a question. For example, the following are all clauses:

```
runs(john).
alive(X) :- heart_beats(X).
?- runs(Who).
```

Code-book excitation:	See **CELP.**
Collocation:	A pair or group of words that are often associated or correlated. For example: *dining table, coffee pot, knife and fork*. 'The company a word keeps' (J. R. Firth).
Comment:	Some text included in a program for the benefit of the reader or the programmer (e.g. to explain what a part of the program does), which is marked so as to be ignored by the compiler.
Compile, compiler, compilation:	A compiler is a computer program that translates computer programs written in a human-level programming language into the numerical instructions that a specific computer can carry out **(machine code)**.
Computational linguistics:	The branch of study that uses computers and computational theory to model various properties of language, or aspects of linguistic processing. Among the main topics studied in this area are **parsing,** language generation, machine translation and natural language understanding.
Conditional probability:	The probability of an event's occurrence given that some prior event or condition holds. For example, suppose that the probability of my cycling to work, $P(cycle)$ is 0.75. That is, I cycle to work three-quarters of the time. However, the probability of my cycling to work if it is raining at breakfast time $P(cycle \mid raining)$ is rather less than 0.75!
Confidence measure:	A quantity (e.g. a rating or a probability) expressing the degree of confidence that a classifier has in the accuracy of its classification. For example, a feature-detector, or a human expert, might judge that a certain portion of a signal is probably voiced, but with a very low level of confidence if they were not very sure.
Constants:	Expressions in a programming language that are fixed terms, not variables. For example, numbers, dates or ASCII characters.
Consulting:	To 'consult' a Prolog program means to load it.
Corpus:	A body of text(s) submitted to linguistic analysis.
Cosine wave:	The shape of the cosine function $y = \cos x$ (see chapter 2).
Cut-off frequency:	The frequency above which a **low pass filter** allows frequencies to pass through or below which a **high pass filter** allows frequencies to pass through. A **band pass filter** has *two* cut-off frequencies, defining the range of frequencies (the **pass band**) that it will let through.

Cyclic rule application: A mode of rule application in which a given rule is applied successively to larger and larger expressions. For instance, stress rules may be applied again and again to a word, whenever a suffix is added to it, as in *TEMpest, temPESTuous, tempestuOSity.*

Data oriented parsing: A method of parsing developed by Rens Bod, which does not use a grammar. Instead, a treebank is broken up into pieces, and those pieces used to try and analyse sentences that were not in the original treebank.

Data structures: Arrangements of information, such as tables, sequences, lists, trees, matrices.

Data types: Many computer programming languages need to be informed what kind of data a particular symbol means. For instance, does the symbol '1' refer to a binary digit, a decimal digit or a printable character? When a variable is employed in a program, it may be necessary to state what kind of data will be stored in that variable when the program is executed. For instance, if the variable x will only ever be used to store an integer between 1 and 255, one byte of memory will be sufficient allocation. If x refers to a larger structure, such as a long decimal number or a parse tree, much more memory will need to be used. The main data types of C are `char, double, enum, float, int, long, short, struct, union, unsigned` and `void`. Prolog is less fussy about the data types of variables, though it discriminates between the following: `atom`, `number` and structures.

Decision tree: A hierarchical structure that takes a program (or a person) through a series of (usually yes/no) questions in order to formulate a decision.

Definite Clause Grammar (DCG): A set of rules written in the special 'grammar rule' notation of Prolog. Such rules have the general form:

```
a(X,...) --> b(Y, ...), ... z(Z, ...), { ... More
clauses ...}.
```

Such a rule is translated into a standard Prolog clause of the form:

```
a(X,...,In,Out) :-
   b(Y, ..., In,Mid),
   ... z(Z, ...,Mid1,Out),
   ... More clauses ... .
```

Depth-first parsing: Consider the four rules (1) IP → NP VP, (2) NP → Det N, (3) Det → 'the', and (4) VP → V NP. In top-down, **depth-first** parsing of a sentence beginning with 'the', the rules would be applied in the following sequence. First, rule 1. Then, the first symbol of rule 1, NP, would be expanded using rule 2. Then, the first symbol of rule 2, Det, would be expanded using rule 3. Successively, the first (leftmost) unexpanded symbol is expanded, even though the remainder of the symbols in the rule first applied (e.g. the VP of rule 1) remain to be expanded subsequently. The **derivational history** thus proceeds: IP ⇒ NP VP ⇒ Det N VP ⇒ the N VP ⇒ etc. In **breadth-first parsing**, the order of rule application, and consequently the derivation, is different. After rule 1 is applied, rule 2 and rule 4 would be applied, before any of the symbols of either rule is expanded. The **derivational history** is thus IP ⇒ NP VP ⇒ Det N V NP ⇒ etc.

Derivational history:	The sequence of forms generated by successive application of the rules of a grammar. Two example derivational histories are given in the previous entry, on **depth-first parsing.**
Deterministic:	A deterministic program or automaton is one in which from any particular point in its operation there is only a single 'next step', i.e. there are no 'choices' to make about what to do next.
Deterministic parsing:	A method of parsing in which it is never necessary to follow multiple choices or to backtrack or to revoke decisions. **Marcus parsing** and **Minimal commitment parsing** are two (closely related) deterministic parsing methods.
Difference list:	In Prolog, a data structure in which an element or a sequence of elements is represented as a pair of lists. For instance, while parsing the string 'the cat sat on the mat', it is often convenient to represent the first 'the' by the difference list `[the,cat,sat,on,the,mat]`, `[cat,sat,on,the, mat]`, the difference between these two lists being the single word `[the]`.
Digital signal:	A representation of a signal as a sequence of numbers, which constitute a sequence of measurements of the signal.
Double:	A **data type** for **floating point numbers,** with twice as much storage as the **float** data type. The term 'double' derives from 'double precision'.
Dynamic programming:	A general method for solving problems that require a search through a range of many possible solutions. **Dynamic time warping** and **Viterbi decoding** are two examples of this method.
Dynamic time warping:	A method of matching two signals or sequences, in order to find the closest-fitting correspondence between successive elements of each.
Earley's algorithm:	An efficient and simple top-down, depth-first parsing algorithm for context-free grammars.
Empty transition:	In an **automaton,** a move from one state to the next that is permitted even though no symbol is read from the input string.
End state:	In an **automaton,** a state in which the automaton halts. There may be more than one such state.
Ergodic:	An **automaton** in which every state can be reached from any of the other states is said to be *ergodic*.
Executable file:	A file that can be executed by the computer as a program. A file of data or text, for example, cannot be executed as a program. A computer program written in a programming language such as C or Prolog also cannot be executed by a computer: it must first be translated into **machine code**. The file that contains the machine code for a particular program is executable, however. In Microsoft Windows, such files typically have the suffix `'.exe'`.
Experimental phonetics:	The scientific study of speech. In its broadest aspects, it includes the study of the physiology of speech production and hearing, the psychology and neurology of speech perception, and the generation and transmission of sound waves (acoustic phonetics). Experimental phonetics often employs instruments, but that does not make it experimental: the key feature of experimental phonetics is its use of experiments to discover facts and test hypotheses.
Fast Fourier Transform (FFT):	A method for computing **Fourier analysis** very efficiently.

Feature detectors: In some methods of speech recognition, a component piece of software with the specific purpose of identifying a particular property of a signal: for example, voicing or silence or high-frequency energy.

Filter: When a digital filter is applied to a signal, it reduces or eliminates certain frequencies while leaving other frequencies relatively unaffected. A **high pass filter** removes low frequencies, so that the resulting signal sounds quite 'trebly' or 'tinny'. A **low pass filter** removes higher frequencies, making the result more 'bassy' or 'muffled'. A **band pass filter** allows frequencies within a certain range to pass through.

Finite-state: An **automaton** with a finite number of states and no auxiliary storage (i.e. external memory) is a finite-state automaton. A language that can be accepted or generated by a finite-state automaton is sometimes called a finite-state language.

Finite-state machine: See **finite-state, automaton.**

FIR (Finite Impulse Response) filter: An FIR filter employs an equation (see chapter 3) in which the output, $y[n]$, only depends on earlier input values $x[n-1]$, $x[n-2]$, etc., and does not refer to previously calculated output values, such as $y[n-1]$, $y[n-2]$, etc. Cf. **recursive filter.**

Float: A **data type** for **floating point numbers.**

Floating point numbers: These are numbers with a decimal point (in various positions). For example, 1.0, 0.043 and 6.02×10^{-23} are all floating point numbers.

'For' loop: A programming instruction for performing a computation repeatedly until a certain condition (the continuation condition) is no longer met. (The continuation condition is therefore also a termination condition.)

Formant synthesis: A method of speech synthesis in which the resonant frequencies of a speech signal (the formants) are modelled using a combination of electronic **resonators,** or by simulating them in software using a combination of **band pass filters.**

Fourier analysis: The mathematical methods by which any signal may be decomposed into and expressed as the sum of a set of sine waves, of various frequencies, amplitudes and phase differences.

Generalized LR parsing: The most efficient method of parsing context-free grammars yet discovered, by Tomita.

Generate: An **automaton** is said to generate a string $abc \ldots x$ if, in traversing from the start state to an end state it moves through transitions labelled with $a, b, \ldots x$. A grammar is said to generate a string $abc \ldots x$ if, by successive application of rules from a start symbol S the string $abc \ldots x$ can be derived. For example, the grammar of two rules (1) S → a S c and (2) S → b is capable of generating the strings $b, abc, aabcc, aaabccc$. In general, it can generate all strings consisting of n as, one b and n cs, for all $n \geq 0$, using n applications of rule 1 followed by one application of rule 2.

Grammar: Informally, a grammar is a set of rules defining (the structure of) a language. More formally, the term 'grammar' is usually understood in linguistics to be a *phrase structure grammar*, i.e. a set of rules that define a certain set of strings by virtue of being able to **generate** those strings. Other formal definitions of grammar are possible: for instance, it is possible to define the structure of a language using statements of logic.

Grammaticality: This refers to whether a string is or is not grammatical. It is used in discussions of judgements by humans concerning the well-formedness of strings, such as when, for example, we ask whether a certain string is grammatical in English. In speech and language processing, we may be interested in the grammaticality of a string, according to some formal **grammar**.

Hanning window: See **windowing**.

Hardware: The physical material of a computer system, including the central processor, the memory, disks, monitor, keyboard and mouse.

Harmonics: Peaks in the spectrum of a periodic sound, occurring at integer multiples of the fundamental frequency.

Hertz: The international standard unit of frequency. 1 hertz (1 Hz) = 1 cycle per second.

Hidden Markov Models (HMMs): A probabilistic finite-state machine in which all symbols in the machine's repertoire can be generated in every state, albeit with different probabilities.

High pass filter: See **filter**.

IIR (Infinite Impulse Response) filter: See **recursive filter**.

Integral: In digital signal processing, the sum of a sequence of numbers. (In calculus, 'integral' means 'the area under a curve'. There are more refined techniques for calculating the integral of a digital signal than simply adding up all the sample values, but I do not go into them in this book.)

Interpreter: In some programming languages, each statement of the program is interpreted into machine code one at a time. This makes it easier to add, remove or change pieces of the program during its development in a very easy way. Most languages, however, are **compiled**. This means that if part of just one line of the program is changed, the whole program must be re-compiled. Although an interpreter is thus a little easier on the programmer, interpreted programs are usually slower than compiled programs.

Kilohertz: A unit of frequency. 1 kHz = 1000 Hz, i.e. 1000 cycles per second.

Klatt formant synthesizer: A **formant synthesis** program designed by Dennis Klatt (see Klatt 1980). It combines both the main approaches to formant synthesis — cascade and parallel arrangements of resonators — in one design, to obtain the combined advantages of both methods.

Knowledge-based speech recognition: A method of speech recognition in which the knowledge of human experts in acoustics, phonetics, linguistics etc. is encoded in the form of rules that the program can use to decode what words, phrases etc. the speech signal conveys.

Language processing: See **computational linguistics**.

Learnability: The degree of ease with which something may be learned, or even just the possibility that it can be learned.

Left recursion: A property of some grammars that causes problems for top-down parsers. If a grammar rule for expression P also has P as its leftmost symbol (e.g. NP → NP PP, as in [[the man][in the suit]]), top-down application of that rule will result in an infinitely long derivation, e.g. NP ⇒ NP PP ⇒ NP PP PP ⇒ NP PP PP PP ... and the parsing task will never be completed! Such grammars have to be modified in order to remove the left recursion before they may be employed by a top-down parser.

Levenshtein distance: The most common measure of the degree to which two strings differ. It is a minimum edit distance, the minimum sum of the number of insertions, deletions or substitutions of one symbol by another. For example, the distance between SHIP and SHOP is 1, between SHIP and SHEEP is 2 (1 substitution and 1 insertion), between THE and THEN 1, and between STOP and START 3.

Library files: contain pieces of computer programs defining useful or frequently used routines of general relevance. In C, for example, the cosine function is defined in the mathematics library, and various useful routines for writing to or reading from a file are defined in the standard input-output library. Library files are often supplied as a supplement to a programming language compiler, to make life easier for programmers.

Linear prediction: Predicting the next value of a signal by linearly extrapolating from n preceding values. The sequence of differences between the predicted value and the actual value is called the prediction residual.

Linear predictive coding: Taken together, a set of linear prediction coefficients and the corresponding prediction residual completely define, without error, the signal from which they were original defined. Therefore, they are an encoding of the signal, from which a completely faithful copy of the original can be reconstructed.

Linking: Typically, a complete program is written in several separate parts, such as **library files** or other relatively self-contained pieces written by someone else. The several parts have to be combined during **compilation**. Usually, each part is partially compiled by itself, into **object code,** and then the several incompletely compiled parts are brought together in the step called 'linking'.

Little endian: See **big endian**.

Logic programming: A method of programming in which programs are composed of statements of logic. A program is 'run' on an input by automatically trying to *prove* the input, using the logical statements of the program. Prolog is probably the best-known example of a logic programming language.

Look-ahead: In attempting to parse a string from left-to-right (irrespective of whether a top-down or bottom-up algorithm is used), it is sometimes useful to look ahead to what word(s) come(s) next, to help decide what rule applies to a phrase. Suppose that a grammar contains two rules for noun phrases: (1) NP → Det N and (2) NP → Det N P NP. From just the first two words of the sentence '*the woman* is reading' it is impossible for the parser to tell which of these two rules correctly describes the structure of the beginning of the sentence. By looking ahead to the next word, 'is', it becomes possible to determine that rule 2 is not appropriate, because 'is' is not a preposition.

Low pass filter: See **filter**. Low pass filters also have the effect of smoothing a rapidly changing signal.

LPC spectrum: A method of calculating the spectrum of a sound from its **linear prediction** coefficients. The spectrum thus derived is much smoother than the more conventional Fourier spectrum.

Machine code: The numerical instructions that a specific computer can carry out. For example, the first two bytes of the machine code for a recent release of Microsoft's WordPad program are 01001101 and 01011010.

Machine language: The language of programs that can be written in **machine code**.

Macro: In C, a macro is an instruction placed in a program as an instruction to the C pre-processor. Macros often abbreviate more verbose expressions.

Marcus parsing: A method of deterministic parsing in which a limited degree of **look-ahead** is used to try and streamline the parsing process, in order to avoid the need for **backtracking** (which is employed in most parsing methods).

Markov assumption: In a Markov model, it is assumed that the route by which a given state was arrived at has no bearing on which step(s) will be taken next.

Markov model: A **probabilistic finite-state** machine in which the Markov assumption holds.

Minimal commitment parsing: A method of **deterministic parsing**, of which **Marcus parsing** is an example, in which grammatical structures and labels are only built if they are certain as one after another word is analysed. Since **backtracking** is prohibited, the parser is required to be circumspect about the addition of any piece of linguistic structure to the overall analysis of a sentence.

Minimum edit distance: See **Levenshtein distance**.

Morphology: In linguistics, the study of words, their parts and structures.

Move: In the theory of **automata** (as in a board game), a 'move' is a step forward through the machine (or game).

Moving average: The average of a short portion of a signal, repeatedly calculated over successive portions.

Multipulse excitation: A method for improving the quality of **linear prediction** synthesis, in which each pitch period in the original signal is modelled by several impulses in the input to the linear prediction filter.

n-gram: A sequence of n symbols, e.g. words or letters, depending on the application. In a **bigram,** $n = 2$; in a **trigram,** $n = 3$.

Nondeterministic: A nondeterministic program or **automaton** is one in which at some point(s) in its operation there is more than one possible 'next step', so that a 'choice' must be made about what to do next. Sometimes all of those choices lead to reasonable outcomes; sometimes some choices lead up blind alleys. This may be a good way of finding a right answer, by ruling out lines of inquiry that do not work out. In order to explore the multiple possibilities engendered by such nondeterminism, Prolog programs employ **backtracking.**

Nyquist frequency: The highest frequency that can be recorded at a particular sampling rate. It is equal to *half* the sampling rate. Thus, with a sampling rate of 16000 samples per second it is not possible to capture frequencies above 8 kHz.

Object code: An intermediate level of representation generated in the first phase of the compilation process. See **linking**. In C, object-code files are usually given the suffix '.o'.

Observation sequence: In a **Hidden Markov Model**, the sequence of symbols (acoustic parameter vectors, words etc.) that the model is given to interpret.

Order: The order of a digital filter, such as a **linear prediction** filter, is the number of previous samples included in the equation. For example, the linear prediction filter $x[t] = -a_1\,x[t-1] - a_2\,x[t-2] - a_3\,x[t-3]$ is of order 3. For most filtering applications, higher orders than this are usually used. For high pass or low pass filtering, for example, 5th-order filters would be not untypical. For linear predictive coding, a rule of thumb is 2 coefficients per kilohertz, up to the **Nyquist frequency**, plus 2. For a signal sampled at 10 kHz, therefore, $(2 \times 5) + 2 = 12$th order is standard. Using a few more coefficients may improve the accuracy of linear prediction, up to a point, but for speech there is little value in using more than 15 predictor coefficients.

Parser: A program for working out the structure of expressions of a language, on the basis of a formally defined grammar of that language.

Part-of-speech tagging: Usually performed as a pre-processing step prior to parsing a sentence, part-of-speech tagging algorithms work out the part of speech of each word in the input. (Usually, they give an estimate of the *most likely* part of speech of each word.)

Pass band: See **cut-off frequency**.

Pattern matching: The process of matching an input 'test' pattern or parameter against a repertoire of stored 'reference' patterns, to find which of the reference patterns is identical to or most similar to the test pattern.

Pattern-recognition approach: An approach to speech recognition based on pattern matching. Rather than trying to analyse and decode the various parts of the input, in order to work out what is being said, this approach is based on the idea of simply looking up the best-fitting example (from a previously collected store of examples).

Phonetics: The study of speech.

Phonology: An area of linguistics dealing with the patterns evident in the spoken form of language. Its key concerns are with patterns of contrast between words, parts of words, and larger chunks of speech; with the serial arrangement of such units; and with the relations between related words, such as *revolve* vs. *revolution*.

Pitch tracking: The process of following (and usually displaying) the details of how the pitch of the voice goes up and down during an input utterance.

Power spectral density: A representation (usually plotted as a graph) of the amplitude (power) of a signal at specific frequencies. The frequency range is usually from 0 up to the **Nyquist frequency**. Such a representation is often called a **spectrum**, for short, though technically this is slightly inaccurate: the spectrum also includes phase information.

Predicate: In Prolog (and in logic), the name of a function, with usually one or more arguments. For example, the structure `is_jolly(ken)` might mean that Ken is jolly, in which case we would say that 'is jolly' is a predicate that is true (or at least is asserted as being true) of Ken.

Prediction residual: See **linear prediction**.

Predictor coefficients: In the simplest form of **linear prediction**, the next value of a signal is linearly extrapolating from the n preceding values by the equation $x[t] = -a_1\,x[t-1] - a_2\,x[t-2] - a_3\,x[t-3] \ldots - a_p\,x[t-n]$. The coefficients a_1 to a_p are called predictor coefficients. In other forms of linear prediction, different kinds of predictor coefficients are obtained: reflection coefficients, for example. Discussion of such other methods lies beyond the scope of this textbook. See also **order**.

Probabilistic: Based on **probability** theory.

Probabilistic grammar: A description or theory of language structure that employs **probability** theory to determine the likelihood of different expressions or their interpretations. Rather than declaring certain expressions to be ungrammatical or ill-formed, probabilistic grammars assign a quantity to each expression according to its likelihood or 'goodness'. According to a probabilistic grammar, the following sentence is not ungrammatical (though it may be rare): *In Norwegian they say things like bread the is on table the* (adapted from Sampson 2001).

Probability: In the mathematical theory of probability (rather than its informal sense), 'probability' is defined in terms of the frequency with which a certain event actually occurs, compared to the rate at which it could, in principle, occur. For example, if you (or a computer program) randomly pick a day of the week, there are seven possible outcomes. The probability of picking one particular day of the week, say Wednesday, is therefore 1 in 7. Expressed as a number, we say that the probability $P = 1/7$. Probabilities are also sometimes expressed as odds ratios (e.g. 4 to 1) or percentages (e.g. a 10% chance of rain).

Program: A sequence of instructions that tell a computer what to do in order to perform some task.

Prolog: A contraction of programming in logic, a computer programming language for logic programming.

Quantization: In signal processing, taking measurements of a continuously varying signal only at specific measurement values. For example, we might record the voltage of a microphone signal at multiples of 0.1 V, even though the signal actual varies through all intermediate values in between x V and $x + 0.1$ V. Quantization is necessary when dealing with **digital signals,** because it is impossible to measure and record the infinite number of values between any two points on a continuum.

Quefrency: The scale of time intervals in a **cepstral analysis**. A quefrency of T seconds corresponds to a frequency of $1/T$ hertz.

Reconstruction: The inverse operation to **quantization**: using a sequence of measured values of a signal to generate a new version that is very similar to the original recording.

Recursive descent: A method of traversing (or constructing) a tree, in which one starts from the root node and moves to each daughter node in turn. As each daughter node is visited, the method is repeated, so that each daughter's daughter, each daughter's daughter's daughter etc. is visited in turn. Since the algorithm is recursive, it is guaranteed to traverse (or construct) any tree, of arbitrary size, without having to specify in advance the size or shape of the tree.

Recursive filter: A recursive filter employs an equation (see chapter 3), in which the output, $y[n]$, depends in part on its previously calculated output values, such as $y[n-1]$, $y[n-2]$, etc. They are also called Infinite Impulse Response (IIR) filters. Cf. **FIR filter.**

Reference parameter: See **pattern matching**.

Regular relation: The kind of mapping that can be computed by a **finite-state** transducer.

Reserved words: Words that have built-in, specific meanings in a computer language, and that cannot therefore be used by the programmer to mean something else. For example, it is possible for a programmer to use almost any sequence of letters as the name of a function. In a program that performs integration it would be fine to define a variable called `integral`, or even `integ`, for short. It would not be allowed to abbreviate that variable to `int`, however, because `int` is a word reserved as the datatype of integers.

Resonator: A chamber or electronic circuit that resonates, i.e. allows sounds or signals at frequencies in a certain range to pass through relatively unaffected, or even amplified, while reducing frequencies outside that range. The centre of the passable frequency range is called the resonant frequency. In software, such an object or circuit can be modelled using a band pass filter.

Resynthesis: The reconstruction of a recorded speech signal using a synthesizer (usually, a **linear prediction** synthesizer). This term is only applicable if the synthetic reconstruction is a very *good* one, such as the synthetic reconstruction of a speaker's voice generated by a mobile telephone.

Root mean square (RMS) amplitude: The square root of the average of the squared sample values. This calculation is spelled out in more detail in chapter 3. For speech signals, the RMS amplitude is a good measure of how the loudness of the signal changes through time.

Sampling, to sample: In speech processing, the act of taking a measurement of a signal at specific moments in time. Each such measurement is a sample of the signal. Each sample usually captures a very fleeting moment, so that a great many samples must be obtained in order to record a signal in detail.

Self-loop: In an **automaton**, a transition from a state to itself, i.e. back to the same state.

Short integer: A two-byte (16-bit) binary number. Sometimes just called a 'short', for short.

Signal: A time-varying recording of some measurable physical property, such as may be recorded using electronic apparatus. For example, speech signals may be recorded using a microphone, visual signals using photocells or a digital camera, or physiological signals such as electro-chemical changes in tissue, using electrodes.

Signal processing: A mathematical and computational study concerned with the analysis of signals. Signal processing methods are typically used to improve the fidelity of signals, or to examine certain properties (such as frequencies, intensity etc.).

Software: Programs or instructions to a computer telling it what to do.

Spectrum: A representation of the frequencies, phases and amplitudes of the components around a specific time interval of a signal. See also **power spectral density**.

Speech recognition: Sometimes used as a shorthand for **automatic speech recognition**, although humans recognize speech too, of course!

Speech technology: The design and production of devices for processing speech, or for producing synthetic imitations of speech. Its main branches are **automatic speech recognition, speech synthesis** and speech coding.

Start state: In an **automaton**, the state at which the automaton starts.

State transition table: A method for encoding a **finite-state machine**. Input symbols are written along one dimension of the table, state numbers along the other dimension, and numbers in the table indicate which state comes next, for a given pair of input symbol and current state.

Stochastic grammar: means the same as **probabilistic grammar**.

Syllabification: The process of dividing words (whether spoken or written) into syllables.

Symbol–state table: See **state transition table**.

Syntax: In linguistics, the arrangement and structure of sentences and other expressions. In computer science, the arrangement and structure of computer programs or instructions. The syntax of a language is usually defined by a set of rules, i.e. a **grammar**.

Test parameter: See **pattern matching**.

Theorem proving: The process of applying a sequence of rules of logic to some basic, given statements of fact (axioms) in order to prove a theorem. In general, attempting to prove that a statement follows logically from other statements. For example, from the statements 'Socrates is an ancient philosopher' and 'all ancient philosophers are dead' we can prove the theorem 'Socrates is dead.'

Token: A single instance of a symbol. See **type**.

Top-down parsing: In top-down parsing, the structure of an input string is found by generating a parse tree that fits the input string.

Training: In **probabilistic** approaches to grammar, the probabilities of rules (or of *n*-grams etc.) are found by analysing a set of examples. This process is called training.

Transducer: In **automata** theory, a transducer is an automaton in which transitions are labelled with *pairs* of symbols from two alphabets. A transducer thus defines a mapping between expressions in the two alphabets.

Transition: A permitted move from one state of an **automaton** to another. In *n*-gram **models**, moving from one *n*-gram to the next is also called a transition.

Tree adjoining grammar: A type of formal grammar in which tree fragments are the primitives. They can be combined by two operations: substitution and adjunction.

Treebank: A database of analysed sentence structures.

Trigram: A sequence of three symbols, e.g. words or letters, depending on the application.

Two-level phonology: An approach to phonology employing **finite-state transducers** to encode rules and to relate different levels of linguistic structure, such as phonology and orthography, phonology and morphology, or phonology and phonetics.

Type: If we ask 'How many letters are there in the *Encyclopedia Britannica*?' one reasonable answer is '26, of course'. That is the number of letter types (if we count 'a' and 'A' as members of the same type). But of course there are millions of letters in the *Encyclopedia Britannica*, if we count each instance separately. Such instances are called **tokens**. We could make the same distinction in respect of words: in a corpus of 10 million word-instances (i.e. tokens), there will be rather fewer distinct words (types), because some words occur many times over.

Variable: In computer programming (as in algebra), a symbol that does not have a fixed value, but can be set to many different values as the program progresses, for example.

Vector quantization: Grouping very similar spectral vectors together, and assigning each such group a code-number, in order to make spectral pattern-matching computationally easier.

Viterbi decoding: A method of determining the most likely sequence of symbols (e.g. in an observation sequence), according to a given **probabilistic** model (usually a **Hidden Markov Model**).

Voicing detection: Automatically working out which portions of a speech signal represent voiced speech and which portions are voiceless.

Warp path: The sequence of pairs of frames generated by the **dynamic time warping** algorithm, constituting the closest match between the test and reference patterns.

Windowing: The selection of successive portions of a signal usually performed prior to subsequent analysis of the portions. The selected portions – windows – are often multiplied by a function (such as the Hanning window) that goes smoothly to zero at the beginning and end, with a maximum in the middle. See chapter 4.

References

*An initial * indicates that a copy of the work, or a link to an associated web-based resource, can be found on the companion website, www.islp.org.uk.*

Allen, J. and M. S. Seidenberg (1999) The emergence of grammaticality in connectionist networks. In MacWhinney 1999, 115–51.

*Antworth, E. L. (1990) *PC-KIMMO: A Two-Level Processor for Morphological Analysis.* Dallas, TX: Summer Institute of Linguistics.

Bailey, T. M. and U. Hahn (2001) Determinants of wordlikeness: Phonotactics or lexical neighborhoods? *Journal of Memory and Language* 44, 568–91.

Bard, E. G., D. Robertson and A. Sorace (1996) Magnitude estimation of linguistic acceptability. *Language* 72, 32–68.

Barton, G. E., R. C. Berwick and E. S. Ristad (1987) *Computational Complexity and Natural Language.* Cambridge, MA: MIT Press.

Bod, R. (1998) *Beyond Grammar: An Experience-Based Theory of Language.* Stanford: CSLI Publications.

Bod, R., J. Hay and S. Jannedy (2003) *Probabilistic Linguistics.* Cambridge, MA: MIT Press.

Bogert, B. P., M. J. R. Healy and J. W. Tukey (1963) The frequency analysis of time series for echoes: Cepstrum, pseudo-autocovariance, cross-cepstrum and saphe cracking. In M. Rosenblatt, ed., *Proceedings of the Symposium on Time Series Analysis.* New York: John Wiley, 209–43.

Broe, M. B. and J. B. Pierrehumbert, eds. (2000) *Papers in Laboratory Phonology V: Acquisition and the Lexicon.* Cambridge: Cambridge University Press.

Brown, P. F., V. J. Della Pietra, P. V. deSouza, J. C. Lai and R. L. Mercer (1992) Class-based n-gram models of natural language. *Computational Linguistics* 18, 467–79.

*Burnard, L., ed. (2000) *The British National Corpus Users Reference Guide.* Oxford: Oxford University Computing Services.

Campbell, J. P. Jr, T. E. Tremain and V. C. Welch (1991) The Federal Standard 1016 4800 bps CELP Voice Coder. *Digital Signal Processing* 1(3), 145–55.

Chao, Y.-R. (1934) The non-uniqueness of phonemic solutions of phonetic systems. *Bulletin of the Institute of History and Philology, Academia Sinica* 4(3), 363–97. Reprinted in E. P. Hamp, M. Joos, F. W. Householder and R. Austerlitz, eds., *Readings in Linguistics: 1925–1957.* Chicago: University of Chicago Press.

Charniak, E. (1993) *Statistical Language Learning.* Cambridge, MA: MIT Press.

Chomsky, N. (1957) *Syntactic Structures.* The Hague: Mouton.

(1965) *Aspects of the Theory of Syntax.* Cambridge, MA: MIT Press.

(1966) *Topics in the Theory of Generative Grammar.* The Hague: Mouton.

Chomsky, N. and M. Halle (1968) *The Sound Pattern of English.* New York: Harper and Row. Reprinted in paperback in 1991 by the MIT Press.

Church, K. W. (1983) *Phrase Structure Parsing: A Method for Taking Advantage of Allophonic Constraints.* PhD thesis, MIT. Distributed by the Indiana University Linguistics Club.

(1988) *Phonological Parsing in Speech Recognition.* Dordrecht: Kluwer.

Clocksin, W. F and C. S. Mellish (2003) *Programming in Prolog.* 5th edition. Berlin: Springer-Verlag.

Coleman, J. S. (1992) YorkTalk: 'Synthesis-by-rule' without segments or rules. In G. Bailly, C. Benoit and T. R. Sawallis, eds., *Talking Machines: Theories, Models, and Designs.* Amsterdam: Elsevier, 43–60.

(1998) *Phonological Representations.* Cambridge: Cambridge University Press.

*(2000a) Improved prediction of stress in out-of-vocabulary words. In *State of the Art in Speech Synthesis.* Meeting Digest 058. London: The Institution of Electrical Engineers.

(2000b) Candidate selection. *The Linguistic Review* 17, 167–79.

(2003) Discovering the acoustic correlates of phonological contrasts. *Journal of Phonetics* 31, 351–72.

*Coleman, J. S. and J. Pierrehumbert (1997) Stochastic phonological grammars and acceptability. In *Computational Phonology. Third Meeting of the ACL Special Interest Group in Computational Phonology.* Somerset, NJ: Association for Computational Linguistics, 49–56.

Coleman, J. and A. Slater (2001) Estimation of parameters for the Klatt synthesizer from a speech database. In R. I. Damper, ed., *Data-Driven Techniques in Speech Synthesis.* Dordrecht: Kluwer, 215–38.

*Dankovičová, J., P. West, J. Coleman and A. Slater (1998) Phonotactic grammaticality is gradient. Poster paper presented at the 6th International Conference on Laboratory Phonology (LabPhon 6), University of York.

Deng, L. and D. X. Sun (1994) A statistical approach to automatic speech recognition using the atomic speech units constructed from overlapping articulatory features. *Journal of the Acoustical Society of America* **95**, 2702–19.

Dinnsen, D. A. (1985) A re-examination of phonological neutralization. *Journal of Linguistics* **21**, 265–79.

*Dirksen, A. (1993) Phrase structure phonology. In T. M. Ellison and J. M. Scobbie, eds., *Computational Phonology. Edinburgh Working Papers in Cognitive Science* **8**, 81–96.

du Maurier, D. (1938) *Rebecca.* London: Victor Gollancz.

Earley, J. (1970) An efficient context-free parsing algorithm. *Communications of the Association for Computing Machinery* **6**, 451–5.

Elman, J. L. (1993) Learning and development in neural networks: the importance of starting small. *Cognition* **48**, 71–99.

(1999) The emergence of language: a conspiracy theory. In MacWhinney, 1999, 1–27.

Embree, P. M. and B. Kimble (1991) *C Language Algorithms for Digital Signal Processing.* Englewood Cliffs, NJ: Prentice–Hall.

Firth, J. R. (1951) Modes of meaning. In *Essays and Studies*, IV, 123. Reprinted in *Papers in Linguistics 1934–1951.* London: Oxford University Press, 190–215.

Frisch, S. A., N. R. Large and D. B. Pisoni (2000) Perception of wordlikeness: Effects of segment probability and length on the processing of nonwords. *Journal of Memory and Language* **42**, 481–96.

Gazdar, G. and C. Mellish (1989) *Natural Language Processing in Prolog: An Introduction to Computational Linguistics.* Wokingham: Addison-Wesley.

Goldsmith, J. (2001) Unsupervised learning of the morphology of a natural language. *Computational Linguistics* **27**, 153–98.

Greenberg, J. H. and J. J. Jenkins (1964) Studies in the psychological correlates of the sound system of American English. *Word* **20**, 157–77.

Halle, M. and K. P. Mohanan (1985) Segmental phonology of Modern English. *Linguistic Inquiry* **16**, 57–116.

Harrington, J. and S. Cassidy (1999) *Techniques in Speech Acoustics.* Dordrecht: Kluwer.

Hawkins, S. and A. Slater (1994) Spread of CV and V-to-V coarticulation in British English: Implications for the intelligibility of synthetic speech. *Proceedings of ICSLP 94: 1994 International Conference on Spoken Language Processing*, I, 57–60.

Hopcroft, J. E., R. Motwani and J. D. Ullman (2000) *Introduction to Automata Theory, Languages, and Computation.* Reading, MA: Addison-Wesley.

Huang, X., A. Acero and H.-W. Hon (2001) *Spoken Language Processing: A Guide to Theory, Algorithm and System Development.* Upper Saddle River, NJ: Prentice Hall.

*Huckvale, M. (1992) A comparison of neural network and Hidden Markov Model approaches to the tiered segmentation of speech. *Proceedings of the Institute of Acoustics Conference on Speech and Hearing, Windermere.*

Jakobson, R., C. G. M. Fant and M. Halle (1961) *Preliminaries to Speech Analysis: The Distinctive Features and their Correlates.* Cambridge, MA: MIT Press.

Johnson, C. D. (1972) *Formal Aspects of Phonological Description.* The Hague: Mouton.

Johnson, K. (1997) *Acoustic and Auditory Phonetics.* Oxford: Blackwell.

Joshi, A. K. (1985) Tree adjoining grammars : How much context sensitivity is required to provide reasonable structural descriptions? In D. R. Dowty, L. Karttunen and A. M. Zwicky, eds., *Natural Language Parsing: Psychological, Computational, and Theoretical Perspectives.* Cambridge: Cambridge University Press, 206–50.

Jurafsky, D. and J. H. Martin (2000) *Speech and Language Processing: An Introduction to Natural Language*

Processing, Computational Linguistics, and Speech Recognition. Upper Saddle River, NJ: Prentice Hall.

*Just, M. A., P. A. Carpenter, T. A. Keller, W. F. Eddy and K. R. Thulborn (1996) Brain activation modulated by sentence comprehension. *Science* **274**, 114–16.

Kaplan, R. M. and M. Kay (1994) Regular models of phonological rule systems. *Computational Linguistics* **20**(3), 331–78.

Karttunen, L. (1983) Kimmo: A general morphological processor. *Texas Linguistics Forum* **22**, 165–86.

Kasami, T. and K. Torii (1969) A syntax-analysis procedure for unambiguous context-free grammars. *Journal of the Association for Computing Machinery* **16**, 423–31.

Kay, M. (1987) Nonconcatenative finite-state morphology. In *Proceedings of the Third Meeting of the European Chapter of the Association for Computational Linguistics.* Association for Computational Linguistics, 2–10.

Kelly, J. and J. K. Local (1986) Long domain resonance patterns in English. In *International Conference on Speech Input/Output; Techniques and Applications.* Conference Publication No. 258. London: Institute of Electrical Engineers, 304–9.

Kernighan, B. W. and D. M. Ritchie (1988) *The C Programming Language.* 2nd edition. Englewood Cliffs, NJ: Prentice Hall.

*Klatt, D. H. (1980) Software for a cascade/parallel formant synthesizer. *Journal of the Acoustical Society of America* **67**(3), 971–95.

Klatt, D. H. and L.C. Klatt (1990) Analysis, synthesis, and perception of voice quality variations among female and male talkers. *Journal of the Acoustical Society of America* **87**(2), 820–57.

Klavans, J. L. and P. Resnik, eds. (1996) *The Balancing Act: Combining Symbolic and Statistical Approaches to Language.* Cambridge, MA: MIT Press.

Koenig, W., H. K. Dunn and L. Y. Lacy (1946) The sound spectrograph. *Journal of the Acoustical Society of America* **18**(1), 19–49.

Kornai, A. (1991) *Formal Phonology.* PhD thesis, Stanford University. Also published in 1995 by Garland Science.

(1999) *Extended Finite State Models of Language.* Cambridge: Cambridge University Press.

Koskenniemi, K. (1983) *Two-Level Morphology: A General Computational Model of Word-Form Recognition and*

Production. Publication 11. Helsinki: Department of General Linguistics, University of Helsinki.

Lari, K., and S. Young (1990) The estimation of stochastic context-free grammars using the Inside–Outside algorithm. *Computer Speech and Language* **4**, 35–56.

Local, J. (2003) Variable domains and variable relevance: Interpreting phonetic exponents. *Journal of Phonetics* **31**(3–4), 321–39.

MacWhinney, B., ed. (1999) *The Emergence of Language.* Mahwah, NJ: Lawrence Erlbaum Associates.

Manning, C. D. and H. Schütze (1999) *Foundations of Statistical Natural Language Processing.* Cambridge, MA: MIT Press.

Marcus, M. P. (1980) *A Theory of Syntactic Recognition for Natural Language.* Cambridge, MA: MIT Press.

Markov, A. A. (1913) Essai d'une recherche statistique sur le texte du roman 'Eugène Onegin' illustrant la liaison des épreuves en chaîne. *Izvistia Imperatorskoi Akademii Nauk (Bulletin de l'Académie Impériale des Sciences de St.-Pétersbourg)* **7**, 153–62.

McLeod, P., K. Plunkett and E. T. Rolls (1998) *Introduction to Connectionist Modelling of Cognitive Processes.* Oxford: Oxford University Press.

Miller, G. A. and N. Chomsky (1963) Finitary models of language users. In R. D. Luce, R. R. Bush and E. Galanter, eds., *Handbook of Mathematical Psychology.* Volume II. New York: John Wiley, 419–91.

*Mitton, R. (1992) A computer-usable dictionary file based on the Oxford Advanced Learner's Dictionary of Current English.

Morgan, D. P. and C. L. Scofield (1991) *Neural Networks and Speech Processing.* Boston, MA: Kluwer.

Mowrey, R. A. and I. R. A. MacKay (1990) Phonological primitives: Electromyographic speech error evidence. *Journal of the Acoustical Society of America* **88**, 1299–312.

Nolan, F. (1992) The descriptive role of segments: Evidence from assimilation. In G. Docherty and D.R. Ladd, eds. *Gesture, Segment, Prosody: Papers in Laboratory Phonology 2.* Cambridge: Cambridge University Press, 261–80.

Noll, A. M. (1967) Cepstrum pitch determination. *Journal of the Acoustical Society of America* **41**(2), 293–309.

Ohala, J. and M. Ohala (1986) Testing hypotheses regarding the psychological manifestation of morpheme structure rules. In J. Ohala and J. J. Jaeger, eds., *Experimental Phonology*. Orlando: Academic Press. 239–52.

Olive, J. P., A. Greenwood and J. S. Coleman (1993) *Acoustics of American English Speech: A Dynamic Approach*. New York: Springer-Verlag.

Peng, S.-H. (2000) Lexical vs. 'phonological' representations of Mandarin sandhi tone. In Broe and Pierrehumbert 2000, 152–67.

Pereira, F. C. N. (2000) Formal grammar and information theory: Together again? *Philosophical Transactions of the Royal Society of London*, A, **358**, 1239–53.

Pereira, F. and Y. Schabes (1992) Inside-outside reestimation from partially bracketed corpora. In *27th Annual Meeting of the Association for Computational Linguistics*. Association for Computational Linguistics, 128–35.

Pereira, F. C. N. and S. M. Shieber (1987) *Prolog and Natural-Language Analysis*. Stanford: CSLI Publications.

Press, W. H., S. A. Teukolsky, W. T. Vetterling and B. P. Flannery (1992) *Numerical Recipes in C: The Art of Scientific Computing*. 2nd edition. Cambridge: Cambridge University Press.

Rabiner, L. R. and B.-H. Juang (1993) *Fundamentals of Speech Recognition*. Englewood Cliffs, NJ: Prentice Hall.

Rabiner, L. R. and S. E. Levinson (1981) Isolated and connected word recognition – theory and selected applications. *IEEE Transactions on Communications* **29**, 621–59. Reprinted in Waibel and Lee 1990, 115–53.

Reetz, H. (1999) Converting speech signals to phonological features. In J. J. Ohala, Y. Hasegawa, M. Ohala, D. Granville and A. C. Bailey, eds. *Proceedings of the XIVth International Congress of Phonetic Sciences*. Berkeley, CA: University of California, III, 1733–6.

Reich, P. A. (1969) The finiteness of natural language. *Language* **45**, 831–43. Reprinted in F. W. Householder, ed. (1972) *Syntactic Theory 1: Structuralist*. Harmondsworth: Penguin Books, 258–72.

Sakoe, H. and S. Chiba (1978) Dynamic programming algorithm optimization for spoken word recognition. *IEEE Transactions on Acoustics, Speech and Signal Processing*, ASSP-26, 43–9.

Sampson, G. (2001) Evidence against the grammatical/ungrammatical distinction. In *Empirical Linguistics*. London: Continuum, 165–79.

Schabes, Y. (1992) Stochastic lexicalized-adjoining grammars. *Actes de Coling-92, Nantes* **2**, 426–32.

Schroeder, M. R. (1985) Linear predictive coding of speech: Review and current directions. *IEEE Communications Magazine* **23(8)**, 54–61.

Scobbie, J. M., F. Gibbon, W. J. Hardcastle and P. Fletcher (2000) Covert contrast as a stage in the acquisition of phonetics and phonology. In Broe and Pierrehumbert 2000, 194–207.

Shieber, S. M. and Y. Schabes (1990) Synchronous tree-adjoining grammars. In H. Karlgren, ed., *COLING 90: Papers Presented to the 13th International Conference on Computational Linguistics*. Helsinki: University of Helsinki, III, 253–8.

Slater, A. and J. Coleman (1996) Non-segmental analysis and synthesis based on a speech database. In H. T. Bunnell and W. Idsardi, eds. *Proceedings of ICSLP 96, Fourth International Conference on Spoken Language Processing*. Wilmington, DE: University of Delaware and Alfred I duPont Institute, IV, 2379–82.

Sproat, R. W., C. Shih, W. Gale and N. Chang (1996) A stochastic finite-state word-segmentation algorithm for Chinese. *Computational Linguistics* **22**, 377–404.

Sterling, L. and E. Shapiro (1994) *The Art of Prolog: Advanced Programming Techniques*. 2nd edition. Cambridge, MA: MIT Press.

Stevens, K. N. (2002) Toward a model for lexical access based on acoustic landmarks and distinctive features. *Journal of the Acoustical Society of America* **111**, 1872–91.

Stolcke, A. (1995) An efficient probabilistic context-free parsing algorithm that computes prefix probabilities. *Computational Linguistics* **21**, 165–201.

Strik, H. and L. Boves (1991) A dynamic programming algorithm for time-aligning and averaging physiological signals related to speech. *Journal of Phonetics* **19**, 367–78.

Tomita, M. (1991) *Generalized LR Parsing*. Dordrecht: Kluwer.

Tremain, T. E. (1982) The government standard linear predictive coding algorithm: LPC-10. *Speech Technology Magazine*, April 1982, 40–9.

Trubetzkoy, N. S. (1969) *Principles of Phonology*. (Translated by C. M. Baltaxe.) Berkeley: University of California Press.

Wagner, R. A. and M. J. Fisher (1974) The string-to-string correction problem. *Journal of the Association for Computing Machinery* **21**, 168–73.

Waibel, A. and K.-F. Lee (1990) *Readings in Speech Recognition*. San Mateo, CA: Morgan Kaufmann.

Wakita, H. (1996) Instrumentation for the study of speech acoustics. In N. J. Lass, ed., *Principles of Experimental Phonetics*. St. Louis, MO: Mosby, 469–94.

Watson, B. W. (1999) Implementing and using finite automata toolkits. In A. Kornai, ed., *Extended Finite State Models of Language*. Cambridge: Cambridge University Press, 19–36.

West, P. (1999) Perception of distributed coarticulatory properties of English /l/ and /ɹ/. *Journal of Phonetics* **27**, 405–26.

Wiebe, B. (1992) *Modelling Autosegmental Phonology with Multi-Tape Finite State Transducers*. Master's thesis, Simon Fraser University.

*Young, S., J. Odell, D. Ollason, V. Valtchev and P. Woodland (1997) *The HTK Book (for HTK Version 2.1)*. Cambridge: Entropic Cambridge Research Laboratory.

Younger, D. (1967) Recognition and parsing of context-free languages in time n^3. *Information and Control* **10**, 189–208.

Index